Arnulfo L. Oliveira Memorial Library

NAPOLEON'S TROUBLESOME AMERICANS

OTHER BOOKS BY PETER P. HILL

French Perceptions of the Early American Republic, 1783–1793
William Vans Murray, Federalist Diplomat
The Elliot School of International Affairs

NAPOLEON'S TROUBLESOME AMERICANS

Franco-American Relations, 1804–1815

PETER P. HILL

Potomac Books, Inc.
Washington, D.C.

Library of Congress Cataloging-in-Publication Data

Hill, Peter P., 1926–
    Napoleon's troublesome Americans : Franco-American relations, 1804–1815 / Peter P. Hill.—1st ed.
        p. cm.
    Includes bibliographical references and index.
    ISBN 1-57488-879-X (alk. paper)
    1. United States—Foreign relations—France.   2. France—Foreign relations—United States.   3. Napoleon I, Emperor of the French, 1769–1821.   4. Jefferson, Thomas, 1743–1826.   5. Madison, James, 1751–1836.   6. United States—Foreign relations—1801–1815.   7. France—Foreign relations—1792–1815.   I. Title.

E183.8.F8H495   2005
327.73044′09′034—dc22

                                                        2004022504

Printed in Canada on acid-free paper that meets the American National Standards Institute Z39-48 Standard.

Potomac Books, Inc.
22841 Quicksilver Drive
Dulles, Virginia 20166

First Edition

10   9   8   7   6   5   4   3   2   1

To Barbara, loving spouse and dearest friend.

CONTENTS

Americans in the
Anglo-French Crossfire

Shortly before Congress declared war on Britain in June 1812, the United States Senate came within two votes of declaring war on France as well. Although the narrow margin suggests a near thing, the targeting of France owed as much to partisan spleen as it did to serious intent. Senate Federalists who backed the motion clearly hankered less for war with France than for the opportunity to smear the Madison administration with the canard that in urging war on Britain, it was bowing to Napoleon's wishes. Partisan politics aside, however, more than a few members of Congress held France guilty of enough offenses against American national interests to make two declarations of war, though inexpedient, not altogether unthinkable. For six years, the two belligerents had nearly equaled each other in seizing American shipping. By any measure, an aggrieved Congress had as much material and emotional cause to declare war on France as on Britain.

Besides explaining why Americans believed Napoleon Bonaparte had treated them so badly, this study will advance the narrative of the era by examining why the French emperor believed Americans deserved such treatment. It does not exonerate him for his unforgiving malevolence, his deceits, or his game-playing with America's vital interests, but it does make the case that he had a great many reasons to resent both the American government and its citizens for what he believed was their deep-seated and sometimes active hostility toward France in his long contest with Great Britain. Though it was not alone among his grievances, he particularly resented Americans' relentless assault on his continental blockade, which he believed was his best and perhaps only hope to defeat Britain by shutting off her European markets. Not only did American merchants, often in collusion with their British counterparts, find ingenious ways to penetrate his "Continental System," but beginning in 1808 they also became the principal suppliers of the British forces he was fighting in Spain and Portugal. In these and other instances, Americans seemed to share a poisonous commonality of interests with his enemy, and no appeals to their sense of honor and self-respect, he believed, would overcome the material importance they attached to their commerce with Britain. He was not surprised, then, at the feebleness of the American response to London's imposition of transit taxes and other controls on American commerce with Europe beginning in 1807. Nor did he accept the supposed evenhandedness of Jefferson's answering embargo or acknowledge the impartiality of its legislative sequel, the Non-Intercourse Act, especially when the latter effectively cut off U.S. traffic with France but did little to hinder American trade with Britain. And when they caught his attention, he chafed, too, at Yankees who ran guns to rebels in St. Domingue (Haiti) where France still claimed a remnant of sovereignty. And to his annoyance, he had to deal with American diplomats of the era who insisted with little evidence to substantiate their claim that the United States had bought West Florida at the time he had sold them Louisiana. At every turn, Napoleon found Americans troublesome or worse.

As the belligerents set out to destroy each other's commerce with neutrals, the Jefferson administration took a stand against what it held to be violations of the protections afforded by the law of nations. Behind such legal arguments, however, was a president who fully understood that any disruption of the nation's commerce with Europe, especially with Britain, would seriously jeopardize its economic well-being. Though not particularly solicitous of the merchant class, Jefferson unquestionably recognized the vital role these commercial exchanges played in the nation's economy,[1] an awareness that sharpened after 1805 with Napoleon's decisive naval defeat at Trafalgar. At this point as noted, the French emperor, now having an enemy his armies could not reach, set out to defeat Britain by attempting to cut off her exports to Europe. His "Continental System," he believed, could so reduce the flow of Britain's exports as to cause her manufacturing base to choke on its surpluses and her economy to collapse. Though he never succeeded in drawing the noose tight enough, he never gave up trying.[2] In the words of one historian, "Napoleon was ready to fight the whole of Europe, if necessary, to prevent English merchandise from reaching it."[3] For American shipmasters and the American statesmen who sought to protect them, this meant that France would seize any vessel suspected of carrying British cargo to a European destination.

On the home front, as both France and Britain began their depredations, the Republican and Federalist parties differed over how best to respond. Spokesmen for the mercantile community, traditionally Federalist, tended to play down the seriousness of Britain's maritime abuses and press for diplomatic solutions. When diplomacy proved unavailing, Jefferson and his Republican Congresses confected a series of economic sanctions designed to coerce the belligerents to mend their ways—measures the Federalists deplored and the belligerents largely ignored. In the end, although France nearly matched Britain in its pillaging of American commerce, the British navy's continued impressment of American seamen and the perception of British intrigue on the northwest frontier led a Republican majority in Congress to decide that Britain was their principal enemy and that war was their only honorable recourse. An unrepentant Napoleon was the principal beneficiary of that decision.

Long before Congress declared war, partisans on both sides could agree that much of their quarrel over lost shipping would not have arisen if Britain and France had seen fit to honor the principle known as "free ships, free goods." Though not fully recognized by the law of nations, this principle held that neutral-flag vessels may carry noncontraband cargoes in safety to any belligerent port as long as that port is not effectively blockaded.[4] Historically, Britain and France stood at opposite extremes with respect to this presumed right of neutral carriers. London, always wary of lessening the advantage conferred by its navy's traditional command of the seas, had rarely allowed neutral ships the right of safe passage to the ports of an enemy.[5] France, by contrast, weaker in naval power and more dependent on foreign carriers, had already twice accorded Americans the right of "free ships," first in the Franco-American commercial treaty of 1778 and again in the Convention of 1800, which ended the Quasi-War. Against this backdrop, Americans naturally expected Paris to outshine London in favoring their maritime rights and consequently were chagrined when Napoleon in late 1806 announced an ostensible blockade of Britain that was patently less effective than those her enemy imposed on France.

American shipowners of the era also had to contend with the British

Admiralty Rule of 1756. Announced at the outset of the Seven Years War, this rule sought to enforce the mercantilist precept that colonial powers should carry the trade of their empires only in their own ships. France and Spain, however, at war with Britain in 1756 and hard pressed by British inroads on their merchant fleets, invited neutral carriers into their colonial ports. Because this resort to neutral carriage diminished Britain's naval advantage, London announced that ports closed by law and custom to second parties in peacetime not be opened to them in wartime, a rule it enforced by seizing neutral vessels caught in the act. But the question later arose: Did the prohibition apply to second parties that had been granted access to colonial ports in times of peace?

In the 1780s, grain shortages in France compelled Paris to open several Antillean ports to the importation of American foodstuffs. Spain, having similar needs, also opened her islands to American suppliers. What followed was predictable. Having brought cargoes to the Caribbean, American shipmasters insisted on being furnished with "return" cargoes, typically sugar and coffee. Because these "colonial" goods more than supplied the needs of American consumers, what was left over constituted a large and valuable re-exportable surplus. In a round-about way, this re-export trade to Europe acquired "legitimacy" from another mercantilist concept that sanctioned the direct exchange of commodities between nation-states in items of their own production or manufacture. All parties saw advantage, for example, in direct exchanges of English woolens for French wines. Now, thanks to an odd twist of mercantilist reasoning, such permissible trade between principals in items of their own production opened the way for Americans to re-export West Indian products to European buyers. The reasoning here lay in the notion that a cargo's most recent port of departure, rather than its place of origin, determined its "nationality." Thus, a cargo of French sugar landed at Charleston (its voyage thereby "broken") became an "American" product that could be re-exported to any port in Europe where commodities truly of American origin were admissible.

Although "broken voyage" enriched those who engaged in it, there were divisive partisan implications. Federalist merchants were pleased to point out that such West Indies cargoes often paid for high-value European manufactures that could not otherwise be "bought" with low-value American raw materials. Republican politicos, however, especially those representing subsistence farmers who had no interest in the export market, questioned whether Congress should spend money to provide naval protection or diplomatic support for cargoes that were not truly "American."[6]

Federalists seemed to have the best of the argument when in May 1800, a "broken voyage" case came before the British jurist, Sir William Scott. The American ship *Polly* captured en route from Havana to Bilbao, Spain, had broken its voyage at Marblehead, Massachusetts, where its cargo had been landed and duties paid. To the dismay of his countrymen, Scott dismissed the captors' claim that the Rule of 1756 had been breached and released the *Polly* on grounds that "[a]n American has, undoubtedly, a right to import the produce of the Spanish colonies for his own use; and after it is imported *bona fide* into his own country, he would be at liberty to carry them on to the general commerce of Europe."[7] American merchants drank grateful toasts to Sir William and exulted as the volume of their re-export trade continued to rise over the next five years.[8]

The windfall was not to last, however. British officialdom, aghast at Scott's decision, sought its reversal. As the historian Bradford Perkins notes pointedly, the *Polly* decision meant that "ship after ship sailed contemptuously past patrolling English vessels, often laden with goods converted only by fraud into nominally neutral property."[9] The halcyon days of "broken voyage" ended abruptly in May 1805 when, under prodding from the Pitt Ministry, Sir William Grant handed down the decision of the Lords Commissioners of Appeals in the case of another American merchantman, the *Essex*. Intercepted with cargo en route from Barcelona to Havana via Salem, the *Essex* was condemned for violating the Rule of 1756. Because a direct voyage to Havana—a port closed in peacetime—had been "falsified" by its "asserted destination" [Salem], Grant said he saw no reason not to condemn it under the Rule of 1756. In the wake of the *Essex* decision, American owners lost an estimated 60 vessels, as well as a profitable trade pattern.[10]

Although the *Essex* decision marked a worsening of Anglo-American relations and evoked the first round of congressional retaliation, it bore only indirectly on American relations with France. It was not long, however, before other British efforts to control American commerce brought France to the realization that her own commercial interests were affected. Thus, whereas Trafalgar may have set off Napoleon's determination to close the continent to British exports, Britain's strictures against neutral commerce would give him a pretext to make it happen.

CHAPTER 1

John Armstrong's
Unpromising Beginning

When Sir William Grant read off the *Essex* decision in May 1805, the future of West Florida, not maritime issues, figured most prominently in U.S. relations with France. John Armstrong, the newly appointed American minister to Paris, spent much of his first six months pressing the French foreign office to admit that West Florida had been part of the Louisiana purchase, thereby seconding Jefferson's obsessive claim to have bought that part of the Florida panhandle lying west of the Perdido river. Few historians can resist quoting Henry Adams's ironic description of Robert Livingston's having been forced "to maintain that Spain had retroceded West Florida to France without knowing it, that France had sold it to the United States without suspecting it, that the United States had bought it without paying for it, and that neither France nor Spain, although the original contracting parties, were competent to decide the meaning of their own contract."[1]

Although this characterization reflected Adams's generally harsh opinion of Jeffersonian diplomacy, his point is well taken: Jefferson's claim to West Florida lacked documentation.[2] For that reason, Armstrong and his fellow diplomats would find themselves hard put to advance it. Indeed, a sizable cross section of the American diplomatic corps—James Monroe, Charles Pinckney, James Bowdoin, and George Erving—all failed in their efforts to persuade Spain that it had ceded West Florida as part of its transfer of Louisiana to France in 1800. The uncertainties sprang from West Florida's having been passed back and forth from France to Britain to Spain, and, as Jefferson would have it, back to France. The question was this: did Spain administer West Florida, the territory between New Orleans and the Apalachicola River, as part of peninsular East Florida or as part of Louisiana when she came into possession of all three in 1763? American claims hung on the supposition that West Florida had accompanied Spain's "retrocession" of Louisiana to France in 1800 and thence by purchase to the United States in 1803.

As to whether Spain administered West Florida as part of Louisiana at the time of retrocession, Madison biographer Irving Brant concludes that it did not. He notes, however, that France had later pressed Madrid to include West Florida on grounds that that province was historically part of Louisiana—a claim Spain had rejected. In that light, Brant sees no impropriety in Jefferson's pursuing a claim, however dubious, which France herself had pressed earlier.[3] How Napoleon would regard such pressure on Madrid when it came from Washington was another matter.

John Armstrong arrived in Paris in late October 1804. When he sailed for home six years later, he looked back on his mission with a sense of satisfaction not wholly shared by his detractors. To his credit, he had kept France's feet to the fire on West Florida until Madison's partial annexation of it in 1810 had more or less mooted the issue. Better yet, he had just received Napoleon's promise to exempt American shipping from the punishing confiscations of his Berlin and Milan decrees. Unfortunately, the exact meaning of this apparent breakthrough was not easy to come by.

Although Armstrong carried out his mission to Paris with a high sense of his country's honor and self-respect, he was not particularly well fitted for diplomatic office. Quarrelsome and abrasive, he was, in the understated words of one historian, "difficult to work with."[4] He also wrote badly in English and not at all in French. Thomas Jefferson, who had a low tolerance for muddy prose, once complained that Armstrong "cannot give a naked fact in an intelligible form," a complaint that Napoleon himself shared on reading some of Armstrong's diplomatic notes.[5]

Obtuse and often mean spirited, the American minister also bickered incessantly with his consuls, charging them variously with either exceeding or abusing their powers, abetting smugglers, profiteering from claims cases, or showing laxity of one form or other. As the president remarked to Madison in August 1807, Armstrong's most recent letters from Paris showed that "the feuds there are not subsiding."[6] The envoy's poor health also affected his mission. Bouts of rheumatic fever, gout, and other unspecified ailments either kept him in bed or taking the waters at Bourbon l'Arcambault often enough that French officials rarely saw him. Nor, as his successor pointed out, was he wealthy enough to indulge the ambassadorial tradition of wining and dining often useful in oiling the wheels of diplomacy.[7] Ministerial salary allotments from a parsimonious Congress, in any case, barely covered everyday expenses.

Given these negatives, Armstrong would seem to have been an unlikely choice for the Paris post, but when Robert Livingston asked to be recalled from Paris, Jefferson welcomed the opportunity to replace one New Yorker with another and thereby continue to bestow patronage on the northern wing of his party. In the same political context, it was Armstrong's good fortune to have married Livingston's sister, Alida. Without this link to the powerful Livingston clan, a Dutchess County landowner who had served briefly in the U.S. Senate would hardly have been a likely candidate for high diplomatic office.[8] This is not to say that Armstrong was entirely without previous public distinction. As a young army major, he had seen wartime service under General Gates, fought at Saratoga, and at war's end gained some notoriety during the army's mutinous stirrings at Newburgh. As author of the so-called "Newburgh Addresses," Armstrong had a major, if fleeting, role in putting Congress on notice that an unpaid soldiery might take matters into its own hands. General Washington's prompt appearance quieted the troops and ended the crisis before it got out of hand. Armstrong's reputation for bellicosity, however, lingered on.

As U.S. minister to France, Armstrong jousted with French officials who tried his frail patience no less than his uncertain talents. Still, the historian Clifford Egan concludes that "if Armstrong was not a brilliant diplomat, neither was he an incompetent amateur,"[9] an assessment, however, that compares gently with that of George Erving, a fellow diplomat who in 1811 wrote that if Armstrong had been "a man of common sense and common honesty," he might have prevented the ills France had visited on American commerce.[10]

Jefferson's fervent desire to obtain West Florida, indeed all of Florida, appeared boldly in the instructions Secretary of State Madison sent to James Monroe in April 1804. Monroe, then in London, was to go to Madrid where it was hoped he could reinvigorate Charles Pinckney's stalled diplomacy, stopping first in Paris to find out if the French government could be persuaded to "interpose" its good offices. Once in Madrid, Monroe was to demand that Spain hand over West Florida without payment, cavil, or encumbrance. For East Florida, as well, he could agree that the United States would pay off its citizens' claims against Spain for earlier maritime depredations, including those committed by French privateers operating in Spanish waters during the American Quasi-War with France.[11] This last, asking Madrid to admit liability for French privateering, would not sit well in Paris.

Like others who tried to pry loose West Florida, Monroe realized from the outset that his best leverage lay in winning Bonaparte's support for American claims. The First Consul, however, had no reason to oblige. Although he counted on Spain to be an active and undistracted ally in his renewed warfare with Britain and Austria in late 1804, he apparently satisfied himself that the United States would not go to war over West Florida and therefore that he need not intercede. At the same time, he was thoroughly annoyed by the spectacle of American diplomats bullying Spain over claims to West Florida which he regarded as groundless. And, as his foreign minister, Charles Maurice de Talleyrand reminded him, they had gone much too far in demanding that Spain indemnify for American property taken by French privateers in Spanish waters during the Quasi-War.[12] Relatedly in the same time frame, Bonaparte also took it seriously amiss that Americans were trading with and ostensibly running guns to rebel forces in Haiti where his troops were now fighting their last losing battles. For a while in 1805, however, it seemed the Haitian and Florida issues might be felicitously resolved in a trade-off. In March, under pressure from both London and Paris, the administration persuaded Congress to ban the clearance of armed merchant ships for Haitian ports.[13] Madison promptly notified Armstrong that although France had demanded a complete trade stoppage, a ban on armed commerce might be enough to cultivate "a disposition in that Government to meet us favorably on other topics."[14] The allusion to West Florida was unmistakable.

In the Haitian background, it might be noted, Americans seeking new markets had responded nimbly when in January 1804 the former slave population declared independence. Although French efforts to restore control had ended disastrously some months earlier her troops still held a few strongholds in the western Spanish sector, and an uptick in French privateering had led U.S. shipowners to arm their vessels. Armstrong was to tell Paris that the ban on arming was as far as Congress could go in deferring to France because an "absolute prohibition" would violate the principle of free ships, free goods.[15] This halfway measure, far from pla-cating, had the opposite effect. Louis Marie Turreau, the French minister in Washington, fired off a barrage of protests,[16] which Bonaparte echoed in August when he annnounced, "I will declare fair prize all [vessels] that shall enter or leave the French ports of St. Domingue."[17] Adding heft to this threat, French and Spanish naval squadrons put in an appearance that fall, and in February 1806 Congress cut off trade completely. By this time, the arguments for not doing so had worn thin. Even the "legal" case was dubious. When Madison tried to lecture Turreau on the right of neutrals to trade at belligerent ports, the French minister rejoined point-edly that the Haitian rebels lacked belligerent status. France was simply putting down an insurrection in which the law of nations forbade other governments to interfere. Turreau scored most tellingly, however, when he noted that the administration's racially motivated refusal to recognize a black government had deprived Haiti of the belligerent status under which the doctrine of free ships, free goods would have applied.[18] Legal arguments aside, Jefferson could only hope that a complete trade em-bargo against Haiti would win Napoleon's good offices in effecting his acquisition of West Florida.[19] It remained to be seen how well Monroe would fare on this issue in Madrid.

───── ⤜⤛ ─────

Armstrong, meanwhile, began to doubt whether any part of Florida could be had unless the negotiations were transferred to Paris where Napoleon and his foreign minister could get a piece of the action.[20] They seemed to be awaiting "some proposition on our part," he wrote, and supposed a cash payment would be the "cheapest way" to bring France into the negotiation. "Half a million would do wonders," he wrote, but added circumspectly, "the mischief would be greater than the miracles."[21] After five months in Paris, he had made no progress on other issues either. Talleyrand had told him that France would not be held accountable for spoliations committed by French privateers operating in Spanish waters during the Quasi-War and continued to reject the notion that West Flor-ida had been part of the Louisiana purchase.[22] Frustrated, Armstrong hinted darkly that war might follow if Monroe failed in Madrid. His threat ignored, he concluded that French mediation definitely had a price tag, that they "will consent to no measure that goes to empty the boxes of his Catholic Majesty, unless it be to fill their own."[23] Not one to shy from thoughts of military solutions, he told Monroe that France might be jolted into taking a mediatory role if the United States were to declare war on Spain.[24]

By the spring of 1805 the administration was taking the Spanish crisis seriously enough to warn Monroe not to create a situation in Madrid that might deprive Congress of its war-making powers.[25] Reports trickling into Paris also suggested the likelihood of war. In early June, General Beurnonville, the French ambassador in Madrid, reported Monroe and Pinckney outraged at the rebuff the Spanish Foreign Minister Pedro Cevallos had given their latest proposal. Monroe was angrily preparing to return to London and Pinckney's recall was imminent. He enclosed a bitter letter from Monroe denouncing Cevallos's rude rejection of their conciliatory efforts and asking him, "as soldier to soldier," why France had said nothing about West Florida's not being part of Louisiana when the United States bought it and now supported Spain's view that it was not. In light of Monroe's anger, Beurnonville thought it possible the United States might take the Floridas by force.[26] At the same time, he scoffed at Monroe's indignation. The Americans' latest offer strained credulity: a demand that Spain cede both Floridas and honor American claims under an 1802 convention, in return for which the United States would agree to a Rio Bravo boundary for Louisiana in the west and forgo claims connected with French privateering. It struck Beurnonville as absurd that Spain should give up Texas and the Floridas to settle claims that were at best dubious.[27]

Hoping to capitalize on Monroe's heated correspondence with Cevallos, Armstrong sent copies to Talleyrand. The latter merely rejoined that the more he thought about it, the more he was convinced "that Spain is right in every point of the controversy."[28] Later, when Monroe returned to Paris empty-handed, Armstrong suggested that the administration might still catch France's attention if it were to levy an embargo on Spain and attack a few of Spain's Gulf ports.[29] In the end, talk of war made little impression on Paris. Beurnonville's warnings were more than offset by intelligence from Washington where French Minister Louis Turreau continued to report an American distaste for armed combat bordering on national cowardice. Paris did, however, anticipate more low-level pressure on Madrid, akin to that of the Mobile Act by which Congress had created a shadow customs district for West Florida in 1804.[30] An unsigned foreign office memorandum of April or May 1805 hinted that the United States might levy a trade embargo on Spain's colonial ports or send troops to occupy territory west of the Mississippi.[31] This tallied closely enough with Armstrong's recommendations to Washington to suggest that the minister had made his militancy known in high places.

Gradually, American officials close to the scene yielded to the idea of buying French support in Madrid with hard cash although Monroe at first resisted it. He blamed Robert Livingston for even suggesting that the United States might have to pay for West Florida. Shortly after the Louisiana Purchase, two foreign ministry officials had told Livingston that Spain might be persuaded to part with West Florida in return for a repayable loan of 70 million livres. How France would figure in this transaction was not clear, but when Monroe heard of it he was sure that any money loaned to Madrid would end up in Paris. He had told Livingston at the time that this would mean "paying twice for the same thing" because Spain would never repay the loan. Later, Monroe's own conversations with the same two officials, Barbé-Marbois and the comte d'Hauterive, met with the same undertone: money would adjust "the differences." About to leave for Madrid, Monroe had rebuffed these overtures, assuring the secretary of state that the French now "know that we are resolved not to give one cent."[32] When Armstrong also rejected the notion of making a cash payment, Madison told him he had done the right thing, that the French wanted "merely to convert the negotiations with Spain into a pecuniary job for France and her Agents."[33] Thus far, American scruples respecting the evils of jobbery still had a few months to run.

In July 1805, the administration resigned itself to a cooling-off period. Jefferson told Turreau that he regarded Napoleon's siding with Spain on the West Florida question as a signal for delay. "Since the Emperor wishes it," he told the French minister, "we can postpone the arrangement to a more favorable time." Alarmed, Turreau warned Paris not to delay too long. American settlers were moving southward in large numbers, and the President had told him frankly, "we are not able to stop our men." Time was on the side of Americans' creeping conquest, he cautioned, and went on to suggest that France might still salvage Spain's territorial assets if it were to send troops to the Floridas. This would have a salutary effect, he rumbled, because Americans "speak of French armies only with a sentiment comprised of respect and fear."[34] Like his counterpart in Paris, Turreau was seldom at a loss for military solutions.

By the fall of 1805, diplomatic currents flowing in both Paris and Washington converged on a money-laundering scheme which, had it been carried out, would have bilked Spain of both Floridas, filled Napoleon's coffers, and made Thomas Jefferson an accomplice to international fleecing on a grand scale. As envisioned by the ever artful Tallyrand, the plan featured the minimal risk of transporting Spanish bullion across waters infested by British men-of-war. It assumed that neutral U.S. vessels could accomplish the crossing in relative safety. Each party, however, envisioned the details of the Florida "job" somewhat differently which may account for its ultimate undoing. Armstrong first got wind of it on 4 September 1805 when he was visited by an unnamed government official who laid out the details. This approach through a subordinate suggests that Talleyrand may have left open the door to deniability, a tactic reminiscent of his conduct during the XYZ Affair. Armstrong's visitor insisted on strict secrecy, urging that if Washington rejected the plan, the president must give it "no public or other notice." Indeed, the miasma of secrecy was so thick that Napoleon himself may not have known the details.[35] The plan was this: Washington would once more make its case to Madrid and on being rebuffed demand that Spain submit the "points in controversy" to the emperor. Thereupon, France would support some five proposals. The nub of the job lay in the last two: the United States would pay Spain ten million dollars and Spain would pay U.S. citizens' claims "by bills [drawn] on the Spanish colonies." That the United States would also be buying East Florida became explicit when Armstrong braced his unnamed visitor for details. In referring the proposals to Washington, Armstrong doubted the administration would pay $10 million for "the barren and expensive province of East Florida," even if three or four million of it were used to settle U.S. claims against Spain. (Apparently, this objection registered because seven million was the figure he relayed to Washington.) Too, he doubted the administration would relinquish various damage claims or look with favor on the proposal to establish a no-settlement zone thirty leagues wide on either side of the Colorado river.[36]

As it turned out, he missed the mark on all counts. A cabinet memorandum, tentatively dated 19 November, accepted the plan in every detail except that it offered five million for the Floridas rather than Armstrong's seven. To set the plan in motion, the United States would threaten Spain to the point where she would agree to French mediation. Once at the table, Washington would offer five million dollars to "cede & confirm to the U.S. East & West Florida." A western boundary on the Colorado River was acceptable, as was a thirty-year no-settlement zone between it and the Rio Grande. Spain, for her part, was to pay off U.S. maritime claimants to the tune of an estimated four million. The plan seemed simple enough:

the U.S. would pay out five million and get back four, along with both Floridas. As to the mechanics of the cash transfers, however, the cabinet memorandum made no mention of Talleyrand's condition that the "bills" for settling U.S. spoliation claims be drawn on Spain's New World colonies.

Nudged by the administration, Congress tacitly consented to the scheme when it passed "the two-million dollar bill" the following spring. Though the figures remained flexible, the U.S. liability of five million would ostensibly be discharged by paying two million out of the U.S. Treasury, the remaining three million to be taken from Spain's New World gold reserves. It was assumed Napoleon would oversee the ultimate disposal of whatever bullion American vessels transported to Spain.

Critics who deplore Jefferson's willingness to gratify Napoleon's greed at Spain's expense must at least admit that by late 1805 Spanish provocations had multiplied to a point where some decisive action seemed called for. Madrid had not only humiliated Monroe and Pinckney, but had also reneged on a claims convention it had signed in 1802. To the south, she had harassed American traffic on the West Florida rivers and built up her armed forces threateningly in the territory west of New Orleans. From a strategic standpoint, too, Spain's weak presence in Florida remained an open invitation to mischief. Should either Britain or France occupy East Florida—a possibility often talked of—Americans could readily anticipate a major threat to their security from these more powerful neighbors. Although some have been scandalized by the near certainty of the Florida purchase money ending up in Paris, the question remains: At what point in responding to Spanish provocations should Jefferson have drawn the line? The president himself answered this question when, referring to what he called the "price of the Floridas," he told Madison, "We need not care who gets that."[37]

CHAPTER 2

NAPOLEON QUASHES THE FLORIDA "JOB"

Conventional wisdom holds that once Napoleon decided to make Spain part of his empire, he naturally acquired an interest in keeping the Floridas for himself. Be that as it may, what was said and done by those closest to the Florida "job" seems to have had a bearing on its demise. Armstrong, for one, quite likely dampened Talleyrand's enthusiasm when asked how "the bills drawn on So. America" were to be redeemed. When Armstrong replied that Spain would have to transport the bullion at her own risk, the Frenchman's reaction was significant. "You do not mean that Spain must bring the dollars to you? That is impossible." While Talleyrand's question was open to alternate emphases, Armstrong's response made clear that the French minister did not balk at the destination of the dollars (i.e., "to you"), but at the seaborne dangers to which Spanish carriers would be exposed, for when pressed further, Armstrong repeated that although he did not know *who* would transport the bullion, it must be done at Spain's risk. This demurrer may have been critical. Given the role the French minister envisioned for neutral-flag vessels in his original plan, he may well have been put off by Armstrong's dismissal of its essential security arrangement.[1]

Talleyrand may also have squirmed uneasily at dickering over the price tag. Even before the administration countered his proposed ten million dollars with an offer of five, he heard Armstrong's deprecating observation that "10 millions or even 7 millions of dollars is a great deal of money for pine trees and sand hills. Were we to give half the sum, we should pay

11

too much for the whistle." Talleyrand, who had dabbled in land speculation during his exile in the United States, tried to break through Armstrong's dismissiveness. "Under your management," he rejoined, "it
would treble the money," and asked, "do you estimate West Florida at
nothing?" No, Armstrong rejoined, "because we have already bought it
[and] Spain can now sell but the jurisdiction—the soil has long since
been sold to individuals." Talleyrand replied vaguely that Spanish land
grants to individuals could always be revoked and then fell back into a
familiar denial that the United States had bought West Florida when it
purchased Louisiana.[2] When the meeting ended, the French minister
himself must have wondered whether the game was worth the whistle.

Too, Madison's stripped-down counter-proposal, conveyed to Armstrong in March 1806, strongly suggested that the only cash likely to be
floated across the Atlantic was the two million dollars Congress had just
appropriated. Moreover, the United States would make no payments
until it had either taken possession of both Floridas or been guaranteed
their possession by a ratified treaty. As for the remainder of the "purchase
price" (the figure was left blank), Madison clearly envisioned the U.S.
government distributing "not less than four millions of dollars" directly
to its citizens. In short, four million would be subtracted from the five,
six, or seven million Talleyrand had hoped would find its way to Europe.[3]
A year and half later, Madison confirmed his intention when he told
Armstrong to specify "a deduction from the sum payable by the United
States."[4] By this time, however, the Florida job had long since died.

Another blighting factor may have been the conduct of James Bowdoin, the Massachusetts merchant and erstwhile diplomatic trouble-
shooter Jefferson sent to Paris that spring to strengthen Armstrong's
negotiating hand. Bowdoin's layover in Paris—he was en route to replace
Pinckney in Madrid—was a disaster. The two men quarreled bitterly over
their respective "powers," with Armstrong jealously elbowing Bowdoin
out of any direct contact with the French government. In late April, the
minister triumphantly denounced his colleague when French postal officials intercepted an uncoded letter in which Bowdoin had represented
France "as usurping over [Spain] an entire sovereignty and even as putting her provinces to sale without her knowledge or consent." This was
too close to the truth. Armstrong later claimed to have smoothed things
over with the foreign office, but not before Napoleon had chided him
testily with the remark that "even your own agents have not only insinuated, but asserted this." Armstrong had barely mastered his embarrass-

ment when Bowdoin again sinned against secrecy. This time, he failed to use cipher in writing of the Florida plan to Manuel Godoy, Spain's chief minister. Angrily to Monroe, Armstrong wondered if Bowdoin had intended this letter "to be read in every post office between Madrid and Paris?"[5] In retrospect, Bowdoin's penchant for writing letters *en clair* may have put too much strain on the need for secrecy surrounding the Florida job. Armstrong thought so and cited Bowdoin's indiscretions as a contributing factor when the Florida negotiation stalled out completely five months later.[6]

Despite these negatives, late spring 1806 found Armstrong momentarily hopeful that France would broker a Florida deal. Paris was pleased, he wrote, that Congress had reacted to the *Essex* decision by passing a non-importation act against Britain, also by the goodwill it had shown in cutting off trade with St. Domingue. Success seemed assured when Talleyrand informed him in early June that the French ambassador in Madrid was instructed to urge the Spanish government to enter into negotiations "whenever the two governments shall have judged it proper."[7] His optimism faded when, in keeping with the equivocal "whenever," Eugenio Izquierdo, a Spanish Counselor of State, turned up in Paris in mid-July ostensibly to negotiate on the Floridas but refusing to do so. Armstrong suggested an early meeting only to have Izquierdo say that certain unspecified ceremonial requirements had to be met. He was put off a second time by the Spaniard's plea for more time to absorb the "bulky" documentation he had recently received from Madrid.

In early September, Armstrong learned from informants that the emperor had ordered Izquierdo not to negotiate.[8] His first impulse, he wrote, was to demand whether the Spaniard "would or would not negotiate" and call on France "to interpose the good offices" Talleyrand had promised in June. He then explained why he took a third course. From Marshal Geraud Duroc, whom he had been urged to consult, he learned that Napoleon would not oppose his making a direct approach to Izquierdo as long as France had no part in it. Send him a treaty, Duroc suggested.[9] Accordingly, on September 30, five days after Napoleon had left Paris, Armstrong braced Izquierdo with both a "treaty of cession" and a claims convention. The former offered Spain $5 million for both East and West Florida, and the latter spelled out the financial terms, once again repeating Armstrong's condition that any funds drawn from Spain's "treasury in South America" were to be transported at Madrid's risk.[10] Not surprisingly, with France no longer in the picture, Izquierdo felt under no obligation to make a substantive reply. He shot back the next day that he lacked the "political powers" to negotiate. There the Florida job ended.

Casting about for an explanation of why Napoleon aborted the Florida negotiation, Armstrong had more questions than answers. Was it, he wondered "a mere freak of caprice, was it delicacy to Spain, [or] was it some new calculation of policy . . . ?" Perhaps the emperor had decided that the "pecuniary consideration was . . . insufficient." Or, perhaps Spain had fallen into disfavor for its recent refusal either to invade Portugal or let French troops do it. And because Talleyrand had underscored the detrimental effect of Bowdoin's epistolary indiscretions, Armstrong added this to the list of possibilities.[11]

The best explanation may be a simple case of Napoleonic impatience with Talleyrand's too eager and possibly corrupt personal interest in the Florida transaction. In early May the foreign minister had sent his master a persuasive argument for taking a mediatory initiative in Madrid. Americans, Talleyrand wrote, earnestly coveted West Florida's southward flowing rivers and were rapidly swelling its population. By contrast, Spain's only interest there was "to prevent other powers from getting new ports on the Gulf of Mexico." What it added up to was that the United States had a greater interest in acquiring West Florida than Spain had in keeping it.[12] Turreau's recent dispatches, moreover, had painted a picture of an American government determined to have the Floridas. Jefferson had been quoted as saying that he would have them "whether by exchange, by acquisition, or finally by force."[13] Still, he believed Washington was willing to negotiate. True, it was still trying to expel Carlos Martinez d'Irujo, Spain's overly outspoken minister; and it had winked at the South American revolutionary Francisco Miranda's blatant arming of vessels in New York for an expedition against Caracas, but the administration had recently moderated its tone toward Spain and was now prepared to settle the Florida issue amicably. In all, Napoleon's foreign minister was telling him the moment had arrived for France to intercede.

It was on 4 June 1806, a month after filing this report, that Talleyrand had promised Armstrong a French initiative in Madrid. By this time, his appetite may have been whetted by news of the "two million dollar" bill, although Turreau did not report its Florida purpose until 10 May.[14] A readiness to mediate lingered until the end of June, most evident in the low-key way Talleyrand and his sovereign handled the potentially disruptive Miranda affair. The would-be liberator had spent two weeks in Washington before his armed expedition left New York on 2 February headed for what was to be a failed assault on Caracas. Both Jefferson and Madison, Paris was told, had "full knowledge" and did nothing to stop him. The administration's subsequent effort to prosecute Miranda's American co-conspirators, however, made it relatively easy to gloss over the incident. When Spain's ambassador to Paris, Prince Masserano, asked how France viewed such "complicity," Talleyrand replied equably that the emperor regretted the administration's inability to stop Miranda but its effort to punish the offenders he took as a sign that "the United States seem disposed to end . . . all the discussions which subsisted between the two powers."[15]

Three days later, Talleyrand wrote Vandeul, the French *chargé* in Madrid, to press Godoy to accept a quick settlement. As June drew to a close, a French-sanctioned negotiation was still afoot. A letter from Vandeul brought word that Godoy seemed eager to conciliate the United States. At this point, sometime during the last week in June, Napoleon made clear to Talleyrand that he had moved too swiftly. The severity of this check can be gauged from the letter Talleyrand sent Vandeul on 3 July, disavowing the latter's diplomacy and serving notice that France would have no part of the negotiation. The emperor, he qualified, would welcome the "return of a good understanding between the two countries; but they alone can judge what means of reconciliation suit their respective interests." A follow-up letter falsely charged Vandeul with having exceeded his instructions.[16]

Thereafter a subdued Tallyrand played the Florida game within the limits Napoleon had set. He instructed Turreau to tell the administration it must deal directly with Madrid on the Florida issue. The emperor, he wrote, "has nothing to prescribe to this. . . ." Why? Because whatever the outcome of the Florida issue he did not foresee an outbreak of war between Spain and the United States. His Majesty would welcome a peaceful settlement but if the administration unwisely resorted to war, it should know that Spain would have the military resources of Europe behind it.[17]

Why Talleyrand's Florida job was still-born and why Napoleon disengaged altogether are susceptible to separate explanations. As has been suggested, the French minister quite likely concluded that little or no money was to be had from the transaction, the scheme too complex, and his American collaborators not sufficiently cooperative. That he continued to take initiatives until the end of June doubtless rode on his hope that if France were to act as an intermediary, these negative factors might be overcome and some skimming of funds still accomplished. Explaining

Napoleon's decision to drop out of the Florida controversy altogether seems to lead in two directions. First, to the truth of what Talleyrand told Turreau: that the emperor doubted the Spanish-American dispute would lead to war and therefore felt French intervention unnecessary. In short, the Florida stew could safely be left to simmer. Second, Napoleon faced crises in Europe that reduced the future of the Floridas to a minor agendum, an issue to be dealt with later in a context he was already planning to alter. By the summer of 1806, although Austria had been cowed at Ulm and Austerlitz, he had yet to make peace with Russia and faced a fall campaign against an angrily mobilizing Prussia.[18] Until the latter were defeated (as it would be at Jena on 14 October), and until Russia was neutralized (as it would be at Friedland the following June), one can assume he preferred to put his plans for the Iberian Peninsula and its New World dependencies on hold.

Not one to give up easily, Armstrong pursued Talleyrand into the field with more correspondence on the Florida issue. Given the intensity of French military operations, however, he was sure his letters were either "lost on the road" or swallowed by the maelstrom. With Talleyrand in close attendance, the emperor and his Grand Army were spending the bleak winter of 1806–07 miserably bivouacked on the frozen plains of Poland and East Prussia where clearly only the most pressing diplomatic business received attention. When Armstrong wrote on 5 February, for example, Napoleon was three days from Eylau, a enormously bloody battle, technically a victory for French forces though it left the czar's army intact. When he wrote again a month later, French forces had taken most of Poland but were desperately regrouping in anticipation of a final showdown with the Russians. Not until after 14 June when Russian forces were decisively defeated at Friedland did he hear from the foreign minister and then only because he wrote once more. His first letter had warned of Spanish troop maneuvers in western Louisiana; his second relayed the latest signal from Madrid that Spain would welcome French mediation.[19] In mid-June 1807, Armstrong made the offer explicit: the United States would pay $5 million for both Floridas and a Louisiana boundary running north from the Sabine River, another $2 million if the line started from the more westerly Colorado.[20] The French foreign minister, obviously much preoccupied with the Treaty of Tilsit, replied offhandedly that the emperor was pleased to hear that Spain and the United States were nego-

tiating their differences. Armstrong was puzzled: he had no ongoing negotiation with Spain because Madrid had deferred to Paris. He jotted a
note at the bottom of Talleyrand's letter to remind him of this when
he returned.[21] Whether he would have greater success with Tallyrand's
successor remained to be seen. In mid-August 1807, the French foreign
minister was abruptly removed from office. Apparently not fallen from
grace altogether, he was sidelined with the title of Vice Grand Electeur.[22]

Though determined to get off to a firm start with the new foreign minister, Armstrong soon discovered that the comte de Champagny (later
made duc de Cadore) had his own ideas of firmness.[23] Champagny lost
no time making himself known and promised to carry forward his predecessor's goodwill. When they first met, however, Champagny sternly demanded that the U.S. consul at Tripoli be reprimanded for failing to
return a social call on his French counterpart. Once past this unpleasantness, the two men talked about Florida and the boundaries of Louisiana,
and four days later Armstrong learned that the French ambassador in
Madrid had been freshly instructed "in relation to our controversy with
Spain."[24] Meanwhile, he asked Champagny to search his archives for documents delineating a western boundary for Louisiana. In a forceful note
dated 28 August 1807, he demanded to know where France held that
western boundary to lie. A truthful answer would confer no "improper
advantages," nor do "any positive wrong to Spain." It was unthinkable
that a boundary description did not exist either in the treaties of Ryswick,
Utrecht, or Rastadt, and certainly at the time France ceded that province
to Spain in 1763.[25]

He was gratified and no less surprised when Champagny promptly
produced the findings of an archival search, a *lettre patente* issued by
Louis XIV on 14 September 1712, which described Louisiana as comprising
"the Mississippi from the Illinois country to the mouth of the river; the
Wabash, the Missouri and all the rivers that flow directly or indirectly
into that of the Mississippi." In short, the entire watershed of the Mississippi basin. Unless Madrid had evidence to the contrary, Champagny
pronounced the 1712 document to be France's most authoritative.[26] Although the West Florida issue still hung fire, Armstrong was elated. This
finding, he wrote Madison, had done more "to open the door to negotiation & adjustment than anything which had been previously done, and I
wait, with much anxiety, the return of the *Revenge,* when I shall prosecute

the correspondence, in the view that our business with Britain, may render necessary." This cryptic reference to business with Britain spoke to the still uncertain outcome of *Chesapeake* crisis, but West Florida was still near the top of Madison's agenda. Writing to Armstrong on 2 August, the secretary had hinted that West Florida might be taken by force unless Spain yielded to diplomacy. Rumor had it that Americans there were ready to strike for independence and if the British moved in that direction, U.S. troops might have to occupy it preemptively. Either way, Spain stood to lose what the United States had been willing to pay for.[27] Armstrong hopefully relayed these warnings to Masserano, although he might not have bothered. The Spanish ambassador merely thanked him for alerting his government to a possible uprising and said he would pass the information along to Madrid.[28]

As 1807 drew to a close, Armstrong saw little hope for either the transfer of the Floridas or the demarcation of the Louisiana boundary. Paris only pretended to be helpful on the Florida question, he mused, her promises all the "more sparing in recent months." Napoleon's contemporary shuffling of dynasties south of the Pyrenees, he believed, might well have a bearing on the future of Spanish and Portugese holdings in the New World. Even if Napoleon did not overthrow the Bourbon and Braganza dynasties, he was sure to hold them "as hostages for the eventual delivery of their colonies." The administration, he believed, would do well to consider imposing "a general embargo [on Spain] . . . accompanied by an attack to the North on Canada . . . & to the south on the Floridas."[29]

Armstrong "for the last time" in late January 1808 requested French mediation on grounds that France "alone can prevent a decision by force."[30] Napoleon's answer, when it came, joined the Florida issue with fast-developing maritime issues. By this time, both belligerents were systematically seizing American vessels. The British ministry's orders-in-council of November 1807 foreshadowed such sweeping controls over American shipping that Napoleon fully expected to hear that Congress had declared war. Accordingly, he baited the Florida hook hoping it would land a defensive alliance. On 4 February, Champagny notified Armstrong that the emperor would welcome a "closer connexion." At the very least, His Majesty would "not look it amiss" if the United States were to defend the Floridas against a British attack. Better yet, in return for a formal alliance he would arrange to have Spain cede those provinces outright and arrange "a convenient western boundary for Louisiana."[31]

Armstrong sniffed the bait and backed away. Washington, he knew, would reject the notion of an alliance, and the idea of a "closer connexion" stood at odds with what he knew was the growing number of detained American vessels. Nor was he deceived by Champagny's accompanying assurance that legal proceedings against these vessels had been suspended and that they were merely sequestered, not confiscated. To Armstrong, as to Madison, the meaning was clear: Americans could have their ships and cargoes back if their government agreed to ally with France against England. For good measure, France would throw in the Floridas and a spacious western boundary for Louisiana.[32]

The American envoy's spirits sank even lower when Champagny told him that France would respect the rights of neutral powers but only when those rights were universally respected. Considering this fanciful appeal to universality in the context of an alliance offer, he wrote on the margin of Champagny's letter: "Make an alliance to-morrow [and] the depredations on your commerce will not cease." A case in point, he noted, was Denmark whose ships were at that moment being seized despite a Franco-Danish alliance.[33]

This offer of what might be called a Florida-based alliance had an opportunistic quality. In this instance, Napoleon presumed too much when he concluded that London's most recent strictures on American shipping had created a *de facto* state of war. Jefferson, it turned out, was not about to take instruction from Paris on how to respond to British orders-in-council.[34] Instead, Congress levied an all-encompassing embargo that left Jefferson's long-protracted Florida diplomacy a subset in a complex web of maritime issues. The most he had achieved by the end of his administration was Napoleon's leave to send U.S. troops into Florida if the British threatened to occupy it. For James Madison, soon to succeed him, what happened to the Floridas would rank significantly lower in the scale of diplomatic imperatives than finding ways to sustain America's maritime neutral rights.

CHAPTER 3

The Cycle of Depredation
Begins, 1806–07

W hy so many American ships and cargoes ultimately fell victim to French corsairs, port officials, and prize courts had something to do with the doctrine of reprisal. To hear it from Paris, London had started this cycle of depredation, having been first to violate the rights of neutral carriers. France was merely responding in kind. What Britain had begun Britain must end. Only then would France follow suit. French officials were explicit on this point: France would stop seizing neutral property whenever Britain left off its own seizures. Thus, the question of which party began the cycle of depredation and therefore should be held responsible for breaking it figured prominently in Washington's diplomatic exchanges with the two European capitals beginning in 1806.

Claiming the right of reprisal, of course, did not disguise that beyond the heated charges of "who started it," both parties profited financially whenever neutral ships and cargoes were condemned and sold. Reprisal provided a pretext but the revenues derived from such depredations gave the belligerents reason enough to fend off American demands for justice. Still, whenever opportunities arose to achieve some easing of this maritime spoliation, American diplomats worked manfully to peel back the layers of justificatory argument in the hope of revealing a core of neutral rights that both belligerents might agree to honor.

———∞———

France was at first a bystander to the neutral rights controversy, unaffected when Congress in March 1806 passed a non-importation act in retaliation for British seizures under the now year-old *Essex* decision. As critics have pointed out, then and since, the law lacked the element of patriotic self-sacrifice because it permitted the continued importation of British goods Americans most needed. It also missed out as a retaliatory gesture because the ban was not to take effect immediately.[1] At the time of its passage, however, postponement seemed to make for good diplomatic strategy: it put London under deadline while affording American diplomats—in this instance, James Monroe and William Pinkney—time to work their magic. Predictably, being threatened with hostile legislation did not sit well with London. Indeed, the Fox-Grenville Ministry insisted to the very end of its negotiations with Monroe and Pinkney that no treaty would take effect unless the threat were withdrawn. Unfortunately, although the ensuing negotiation produced a treaty with remarkably favorable commercial clauses, Jefferson declined to submit it to the Senate largely because it failed to resolve the impressment issue.[2] As Secretary Madison later told Monroe, the public felt too strongly about impressment to settle for anything less than full renunciation.[3] The cast-aside treaty would have re-legitimized the Caribbean re-export trade, which meant that Jefferson's rejection of it left American shipping still exposed to the rigors of the *Essex* ruling.[4]

Armstrong had difficulty explaining to French officials what was transpiring in London. Progress reports from Monroe and Pinkney arrived infrequently and were usually couched in generalities. This was only one of his worries. Monroe and Pinkney had hardly begun to negotiate when London fired the opening round in the neutral rights controversy. In mid-May 1806, the ministry announced its intention to levy a naval blockade along a sizable stretch of Europe's Channel coastline. Fox's Blockade, as it was called, unquestionably supported the French charge that Britain was the initial offender against the rights of maritime neutrals. When Napoleon responded with his Berlin Decree the following November, he cited its irregularities; and so did others. Given its scope, few believed it could be sufficiently enforced to meet the accepted test of a blockade's legality. On this flaw both Paris and Washington agreed.[5] Moreover, as a "first cause," it remained a focus of debate until 1812, at a time when both belligerents appeared to be on the brink of renouncing their antineutral decrees and the question arose as to whether Fox's Blockade was still on the books or had also been renounced.

As noted above, the doomed Monroe-Pinkney treaty would have reversed the *Essex* decision and constituted a major concession to American shipowners. Although Charles James Fox tried to hide this fact from his political enemies—a concealment which lessened its usefulness as a gesture of goodwill—Monroe and Pinkney were pleased at the time to have won it. Explaining the ministry's retreat, the historian Bradford Perkins finds that it was most likely aimed at relieving British court dockets overloaded by the litigation attending the seizure of American vessels under the *Essex* decision.[6] In effect, the Fox-Grenville Ministry proposed to give with one hand while it took away with the other. Neutral vessels might once more re-export Caribbean cargoes to European destinations but would be denied access to ports between the Elbe River and Brest. Hoping perhaps to certify the blockade's effectiveness, the ministry announced it would be rigorously enforced only between Ostend and the mouth of the Seine. Even so, Fox's Blockade met with the objection that no naval force could effectively prevent cargoes from being landed at all places between these two points. Critics argued that to pretend otherwise was absurd. Monroe sweepingly characterized the blockade as "a monstrous attempt . . . to treat all of Europe as in a state of Blockade. . . ." Tenche Coxe, a former treasury official and perennial advice-giver, assured Madison (who needed no convincing) that the new blockade was "unwarranted by the Law of Nations" because "the coastline it pretended to put under interdiction was too extensive."[7] In France, Champagny later claimed that Britain had put "not a single warship" on the supposedly blockaded coast.[8] Ironically, he had in hand a French-language version of a note handed to Monroe and Pinkney on 31 December 1806, asserting that Britain had "never declared any port in a state of blockade without sending there a force sufficient to render entry patently dangerous."[9] Between these opposing assertions, nothing short of a search of British naval archives is likely to reveal whether in fact London backed up Fox's blockade with enough warships to make it effective. Perkins doubtless has it right when he concludes that "All but the most partisan Federalists refused to believe that even the Royal Navy could maintain a blockade according to the old standards along such an extensive stretch of coastline."[10]

━━━━━━━━━━

Napoleon's retaliatory Berlin Decree lacked symmetry to the offense and was slow in coming.[11] Somewhat preposterously, it declared a blockade of the entire British Isles and, until its underlying purpose became clear, seemed to express little more than the emperor's view that one paper blockade deserved another. Six months elapsed before Napoleon struck back. Significantly, his Berlin Decree of 21 November 1806 burst on the scene only after he defeated the Prussians at Jena. Military events appear to explain the delay insofar as the historian Eli Heckscher makes a compelling case that Napoleon would not have waited from May to November if he had meant merely to respond to Fox's blockade. Rather, he contends, the emperor realized that his forces now having occupied the northern ports of Lubeck, Hamburg, and Bremen had made his "system" continentally feasible.[12] Thus, while the Berlin Decree was nominally retaliatory, it sounded the opening gun in Napoleon's long battle to make all of Europe proof against British commerce.

The decree itself charged London with having created a flimsy and wholly unjustified pretext for seizing persons and property and went on to declare a retaliatory blockade that would be enforced by closing French ports to all vessels coming from Britain or any of its possessions. Three years later, Champagny recalled to his master how felicitously the Berlin Decree had advanced the purposes of the Continental System in its early phases. By threatening to seize all ships and cargoes coming from Britain and her colonies and later requiring Spain, Holland, Naples, and Tuscany to do the same, France had made a good start toward its ultimate objective of cutting off British imports entirely.[13] Armstrong, to his credit, foresaw this larger purpose when he noted the previous March that Napoleon's peace with Prussia had stipulated that Britain be excluded "from all commercial intercourse with the North of Europe." A few weeks later he predicted the emperor would likely try to close all European ports to the British. Should this happen, he wrote prophetically, between "the occlusion of the French and the blockade system of the British our commerce will be in a pretty situation."[14]

How France intended to carry out the Berlin Decree touched off a controversy troublesome to Franco-American relations until the end of the Napoleonic era. Armstrong first put his finger on the central issue when he wondered whether France would seize vessels on the high seas or only after they entered a French port. From Bordeaux U.S. Consul William Lee told him that privateers were being fitted out, ostensibly to prey on American vessels doing business with the British.[15] The venue of capture soon became a critical issue. Washington from the outset was prepared to accept as a warrantable exercise of domestic regulation the detention of vessels caught entering French ports with British cargoes.

Captures on the high seas, however, it would view as a violation of Americans' maritime neutral rights. Thus, whether French port officials or, alternatively, the captains of French privateers were to be the agents of enforcing the Berlin Decree dominated the near-term dialogue between Washington and Paris. Most remarkable, perhaps, was how often it had to be repeated before Paris officialdom understood how seriously Washington regarded the difference between acceptable port-side seizures and unacceptable seizures at sea. Three years later Madison remarked that Napoleon had not yet understood "the difference between the external & internal character of his Decrees."[16]

———— ✺ ————

Armstrong at first saw no cause for alarm on this score. He told Lee he had no official information but assumed the decree was merely intended to stop British commodities at their point of entry and would not be enforced by captures at sea.[17] His optimism was borne out four days later when Minister of Marine Denis Decrès assured him the decree "will in no respect disturb the existing regulations of Commerce between France and the U.S. of America." From this he inferred that no American vessels would be taken at sea merely for having touched at a British port. Talleyrand, too, assured him that American shipmasters coming from British ports would simply be turned away, their cargoes confiscated only if they were caught trying to land them under false declarations. Satisfied, he sent Madison a copy of Decrès' assurances.[18] Armstrong's quick action, it turned out, relieved tensions. From Washington, Turreau wrote that the announcement of a French blockade of the British Isles "has not put us in the best posture," but the subsequent publication of Decrès' letter to Armstrong had had a calming effect.[19] In France, meanwhile, events appeared to bear out the nonthreatening nature of the decree. In March 1807, Armstrong confidently reported that as far as he knew, the only U.S. vessel to be seized, the *Hibernia*, had been released. That the Council of Prizes had subsequently awarded interest and damages to the plaintiffs, he wrote, "cannot fail to give satisfaction to the trading part of our community."[20] Until late 1807 Armstrong's assessment proved accurate: Napoleon's earliest implementation of his "System" caused no serious rift with Washington.

———— ✺ ————

Napoleon's reaction to the short-lived Monroe-Pinkney treaty is not recorded, but French officials clearly took it as evidence that Americans

were much too willing to accommodate their enemy. What caught Turreau's disapproving eye was a "declaratory statement" that if the treaty
were ratified, the United States would join Britain in resisting the Berlin
Decree.[21] All told, he was satisfied to see the treaty shelved and boasted of
having had a hand in persuading Jefferson not to send it to the Senate. In
the aftermath, he snickered at the readiness of Congress to accede to the
president's request to put off implementing the Non-Importation Act for
another nine months. "These people do not take a step forward against
England," he wrote, "without hastening to take two backward."[22] In fact,
Jefferson had not despaired of having a treaty with Britain. In May 1807,
he sent Monroe and Pinkney fresh instructions designed to remedy the
flaws in the one he had cast aside.[23]

   While only the fact and not the fate of treaty was known, Armstrong
feared a reflexive blowback. French hatred of Britain was too deep for
Frenchmen not to resent any power that treated with her. No American
diplomat, he knew, could afford to forget how viciously France had reacted to Jay's Treaty a decade earlier. Hoping then to put the best face
possible on what had transpired in London, he mailed Talleyrand an outline of the treaty, gingerly touting it as "a liberal and successful endeavor
to better the condition of both neutrals and belligerents."[24] He waited
uneasily for word of official displeasure, though he could not help but be
reassured by the absence of anyone in the French capital empowered to
respond authoritatively. As noted earlier, Napoleon had taken up residence in Germany and Poland that winter, tensely girding for the showdown that would come with the battle of Friedland. That Armstrong's
Florida correspondence also went unanswered that spring meant that the
emperor's preoccupation with military matters left little time for considering the most recent developments in London. Possibly, too, the emper-
or's camp remained silent because Louis Pichon may have persuaded
Talleyrand that the Monroe-Pinkney treaty would have little or no bearing on French relations with the United States. Recently returned from
Washington where he had served as *chargé*, the well-informed Pichon
noted that although the treaty appeared "to have ended all the differences
between these two powers," it contained nothing prejudicial to French
interests. Quite likely, too, French officials were waiting to see how Washington would react to London's most recent order-in-council—that of
7 January 1807.[25]

Following a tit-for-tat pattern, the British ministry's January order took aim at that part of the Berlin Decree which closed French ports to British goods. Accordingly, it threatened to confiscate any neutral ship together with its cargo caught in transit between French (or French-controlled) ports from which British merchantmen were excluded. Aimed at neutrals engaged in Europe's coastwise traffic, the order responded not so much to the closing of French ports as to France's efforts to close Spanish, Dutch, and other "French-allied" ports where British ships were accustomed to dropping cargoes. As such, it warned neutral shipmasters not to fall in with the continental dimensions of Napoleon's "System."[26] The order seems also to have been self-defeating. As Henry Adams notes ironically, British exports to the continent depended heavily on American carriers.[27]

In Washington, reaction to the January order varied. Madison thought Jefferson had shown great restraint in asking Congress to put off imposing the Non-Importation Act. At the same time, he instructed Monroe and Pinkney to cite the postponement as proof of the President's wish "to smoothe the path of negotiations." Fresh instructions were on their way. Speaking for himself, the secretary of state fumed at London for having agreed not to retaliate against the Berlin Decree unless the United States failed "to controul its operation" and then had acted before it could possibly have known what the administration's response would be.[28] All in all, although the activities of both belligerents had affronted the administration by early 1807, Britain had for the moment outdistanced France in giving offense.

—⁂—

Napoleon's benign enforcement of the Berlin Decree, however, continued to bear watching. Axiomatically, the farther from Paris the writ of any French decree ran, the more loosely it was construed. By late spring 1807, French and Spanish privateers operating in the West Indies belied the assurances given to Armstrong that no captures would be made on the high seas. Lest Paris itself be unaware of such activity, Madison told Armstrong to request that its officials in the Indies and elsewhere be notified that American vessels were "exempted" from captures at sea. Worrisome, too, was George Erving's alert that privateers sallying out of Spanish ports were operating under a Spanish version of the Berlin Decree. Unless Spain conformed to the French interpretation of the decree's limitations,

Madison warned, Americans could expect a growing number of losses in those waters as well.[29]

Throughout the summer of 1807, Armstrong basked in what he believed was reliable evidence that France would act only within bounds of "domestic regulation." He told Monroe, now in London, not to believe rumors of French corsairs on the prowl and again mentioned the lone capture and release of the *Hibernia*. As for reports of privateers operating out of Spanish ports, he had the French government's promise to pay for their depredations. French conduct, in his view, was moderate to a fault. American vessels arriving from Britain might have their cargoes sequestered, he told Monroe, but the carriers themselves were being released. Cargoes, too, might be restored if their owners could prove absence of intent to violate the decree. What rules of evidence might apply in such cases he was still looking into.[30] In short, by midsummer 1807, Armstrong's only major complaint against France was its reluctance to lend a hand in the Florida negotiation. Britain was still the principal offender, France a paragon of restraint.

Spain's co-enforcement of the Berlin Decree, meanwhile, proved so comically disjointed as to raise doubt whether European statesmen bothered to read one another's official pronouncements. Even as Armstrong rejoiced in the mildness of France's enforcement of the Berlin Decree, Prince Masserano, Spain's ambassador in Paris, made it quite clear that his government had it backwards. Madrid, Talleyrand was told, had ordered its port officials to detain any vessel outbound for a British port; he said nothing about vessels inbound. Having turned the Berlin Decree on its head, Masserano asked how Spain should deal with George Erving's objections that such detentions violated the principle of free ships, free goods. Spain's "tranquillity," he wrote, depended on getting a quick answer. Six weeks later Talleyrand, having just returned from Napoleon's long campaign in the east, referred Masserano's questions to Denis Decrès who, as navy minister, had been charged with enforcement in the emperor's absence. Decrès replied that he had sought instructions the previous May but had received none. Now that the emperor had returned to Paris, he urged the foreign minister to go to the source.[31] A week later, however, Talleyrand was ousted from the foreign ministry, leaving the comte de Champagny to respond to Armstrong's request that Madrid be told that only cargoes of British origin be sequestered, not the vessels that brought them. Although the new foreign minister promised to do so, little evidence exists that France worked any change in Spain's construction of the Berlin Decree or even cared how others might construe it.[32]

———— ∞∞∞ ————

Relative quiet reigned on various diplomatic fronts as the summer of 1807 began. Napoleon savored the military ascendency gained from his victory over and subsequent alliance with the czar, and across the Channel his only remaining enemy acquired a new ministry under Lord Liverpool whose composition cast doubt on whether Monroe and Pinkney could pick up the pieces of their rejected treaty. They could not. In Washington, Turreau still puzzled over whether Jefferson's passion for annexing Florida might lead to war, but Americans generally, he reported, seemed more interested in following the final stages of Aaron Burr's treason trial.

The diplomatic quiet broke abruptly to the thunder of cannonades when on June 22 the British Frigate *Leopard* hailed, hulled, and sent a press party aboard the U.S. frigate *Chesapeake* shortly after it had left Norfolk Roads. That the *Leopard's* broadsides killed three Americans and wounded eighteen caused less public outrage than that four alleged British deserters had been removed from the deck of an American man-of-war. This insult to the flag ranked as a potential *casus belli*, for it was widely accepted that merchant vessels might suffer such boardings, but naval vessels never, not without dishonor to national sovereignty. Conventional wisdom holds that if Jefferson had opted for war and promptly called Congress into session, that body would almost certainly have obliged him.

Instead, unwisely perhaps, although wisdom owes much to hindsight, the president chose a less militant course. First, as a stopgap befitting the nature of the offense, he ordered all British warships to leave U.S. territorial waters. Then, with studied calculation, he turned to London for the apology he knew must be forthcoming and which, from the enormity of the affront, he hoped to parlay into a British commitment to give up recovering deserters from all American vessels.[33] Unfortunately, this broader diplomatic objective fell on the hardened ground of Britain's perennial concern for her undermanned navy. In effect, London's response was yes, we probably owe an apology; but no, impressment is not up for discussion. Haggling over the terms of an apology dragged on until late 1811, and although impressment tended to slacken, the reasons had more to do with the British navy's downsizing after its victory at Trafalgar than with any thought of retreat from principle.

Napoleon, though gleeful at the *Chesapeake* affair, doubted much would come of it. He denounced the *Leopard*'s attack as unmistakable evidence of Britain's hostility toward neutrals, but after telling a diplomatic audience that "this is most abominable," he predicted to Armstrong privately that London would settle the affair because (Armstrong quoted him) "they are afraid to go to war with your country."[34] Reports from Washington bore out Napoleon's prediction that there would be no war. Turreau's jaded reading of the American reactions ran the gamut from repugnance to disgust. Word of the attack had spread rapidly, he reported, evoking a number of warlike demonstrations, but Jefferson's refusal to convene Congress signaled a preference for negotiation. If Washington became distressed enough to ask for an alliance, he urged it be rejected. This government, he wrote, is "totally skittish." From members of the cabinet he heard that the administration would demand reparations, the restoration of the abducted seamen, and punishment of the offending captain. Turreau predicted they would fail on all counts,[35] and in the short run he was correct. Still, hoping for a first-hand reading of the administration's reaction, the French minister left his off-season retreat in Baltimore and turned up at an official reception in Washington in mid-July. Jefferson greeted him "more warmly than was his custom," he wrote, "but left me a little time afterward to pursue with the English minister a conversation that my entry had interrupted." Rejoining Turreau, the president told him: "If the English do not give us the satisfaction we demand, we will take Canada which wants to join the Union, and when with Canada, we shall have the Floridas, we will no longer have any difficulty with our vessels, and this is the only way to stop them."

If the logic of this sequence escaped Turreau, his understanding of English, always shaky, must have been overwhelmed when a voluable Jefferson went on to speak of "twenty different subjects in a conversation of half an hour." What Turreau did learn from this encounter was that Jefferson counted on the public's anger to last until Congress met in the fall, at which time if London had not given satisfaction, he believed he would still have public support for a declaration of war should he ask for it. Turreau doubted the president's strategy would succeed. Public outrage would fade, and Congress when it reconvened would be bitterly divided. In the end, he predicted, the administration would do everything in its power to keep the peace because it "has nothing to gain and everything to lose from war." Moreover, if peace now came to Europe, as seemed likely, the prospect of fighting Britain alone, "will cool the zeal of those who really want war." The most France could expect from the *Chesapeake* affair, he observed, was that Washington was not likely to attempt another treaty with London in the near future.[36] Again, he was right on all counts.

By early September, after listening to much heated oratory, the French minister shrugged scornfully at the many good reasons Americans were finding not to go to war. This was to be expected, he wrote, of "a people who have no idea of glory . . . and are disposed to suffer all kinds of humiliation."[37] Turreau clearly had no use for un-self-respecting Americans. His correspondence bristles with disdain for the impotence of partisan democracy and for Jefferson's all too "philosophical" approach to problems that in his view called for military solutions. He seldom failed to picture Americans as a spiritless lot, divided and ill-led, who valued their material prosperity above honor. To the extent that Napoleon read whatever diplomatic correspondence came within his reach, Turreau's depiction of the *Chesapeake* affair and its aftermath almost certainly reinforced the emperor's low esteem of Americans.

While the *Chesapeake* crisis lasted, Madison warned Armstrong that the cost of arming for war would mean putting off the purchase of the Floridas. If Spain had already agreed to sell, he must delay the first payment until London and Washington "shall have settled their differences."[38] If war did come, he should press France to re-open her ports in St. Domingue and seek out Dutch bankers for wartime loans. The latter, he noted, had recently been forbidden to make loans to foreign governments, but Armstrong should try to get an exception. And unless Paris objected, he was to explore the loan market with bankers in Antwerp. In sum, with his customary attention to detail, Madison made sure to leave no contingency uncharted. Otherwise, the *Chesapeake* affair had no effect on French-American relations, which by and large remained relatively placid.

CHAPTER 4

NAPOLEON TAKES EXCEPTION
TO JEFFERSON'S EMBARGO

Americans relations with both belligerents worsened perceptibly in the fall of 1807. In mid-October Armstrong learned that Monroe and Pinkney had once more failed to get Britain to renounce impressment, and although London planned to send a special envoy to Washington, there was little reason to expect he would concede on issues relating to either impressment or trade. In England, meanwhile, American shipmasters alarmed by the failure of Jefferson's diplomacy were clearing British ports in ballast.[1] American commerce with France also became more chancy when Napoleon handed down fresh instructions for enforcing his Berlin Decree, a crackdown that began when he had occasion to answer questions from his Navy Minister. This imperial response passed from his Minister of Justice to his Prize Council's Procurer General who, in turn, conveyed it to Champagny. What emerged from this bureaucratic filtration was that any vessel known to have touched at a British port, irrespective of its cargo's origin, would be sequestered but not confiscated pending the emperor's further disposition.[2] When Armstrong requested clarification, Champagny said nothing of the perils of merely "touching" at a British port, but did warn that "all neutral vessels leaving English ports with cargoes of English or English-origin merchandise" would be detained. Foreseeing that American merchantmen would now be taken at sea as well as on arrival, Armstrong urged that the emperor hold off at least until the U.S. negotiations in London had played out. He reminded Champagny that one of the announced purposes of the Berlin Decree had been to force Britain to respect the rights of maritime neutrals. Now, with Americans "on the brink of war with that power expressly in defense of those neutral rights," surely the emperor would not wish to weaken their negotiating position.[3] Nothing came of this plea, but had he got wind of it, Napoleon would surely have scoffed at the notion of fostering the cause of American neutral rights at the Court of St. James at a time when his most obvious course lay in keeping Americans and Britons at each other's throats.

For several weeks the American minister knew more than Champagny had told him on 7 October, specifically that French privateers would seize American vessels known to have put into a British port irrespective of their cargoes.[4] Accordingly, he warned his consuls that the Berlin Decree "is about to be literally executed," and because the British might retaliate by seizing American vessels, they should urge shipmasters to make sail for home as quickly as possible.[5]

At a diplomatic audience on 15 October, Napoleon dashed any hope that he might wait for Monroe and Pinkney to string out their talks in London before enforcing his decree more stringently. As the American minister listened uneasily, the emperor denounced Britain's "maritime usages and tyranny," and vowed to crush her. "Great Britain shall be destroyed," he told the assembled diplomats. "I have the means of doing it, and they shall be employed." His collateral targets, Armstrong supposed, were the neighboring powers whose ports regularly welcomed British cargoes. At the very least, Napoleon meant to halt the parade of neutral vessels slipping across the channel to Dutch ports. The emperor's more rigorous enforcement, he suspected, was intended to prevent the likelihood of the United States coming to any "amicable arrangement" with Britain.[6]

Armstrong's first guess seems nearer the mark. For Napoleon, halting the influx of British goods through Dutch ports clearly figured more important in his calculations than roiling the waters of Anglo-American relations. Shortly before his tirade to the diplomatic corps, he lashed out angrily at the reported complicity of French consuls in Holland who were certifying British imports as Dutch and allowing them to be re-exported to French and Italian destinations.[7] To the emperor's obvious distress, his Continental System never quite stopped leaking.

Ironically, as Armstrong and U.S. consuls prepared for a more damaging French assault on American shipping the next blow came from London and made it certain. Of the three ministerial orders-in-council dated 11 November 1807, one is best described as a tax and licensing order. It lifted the ban issued the previous January—the one forbidding neutrals to trade at European ports closed to British vessels—and ruled that neutral carriers inbound with colonial goods must first stop at a British port, pay a transit tax, and purchase a license before proceeding. These three orders-in-council were just the beginning. The historian Eli Heckscher counts no fewer than twenty-four subsequent orders, either clarifying, delimiting, or expanding those of 11 November, but all in support of the dictum that all neutral vessels laded with colonial produce make the "obligatory call at a British port."[8] The Royal Navy made sure they did so. With good reason, Bradford Perkins calls the November orders "the Portland ministry's greatest single contribution to eventual war."[9] Americans were particularly galled by London's announced rationale: that they must pay a price for not having forced Napoleon to revoke his Berlin Decree. Because that decree had not been strictly enforced for more than a year, Henry Adams offers more plausible motives. He points to persons close to the ministry who profited notoriously from privateering but also credits the explanation given by Lord Bathurst, president of the Board of Trade, who argued that a "tax" on imports to the continent would assure that France did not obtain colonial produce more cheaply than Britain, a motive the British emissary David Erskine later confirmed to Madison.[10] As a clincher, Heckscher notes that British duties on Europe-bound colonial goods did, in fact, achieve the intended price result.[11]

Reactions to the November orders were sharp. In Washington, a thoroughly fed-up Congress found an additional reason to enact a general embargo. And from Napoleon's headquarters in Milan came a blistering decree that spelled bad news for any American vessel that bowed to London's financial controls. But even before the emperor learned the details of the British orders, he made sure that Armstrong knew how important it was for Americans to resist British visit and search and other insults to their "dignity and independence."[12] Here began a soon familiar refrain of blaming and shaming neutral nations for allowing themselves to be victimized, an incantation which may have satisfied Napoleon's sense of righteousness but left the victims wondering how much resistance to "British tyranny" short of war would meet the imperial criterion of enough. By way of answer, the Milan Decree set the first hurdles and they were high.

Dated 17 December 1807, the Milan Decree targeted the November orders with scrupulous exactitude. Any vessel that submitted to British search, touched at a British port, or "paid any tax whatsoever to the English Government," was declared to be "denationalized," thereby losing the protection of its flag and becoming fair prize. On its flip side, the Milan Decree offered immunity to those powers "who shall have the firmness to compel the English government to respect their flag."[13]

In operational terms, the decree plainly foreshadowed captures on the high seas. It also faced the masters of incoming merchantmen with the nearly insuperable task of proving they had not been visited, or touched at a British port, or received a British license. Especially vexing was the liability implicit in having been visited, a procedure no unarmed merchantman could resist and for which no third party had ever before imposed a penalty. Alarmed, Armstrong wondered if Napoleon meant the decree to provoke London to even greater violations of neutral rights. Persons he spoke to deplored it, he wrote, "but no one will voice objections." Even Talleyrand "who is permitted to go farther than any other person, dares not avow his opinion of it."[14] As usual, rumors abounded. On hearing that all vessels belonging to "friendly and allied powers," were about to be interned, Armstrong turned anxiously to Denis Decrès. He waited a month before the navy minister assured him the order did not apply to American vessels; they were free to depart.[15] He relaxed even more when Lee reported from Bordeaux that U.S. vessels detained since early January had now been permitted to leave. Less welcome, however, Lee told of privateers fitting out in large numbers and port officials zealously grilling the crews of recent arrivals. By his count, the officers and crew of six U.S. vessels had already undergone a tortuous sorting-out of evidence against them. Port officials probed relentlessly. "The crews of all our vessels," he wrote, "are all now strictly examined, each man separately, in order to ascertain if they have been in English ports *since* the decree of 21 Nov. 1807, or have been boarded or spoken with by English cruizers on the passage out."[16] As Lee implied, such questioning of individual crewmen played into the hands of officials who found ways to reward the disgruntled for bearing false witness. Armstrong's successor, Joel Barlow, was still protesting such inquisitions six years later.

Meanwhile, the French judiciary was gearing up for the trial of more American prize cases. An unsigned memorandum addressed to Champagny on 12 January asked if the emperor had decided whether local courts or the Council of Prizes would process the large number of U.S. vessels now being taken into custody.[17] In fact, the number of "sequestered" vessels mounted in the early weeks of 1808, but none had yet been confiscated, leading Armstrong to speculate they might be released if Congress were to cut off trade with Britain.[18] A few days later, his speculation was put to the test. News reaching Paris in early February announced that Congress had locked down all vessels of U.S. registry. Jefferson's famous embargo, together with the belated implementation of the Non-Importation Act against Britain, meant that only vessels still at sea, summoned home by Congress but urged by their owners to stay abroad, would continue what commerce was left in American bottoms.[19]

On its face, the embargo should have brought better relations with Paris. Not only did it dovetail with Napoleon's Continental System by closing off a major British market, but it also held out the prospect that fewer Americans would be trying to slip British goods into the European ports he had closed to such traffic. On balance, too, France could easily afford to lose her American trade, knowing that Britain would suffer disproportionately because her own commerce with the United States was many times greater. In short, by early 1808, France and the United States appeared to have in hand the makings of a rapprochement, one that Jefferson also hoped might facilitate his acquisition of the Floridas. In this, however, he was once more destined to be disappointed. As Lawrence Kaplan wryly observes: "The Embargo Act, intended as a fair exchange for the Floridas, in effect made America an ally in the Continental System without securing one square foot of Florida soil in return."[20] In the end, neither party seemed able to muster the goodwill or steadiness of purpose to effect what might have been at least a détente. Too, the time-lag in transatlantic communication worked against it. Because London was closer than Washington, Napoleon knew of the November orders before he had news of the embargo. His impulsive reaction set a harsh tone for French policy for months to come. He could not imagine, he told Champagny, that Americans would brook such humiliation without declaring war. How else could they respond? But until he knew their response, he would continue to sequester their vessels and dispose of them "according to circumstances."[21] What those circumstances were Champagny made clear to Armstrong on 15 January. The emperor, he wrote, fully expected an American declaration of war, indeed believed a state of war already existed, and because he now regarded the United States "as associated in the cause of all the powers that must defend themselves against England, [he] has taken no definitive actions against American vessels brought into our ports; he has ordered that they remain under sequestration pending the express wishes of the United States government in this regard."[22] As noted earlier, neither Armstrong nor Madison when he learned of it had any difficulty reading Napoleon's blackmail for what it was: American vessels might be freed, but only if the United States declared war on Britain.

Manfully, Armstrong played the embargo to Champagny as a reasonable alternative to the war declaration the emperor had expected. France, he reminded, had promised to release American ships and cargoes if the United States took "measures against G.B. similar to those of the Continent." Now, having closed its ports to British goods and laid "a general embargo on their own vessels," his government expected the promise to be fulfilled. Champagny's written reply, unfortunately, stood squarely on Napoleon's all-or-nothing instructions of 12 January. Nor, as also noted earlier, was Armstrong heartened by its appeal to universality. France, Champagny wrote, would honor the principle of free ships, free goods, but only when Britain had ceased violating the rights of all neutrals. Only when those rights were universally respected could France agree to respect them.[23] The message was clear: an embargo did not go far enough to warrant revoking the French decrees. By implication, only a U.S. declaration of war would meet the emperor's requirements. Napoleon dispelled any doubt on this score when several days later he met with his Council of Administration of the Interior, a venue in which Armstrong had hoped his advisors might persuade him to moderate his decrees. Instead, the emperor stiffly refused to consider any changes in policy and was quoted as saying that "the Americans should be compelled to take the positive character of allies or of enemies."[24] His roll-call mentality simply refused to accept that the United States would calmly allow Britain to tax and license its commerce with Europe. And that Washington could rebuff his offer of alliance—with the Floridas thrown in—he clearly found baffling.

But Napoleon also had reason to fault the embargo for its supposed evenhandedness. In meting out equal treatment to both belligerents, Champagny pointed out, Congress had not differentiated between the gravity of their respective offenses. Washington made much of the law's impartiality, cutting off commerce with both belligerents while offering each the same opportunity to restore that commerce. But France had done nothing, he reminded the emperor, to compare with Fox's Blockade, or Britain's wanton attack on the *Chesapeake*, or her systematic impressment of American seamen. Not only did the punishment of France exceed her offense, but it soon became apparent that the embargo had left scores of American vessels still at large, still trading with Britain and still using their flag to falsify the importation of British commodities.[25] The American embargo had made his continental blockade only relatively tighter.

Napoleon's offer of an alliance, plus the release of U.S. vessels, plus the Floridas, met a swift death in Washington. Madison told Armstrong to inform the French government that "no independent and honorable nation" could submit to such terms; and although the president still hoped to acquire the Floridas, his administration was committed to a neutrality which forbade it to join against England "for the purpose of obtaining a separate and particular object." Armstrong should nevertheless "leave the way open for friendly and respectful explanations." In any event, the president was gratified to learn that France would not object if the United States found it necessary to defend the Floridas against a British attack.[26] Mindful that defending might lead to annexation, Jefferson still hoped for Napoleon's acceptance of that as well.

The Administration, meanwhile, set out to show its home front critics that the ploughshare of embargo could be beaten into the spear of coercion. Four months after its passage, Madison reminded Armstrong that the president had authority to restore trade if either power modified its antineutral decrees.[27] Two months later he made the case for a French retreat more explicit. The president would lift the embargo on France if she were to return to her earlier mode of enforcing the Berlin Decree, that is, by detaining U.S. vessels only on arrival. Armstrong was to point out that France had little to lose by forgoing captures at sea because she lacked the naval capacity to make any but random seizures. Even if London did not follow suit by repealing her "whole illegal system" (which Madison thought unlikely), France's return to this self-imposed restriction would remove a troublesome issue.[28] Curiously, Madison did not call on France to revoke the Milan Decree by name. That would come later, much later. Rather, in May and June 1808 the administration seemed more intent on milking Paris for leverage it might use in its dealings with London. Because the British crisis still held center stage, Washington hoped to hold up concessions from Paris as an example of goodwill worthy of emulation. It was a slim hope, but one that Jefferson and his secretary of state thought worth pursuing.

Position-taking, voluably defended by statesmen on both sides of the Atlantic, highlighted the diplomatic correspondence of early 1808. Instructions and despatches, of course, came and went in cycles of five to nine weeks depending on the length of time it took despatch boats to make winter crossings. Remarkably, the Atlantic time-lag mattered very little. Both sides by this time had so fully digested their major complaints that Madison, for example, writing on 8 February to denounce France for violating the principle of free ships might have been just across town from Champagny who, on the 15th, was writing Turreau to explain to the administration why that principle no longer obtained.[29] Likewise, by early April, Armstrong had already registered most of the complaints Madison formally charged him to make when he wrote him in early February.[30] Similarly, on 30 January, Turreau reported having justified the Berlin Decree in terms strikingly like those Champagny was to outline to him two weeks later.[31]

Unraveling the skeins of argument made familiar by repetition, both sides repeatedly fetched up on hard knots of frustration. Madison, impatient with "who started it" and indignant over the premature loosing of retaliatory decrees, summed up the administration's exasperation when (through Armstrong) he demanded to know why the legitimate commerce of neutrals should be "the sport of belligerents contesting with each other the priority of their destructive innovations." Innocent neutrals, he continued, had not been given an opportunity to disprove "that culpable acquiescence which is made the pretext by both for the wrongs done to them."[32] Armstrong who needed little prompting relayed these grievances even more forcefully. How, he asked Champagny, could France accuse his countrymen of "acquiescing" in British abuses when both belligerents had victimized American vessels, diverting them from their destinations, dragging them in for adjudication, and even in several instances, burning them on the high seas? If British blockades were "monstrous and indefensible," as Talleyrand termed them, then "what can be said for the policy of France, which differs in nothing from that of England?"[33]

American officials particularly resented the charge of "acquiescence." No reminders of Pinkney's stern protests to London or allusions to Britain's being the principal victim of the embargo could drown out the French reproach that Americans were not self-respecting, had not stood up to "British tyranny," or at least had not done so with sufficient vigor. Jefferson himself suffered Turreau's backhanded slur that France had always shown respect to "governments that uphold their dignity."[34] Especially afflicting was the inclusion of visit-and-search among the indignities to which Americans had ostensibly bowed. Time and again, American spokesmen protested the injustice done to shipmasters who, having neither touched at a British port, nor shipped a British cargo, nor bought a British license, nor submitted to British taxation, could not prevent British men-of-war from visiting and searching their vessels and had nonetheless been taken into custody for having "acquiesced."

Answering this complaint came the French reply that Americans deserved to be punished for submitting to searches in pursuance of British blockades that even they admitted failed to meet the standards of effective interdiction. In plain language, they were guilty of abetting British lawlessness. Nor was "being visited" an offense the French took lightly. In February 1808, William Lee counted some thirty American vessels detained in French ports, most of them, he wrote, solely "for having been boarded by English cruizers."[35]

Frustration on the American side had its counterpart among French port officials who found it virtually impossible to tell the difference between Americans and Englishmen. Champagny called Armstrong's attention to this confusion when he first defended the Milan Decree, noting how difficult it was to ascertain the nationality of Americans who had "habitual relations with England, using a common language, and often mixing their interests." Not unreasonably he suspected them of conniving with the British.[36] Mild at first, this tone of mistrust grew in time to the widely-held belief that every American ship's company, master and crew, should be deemed British until proven otherwise. In support of this mistrust, U.S. consuls themselves uncovered more than enough irregularities in ships' "papers" to substantiate the existence of a pervasively fraudulent collusion between American shipowners and British exporters.

In late 1807, Lee explained why he had refused clearance papers to U.S. vessels preparing to sail from Bordeaux under French colors. "As those vessels assume the french character merely to get out of port and when at sea are . . . protected by their American papers & a British license, it would be extremely dangerous for me if it was discovered by this Government that I had lent my authority to such transactions."[37] Later, almost a year into the embargo, Lee still had no instructions as to whether he should deny clearances to American vessels that entered French ports with suspicious documents. Had he received such instructions, he said, he might have "put a stop to the nefarious practices of the English who send shoals of American vessels from their ports whose owners never saw America, and whose papers are manufactured in London." He also told of having set out for La Rochelle to examine what he believed were the forged papers of some ten American vessels supposedly arrived from Norway, but turned back when news reached him that the crews had ratted and all the vessels had been seized. To Madison he wrote, "our vessels papers with all their private marks are so completely copied in London that it is almost impossible to detect them."[38] Similarly, as the embargo took hold in April 1808, David Bailie Warden, Skipwith's successor in the Paris consulate, remarked that arrivals showing U.S. registry were in fact "navigating by British license, or British protection, and consequently ought to be condemned."[39] That Napoleon that same month should order them seized without making fine distinctions seems arguably justifiable.

CHAPTER 5

CAPTURED SHIPS AND
STRANDED SEAMEN; NAPOLEON
REACTS TO THE EMBARGO

Until Napoleon added embargo-evasion to his reasons for detaining American vessels, Armstrong spent the early months of 1808 trying to free those detained earlier while doing his meager best to ease the hardships of stranded American crewmen. Some of the latter, he knew, were locked up when French officials decided they were British subjects. Others whose captains could no longer pay their wages looked to his legation for food and shelter. Captains and supercargoes, meanwhile, clamored for his assistance in getting their vessels released.[1] Inevitably perhaps, his efforts on behalf of shipowners and distressed seamen racheted up his longstanding feud with Consul General Fulwar Skipwith. In February, for example, five sea captains detained at Calais wrote him that Skipwith had offered to hire legal counsel at a cost of 1200 livres per lawyer. This was outrageous, he told Madison, because the consul-general himself had earlier quoted the lawyers' fees at half that amount. Moreover, Skipwith had given them bad advice: legal counsel was "unnecessary and even useless" because prize case decisions were usually "political" and there was no way of telling whether they would be tried by the Prize Council or some local tribunal. He told the captains not to hire lawyers or agents until the legal situation had cleared.[2]

Minister and consul-general also differed over how to rescue American crewmen, some mistaken for British deserters and jailed as prisoners of war. Certain that many were native-born or naturalized Americans, Skipwith proposed to verify their U.S. citizenship by sending someone to interrogate them at various prison "depots." When Armstrong vetoed the proposal, Skipwith complained to Madison that the minister had authorized such interrogations two years earlier but now, apparently to avoid the expense, had reneged.[3] Amid these and other heated exchanges, Skipwith quit his post that summer but not before Armstrong had tried to have him declared *persona non grata* and then denied him passage home aboard a U.S. despatch boat. In revenge, Skipwith tried to persuade Jefferson, a fellow Virginian, to appoint Isaac Cox Barnet his successor, knowing that Armstrong detested him.[4] Armstrong got rid of Barnet, too. Such ministerial feuding with consuls was not uncommon in this era. Typically, the consuls were politically-connected businessmen who sometimes over-worked the perks of their office for private gain. During Armstrong's watch, they appear to have been more than ordinarily defensive.

As for stranded seamen, Armstrong seemed principally intent on dodging their hotel bills. He did, however, suggest to Champagny that crews might be fed and housed on shipboard if their captains were permitted to sell off part of their sequestered cargoes. Here the evidence is spotty but suggests that permission was sometimes granted. The alternative was repatriation. In February, for example, William Lee identified an inexpensive charter vessel in which he hoped to send home the dozens of sailors who had "besieged" him in Bordeaux. Armstrong would have to foot the bill, he added, and Pinkney would have to get assurance of their safe passage. The following November, he told of having placed eighteen on board a vessel whose captain had agreed to give them free passage in return for Lee's having arranged for the vessel's release. Others, he assumed, weary of waiting or hopeful of prize money, would sign on board French letters of marque.[5] By early 1808, the problems afflicting imprisoned or stranded seamen were just beginning to surface. Only after Napoleon left for Elba would American diplomats in France be rid of them.

On the larger stage, meanwhile, the French emperor was preparing a response to Jefferson's first major experiment in economic sanctions. The embargo was four months old when Napoleon announced he would seize any and all U.S. vessels that had managed to elude it.[6] Not unexpectedly, Americans found his Bayonne Decree of 17 April 1808 insufferably high-handed, but Napoleon made the case that Americans who evaded the laws of their own government had put themselves beyond its protection. No matter who caught them, they deserved to be punished. Though his rationale was presumptuous, painting them as law-breakers clearly went down more easily than admitting that American captains still at sea were conniving with the British to slip forbidden goods through his continental blockade. Thus, although his announced reasons smacked of some sort of inverted legalism, the Bayonne Decree reflected a settled conviction that American ships still in European waters were little more than wedges for British exporters seeking to widen the chinks in his system.[7] Madison, on hearing of the Bayonne Decree, made a mental note to add its victims to the roster of others for which the United States would demand indemnification. The French emperor had offered an "ingenious" rationale, he wrote, although he was more disturbed by what the decree revealed of his "temper."[8] According to one estimate, the Bayonne Decree ultimately took a toll of $10 million in American property losses.[9]

Relatedly perhaps, the decree coincided with Napoleon's visit that spring to the depression-struck seaport of Bordeaux where he witnessed at firsthand the ruinous effects of his continental blockade. The devastation he saw there helps to explain not only why he lashed out at American carriers but also why he began to cast about for ways to revive at least a portion of France's overseas commerce. Bordeaux typified on a large scale what his system had wrought elsewhere. Until recently, the port's incoming cargoes had come mostly in U.S. vessels, but the gradual disappearance of the latter, either embargoed or sequestered, had nearly emptied its harbor. Shortly before Napoleon passed through, Lee observed that "Grass is growing in the streets of this City. Its beautiful port is totally deserted except by two Marblehead fishing schooners and three or four empty vessels which still swing to the tides."[10] The emperor also heard at secondhand from local merchants how bleakly their distress was mirrored in the French Antilles where for lack of American shipping, a swath of depression had cut through the island economies. Thus, whatever else he may have thought of the embargo, the havoc it created in the French islands gave him still another reason to avenge himself on what remained of the American merchant fleet. Nor were Bordelais businessmen slow to exact their own vengeance. Responding to the Bayonne Decree, they lost no time diverting their capital investment from the Antilles trade to privateering.[11]

The summer of 1808 passed in desultory diplomatic exchanges, fretful but of little moment. Public attention fixed primarily on Spain where Napoleon had finally met an enemy he could not decisively defeat. Having tricked both King Charles IV and his son Ferdinand VII into abdicating, he named his brother Joseph to the Spanish throne, an act that met with widespread popular resistance. Insurgency, in turn, gave birth to a Spanish Junta claiming sovereignty both at home and overseas and presented the United States with both dangers and opportunities. The Junta's ties to London revived instinctive fears of a British military appearance in Florida, but the chaos in Spain itself had the more immediate effect of rekindling Jefferson's drive to annex that province. Heartened by Pinkney's recent reports from London, he wrote Secretary of War Henry Dearborn that "Should England make up with us, while Bonaparte continues at war with Spain, a moment may occur when we may without danger of commitment with either France or England seize to our own limits of Louisiana as of right & the residue of the Floridas as reprisal for spoliations."[12]

Even as Jefferson speculated on when that "moment" might occur, Napoleon snatched it away. Having allowed in February that American troops might defend Florida to ward off a British threat and more recently offered the Floridas in return for an alliance, he now reneged, claiming the administration had misunderstood. Armstrong got the bad news shortly after he explained why his government had rejected a "more intimate connexion." To soften the rebuff, he expressed Jefferson's gratitude for the emperor's sanctioning "a precautionary occupation of the Floridas against the hostile designs of G.B. . . . , should it be necessary." No, no, came the reply: only if France herself were invited to intervene would U.S. troops be welcome, and the invitation must come from Madrid. As Champagny explained smugly, the emperor "has neither the right nor the wish to authorize a violation of the law of nations." Frustrated, Armstrong quoted back to him the text of his February 3 note. To Madison he suggested that Napoleon's war in Spain had enlivened his interest in the Floridas. He had no doubt the emperor's change of heart stemmed from "the new relations which the Floridas have to this government since the abdication of Charles the 4th."[13]

Context also has to be considered in Napoleon's stand on the Florida issue. The United States had, after all, just rejected a French offer of alliance and shrugged off suggestions that it join a French-sponsored league of armed neutrals. Too, there is no reason to suppose that Napoleon felt any less pique at the freewheeling conduct of American shipmasters in June than he had in April when he issued the Bayonne Decree. Topping these residual grievances were fresh rumors that American carriers still on the loose were supplying foodstuffs to British and insurgent forces through ports in Spain and Portugal still open to them.[14] In sum, Americans were becoming increasingly troublesome.

———— ∞∞∞ ————

Louis Turreau, meanwhile, reported a commensurate hardening of American attitudes toward France. At one of his weekly meetings with Jefferson, the French minister had expressed dismay at the administration's publishing the correspondence between Armstrong and Champagny of the previous January. Here for all to see was the American minister's protest against the Berlin Decree published alongside Champagny's letter bluntly rejecting it. He understood why the administration needed to quiet Federalist charges that it was pro-French, but the consequences were lamentable, he went on, because the public now equated France with Britain "respecting the grievances the United States complains of." Newspapers once consistently pro-French now praised the administration for its firmness in embargoing both belligerents.[15] How long that embargo might last and what might follow also weighed on Turreau's mind. When Madison reminded him that the law provided for restoring commerce with the power that repealed its decrees, the Frenchman hotly denied an equivalency. Restoring trade with France meant little as long as the British were allowed to interfere with it.[16] In this, Turreau showed he had correctly read the "universality" argument in Champagny's letter of 13 February, that is, that London must do more than show favor to Americans; it must give up all efforts to control neutral traffic with the continent if Americans were to expect any relief from the French decrees. Then, echoing a complaint from Paris, he asked Jefferson why the embargo had punished both belligerents without distinction despite France's having given less offense. To this, the president had replied mildly that comparing the conduct of the two powers had never entered into its rationale. Besides, Britain had obviously suffered greater deprivation than France because it had a larger stake in the Atlantic trade. But even if the embargo had weighed equally on both, the president continued, the United States had imposed other punitive measures on France's enemy as, for example, his closing U.S. ports to British warships after the *Chesapeake* incident and the imposition of non-importation only against Britain. Do not these measures, he asked, so hurtful to Britain, also "serve your cause?" Turreau did not record his response, but he welcomed Jefferson's repeated assurances that whatever followed the embargo, France could rest assured that the United States would never make an alliance with England. The president spoke so forcefully on this point, Turreau reported, that he paused, embarrassed at having made promises "beyond his powers."[17] Jefferson may also have spoken beyond the dictates of good policy. Napoleon, if this outburst of presidential anglophobia reached his ears, may well have concluded that no further harm could come of squandering whatever goodwill remained in his relations with the United States.

But was Jefferson's anti-British fervor genuine? Turreau obviously thought so. One cannot put "absolute faith in all that Mr. Jefferson says," he mused; "I must admit, however, that he seems to me sincere and truthful in everything he said to me with respect to France and England." Hoping to corroborate Jefferson's insistence that Britain must give up impressment as well as its orders-in-council, Turreau sounded out Madison. The secretary, however, replied cryptically that he "did not go as far as M. Jefferson," only that an arrangement with London would be difficult at the present time. Recalling the leeway Monroe and Pinkney had taken with respect to impressment in 1806, Turreau suspected these two English-speaking peoples might still reach a compromise on this as well as other issues. As long as their differences persisted, however, he urged his government to be more lenient toward American shipping.[18]

Common to Washington and Paris that summer was each party's growing conviction that the other had exaggerated its grievances. In simplest terms, Americans believed their embargo less hurtful to France than to Britain, whereas Frenchmen believed the emperor's decrees did less harm to Americans than did Britain's orders-in-council. Nor would either side accept the other's proposed remedies. Washington had rebuffed Napoleon's offer of a "more intimate connexion," and there appeared to be no common ground for ending the French seizures of American vessels. By early April 1808, Armstrong had protested more than twenty specific detentions, only to meet with Champagny's explanation that "large numbers" of U.S. carriers had arrived laden with British goods. Those claiming to have sailed from U.S. ports, closed for the past five months, had undoubtedly falsified the origins of their cargoes. Some even had British passengers on board.[19] In sum, both parties felt aggrieved over the operation of the Continental System from which Napoleon showed no signs of retreating.

───── ∞ ─────

With most American carriers locked in the embrace of the embargo, Napoleon began to look elsewhere for ways to lessen the blighting effect of his system without serving his enemy. Some of the innovations he toyed with in late summer 1808 were later acted on. All of them foreshadowed modest changes in French policy-thinking over the next four years. Frank Melvin, the first historian to track the documentary stream of policy recommendations Napoleon either asked for or received unsolicited in late 1808, labels this period one of "ameliorative experiments." Melvin credits Armstrong's note of 6 August with setting off this spate of recommendations when, soon after receiving it, Champagny discussed its contents with a recently arrived American sea captain named Nathan Haley whose only official mission at the time had been to deliver State Department despatches. Perhaps because Haley had some standing—he had once been a French naval officer—Champagny forwarded the courier's analysis of Armstrong's August 6 note to Napoleon who in turn requested an opinion from his Director General of Customs, Collin de Sussy. The latter's views, in turn, were critiqued by Champagny and Navy Minister Denis Decrès. The question they addressed was how France might use neutral-flag carriers to revive her external commerce while retaining intact the exclusionary intent of the Continental System.[20]

One of the major proposals can be traced to Madison, the other, in all likelihood, to Haley. What it owed to Madison was the familiar observation, now officially restated, that if France were to adjudicate ships only after they arrived, the United States would accept any resulting confiscations as being within the scope of "municipal regulation."[21] Champagny may have been deliberately obtuse when he asked Armstrong to be "more explicit on this point," noting that in-port seizures seemed "more rigorous" than current practice. Armstrong's August 6 note also supported the idea that France should require incoming carriers to export cargoes of equal value, thereby creating favorable balances of trade for both parties while tipping the balance against Britain. A month later, Armstrong repeated, this time in French, that France should restrict itself to portside enforcement of its decrees, welcome all U.S. vessels bearing cargoes certified as products of the United States and after offloading require them to take away cargoes of equal value. He repeated the presumed advantages: a reliable channel for French exports, safeguards against British imports, and trade balances favoring France and the United States.[22]

Haley's input came shortly after Armstrong had left Paris to take the waters at Bourbon l'Archambault. In opting to nurse his gout, while away from the capital, the American minister may have missed playing a major role in a review of French maritime policies. Certainly he did not foresee that Haley's gloss on his note of 6 August would spark so lively a debate among the emperor's advisors. Haley, after meeting first with Decrès and then with Champagny in early September, wrote a memorandum clarifying what Armstrong had written. Napoleon, however, asked for further clarification.[23] Before Haley could reply (he had business in Le Havre), the emperor, as already noted, asked his customs chief to report on the American situation generally and may have sent him a copy of Haley's memorandum. When de Sussy responded on 11 September, his report was sent to Navy Minister Decrès for his opinion. Haley's before-and-after analyses, combined with what is probably de Sussy's intervening critique, brought together the most fully developed arguments for and against modifying the French decrees.[24]

Haley, analyzing the diplomatic scene in his first memorandum, predicted an imminent rupture in Anglo-American relations. Pinkney's despatches telling of London's refusal to revoke its orders were now aboard the *St. Michel*, about to depart from L'Orient. Armstrong's despatches would soon join them. Congress, on learning of Pinkney's failure, would have to decide on a course of action. France, he argued, still had time before the *St. Michel* sailed to focus congressional hostility on Britain. The French decrees, he argued, could be enforced just as effectively through purely "municipal regulations." Just as effectively as what? Unfortunately, Haley's first memorandum failed to spell out the American objection to seizures made on the high seas, an omission that may explain why Napoleon asked for clarification. As before, this distinction between pelagic and portside seizures remained extremely difficult to put across, although one suspects the French emperor may have deliberately chosen not to understand it. He may have concluded what became increasingly apparent in his overall strategy: that any concession made to American shipping, if matched by the British, might lead to an Anglo-American rapprochement.

Haley's second memorandum repeated what Armstrong had already stated twice: that the United States did not object to the French confiscating British goods on arrival; it asked only "not to be exposed to the capture of their vessels on the high seas." Haley also analyzed more fully Armstrong's allusions to balance of trade issues. Britain's "great advantage," he wrote, lay in having a favorable balance with the United States which the latter offset by re-exporting high-value West Indies cargoes to Europe. The result had been a debilitating flow of specie away from Europe. At the same time, French decrees had reduced the number of carriers, thereby raising prices on imports while depressing prices on exports. Consequently, he estimated, French customs revenues had dropped by two-thirds. France, however, still had the means to shrink Britain's advantage. She need only restrict herself to detaining suspicious U.S. vessels when they arrived and require others to lade outgoing cargoes of equal value. Commerce in American bottoms would revive, specie would remain in Europe, and France would enjoy lower prices on imports and fetch higher prices for her exports. The political fallout would be equally salubrious because Americans would have no further cause for complaint. Moreover, if France agreed to forgo such captures, Haley thought Armstrong might be able to interpret his instructions loosely enough to incorporate these proposals in a treaty.

Whether the anonymous critic (probably Collin de Sussy) saw one or both of Haley's memoranda, he spotted their essential flaw. Both Armstrong and Haley had insisted that American vessels not be hindered in their commerce with other powers. But leaving them free to carry on "all other commerce" would defeat what the writer conceived to be the emperor's central purpose of cutting Britain off from all commercial intercourse. Moreover, calling back French privateers would likely throw American carriers into even greater servitude to British commerce. Brushing aside as problematic Haley's assurances of a more favorable trade balance, the writer also dismissed the argument of political advantage. He saw no sign that Congress was on the brink of war with either belligerent and every likelihood that whatever followed the embargo, Washington would continue its ban on British imports as long as the issue of impressment remained unresolved.[25] Champagny, knowing that Napoleon already had critiques from other sources, merely forwarded Haley's second memorandum, his cover letter noncommittal to a fault.[26]

More pressing business that fall swallowed whatever consideration Napoleon might have given to these proposals. Between trying to mop up Spanish insurrectionists and facing Habsburg Austria's anger at how badly he had treated the Spanish Bourbons, the French emperor had little time to weigh changes in maritime policies. On 22 September, he left Paris for Erfurt where he met with Czar Alexander, failed to win the latter's support against Austria, and dashed back to cope with Spanish partisans who refused to be put down. Both during and after the Erfurt Congress (so-called because dozens of German princelings also put in an appearance), time was the critical factor. On 20 October Armstrong wrote that despite Napoleon's disposition "to remove all difficulties . . . time was wanting at the moment to enter upon the business."[27] A month later, he reported that the emperor on his return from Erfurt had devoted all his attention to Spain and, according to Champagny, had still not found time to read his letters. By December, a temporary French victory in Spain meant only that Napoleon was now taken up with mobilizing for an Austrian offensive. Well into 1809, Armstrong despaired of any fundamental change in French maritime policy. The moment had passed. Without some overriding imperative, suggestions for policy changes were too readily shunted aside. Absent compelling reasons, neither the diplomat nor the courier had persuaded the emperor to forgo depredations on the high seas. Still, their openness to the idea of requiring return-cargoes to be of equal value and their endorsement of consular certification were to gain a firm foothold in the near-term of French policy. Whether, as Haley believed, Armstrong might have negotiated a treaty on these bases seems doubtful. Armstrong himself was dubious.[28]

How little the American minister knew of Haley's "diplomacy" he revealed in late November. Someone named "Hayley," he wrote Madison, had spoken with Champagny and Decrès and put his ideas in writing. As far as he could tell, the foreign ministry had subsequently broken off after finding Haley "leaky and incapable of keeping his own secrets."

News of Haley's unsolicited diplomacy reached Washington shortly after James Madison had left the State Department to take over the presidency in March 1809. Long regarded as Jefferson's heir apparent, the secretary of state moved effortlessly into his role as chief magistrate. Having easily defeated Charles Cotesworth Pinckney of South Carolina, his Federalist opponent in the election of 1808, Madison was to face relentless opposition from anti-administration members of his own party from the moment of his inauguration. Hoping to mitigate the hostility of this faction, most visibly led by Senator Samuel Smith of Maryland, he appointed the senator's brother, Robert Smith, to succeed him as secretary of state.

It was Smith, then, who expressed the new administration's "surprize and regret" that Haley had presumed to speak for it. Armstrong was to tell the French government that the courier had had no authority to hold talks with French officials. Then, perhaps reflecting President Madison's lack of confidence in Armstrong himself, Smith entertained the possibility that Haley's "proceedings" might not have been a dead loss. Armstrong was to disavow anything the captain had proposed unless, of course, it coincided with administration policy.[29]

Before long, Smith himself lost Madison's confidence, proving to be little more than a mole within the Madison cabinet, an informant to political enemies and particularly indiscreet in his dealings with the British *chargé d'affaires.* Intellectually deficient as well, Smith needed considerable coaching from the president in the performance of his duties. In the sardonic phrase of Irving Brant, when Madison replaced him with Monroe in the spring of 1811, the president finally "had a secretary of state who could write his own despatches."[30]

Unfortunately, as Madison's presidency got under way, no doubt remained of Napoleon's intent to continue pelagic enforcement of his continental blockade. As Champagny told Turreau, the emperor could show no special favor to Americans lest other maritime neutrals feel themselves unfairly treated. Moreover, he added, Americans continued to offend France by their unwillingness to honor his Continental System. As long as their shipmasters found ways to sneak in British cargoes, the emperor's grievance on this score would remain.[31]

CHAPTER 6

INCREASING TENSIONS, 1809

B y early 1809 Napoleon's makeshift maritime policy stood uncertainly on three legs. Most of the weight rested on certificates-of-origin and specified export requirements. Armstrong and Haley, if they accomplished nothing else, had focused Bonaparte's attention on the need to strengthen these elements. The third prop—a nascent licensing scheme—was added shortly.

Requiring French consuls to certify the non-British origins of France-bound cargoes had been somewhat haphazardly enforced until Napoleon ruled on 9 May that consuls must be physically present during the loading of such cargoes to make sure they were not of British origin or manufacture. He also ruled that if cargoes arrived uncertified because no French consul resided at the port of embarkation, they would be admitted only if French customs officials could identify them as "products of the north." "Colonial" goods like sugar and coffee, however, were not to be admitted without certification because determining their origin was too difficult. London, incidentally, had first taken notice of French-certified cargoes in one of its November 1807 orders-in-council, threatening to confiscate any vessel found carrying them. This sat well enough with Paris for it meant that American vessels once laded with such cargoes would likely steer clear of British ports. Certification went down less well in Washington because it restricted the freedom of Americans to seek out optimal markets and might, some thought, infringe on U.S. jurisdictional authority.[1] American exporters, eager to have a piece of the French market, welcomed certification as a security against delays at the other end. By the spring of 1809 Champagny, hoping to override the administration's objections, proposed a draft treaty by which the United States would acquiesce in the practice.[2] Nothing came of this proposal and to the dismay of French officials, British-forged certificates began to turn up in late August.

In a further effort to tighten controls, consuls were warned to certify only those cargoes destined for French ports; ships cleared for other continental destinations had been landing British cargoes falsely certified as French.[3] Like most documentary safeguards, certificates were not tamperproof even when consuls accompanied them with coded letters and copies of American newspapers bearing the date of a vessel's departure. The widespread use of forged documents undoubtedly added fuel to Napoleon's smouldering dislike of American merchant-adventurers who conspired with British exporters to punch holes in his Continental System.

The May 9 decree also required neutral importers to carry away French cargoes of equal value, a requirement designed to prevent the flight of specie. Haley's warning had underscored that if the captains of American vessels exchanged their goods for cash instead of cargo, not only would they deplete France's specie reserves, but, in all likelihood, they would spend the cash rounding out their cargoes in British ports on the voyage home. Over time, what might be called the equal-value export requirement produced some bizarre results. In early 1813, David Warden reported that French silks, a required export commodity, had so overstocked the market that outgoing cargoes of silk goods were being sold to smugglers or simply dumped overboard.[4]

⸻ ❧❧❧ ⸻

Licensing, another prop to French maritime regulation, gained a foothold in April 1809 when Napoleon authorized a small number of "permis" for the export of grain to Britain. Because trading with the enemy ran contrary to his system, some historians ascribe this anomaly to the distress of French grain farmers whose bumper harvests and low prices that spring coincided with a grain shortage in Britain.[5] What Napoleon intended as a temporary measure to exploit this conjuncture of supply and demand, however, ultimately grew to become an unwieldy mechanism for micromanaging France's external commerce. Besides opening a sizable hole in his system, licensing also created a bureaucratic mare's nest that Napoleon himself came to regret. From his exile on St. Helena, he admitted that "The system of commercial licenses was no doubt mischievous. Heaven forbid that I should have adopted it as a principle. It was the invention of the English; with me it was only a momentary resource."[6] Whatever Napoleon's later misgivings, this "momentary resource" of April 1809 soon proved addictive. By January 1810, some 300 licenses had been issued, and in July and August of that year a series of imperial decrees formalized the procedures for acquiring them.[7]

Napoleon also let it be known in mid-February that he might release detained vessels not *sub judice* if their captains bought licenses and gave bond that they would sail directly to their home ports. Armstrong doubted many would qualify. Only about twenty were free of legal process, he observed sourly, and even these were of such dubious "character and connexion" as to make freeing them unlikely.[8] His pessimism deepened when he learned how the French planned to guarantee their return to home ports. Having assumed that U.S. consuls would handle the bonding arrangements, he was unpleasantly surprised when word came back from Marseille that the Imperial Customs House intended to hold the bond, moreover at "double the value of the ships and cargoes." Armstrong objected vehemently, both to the excessive cost and the likely results. The British, he wrote, would surely seize carriers found to have been bonded by the French government, adding wryly that such controls differed little from Britain's.[9]

His objections registered strongly enough that for a while American vessels were left outside the French licensing system. Paris for the moment turned instead to the more pliant city-states of north Germany where the Hanse towns furnished more than enough "neutral" licensees.[10] The principal result of Armstrong's protest was to thicken the atmosphere of distrust in Paris. By the end of April, Finance Minister Martin Gaudin, having read his objections, reminded the emperor that if he intended to maintain his continental blockade, he would do well not to favor Americans, given their ties of language, family, and commerce with the British. Armstrong's insistence that U.S. consuls be the bonding agents, he added, would by no means guarantee the American vessels' destinations.[11] In all this, he mirrored the jaundiced view of many French officials that Americans were not to be trusted where their material interests were concerned.

Early in James Madison's presidency, two events occurring in rapid succession jarred the already unstable state of Franco-American relations. In

March 1809, Congress replaced the embargo with the Non-Intercourse Act which, like its predecessor, Paris found unjustly punitive; and in April David Erskine, the British envoy to Washington, signed an agreement that appeared to herald an end to Britain's offending orders-in-council. Both events drew hostile fire from Paris: the Non-Intercourse Act because it was seen to be more injurious to France than to Britain, and Erskine's diplomacy because it held out the unwelcome prospect of an Anglo-American détente. Although the Portland ministry quickly disavowed the Smith-Erskine Agreement, its brief promise of a better day for neutral commerce was enough to move Napoleon to take another look at his own offending policies.

The Non-Intercourse Act banned trade with both belligerents while re-opening commerce with all other nations. The law also explicitly author-ized the president to renew commercial intercourse with whichever bel-ligerent ceased to abuse American shipping. This sequel to the embargo had few believers in Congress. Nearly every opponent of the bill predicted rampant violations, but no one foresaw how sorely France would resent its one-sided consequences. A largely silent and half-hearted majority passed the measure, 81–40, on 17 February.[12]

From Napoleon's vantage, when it was called to his attention, this latest wrinkle in coercive legislation damaged French interests in three respects. First, as was widely foreseen at the time, American merchants effectively resumed dealings with their British counterparts simply by swapping car-goes in neutral ports. Reportedly, nearly eighty ships sailed from New York that spring for a rendezvous of cargo-exchanges in the Azores.[13] As Champagny later noted, even this subterfuge proved unnecessary: Ameri-can shipmasters merely allowed British warships to escort them to British ports where they promptly sold off cargoes that were intended for the British market in the first place. It rankled Paris, too, that those same British warships effectively denied France a like opportunity to engage in such indirect traffic.[14] A year later Napoleon was overheard to remark bitterly that he could not "see with indifference" a law whose unequal operation works "much to my prejudice and greatly to the advantage of British Commerce."[15]

Second, the law did not ban U.S. commerce with Napoleon's satellites, most significantly the Dutch whose leakages in the Continental System were already so porous as to threaten a dyke-burst. Such congressional indifference to the integrity of his system added measurably to the irritation the emperor already felt at the unwillingness of his brother, the Dutch King Louis Napoleon, to crack down on such interlopers.

Finally, the law imposed what Paris viewed as an undeserved penalty by closing U.S. ports to French naval vessels. Worse in the long run, it threatened confiscation of any French (or British) cargo vessel caught entering a U.S. harbor. What Congress touted as even-handedness in this respect Napoleon would later seize on as a pretext for retaliation. Although it took some time for the threat to register in Paris, when Napoleon finally decided to confiscate American vessels that had been merely "sequestered," he would cite as his rationale the confiscatory section 3 of the Non-Intercourse Act.[16]

Initially, the French emperor took greatest offense at what he believed was the unwarranted closure of U.S. ports to French warships, a congressional response to the French Navy's alleged burning of several American merchantmen nearly a year before. Because the ban came so long after the fact, the French emperor quite possibly missed the cause and effect relationship. In April 1808 he was deeply immersed in opening his Spanish campaign and may not have paid particular attention to Armstrong's alluding to American ships having been "burnt on the high seas" when it appeared in a single sentence buried among more fully-developed protests leveled against French maritime policy. Although by late August Armstrong had conclusive "evidence" of the burnings, he had let the matter drop, flatly refusing to return to Paris. Writing from Bourbon l'Arcambault where he was taking the waters, he allowed peevishly that any renewed contact with the foreign office at that time "would certainly be useless, and probably injurious." Informants had warned him the emperor was in no mood to discuss relations with the United States and to try would likely irritate him. Thus, the connection between ship-burnings and the exclusion of French warships from U.S. harbors may have escaped imperial notice.[17] When Congress amended the Non-Intercourse Act in June, it lifted the ban on the warships, but not merchant ships.[18] The door to French retaliation remained open.

⸻

Armstrong would have a lot of explaining to do when the adverse impact of the Non-Intercourse Act registered with the foreign office in the late spring of 1809. His mission was further complicated by a momentary uptick in U.S. relations with London. The Smith-Erskine Agreement, signed in Washington on 19 April, appeared to put an amicable end to nearly all disputes with Britain. What the consequences would be for his dealings with the French government the American minister could only guess. His situation might have become untenable if the British foreign minister had not subsequently disavowed the agreement. In explaining George Canning's disavowal, historians have questioned the motives of all parties: Canning for having burdened his emissary with conditions he knew Madison could not accept, David Erskine for ignoring them, and Madison for disregarding the warning signs.[19] Secretary of State Robert Smith, who gave his name but little else to the agreement, played the president's proxy, while Erskine, yielding to youthful eagerness for a diplomatic breakthrough, made at least three major mistakes, all errors of omission. First, he omitted an important condition from that part of his instructions which authorized him to withdraw the January and November 1807 orders-in-council in return for the United States lifting its nonintercourse. Canning's additional qualification was that the United States allow British warships to seize American vessels caught trading with France, a stipulation Erskine dropped when Madison and Smith rejected it as dishonorable. The envoy also accepted the administration's argument that he could reasonably leave out Canning's requirement that the United States acquiesce in the Rule of 1756. His most feckless omission, however, lay in disregarding Canning's *sine qua non* that as a condition to Britain's repeal, the United States bind itself to maintain non-intercourse against France—in effect, forgo future efforts to patch things up with Britain's enemy—as long as the two were at war.

Whether Madison and his advisors realized the appalling extent to which Erskine had violated his instructions is a matter about which historians of Anglo-American relations have reached variously shaded conclusions. What seems clear, however, is that Erskine and various administration figures persuaded themselves they could set aside Canning's requirements if, as they believed, London were fundamentally sincere in its wish to restore good relations. Although Erskine later claimed to have honored the spirit of his instructions, George Canning decidedly disagreed.[20] He publicly denounced his emissary, repudiated the agreement, and recalled him forthwith, thereby bursting the bubble of elation that had initially greeted news of the accord.

While the euphoria lasted, Turreau worried over rumors that a full-blown treaty might follow. When Gallatin told him that vessels with $200 million in cargo had already sailed, the French minister observed dryly that with so much at stake, London might ask more of Washington than it would be willing to concede when it came to treaty-making.[21] Though angry and depressed, the French minister showed an uncharacteristic sensitivity to countervailing political factors that spring. In March, he had lulled himself into believing that if the embargo were lifted, Congress would follow it by declaring war on Britain. When instead it voted for non-intercourse, he counseled restraint even as he grumbled at the parade of U.S. vessels setting out for Madeira and St. Barthelémy where he knew they would exchange cargoes with the British. A recently inaugurated Madison, he reflected, would probably call Congress into session within two months, and until the political situation cleared, he urged Paris to hold fire.[22] A month later, unaware that Smith and Erskine were preparing another blow, he reported sourly that American merchants not only consorted with their British associates in neutral West Indies ports, but shipmasters headed for European ports fully expected to be intercepted, their cargoes taken directly to British ports. Indeed, insurance companies were guaranteeing delivery to British destinations.

In retrospect, he was not sure whether Congress had set out deliberately to favor Britain or had simply failed to foresee the law's one-sided result. In any case, he estimated that 90 percent of the recent ship departures would benefit France's enemy.[23] When, five days later, news broke of the Erskine Agreement, he brushed aside his earlier cautionary advice. Now claiming prescience, he wrote that he had suspected all along that Britain would triumph in American councils. "It can no longer be doubted that today the Americans are entirely delivered to the English."[24] Insult having now been added to injury, on June 10 Turreau sent Smith a letter of protest so strongly worded that he was forced to withdraw it. Four years later, the supposed insults he had flung at the administration came back to haunt his successor. When the note was published in the fall of 1813, congressional Federalists eagerly seized on the administration's delay in rejecting what came to be known as the "Turreau Letter" as further proof of its subservience to France.[25]

Unlike the embargo, the Non-Intercourse Act offered the belligerents a clearer set of incentives. If one revoked its decrees and the other did not, commercial ties would be renewed with the complying party. Madison was barely two weeks in office when he wrote Pinkney and Armstrong that if only one belligerent complied, Congress would likely force the issue by declaring war on the other. Decisions for war lay with Congress, of course, but the belligerent that refused to revoke its antineutral measures should know that the president believed Congress would probably declare war against it. Cautiously, in nearly identical letters, he told the two emissaries to say as much, orally, not in writing, and to put it forward only as the "opinion of the Executive."[26] Like Woodrow Wilson's tentative offer of armed mediation in Europe's war 107 years later, Madison refrained from promising a war that only Congress could declare. In 1809, it turned out that a presidential "probably" as to what Congress *might* do carried even less weight, as Armstrong discovered when, conveying the executive's "opinion," he met with no response. Having ventured warily into an unexplored area of presidential discretion, Madison clearly felt himself on firmer ground when he underscored the authority Congress had given him to restore intercourse with the power that revoked its decrees. This he assured the two ministers he would do.

Armstrong at first got little guidance from Washington on how to reconcile Paris to this latest piece of legislation. Like Congress itself, Madison appears to have looked on the operational aspects of non-intercourse more with an eye to their effect on London than on how they might complicate relations with France. Armstrong could hardly have seen much merit in a letter Smith sent him on 15 March instructing him to urge France to revoke its edicts because they violated American maritime rights. He had, after all, been making this point to the foreign office for nearly a year. Nor was it helpful for Smith to tell him that French decrees had provided London with a pretext for its orders-in-council when Armstrong already knew—and Smith should have known—that Paris saw it the other way around.[27]

A month later, the administration told him in more detail how he should deal with the Erskine Agreement. A formal treaty with Britain would follow, Smith warned him, but he must assure Paris that neither the agreement nor "the proposed Treaty [were] . . . in any degree inconsistent with the friendly adjustment of our differences with France." Indeed, Britain's revocation of its orders should be pictured as removing "every motive for the continuance of the illegal parts of the French decrees." It took less than a week for Smith (or more likely Madison) to realize that their man in Paris would have to do more than make soothing pronouncements. They wrote him again, suggesting a number of options that might direct attention away from the Erskine Agreement. He might, for example, offer to renegotiate the Franco-American Convention of 1800 and once more probe France's willingness to cede the Floridas now that the emperor had ostensibly conquered Spain. Most important, he was to promise an immediate presidential proclamation lifting non-intercourse if France revoked her decrees.[28] He was to point out that the Milan Decree was now obsolete because the Erskine Agreement had rescinded the orders-in-council that had provoked it. Beyond this, France need enforce only those parts of the Berlin Decree that did no violence to neutral rights. Neither Madison nor Smith had to spell out what those "parts" were. A critical distinction had come full circle.[29] It remained to be seen whether Napoleon would forgo captures on the high seas in return for a restoration of commercial relations once he had had the chance to assess the impact the Non-Intercourse Act on Britain and to examine the wreckage of the Erskine Agreement.

CHAPTER 7

Napoleon Shifts the Diplomatic Initiative to London

Spring with its swifter and more frequent crossings might have fired up both the tempo and temper of diplomatic exchanges had Napoleon not left his capital in mid-April for another campaign against Austria and before he had an opportunity to weigh the implications of the Non-Intercourse Act. His departure afforded Armstrong a welcome respite. News of the act, he wrote, had reached Paris just as the emperor was setting off to join his armies in Germany. Wary of what parting instructions Napoleon might have left, he was tempted to delay the return of his despatch boat. If war came, he wanted to have it handy for a speedy return home. Meanwhile, to avert any gratuitous misunderstandings, he immediately wrote Champagny a short and placatory note explaining what the act contained.[1] A few days later, knowing the foreign minister had left for Munich, he pursued him with a plea that France avail herself of the new law's opportunities. Casting aside Smith's enjoinder not to put the executive's "opinion" in writing, he wrote that if France agreed to a "mere modification" of its decrees and Britain persisted in hers, the president would "advise" Congress to declare war. Outright repeal was not required or even the restoration of property already confiscated. The United States would renew commercial relations if France would simply "hereafter exempt Americans ships from future vexations and capture." What the Non-Intercourse Act meant, he continued wordily, was that "if Great Britain should not give a construction of similar character and extent to her orders of Council on the same subject the President of the United States would, in that case, advise to [sic] an immediate war with the latter."[2]

Armstrong's message was as clear and forceful as his verbosity could make it: France could bring America to war against Britain by revoking the Berlin Decree and easing her enforcement of the Milan Decree. Only later would Madison require that both decrees be revoked. Meanwhile, hoping to hasten a reply from Munich, Armstrong contemplated asking for his passports, but in a way "calculated to avoid offense," he told Madison.[3] He relaxed a bit on hearing that his note of 2 May would be forwarded to the emperor. On reflection, he thought it likely Napoleon would follow Britain's lead. If London's "system" held firm, "he will no doubt persevere in his"; but if the Erskine Agreement signaled a British retreat, the emperor would follow suit.[4]

Although Armstrong welcomed the silence from Munich, he grumbled at hearing nothing from London, complaining that his colleague's secretiveness was "extraordinary," especially since he knew Pinkney had told Washington that a breakthrough might be at hand.[5] Curiously, he took little notice of the Portland ministry's order of 26 April extending Britain's blockade to all French, Dutch, and German ports as far north as Ems. Significantly, although this blockade order still required neutral vessels bound for Europe to stop at British ports, it eliminated onerous transit duties—the so-called payments of "tribute" Napoleon had taken such strong exception to. Because the order failed to jibe with Erskine's promise of a clean sweep, news of it reaching Washington cast serious doubt on British intentions, not to mention Erskine's good faith.[6]

If Armstrong was inattentive to the April 26 order, it was because he was suddenly jolted by press rumors, subsequently proved false, that Pinkney had persuaded London to rescind all of its offending orders-in-council, perhaps even negotiated a British alliance. If there were any truth to these reports, he assured Champagny, his colleague in London would surely have notified him. Ten days later, however, flushed with embarrassment, he admitted having learned unofficially that London had revoked its orders and Washington had lifted its non-intercourse measures. What he heard, of course, was breaking news of the Erskine Agreement. Disclaiming any intent to deceive, Armstrong blamed Pinkney for failing to keep him informed. He even quoted to the foreign minister that part of their instructions in which he and Pinkney were ordered "to loose [sic] no time in transmitting this [kind of] information" both to the State Department and to each other.[7] Typically, Armstrong's biting censure of

Pinkney was too quick off the mark. The latter could not have foreseen the terms Erskine negotiated in Washington; even George Canning had been taken by surprise. The sparse flow of communication from London to Paris that spring meant simply that until the Erskine Agreement arrived, Pinkney had little of substance to report.

Caught off guard once more, Armstrong worried about how to reconcile the French government to the uncertainties left by Canning's repudiation of the agreement. He sensed the emperor would not take lightly even a failed effort at Anglo-American reconciliation. And if Napoleon were to foresee a reprise of Erskine's diplomacy, there was no telling his hostile reaction. Making the best of it, he touted the agreement to Champagny as gratifying evidence of Britain's willingness to meet American complaints, however briefly, and proof of the American government's commitment to neutral rights. London's disavowal, he added hopefully, did not detract from the propriety of the intent.[8]

While showing a brave face to Champagny, Armstrong told Smith he had been completely undone by events. He had not renewed his efforts to get France to modify her own maritime decrees, he explained cryptically, because he had been put off by London's disavowal of the Erskine Agreement. This failure to pursue the most important part of his instructions is puzzling, but possibly explained by his earlier stated belief that Napoleon's treatment of the United States, for better or worse, would march in lockstep with London's. Now that London had opted for no accommodation, he may have assumed that neither would the French emperor. And yet, in a second letter to Smith of the same date, Armstrong reported a glimmer of hope in a recent visit he had had from the Comte d'Hauterive, a high level foreign office figure.[9]

Napoleon almost certainly expected no more from the ensuing Armstrong-Hauterive talks than to offset Britain's apparent abandonment of transit taxes. Champagny initiated this low-level negotiation when he briefed the emperor on the implications of both the Non-Intercourse Act and London's most recent blockade order.[10] He characterized the former as "an act of reprisal for the prohibitive decrees of France and England," under which France would continue to lose significant import and export opportunities. Armstrong had made clear, however, that if France interpreted its decrees "a bit more favorably," detaining American vessels only after their arrival, Washington would restore trade with France. He went on to point out that London's elimination of transit taxes in her blockade order of 26 April had put France in an unfavorable light. He then turned to a related problem. Americans complained of vessels being detained simply because British warships had boarded them. He understood the emperor's suspicion that during such visits American skippers were yielding to London's financial impositions. Or, as he put it, "How can we be sure they are not paying tribute to England?" It might be true that Britain no longer imposed transit taxes, but the fundamental question Hauterive should put to Armstrong was this: Could the United States give credible guarantees that American shipmasters would not in the course of being visited pay any kind of "tribute" to France's enemy? Wittingly perhaps, neither Napoleon nor his foreign minister defined what elements of "tribute" they had in mind, whether they meant customs duties, transit taxes, and/or licensing fees. Given this focus on "tribute," however, the emperor agreed that Armstrong should be pressed for answers and ordered Hauterive's instructions forwarded to Paris.[11]

In launching this démarche, Champagny acted boldly in view of Napoleon's first snarling reaction to Armstrong's explanation of the Non-Intercourse Act. Having earlier declared "denationalized" any vessel that submitted to British visit and search, he now likened such vessels to "floating colonies," whose boarding by a hostile party he compared to an invasion of one's territory, an act of war. If Washington could not protect French property aboard its floating colonies, he would consider their vessels as "no longer belonging to the United States."[12] Because such wrathful pronouncements did not at all respond to the specifics of Armstrong's May 2 letter, Napoleon may have seen only Champagny's summary of it, written from Munich a week earlier.[13] But if he missed law's implied offer to restore commerce, he had the excuse of more pressing matters. Four days later at Aspern and Essling he would face evenly-matched Austrian forces under the Archduke Charles. Only after that inconclusive battle did Champagny's moderating influence begin to be felt. By early June, however, the foreign minister had not only persuaded him to put Hauterive in play, but had also drafted an imperial decree which, had it been promulgated, would have exempted American vessels from the enforcement of the Milan Decree. This draft document, though it served no immediate purpose, clearly reflected the foreign minister's determination that France not be outmaneuvered by London's apparent concessions to maritime neutrals.[14]

From the outset, the Hauterive-Armstrong conversations lost their intended focus on "tribute." Neither man left a record of having addressed this issue directly. Not only did they talk past each other, but also their meetings became less meaningful once it became apparent how little London had conceded. The April 26 order-in-council had, after all, created another illegal "paper" blockade which meant that neutrals submitting to it could hardly expect favors from France. Moreover, the collapse of Anglo-American negotiations removed the element of immediacy. As Hauterive observed, London's disavowal of Erskine had placed Armstrong "in a very bad position." Their talks, he believed, "will be more embarrassing for him than for me."[15] Privately, Armstrong agreed. Hauterive nonetheless promised to draw out the American on specific issues, and at their first meeting, Armstrong found the Frenchman's manner "particularly friendly & free" and was relieved that he spoke English. He repeated at length Washington's readiness to accept portside seizures and at one point remarked bluntly that if American vessels traded with the British and subsequently entered a French port, they should get what they deserved. Vessels at sea, however, powerless to resist visit and search should not for that reason be punished. At this point, where logically it might have come up, neither man talked specifically about guarantees against paying "tribute." Likely, they realized that no one could tell for sure what passed between American shipmasters and British boarding parties and that treaty guarantees would have little effect on such occasions. Assuming that Napoleon knew this as well—and later evidence suggests that he did—then he expected no more from the Hauterive talks than to counter Britain's apparent concessions to maritime neutrals.

Emboldened by news that Napoleon had decisively defeated Austria at Wagram on 6 July, Armstrong drove out to Hauterive's country house in Bagnieux where, to his gratification, the division chief divulged the contents of Champagny's draft decree repealing that of Milan. If promulgated, they agreed, it would go a long way toward meeting American complaints. He was put off, however, when Hauterive told him that any change in imperial policy would depend on London's response to the Erskine fiasco.[16] Hauterive later explained to Champagny why he saw fit to dampen Armstrong's expectations. Canning's critics in Parliament were predicting that American indignation at the repudiation of the Erskine Agreement might lead to war. Consequently, Canning had lost no time in sending a replacement. If the new minister, Francis Jackson, were to foist on Washington even part of Erskine's original instructions, good policy suggested France should await the outcome of this next mission.[17]

Armstrong came away from Bagnieux deeply discouraged. Hauterive's message, "when translated into plain English [he wrote Smith], amounts to this, that unless you resist the British doctrines of *search* and *blockade*, you need expect no relaxation on the part of the Emperor. . . ." Napoleon, he concluded bitterly, had returned to his "old offensive system." Too, he realized that for Washington even to have considered Erskine's terms had revived suspicion among French officials that the two English-speaking peoples might yet reach an accord on some variation of that disgraced minister's instructions.[18]

In mid-summer 1809, timing became the most conspicuous factor in Napoleon's dealing with the Anglo-American nexus. In June, Champagny previewed to Hauterive the emperor's determination to avoid making concessions in the wrong sequence. "If we revoke our measures before the English revoke theirs," he explained, "we remove any reason for them to recall their orders in council."[19] This dictum—that London make the first retreat—became the bedrock of French policy on 22 August when Napoleon ordered his foreign minister, then in Altenberg, to lay out the proper sequence to John Armstrong.[20] Predictably, Napoleon began his "Altenberg Letter" by denouncing Britain's "repugnant" blockades, but for some reason singled out for its particular repugnance only Britain's initial blockade of 1806, the one that had evoked his Berlin Decree. The strange singularity of the target later led Madison to try to find out whether Napoleon was serious about revoking this decree on the simple recall of a three-year-old British interdiction which had been superseded as recently as the previous April by a blockade just as ill-enforced as that of 1806.[21]

The emperor then turned his fire on the Non-Intercourse Act for permitting U.S. trade with France's European dependencies, especially the Dutch and made clear he intended to retaliate.[22] Note, both belligerents wanted Americans out of the Dutch trade: Napoleon because British goods smuggled into Dutch ports punched gaping holes in his system; London because American contrabandiers competed too vigorously with their own. Napoleon's Altenberg Letter and London's April 26 blockade order posted the same warning: Americans, keep out.

Although threatening another round of seizures, the emperor promised Americans relief under the same sequence of actions Champagny had spelled out to Hauterive in June, this time in more explicit terms. The

Altenberg Letter read: "Should England recall her declaration of blockade of France, France will recall her decree of blockade of England [the Berlin Decree]; should England recall her orders-in-council of 11 November 1807, the decree of Milan will likewise fall; American commerce will recover all its liberty, and it will be sure to find favor in the ports of France. . . . But it is for the United States by their firmness to bring about these happy results." Thus, with apparent magnanimity, Napoleon neatly passed responsibility for a diplomatic breakthrough to London and Washington. On reading the letter, Armstrong wondered (to Smith) why the emperor had had it printed in the Paris press unless its publication was "a direct invitation to G.B. to maintain her system." Armstrong's point was well taken. Napoleon's pronouncement gave London no reason not to maintain that system. Dispirited as autumn lengthened, Armstrong characteristically reverted to military solutions. With more certitude than was warranted, he regaled a skeptical Champagny with the imminence of an American war on England. At the same time he urged the administration to declare war on both belligerents.[23]

———— ⊷⊶ ————

The Altenberg Letter raised the question of how soon and with what severity France would close down the European ports she controlled and which the Non-Intercourse Act had fecklessly left open. Napoleon was already toying with the most sweeping of interdictions. Although he neither signed nor published it, a draft decree dated 4 August 1809 would have confiscated outright all American vessels attempting to land cargoes at European ports under French control. His justification was the threat of confiscation posed to French merchantmen by Section 3 of the Non-Intercourse Act.[24] Thus, whereas the Altenberg Letter suggested a certain flexibility in French policy, the unpromulgated decree of 4 August meant that Napoleon had come up with a brand-new justification for seizing American shipping. Reprisals until then pictured as responses to Britain's wrongdoing could now be justified by Section 3 of the Non-Intercourse Act. Congress had played haplessly into his hands. But why did Napoleon hold back his 4 August decree? Henry Adams ascribes the delay to his ministers' advice that he not make sweeping confiscations "founded on the phrase of a penalty which the customs laws of every country necessarily contained."[25] Champagny later recalled that the August decree had been shelved because the emperor wanted to see what happened next in Anglo-American relations.[26] Whatever the reason for Napoleon's restraint at this point, Congress had furnished him ground for retaliation whenever he chose to act on it.

———— ⊙⊛⊙ ————

Meanwhile, London's disavowal of the Erskine Agreement made it incumbent on Madison to reinstitute non-intercourse against Britain lest France take further offense. He also needed to quash speculation that he might accept from Francis Jackson so much of Erskine's original instructions as had been clearly hostile to French interests. A letter from Albert Gallatin in late July warned that any delay in reimposing non-intercourse would expose France to a "very injurious inequality." Jackson's intentions must also be ascertained because Canning had hinted in the press that Washington had nearly accepted Britain's original terms. The administration, he urged, must "hear without delay what Mr. Jackson has to say & no less so to answer him immediately."[27]

Reluctant to quit Montpellier for the heat of Washington, the president nonetheless made a quick trip to the capital and on 9 August issued a proclamation once more suspending commerce with Britain.[28] His action did not pass unchallenged, however. Dissension within his cabinet flared briefly when Robert Smith questioned whether Congress, in authorizing the president to lift the trade ban, had also empowered him to reimpose it. The secretary of state clearly thought not. The president, knowing his (other) political enemies would echo this view as well, nonetheless heeded Gallatin's sensible advice. As he told a sympathetic Jefferson, reimposing the trade ban on Britain was a "manifest necessity."[29]

Divining Francis Jackson's intentions despite the slow motion of early nineteenth century diplomacy took remarkably little time. Canning's unpromising appointee, known reproachfully as "Copenhagen" Jackson for his role in the Royal Navy's discreditable bombardment of that neutral capital two years earlier, quickly lived up to the administration's worst expectations. Haughty, disdainful of all things American, and determined not to show any of Erskine's softness, Jackson raised hackles from the moment he arrived in early September. He brought no new proposals, persistently refused to explain Canning's disavowal of the Erskine Agreement (in terms that Madison could accept), and three times accused the administration of tricking Erskine into making an agreement it knew violated his instructions. The third time he did this, in early November, Madison notified him bluntly that "no further communications will be received from you."[30] In sum, within the space of two months and for whatever it might count toward relieving French mistrust, Jackson had managed to dispel any prospect of Anglo-American détente.

What French officialdom knew of Jackson's failed mission was fragmentary at first. Only toward year's end, when Congress took up and angrily debated the British minister's "arrogance," did press accounts crossing the Atlantic convey how far he had fallen from favor. Armstrong appreciated being able to confirm as early as 16 September that American intercourse with Britain had once more been suspended. Even before Jackson arrived in Washington, he was authorized to tell Paris there would be no "amicable adjustment" if the new British minister sought to revive Erskine's original terms.[31] Subsequent press reports from America bore out the certainty of it.

Standing up to London may have served the administration's need to restore a semblance of impartiality but, as Armstrong well knew, stern actions from Washington gave Paris no reason to reconsider its own policy toward neutrals. Meanwhile, he ruminated on Europe's larger scene, pondering possible outcomes for a recently defeated Austria, a Russian ally worried over the future of Poland, a divorced empress, and a still undefeated Spain. That same August of 1809, as Champagny crafted the Altenberg Letter and Madison reinstituted non-intercourse, Armstrong, apparently feeling the need for action, left Paris for Amsterdam where he hoped to encourage the emperor's brother Louis to keep French privateers from preying on American shipping. In view of the Dutch king's well-known laxity in enforcing his brother's maritime decrees, Armstrong's optimism seemed warranted. Despite the emperor's repeated warnings, Louis had sought popular support, perhaps even a measure of independence, for his satellite realm by condoning as many breaches in the Continental System as might help keep its battered mercantile economy afloat. Consequently, carriers of contraband, mostly British and American, conducted a lively cross-Channel traffic running a gauntlet of French corsairs.

When they met, Louis confided uneasily that his efforts to suppress French privateering had caused a "very serious quarrel with the Emperor." He reminded Armstrong that many of the captured American vessels had been released, and some taken more recently would also be restored. When the American minister described the spectacle of widespread smuggling as a "triumph of contraband over honest industry," Louis added helpfully that it was also a triumph "of immorality over justice." The illicit trade, they solemnly agreed, would continue as long

as Napoleon persisted in his misguided system.[32] Before he got back to
Paris, Armstrong decided to renew his request for a "temporary congé,"
hoping to elicit a conciliatory gesture from Paris. He assured Smith, however, that he would leave the administration "an entire freedom of choice
with regard to your future conduct." What that choice should be Armstrong left no doubt. His patience frayed by diplomatic deadlock, he
meant to send signals to Washington as well.[33] When Champagny refused
his request for leave, Armstrong decided not to press the matter. He worried that his departure might provoke the government to confiscate
American property that until then had been only sequestered. Too, that
leaving his post might give the administration less rather than more "freedom of choice" seemed to catch up with him as a sober afterthought.[34]

Adding to Armstrong's malaise, Hauterive took advantage of his absence from Paris to turn over future meetings to Jean-Baptiste Petry, an
attaché at the French legation recently returned from Washington. The
American minister, he told Champagny, had nothing to offer but "po-
lemical conversations;" moreover, Petry fully understood the issues and
spoke English better than he.[35] For what it was worth, Petry's appearance
on the diplomatic scene added a voice for moderating French policy during the months to come. A self-professed expert on American matters, he
usually gave advice that was temperate, well-reasoned, and just as routinely ignored. Champagny at the time raised no objection to Hauterive's
putting him in play, most likely because he believed the emperor had
set his course in the Altenberg Letter. Until either Madison or London
responded to its imperatives, Petry could go through the motions of responding to American complaints.

CHAPTER 8

Fleeting Hopes for
Conciliation, 1809–10

In late 1809 Madison wrote to find out whether Napoleon seriously meant to revoke his Berlin Decree solely on the strength of London's revocation of its 1806 blockade. If Armstrong could verify this minimal condition, then the president also needed to know from Pinkney whether that blockade was still in force.[1] The answer from Paris was affirmative. In late January 1810, Armstrong relayed Petry's assurance that "the only condition required for the revocation [of the Berlin Decree] will be the previous revocation by the British Government of her blockade of France, or part of France (such as that from the Elbe to Brest. . . ." This reference to the Elbe and Brest unmistakably identified Fox's blockade.[2] Getting London to clarify the status of that blockade, however, plunged William Pinkney into protracted and frustrating exchanges with Britain's new foreign secretary. Repeated inquiries finally elicited from Lord Wellesley the unhelpful inference that although the 1806 blockade had never been formally withdrawn, it had been "merged and comprehended" within the blockade order of January 1807.[3] Pinkney's efforts to squeeze from the foreign office even the barest hint that Fox's blockade might have expired, lapsed, or been "virtually revoked" proved futile. Armstrong, who shared his colleague's exasperation, concluded dryly that Wellesley was unlikely to admit to anything that might improve U.S. relations with France. Back in Washington, Smith gave up on London's refusal to "originate the annulment" of Fox's blockade and urged Pinkney to "press the other experiment held out in the late act of Congress." What he referred to was Macon's Bill, No. 2, a legislative enactment restoring commerce with both belligerents while enticing each to retreat from its maritime strictures by promising to reinstitute non-intercourse against the other. With American diplomacy at a standstill in both London and Paris, the last major phase of congressional experimentation with economic sanctions was about to begin.[4]

Ruminating over the failed Erskine Agreement, Madison concluded that its failure to close the Dutch trade to American shipping best explained Canning's disavowal. That the ministry's April 26 order had put Dutch ports under blockade confirmed it. All other objections to Erskine's Agreement could be explained away, he believed, leaving only Britain's highly profitable traffic with the Netherlands to account for its repudiation.[5] Since that rebuff, diplomatic activity had slowed on all fronts. The administration wisely declined to recognize either the British-backed Spanish Junta or the puppet regime of Joseph Bonaparte. Republicans in Congress angrily denounced Britain for its wrongheaded rejection of the Erskine Agreement and lashed out at Jackson's insulting charge that the administration had shown bad faith during its negotiation. Relations with France were seldom mentioned on the floor of either house. Nor did Armstrong's reports give Washington any hint of movement in French policy.[6] At least for the moment, Napoleon's Altenberg Letter had succeeded in quieting Franco-American relations by specifying that London take the first placatory step.

Unable to resolve the big issues, figures near the centers of power turned to lesser and sometimes more personal activities. John Armstrong roused himself long enough to report on the Empress Josephine's divorce and Austria's sadly fallen state, but seemed to prefer belaboring his consuls for their shortcomings.[7] Turreau, too, complained of consular deficiencies and like Armstrong wished he were home. In a year-end summary of congressional activity, he grumbled that his consuls, "most of whom are absolutely incapable of any political work," had been no help. Thanks to their ignorance he knew about as much of the politics in New York, Philadelphia, and Charleston, he wrote, as he did of China.[8]

In December, his private correspondence sounded a desperate note. He begged an unidentified friend to tell the foreign office that his eyesight was failing to the point where he could no longer read by candlelight; his personal finances were exhausted; and worst of all, his appalling wife whom he had hoped to leave in France had followed him to Washington where even the "authorities" could not prevent her from ruining his reputation. If all this could be explained to Champagny, he hoped his recall would soon follow. Looking toward a peaceful retirement, he asked his anonymous friend to take what remained of his funds and buy him a house in the country, no matter how far from Paris.[9]

The slack season also brought out the worst in Robert Smith who saw fit to needle Pinkney about the all too familiar problem of British ship-masters using forged American papers. He pointed out, superfluously, that forgeries had led officials on the continent to confiscate American vessels that exhibited the genuine article. Pinckney was to ask the ministry to suppress both the forgers and the use of forged papers. From across the Channel, meanwhile, came intimations of how widespread the prac-tice had become. William Lee, on hearing rumors that Napoleon had sequestered all vessels detained in northern Europe, wrote his wife that he was not alarmed "because out of 100 [vessels] it is proved that 80 are English with American forged papers." Even allowing for Lee's tendency to exaggerate, his firsthand experience in detecting false documents showed the problem to be as intractable as it was troublesome; forged ships papers would remain a source of anguish to all except those who found them useful.[10]

When the French Council of Prizes suspended its hearings in early September, Americans still doing business in France began to adapt to changed circumstances.[11] Those who still bought and sold cargoes in France, Armstrong noted, were teaming up with French houses that had secured licenses. Licensed traffic, he observed, was known to yield high profits at considerably less risk than trading on private account. Whether American vessels lacking such protections would be seized on entering French-controlled ports elsewhere remained uncertain. In Amsterdam, a shipload of U.S. cotton destined for Paris was turned away, and to the south Armstrong heard rumors that ships entering French occupied ports in Spain would likely join the ranks of the sequestered.[12]

The lull that began in August broke in late December 1809 when Napo-leon once more turned his attention to neutral shipping and began cast-ing about for what Henry Adams wryly terms "a theory on which neutrals could be at the same time plundered and encouraged."[13] Adams's judg-ment of motives aside, the emperor at least managed to confuse matters when on the 19th he ordered General Berthier, commanding French forces in Spain, to confiscate all American vessels and cargoes found in Spanish ports, then two days later told his interior minister that he had merely ordered them sequestered.[14] Champagny compounded the confusion when he used the term "seized" in a letter to Armstrong on 14 February. Because this letter made no mention of confiscation, President Madison later read it to mean that American property there might be restored.[15]

The emperor's ministers, meanwhile, took what was for them a remarkable initiative, emerging briefly from policy-making obscurity to strike a blow for better treatment of neutral carriers. Apparently unbidden, Joseph Fouché and the duc de Montalivet, his ministers of police and interior, respectively, joined with Champagny (recently elevated to become the duc de Cadore) to present the emperor with options for easing the rigors of his maritime decrees.[16] Armstrong, heartened by rumors of what was afoot, nevertheless cautioned Smith that "the sunshine of this climate is always doubtful."[17] On New Year's Day, however, his optimism peaking, he wrote that he had "but a moment to say that appearances are favorable. By the 10 of Jan'y [the date scheduled for a meeting of a Council of State] the present system will be irretrievably fixed, or entirely altered. Of the two events, the latter is most probable." Fouché and Montalivet had let it be known that the emperor was about to accept their case for eliminating some of the self-destructive elements of French maritime policy. A new imperial decree on American commerce, Armstrong's informants told him, would produce "the happiest results." Hedging against disappointment, the envoy warned himself that persons close to the emperor were sure to predict a disastrous price-collapse if France were to fling open its doors to American shipping. Too, any change in the status quo would meet with strenuous opposition from those well-connected persons who had a vested interest in privateering and the lawyers who had a financial stake in "prosecuting and defending our vessels." Still, he wrote, Bonaparte "sees things in a way almost peculiar to himself . . . and may override this opposition."[18]

January 10 came and went without incident. When a Council of State did not meet, Armstrong concluded bitterly that the opponents of change had prevailed. William Lee, then visiting Paris from his consular post in Bordeaux, agreed: "interested persons," he believed, had dissuaded the emperor from taking the advice of his "best ministers." January 10 did not pass altogether unmarked, however. That day Napoleon shattered whatever hope remained for a more benevolent maritime regime by disclosing the confiscation order he had sent Berthier three weeks before. Even his ministers were shocked, Lee reported, and groping for an explanation, both he and Armstrong thought it likely the administration's recent "rupture" with Francis Jackson had persuaded the emperor that he had no compelling reason to conciliate the United States.[19]

Henry Adams admires how fully John Armstrong kept himself informed of ministerial activity throughout the excitement of early January. Very likely, Lee's presence at Armstrong's elbow and his almost daily contact with ministry figures go far to explain that good intelligence. The 37-year-old merchant-consul happened to be in Paris promoting construction of a bridge over the Garonne when Armstrong enlisted his services. A mobile and energetic figure, Lee spoke French fluently and possessed social graces that gave him easy access to the upper reaches of Paris society. On this occasion, he clearly relished enlivening what he regarded as Armstrong's too sedentary diplomacy, though he almost certainly attached too much importance to his own role. On 2 January, having just written a lengthy memorandum to the foreign office explaining why France should do more to encourage its American trade, he boasted exuberantly to his wife: "I can hardly credit myself with what I have brought about. The thing is finished and you may hourly expect to a see a decree in favor of American commerce."[20] Even after news broke of the confiscations in Spain, Lee was buoyed by Montalivet's assurances that he and Fouché were still trying to persuade the emperor to accommodate the United States. When nothing materialized, he predicted gloomily that Napoleon would likely top off his Spanish confiscations by confiscating U.S. vessels in French ports thus far only sequestered. If this happened, he estimated a property loss in the millions and doubted a politically-isolated Armstrong could prevent it. In Lee's mind, the villains and accomplices were easily identified. The emperor was surrounded by "a set of men . . . who are concerned in licenses, shares in privateers, &c.&c.&c," and Armstrong, "by remaining in his cabinet, has no means of combating the machinations of these men. . . ."[21] Although Lee's premonition of outright confiscations anticipated Napoleon's Rambouillet Decree by several months, experience had conditioned him to expect the worst. In fact, harsher measures were already brewing.

Henry Adams, whose judgment is not to be taken lightly, pictures Napoleon in January 1810 more intent on finding plausible grounds for selling off the U.S. vessels than in finding ways to pacify Washington. On its face, the Rambouillet Decree of March 23, which ordered the confiscation and sale of those vessels,[22] supports this view of long pent-up avarice finally triumphing. The case can be made, however, that in January and February of 1810, the French emperor was still looking for some means of accommodation. On 10 January, the day his Council of State did not meet, he asked Champagny, the newly elevated duc de Cadore, to review Franco-American relations and tell him "what it is necessary to do to get us out of the position in which we find ourselves." Was it true, he asked, "that the English are pulling back, that they no longer levy taxes on vessels; let me know if there is an authentic act which announces this . . . for, once I am assured that an 'octroi' on navigation is no longer imposed by England, I shall be able to give way on many things." Moreover, he continued, if Armstrong could guarantee by treaty that Americans would not submit to such taxes in the future, French warships would thereafter stop U.S. vessels only to verify their registry. He would welcome them so long as they came "directly from the United States, from another port of France, or from a neutral country."[23]

Something was amiss in this directive. Napoleon had already signaled a readiness to revoke his decrees (the previous April) if London dropped its "octroi" on U.S. vessels. Was his memory so flawed, as Henry Adams suggests, as to have forgotten this earlier offer?[24] One answer may be that he was genuinely confused by the profuse and often overlapping British orders-in-council. The British themselves may not have had a clear idea of what they meant. Cadore certainly did not. In the closing paragraphs of his thirty-four-page "rapport" he observed that whatever London may have intended by its order of April 26, British admiralty courts "have produced a multitude of arbitrary dispositions often contrary . . . making the English system of maritime legislation so complicated that it can be truly said that there is no recognized legislation at all."[25] Any attempt to sort out these ministerial edicts, he concluded, led to "opposing results." Still, if he read the April order correctly, Americans were no longer required to pay "tribute." Rather, they were merely required to buy licenses to trade with ports the British had ostensibly blockaded. French consuls, he noted, were reporting American vessels licensed to trade with Amsterdam which lay within Britain's April blockade zone but those trading with Hamburg, which lay beyond it were not licensed.[26] Perhaps because he was unaware of it, Cadore neglected to mention the enormous amount of revenue London was beginning to derive from this rapidly expanding licensing regime. Nor did he seem to realize that by licensing trade to blockaded ports, London had usefully muddied the concept of what constituted a "legal" blockade. From the standpoint of producing revenue,

Frank Melvin estimates that the British government had sold no fewer than 18,000 licenses by the end of 1810.[27] Once Britain's windfall from this source became better known, it was not surprising that Napoleon responded in kind to its attractions.

Even as Cadore gathered data for his report, he asked Petry to find out if Armstrong had authority to negotiate a treaty. When Petry asked what "powers" he had, the American minister said he was authorized to re-negotiate the Franco-American Convention of 1800 with certain changes. But when Petry asked what else might be included, Armstrong made the mistake of jotting down in fractured French the treaty terms that came most readily to mind. They included restoration of American property not yet definitively condemned, agreement on the principle of "free ships, free goods," and a reciprocal pledge not to pay "tribute to any foreign power."[28] Unfortunately, this exercise in instant-note writing put too much strain on Armstrong's command of the language. When Napoleon read it, he exploded to Cadore: "You must see the American minister . . . it is too ridiculous that he writes things one cannot understand. I prefer that he write in English, but at length and in a manner that we may understand." And "write to America," he ordered, so that "the President may know what an imbecile he has sent here."[29]

Events unfolded swiftly at two levels in late January. While Napoleon and his foreign minister planned a final solution for disposing of Ameri-can property, Petry asked Armstrong for a fuller statement of treaty terms. Together they drafted a document (marked "D," in Armstrong's correspondence) which they believed the emperor might find acceptable. Meeting Petry half way, Armstrong agreed that as long as Britain flirted with paper blockades or exacted "tribute" from neutral shipping, Ameri-can vessels caught trading with her should be "liable to confiscation." Petry, for his part, seemed willing to have France restore all U.S. ships except those taken with false papers or British cargoes.[30] Their meetings were not without tension, however. Armstrong fumed silently when Petry explained that the emperor had sequestered American vessels in Spain because he could not permit Frenchmen to suffer greater deprivation than his allies. Nor did he object, though he might have (he told Smith), when Petry indicated that the ultimate fate of those vessels would have to be negotiated.[31]

Even as treaty talks got under way, Napoleon and his foreign minister were examining rationales for sterner measures. The "new" element they hit on was the infamous Section 3 of the Non-Intercourse Act, the clause which threatened to confiscate French vessels entering U.S. ports. Although Napoleon had cited Section 3 as sufficient grounds for reprisal when he drafted his unpromulgated decree of the previous August, it had not been heard from since. Now, six months later, Cadore brought it to his attention.[32] Whether from bad memory, or some long-postponed design, only in January of 1810 did Section 3 become an active pretext for France's past and ongoing sequestrations.[33] Cadore made the linkage explicit when he told Armstrong that "If American vessels have been sequestered in France, France is only imitating the example which has been given it by the American government."

Henry Adams, it may be recalled, argues that in August Napoleon's advisors had counseled him not to take reprisals on so flimsy a basis.[34] Also, as noted earlier, the emperor may have decided to await the fallout from the Erskine fiasco. By early 1810, however, Adams finds Napoleon's Rambouillet Decree simply a release for long suppressed rapacity. Others, however, tend to blame Armstrong for provoking it, arguing that the American minister had angered the French emperor by too openly questioning his motives while insisting too belligerently that France must either restore American property or indemnify the owners.[35] Such allegations aside, Napoleon dictated a note on 14 February that offered to rework the Franco-American Convention of 1800 so as to "consolidate the commerce and the prosperity of America," in return for treaty guarantees that the United States would resist the British orders-in-council and ignore any blockade not effectively enforced.[36] With these broad terms before them, Armstrong and Cadore prepared to do business.

CHAPTER 9

Both Sides Charge Bad Faith

A rmstrong's treaty talks with Cadore did not go smoothly. Nor were they marked by much give and take. He proceeded, he told Smith, "with little hope and much circumspection." He would ignore the errors of fact and argument in Cadore's note of 14 February and merely reply with a list of his own treaty articles. Whatever the emperor had in mind, the American minister promised to make no firm commitments or even preliminary "engagements." He would accept past confiscations as irrevocable but would insist that all American property "not yet definitively condemned" either be restored or their owners indemnified.[1] He repeated this *sine qua non* to Petry several days later when the latter came to tell him that the emperor had seen his initial treaty proposals and that a "contre-projet was being prepared."[2] Whether Armstrong's insistence on restoration or indemnification had anything to do with provoking the Rambouillet Decree, he at least read Washington correctly. Like his envoy, Madison insisted that France either restore or indemnify.[3] Here, for the first time, an American diplomat officially inserted his government's demand for indemnification into a treaty negotiation. Insistence on this score would soon become the central issue in Franco-American relations. Looking back on the Rambouillet Decree, Armstrong wondered if his willingness to acquiesce in "confiscations already pronounced" had encouraged the emperor to order more.[4] The Rambouillet Decree had many explanations.

Napoleon bridled at what emerged from this second round of talks. He termed Armstrong's draft "incomplete and full of reticences." Then, in a curious flight of logic, he attacked the envoy's apparent show of bad faith on the issue of "tribute." Armstrong, he expostulated, "knows very well that no one can prove whether or not they [American vessels] have paid tribute." Coming from Napoleon this admission was all the more astonishing, for he had repeatedly insisted on such proofs. To say they were not obtainable while having held them up as the test of American fidelity made sense only if the emperor had no intention of treating. Still, it seems likely that as late as 22 February, Napoleon still hoped to arrange a *modus vivendi*, if not with Armstrong, then through other channels. The means he suggested for the near term must have puzzled Cadore, whom he instructed to revise Armstrong's treaty articles "according to our principles," but at the same time "re-draft the treaty as he [Armstrong] would have it, and you will propose that he sign it."[5]

Napoleon also had in mind getting rid of those diplomats who in his view lacked the wit to break the impasse with the United States. He ordered Cadore to seek Armstrong's recall on grounds that the American envoy was too secluded, inactive, out of touch with current affairs or, as Napoleon described him, "a morose man with whom one cannot deal."[6] He also planned to recall Turreau who, sick and aging, he believed had been out of France too long and should be replaced by "a man of confidence who knows my intentions and who will give energy to the important matters I would charge him with."[7] Pending Turreau's removal, he toyed with the idea of sending a special envoy to Washington. Thus, while Cadore and Armstrong sparred over treaty-related issues, Napoleon ordered instructions drafted for the marquis du Moustier. Cadore would have preferred to send the more experienced Petry but acknowledged that the son of the former French minister to the United States "would be seen with pleasure in a country where his father has been."[8] The plan envisioned young Moustier staying in Washington no more than six weeks, only long enough to present a letter "proposing an arrangement."[9] For reasons not recorded, Moustier never sailed.

The charge that Armstrong himself provoked the Rambouillet Decree rests in large part on the intemperate note he sent Cadore on 10 March in response to the latter's of 14 February. Flinging caution to the proverbial winds, he tore into Cadore's most offensive passages. He could hardly have chosen a worse time: Cadore's "contre-projet" had just reached Napoleon's desk. What sparked his outburst was news confirming the sale of American cargoes detained in Spanish ports. Once past his protest on this score, he launched into a biting critique of French motives.[10] Did France, he asked bitterly, intend to hold hostage the proceeds derived from the sale of American property in Spain until such time as a treaty had been concluded? Meanwhile, her retaliatory rationale was outrageous. He admitted that the Non-Intercourse Act had closed U.S. ports to French vessels on pain of confiscation, but as far as he knew, none had actually been taken. Moreover, the penalty for violating the Non-Intercourse Act stood on its merits as a proper exercise of municipal regulation, evenhanded toward both belligerents and amply justified by French violence to American shipping, instances of which he detailed at length. What he found most inexplicable, however, was the time lag. Why, he asked, after nine months of "no previous complaint," had Section 3 of the Non-Intercourse Act suddenly become a pretext for reprisal? French authorities had known of it since June or July and until now had not shown "the slightest trace of complaint." In August, the emperor's Altenberg Letter had held out hope of friendlier relations by prescribing the circumstances under which he might revoke his decrees. Because nothing thereafter had suggested that Section 3 might be grounds for retaliation, he had to suppose that it was "merely found for the occasion . . . and made to justify seizures not otherwise justifiable."

John Quincy Adams later wrote from St. Petersburg that Armstrong's note had been widely published and "admired wherever it was read." He added, however, that Armstrong had a reputation among French embassy officials for being "captious and petulant." True or not, Adams felt the administration should know how the French regarded him. The French ambassador himself had complained that Armstrong wrote "peevish notes" when oral representations would have better served his purposes.[11] From Washington, however, Robert Smith tacitly approved Armstrong's outburst, observing that France's feeble justification for seizing American property had roused "high indignation." But Smith also conveyed the president's view that the time was not right for "animadversions," presumably because the recent passage of Macon's Bill was expected to change the face of U.S. relations with both belligerents.[12]

The vehemence of Armstrong's assault obviously caught Cadore off guard because he had just assured the emperor that the American minister "calms himself with the hope that the proceeds from the sale of American vessels, which are put in escrow [*en depot*], may one day be restored to the United States."[13] How little Armstrong had been tranquillized was now all too evident. Hoping to soften the impact of the American envoy's note, Cadore tried to explain it in terms of Armstrong's difficult personality. He told Napoleon that the American minister was ordinarily well-disposed toward France, but added insightfully that "if the language of his note is not conciliatory, it is that he did not know how to make it so."[14]

Napoleon, particularly irked by Armstrong's sarcastic questioning of the long delay between passage of the Non-Intercourse Act and the French decision to retaliate, wanted him to know that despite the passage of time, the punitive section of the act "came to our knowledge only a short time ago, and only when I had knowledge of it did I immediately prescribe the same measures." To lend credence to the phrase, "a short time ago," Cadore reminded the emperor—and doubtless Armstrong as well—that the text of the act had arrived just before the battle of Wagram.[15] By implication, military exigencies in June 1809 could account for the emperor's inattention to Section 3. Even Henry Adams is prepared to concede that Napoleon's memory might have lapsed in such circumstances.[16] Or, as already noted, the emperor may never have read the text in full. Cadore was in Vienna and Napoleon in Munich when a copy of the act arrived. Cadore's cover letter to the emperor had described it in general terms, and although the two men had discussed it on the eve of the battle, it is possible neither picked up on Section 3.[17] Still, the unpromulgated decree of the previous August—the one his ministers talked him out of—had explicitly cited that section as grounds for French reprisal. Had the emperor forgotten that occasion, as well? Perhaps, because since August there had been no reports of the United States actually confiscating French vessels. Without a live case before them, neither man would have had reason to recur to specific articles.

Cadore's formal reply stood firm on principle: although France had seized many more vessels than had the United States, "this difference in results changes nothing in the character of the act itself; it tends only to show that it would have more suited the interests of the United States not to have exposed itself, by the order to seize French vessels, to a reciprocity so prejudicial to them."[18] With this parting shot, both sides were left with little more to say. March 21, 1810, seemed to mark the end of hopes for an accommodation. Cadore's high-handed policy statement of 14 February, Armstrong's biting reply of 10 March, and Cadore's defensive response of 21 March had strung out the dialogue as far as either party wished it to continue.

Cadore made one last attempt to persuade his master to shift negotiations to Washington. Armstrong, he wrote, "wants passionately to breathe his natal air," and Moustier could sail from La Rochelle in early April.[19] Instead, two days later, Napoleon's Rambouillet Decree effectively ended diplomatic dialogue for the foreseeable future, although as Henry Adams points out, this stunning order to sell off all U.S. vessels within his reach exhausted the emperor's arsenal of punitive measures and left him with no future recourse except diplomacy.[20] To review briefly, the previous December Napoleon had ordered the confiscation and sale of American ships held in Spanish ports. Now, on 23 March 1810, he extended the "sell order" to American vessels detained in French ports as well, citing Section 3 as justification. The order struck retroactively at all U.S. shipping detained since 20 May 1809, presumably the earliest date Paris could have known the terms of the offending act. And although publication of the Rambouillet Decree was delayed for nearly two months, Napoleon charged his ministries of justice and finance to begin executing it immediately.[21] Proceeds from the sales were to be deposited in the *caisse d'amortissment*, that is, put in escrow, only one step short of outright expropriation. That would come later.[22]

How much American tonnage fell victim to the Rambouillet Decree can only be estimated. One source, printed in English and found in the French archives, offers what purports to be the U.S. consul-general's tally of vessels seized in the twelve months preceding the decree. David Baillie Warden had listed 133 vessels by name. Of these, France had released thirty-eight after confiscating their cargoes, sequestered forty-four in Spanish ports, and still detained fifty-one in French, Dutch, and Neapolitan ports.[23] These figures, however, appear to be too conservative. William Lee, for example, counted forty-six vessels sequestered in the "Ports of Biscay" alone.[24]

Despite the harshness of his latest decree, Napoleon did not intend to cut off or even discourage future trade with the United States. Instead, he would license it. The Rambouillet Decree was barely two weeks old when the foreign office circularized French consuls with an updated explanation of how the licensing system was expected to work. Only French exporters would be issued *permis* although French firms overseas might seek consular assistance to ship licensed cargoes back to France.[25] Armstrong at first scoffed at how few American products had been approved for licensed importation. "What think you," he wrote Smith, "of a plan which should admit to French ports of our Staples but Codfish, Potashes, rice and Indigo . . . ?" His scorn, however, proved premature. Given the growth potential for projects in which bureaucracies have a hand, he had witnessed only the beginning. Before long, Napoleon would authorize more licenses, more U.S. ports of exit, and a greater volume and variety of importable U.S. cargoes. To oversee its operation, he named Collin de Sussy to head a new Council of Commerce and Manufactures in early June.[26] Simultaneously, he moved to close down the leakage of British goods his brother Louis had so long tolerated through Dutch ports. The latter's unrepentant complicity with contrabandiers now cost him his throne. By June of 1810 the annexation of Holland underscored the emperor's grim determination to close Europe's doors to all but licensed imports. Licensing hereafter became an integral part of his system.

Armstrong at this point saw no clear road ahead. In April he prodded Cadore to bring forward a treaty "projet" only to be told that no diplomatic business was being transacted during the emperor's wedding preparations.[27] Also in vain, he revisited the policy options of the Altenberg Letter, asking Pinkney whether London had clarified the status of Fox's blockade. The latter replied that the British ministry either would not or could not.[28] In London as in Paris, American diplomats had reached an impasse in the spring of 1810.

CHAPTER 10

NAPOLEON TOYS
WITH MACON'S BILL

Across the Atlantic that spring Madison's Republican supporters in Congress were preparing a fresh initiative. Having thus far failed to curb the predatory conduct of the belligerents, Congress on 3 May 1810 performed a legislative about-face that seemed to signal a last-ditch effort at economic persuasion. It restored commerce with both Britain and France but threatened to reimpose non-intercourse on the still-offending party if one should repeal its antineutral measures and the other did not. In the minds of its critics and in the oft-quoted words of an obscure Virginia congressman, Macon's Bill No. 2, as it was called, "held up the honor and character of the nation to the highest bidder."[1]

This unflattering judgment has pretty much weathered the test of time.[2] It depicts a weak and divided Congress acting with ultimately disastrous results when Napoleon Bonaparte stepped forward as the high bidder. When the French emperor subsequently appeared to revoke his Berlin and Milan decrees, Madison accepted his word for it; and when London failed to follow suit within the grace period of three months, the president asked Congress to reimpose non-intercourse on Britain. Thereafter, from February 1811 to June 1812, French diplomacy can be pictured as skillfully deflecting American anger long enough for Congress to decide that Britain, after all, was the enemy it preferred to fight.

Though a worst-case example of unintended consequences, the near-term fallout from Macon's Bill was not altogether unsalutary. British manufacturers once more enjoyed a market among American consumers, and American merchants in the British trade no longer had to put up with the delays and additional costs of exchanging cargoes in neutral ports. Nor could either belligerent, it was believed, charge the administration with trying to coerce it. Congress, however, could take little pride in its inability to flex a more muscular response to the belligerents' unremitting insults. Before enacting Macon's Bill it had rejected such alternatives as arming convoys, renewing the Non-Intercourse Act, returning to the embargo, or even voting funds to keep the navy fit. Instead, faced with doing something or nothing, Congress opted to let their abusers decide the future of economic coercion. It was not a pretty sight.

Macon's Bill also prefigured the propensity of American statesmen to offer legalistic solutions to international problems. Such an approach says in effect: if you do this, we'll do that, and our differences will be resolved. Often enough, however, the other party will put its own spin on what the "contract" proposes and fail to show a decent Anglo-Saxon respect for its letter and spirit. In passing Macon's Bill No. 2, the 12th American Congress offered an early example of how impercipient the people's representatives can be when they solicit the pledged word of another government in presumed good faith. In this instance, only if the French emperor's conduct had been as honest as that which Americans believed their own to be could Macon's Bill have earned a less severe judgment. Not that many of Napoleon's contemporaries, including members of Congress, expected him to be a model of fair play, and there was a certain irony in their equally characteristic American outrage in discovering their trust had been betrayed.

Speculating on the belligerents' likely response, Madison ventured hopefully to Pinkney that each ought to see Macon's Bill "as a promise of attack on the other." Within that promise, he admitted, lay an obvious "inequality," because Britain had little to gain from an American "attack" on French commerce so long as the Royal Navy was already doing a good job in that respect. France, however, could "turn the tables on G. Britain by compelling her either to revoke her orders, or to lose the commerce of this country," which, he reminded Pinkney, the British had just regained at no cost. Napoleon, he believed, could scarcely miss the bill's potential for reinforcing his Continental System, for if he acted on it, the resulting shutdown of American commerce with Britain would be "the very species of resistance most analogous to her [France's] professed views." Otherwise, he mused, Britain "has every earthly motive to continue her restrictions agst. us."[3] French compliance was a "possibility," he wrote Jefferson, although under the circumstances it would certainly not be received with goodwill. The *National Intelligencer* had just published Cadore's letter of 14 February, justifying the seizure of American vessels in Spanish ports.[4]

When Madison instructed his diplomats on how to implement Macon's Bill, he added some essential refinements. London's repeal, if it came, must be all-inclusive, not just a revocation of its most recent orders-in-council, but the recall of all offending maritime measures dating back to and including Fox's Blockade of 1806. He warned Armstrong that France must not only revoke or modify her decrees; she must also make "satisfactory provision for restoring the property lately surprised and seized."[5] Five months later, however, Madison dropped this demand when he accepted the terms of the Cadore Letter, causing Henry Adams to suggest an unseemly presidential willingness to abandon just claims.[6] Madison, in his own defense, mistakenly assumed that the vessels seized in Spain would be released as part of the overall accommodation. Somewhat abashedly, he told Armstrong he hoped "the sequestred vessels will have been restored; without which the Executive may be charged with violating their own instruction to you." But he may also have concluded that in demanding restoration he had exceeded the letter of Macon's Bill. As Joel Barlow pointed out, no similar demand for restoration had been made of London.[7]

As it turned out, Napoleon's response to Macon's Bill would put Madison to one of the severest tests of his administration. In accepting that response, conditional at best, he would bring down Federalist charges that he had been duped.

Napoleon complained peevishly at having to read Macon's Bill from Armstrong's copy of a newspaper clipping, but even in newsprint he saw opportunities for France where Madison supposed he would. In this, he was more perceptive than those around him. Cadore, for example, forwarded Macon's Bill without comment; Turreau merely described it; and Armstrong fretted at the likelihood that reimposing sanctions on one belligerent would evoke harsher measures from the other.[8]

Eyeing this latest devolution in congressional legislation, the emperor toyed with options, none of which envisioned a simple, unconditional repeal of his decrees. He wrote at length to his minister of interior that he might announce their repeal on 1 September if by that time London had revoked its orders-in-council. Or, he might await British revocation and then decide on a response. In either case, London must take the first step. Whatever his enemy's next move, however, he gave no thought to slackening his efforts to bar British exports from European markets. Even if he revoked his decrees, he told Montelivet, there were other ways to prevent Americans from breaching his system. He meant licensing; and he spelled out the specifics. Hereafter, Americans might buy a limited number of *permis* to import such items as fish oil, codfish, Georgia cotton, and French West Indies sugar. Any vessels arriving without licenses and without certified cargoes would be deemed British and confiscated.

Having set the framework, Napoleon told Montelivet to work out the details. Even here, the emperor could not resist being explicit: only twenty vessels would be licensed; they must depart from a single U.S. port, bring consular "certificates of origin," and land at one or two designated French ports. Licensees must also lade a return-cargo of French commodities equal in value to the cargoes they had imported. An imperial decree, dated 25 July, set this system in motion.[9] For Napoleon this was a manageable beginning, a first step toward luring American shipmasters into a controlled commerce that promised to be profitable to them, useful to France, and proof against British taint. The enactment of Macon's Bill No. 2 may have done more to quicken the growth of French licensing than any other factor in the emperor's consideration of how to exploit American trade without breaching his system. For the United States, committed to the principle of unfettered trade, French licensing was another of the unintended (and unwelcome) consequences of its most recent legislation.[10]

Significantly, Napoleon's decision to license France's external trade meant that he had no need to rely on his Berlin and Milan decrees to wall out British imports. By admitting only licensed arrivals, he could avoid troublesome controversies over captures at sea. American spokesmen having repeatedly offered no objection to in-port seizures, licensing could be portrayed as merely an enhanced form of "domestic regulation." In sum, he came up with a means of maintaining his system without reference to his earlier decrees, and what came to be known as the "Cadore Letter" dated 5 August set forth his conditions for revoking them, and they were tricky. The crucial paragraph, as Cadore crafted it and sent it to Armstrong, read:

"In this new state of things, I am authorized to declare to you, sir, that the decrees of Berlin & of Milan are revoked, and that after the 1st of November, they will cease to have effect, provided that as a consequence of this declaration, the English shall revoke their orders in Council and shall renounce the new principles of blockade they saw fit to establish, or that the English [he meant the United States], conformable to the act you have just communicated to me, shall cause their rights to be respected by the English."[11]

Among the several quirks of the Cadore Letter was the latitude Napoleon allowed himself in specifying what action(s) would satisfy him that the United States had effectively caused "their rights to be respected." What rights did he have in mind? For Madison, relying on the language of Macon's Bill, the reimposition of non-intercourse on Britain was all that was promised. This Madison did, and Congress backed him up. The question that lingered into the spring of 1811 was whether the reimposition of non-intercourse would sufficiently meet the emperor's requirement that the United States had made its rights respected? This uncertainty would persist. Cadore himself may have been the author of this imprecision. Napoleon's original draft had specified that Washington need only "re-establish its prohibitions against England." Later drafts, however, had introduced the vaguer requirement of causing Britain "to respect their rights."[12] Also equivocal, though hidden from view, was Cadore's hint to French consuls that the decrees might not be definitively revoked unless the United States followed up its reimposition of non-intercourse with a declaration of war.[13]

Timing also figured problematically in the Cadore Letter and echoed the sequence of actions prescribed by the Altenberg Letter. Only after London had revoked its orders (or the United States had reimposed non-intercourse) were the French decrees to "cease to have their effect." London, however, could not reasonably be expected to revoke its orders before it had proof that the French decrees were inoperative. Each action depended on the other occurring first, which left American diplomats straining to produce evidence of the non-enforcement of the French decrees (which had not been unconditionally promised) in an effort to persuade London to revoke its orders. Without such proofs from Paris, the course of American diplomacy was stymied from the moment Lord Wellesley first saw the Cadore Letter in late August. The British foreign secretary assured Pinkney that His Majesty would gladly relinquish his system "whenever the repeal of the French decrees shall have actually taken effect."[14] Thereafter, each belligerent's perception of what the other had done or not done in pursuance of the Cadore Letter provided all parties with ample grounds for recrimination.

Uncertainty, too, hung over what exactly was supposed to happen before (or after) November 1. Was this a deadline for both British repeal and, failing that, for the reimposition of non-intercourse as well? Cadore obviously thought so. Extrapolating for Napoleon, he assumed that the Berlin and Milan decrees "will be revoked if, between now and 1 November England recalls her orders-in-council, or if, in case of refusal, the United States have taken effective measures to make their rights respected." Despite the conjunction "or," Cadore clearly envisioned two sequential actions having to take place before 1 November: London must decide whether to say yes or no and, if the latter, the United States must impose its penalty.

Alternatively, November 1 might be read merely as the date after which, at any time, either British or American compliance would result in the French decrees ceasing to have effect. Madison certainly construed it this way. For him, November 1 was a deadline, but only for signaling his administration's acceptance of the terms of the Cadore Letter. His proclamation of that date reasonably extended to Britain a three-month grace period in which to repeal its orders before Congress would be asked to implement non-intercourse.[15] This construction, however, left uncertain how France would treat American shipping in the three-month interim. And how would France respond, Madison wondered, if Britain were to announce the repeal of her orders, but "without discontinuing her Mock blockades?"[16]

Armstrong at first hailed the Cadore Letter as a fitting capstone to his mission and hastened plans for a triumphal homecoming. He told Smith, however, that before he left Paris he would press Cadore to find out how France planned to deal with vessels arriving before 1 November, and whether those now detained in Spanish ports were to be considered confiscated or merely sequestered. He would also find out if the Rambouillet Decree had been revoked.[17] Cadore, who had already briefed Napoleon on what questions to expect, answered Armstrong obliquely.[18] The Berlin and Milan decrees would remain more or less in force until 1 November; that is, vessels found to have submitted to British controls would be detained but not necessarily confiscated.[19] Those now held in Spanish ports would be processed under what Cadore vaguely referred to as "the principles of reprisals;" and the Rambouillet Decree, Armstrong was told, was not explicitly repealed but its enforcement could logically be considered to have lapsed when the Non-Intercourse Act was superseded.[20]

Hoping for more explicit answers, Armstrong pursued Cadore with unaccustomed zeal. Piecing together the responses, he concluded that while U.S. vessels arriving between 5 August and 1 November would not be confiscated outright, some might be detained. Those already being processed under the Berlin, Milan, or Rambouillet decrees, however, would continue to undergo legal proceedings that might result in confiscation.[21] In short, French policy remained almost as hostile as it had been.

Resentful at being importuned, Cadore derided Armstrong's eagerness to quit Paris lest anything "tarnish the glory he attaches to having obtained the note of 5 August." In fact, though the American minister went forward with plans for departure, he had begun to doubt whether the Cadore Letter heralded much change for the better. He confided to Smith that the "old system . . . is fast recovering the ground it had lost & I should not be astonished, were it soon to become as great a favorite as formerly."[22] Cadore chafed at Armstrong's last-minute unwillingness "to engage in any of the difficult questions" he had raised. And yet his own answers were off-putting. When Armstrong asked whether departing vessels would require licenses, Cadore advised Napoleon to tell him that the future of licensing depended on how the parties responded to the Cadore Letter. Napoleon opted instead to hold up licensing as a favor conferred on Americans exclusively. Cadore's reply of 12 September announced smugly that as far as licenses were concerned, the American "is the only [other] flag that has obtained them."[23]

Cadore was right about one thing: the American minister's haste to depart did distract him from some major issues. Licensing, the prospect of which had incensed him in July, now became a subject of perfunctory inquiry.[24] Indemnification, a *sine qua non* during his abortive treaty talks only a few months before, dropped altogether out of his official correspondence. And, as if to assure himself that he had left no unfinished business in Paris, he insisted to Pinkney that no one should mistake the direction France had taken in the Cadore Letter: the next move on the diplomatic chessboard lay with London.[25]

Armstrong even managed to brush aside Cadore's triumphant discovery of *La Franchise*, a French despatch boat netted by the Non-Intercourse Act some nine months earlier and held at New Orleans. Its detention

ostensibly furnished France with the live evidence she needed to justify
the Rambouillet Decree. From a policy standpoint, the incident had both
strengths and weaknesses. Privately Cadore admitted that the *aviso* had
"ended up being released." However, the circumstances of its capture, its
character as a public vessel, and its treatment during detention vindicated
past reprisals. From reports reaching Paris, the incident was custom-
made to give affront. Turreau described *La Franchise* as having been detained when she innocently put into New Orleans for repairs. During
the ensuing litigation, remarks had been made insulting to the French
government. Napoleon, taking all this in as he perused Cadore's draft of
a protest, added some testy marginalia (in red pencil) and ordered Cadore
to cite this offense "when they demand all the vessels that I have taken."[26]
Armstrong, now in the last phases of packing for home, chose not to join
battle. He would ask his government for an explanation, he replied
mildly, but suggested that Turreau's account, unmentioned until recently,
might be "either less ample or less correct than it may become under a
new examination of the case." Armstrong's coolness proved warranted.
The furor over *La Franchise* did recede as more facts surfaced. As Smith
later explained, its captain had offered cargo for sale, had no naval commission, and was suspected of having plundered U.S. vessels in nearby
waters. When Turreau vouched for its public character, however, legal
proceedings were dropped and the vessel freed, but not before Cadore
had compared France's righteous indignation to that which Americans
had felt at the attack on the *Chesapeake*.[27] Three days later, Armstrong
left for Bordeaux, convinced that his mission had accomplished all that it
could. He took with him twenty Merino sheep and left behind a number
of unanswered questions relating to the status of American shipping in
French ports.[28]

   As Armstrong prepared to leave, Napoleon completed the cycle of confiscation heralded by his Rambouillet Decree. His Trianon Decree of 5
August 1810, which some called larcenous, at least forecast how American
ships and cargoes might fare at his hands in the immediate future. For
the past three years, American property had been detained and sequestered, some of it confiscated and later sold. Now, from his Trianon palace,
the emperor decreed that the proceeds from the most recent sales, till
then held in escrow, be transferred from the caisse d'amortissement to
the French treasury. Thus, with a finality ill-befitting the tone of the Cadore Letter, ironically of the same date, American property valued at
perhaps as much as $10 million disappeared into the imperial pocket.[29]

As a target of outrage, the Trianon Decree would take a prominent place on the list of American grievances toward Napoleonic France. It also confirmed the stereotype of an upscale Corsican bandit who would steal whatever he could to feed his cash-strapped empire and its expensive war machine. This view of imperial rapacity, however, should take into account the emperor's long-held perception that vessels arriving in French ports flying the American flag were either British exhibiting forged American "papers," or, if American, tainted by contact with the enemy. But besides these long-standing grievances, the Trianon Decree drew its specific rationale from Section 3 of the Non-Intercourse Act. With a fine show of precision, the order to sell off and pocket the proceeds applied only to those vessels arriving in French ports between 20 May 1809 and 1 May 1810, the period during which the Non-Intercourse Act had been known in France. Presumably, ships and cargoes detained prior to May 1809 would continue to be adjudicated on a case-by-case basis. And those arriving since 1 May would be cleared for departure if Napoleon saw fit to license them.

If the Trianon Decree sealed the fate of U.S. property seized in the year preceding 1 May 1810, American merchants and shipowners were not without future recourse. Because spoliation claims seldom die, the Trianon Decree would take its place alongside other predatory acts of the French emperor for which satisfaction would be pressed at a later day when the United States found itself in a better position to expect success. For the time being, however, claimants had to face the reality that Napoleon had taken their property on grounds he believed deserving.

CHAPTER 11

MADISON BETS ON
THE CADORE LETTER

B efore he took over the Paris legation as *chargé d'affaires,* Jonathan Russell was one of those overseas businessmen who, favored with the right political connections, was able to augment his income with consular fees. In Russell's case, earlier prominence in the Jeffersonian politics of his native Rhode Island combined with a moderately successful business enterprise accounts for his holding the consular post in Hamburg when Armstrong summoned him to the French capital in the late summer of 1810. Thrust suddenly into the diplomatic arena, Russell performed ably enough to find himself among the giants who later negotiated the Treaty of Ghent, and in 1814 was appointed the first U.S. minister to Sweden. His later career was less distinguished. On returning home to enter the national political arena, he stumbled fatally when, in a bid for support among western Republicans, he published a letter he had written from Ghent during the peace negotiations but altered it in such a way as to falsify his position on the politically-divisive fisheries issue. To his dismay, his fellow peace commissioner and fisheries defender John Quincy Adams caught the discrepancies and hastened to set the record straight. Adams not only had an original copy of Russell's letter but proceeded to publish both texts side by side. Devastatingly discredited, Russell faded quickly from public life but not before suffering the dubious distinction of having his name become a verb of local usage, as in being "jonathan russelled," which is to say, confronted with irrefutable evidence of one's wrongdoing.[1]

Russell in his Paris phase, however, exhibited a degree of patience and perseverance for which even John Adams's acerbic great-grandson has praise. Until Joel Barlow arrived in the fall of 1811, the merchant from Rhode Island bore up gamely under burdens of increasing weight and complexity, enjoying little of the respite usually associated with interim appointments. Rather, he was beset by American shipmasters seeking clearances, stranded crewmen clamoring for repatriation, and a growing number of troublesome political issues. French licensing procedures, his most vexing problem, he found so disordered that not even French ministers could fully explain them; and the questions he felt compelled to raise about the conditions set forth in the Cadore Letter met with predictably evasive answers.

Russell began his mission with the relatively pleasant task of arranging passage for the newly appointed French minister to the United States, Louis-Barbé-Charles Serurier.[2] A young diplomat fresh from a posting in Holland, Serurier was to prove a welcome successor to the sick and surly old general whose Washington legation he took over in February 1811. Personable and experienced, the thirty-five-year-old diplomat conveyed enough goodwill to mitigate his master's later shows of ill-will. He made a favorable impression on Russell, although the latter wondered how a man of such "benevolent" demeanor could be loyal to a tyrant. What Russell missed, though it soon became apparent, was Serurier's competence as a professional diplomat, a man who was respected for his candor and restraint and who survived the Hundred Days to remain at his Washington post well into the Bourbon Restoration.[3] His lively intelligence, moreover, opened itself to an understanding of Americans and a readiness to accept them on their own terms. Gone now were Turreau's scornful iterations of American failings and in their place gracefully written reports, perhaps not as insightful as de Tocqueville's but illuminating as to both the political culture and the temperament of his host country. Unfortunately, Paris seldom heeded either his insights or his advice.

Gale-force westerlies delayed the French minister's departure until the end of December, allowing Cadore time to fine-tune his instructions. If licensing worked as intended, Cadore told him, the resulting growth of Franco-American commerce would likely invite more British attacks so that eventually the United States would be drawn into war "without their having been the aggressors." Until that happened, Serurier was to avoid bickering over detained shipping and find out what he could about annexationist activity in West Florida (the so-called Baton Rouge revolution had taken place in August).[4] Russell also offered advice, urging Serurier to announce on his arrival that the Berlin and Milan decrees had been "definitively repealed." He also asked Petry why, if revocation had occurred, neither the Prize Council nor the Director of Customs had been notified. Both men reminded him that London and Washington had yet to fulfill the conditions by which revocation would become definitive.[5] Russell expected as much but still hoped that his bid for a more friendly interpretation of the Cadore Letter would find its way into the French minister's instructions. It did not.[6]

The first major item on Russell's docket was to inquire into French licensing. In early October he called Cadore's attention to the scores of American vessels lying at anchor in ports from Bayonne to Amsterdam apparently denied clearance for want of licenses. But even if licensed, he added pointedly, obliging them to give bond for a return voyage to France would subject them to "the same *denationalizing* circuit" that France claimed Americans were submitting to under British orders-in-council. How, if licensed by France, could American shipmasters expect their flag to protect them? Cadore bristled at the suggestion of a British parallel and told the *chargé* he was mistaken: only French-flag vessels were being licensed: all others were free to depart. Neither statement was true. Cadore had already told Serurier that plans were afoot to license some thirty vessels in Charleston and New York for voyages to France. A great majority of them would inevitably be of American registry. In fact, Serurier had instructions to trumpet the fact that "only Americans" had been privileged to receive such licenses.[7] As for Cadore's assurance that others were free to depart, Russell promptly produced affidavits from American consuls and sea captains testifying that French port officials did require licenses for the departure of all vessels. The prevailing rule was: no license, no clearance. Having made his case, he added tactfully that perhaps some other governmental authority had misinformed them.[8] After that, he could only wait. The large-scale licensing of American merchantmen still lay in the future.

❈

As the year 1810 drew to a close, Russell puzzled over the direction of French policy. "No one here except the Emperor," he wrote Smith, "knows if the Berlin and Milan decrees be absolutely revoked . . . and no one dares inquire of him concerning them." But if not revoked, neither could he find evidence of enforcement. As far as he knew, no American

vessel had been detained in their name since the first of November.[9]
Plainly at a loss, he asked Pinkney how one could prove the non-existence
of an edict, "except by the promulgation of its repeal & its subsequent
non-execution." Evidence abounded of non-execution, but whether the
decrees were still on the books he had no way of knowing. And as Pinkney
sourly reminded him, without documentary evidence of repeal, London
would not revoke its orders-in-council.[10] On further reflection, Russell
concluded gloomily that even if Britain did revoke her orders, the French
decrees would be followed by "measures of equal violence."[11] To expect
any concession from Bonaparte, he mused, "must, I fear, be precarious &
uncertain," coming from "a spoilt child of fortune who regards neither
the sanctity of principle or the decency of forms." Napoleon might make
"occasional modifications," but his Continental System would remain
intact, even though, he noted ironically, it had already bankrupted a host
of French banks and commercial houses and caused "more misery to the
continent than to England."[12]

For his own part, Russell routinely rebuffed French officials who asked
whether American shipowners would accept import licenses to bring in
much-needed grain. The latter, he replied, would obviously consult their
own interests but his government would not be a party to this sort of
"partial intercourse." Likewise, he rejected Cadore's suggestion that he
might get clearance for individual vessels if he petitioned for their release
separately. This sort of dickering, he told Smith, would be undignified
although he promised to assist beleaguered shipmasters "as far as may be
compatible with national honour."[13] Attentive to his own honor, Russell
refused Americans who sought his assistance in obtaining licenses. He
later told Sylvanus Bourne, the longtime U.S. consul in Amsterdam, that
"I have had many applications of this kind & have uniformly rejected
them."[14]

───────── ◦◦◦◦ ─────────

News that Madison had accepted the terms of the Cadore Letter reached
Russell on 13 December. The offsetting bad news was that an American
merchantman, the *New Orleans Packet*, had just been seized in the name
of the Milan Decree, thereby casting doubt on the promise of the Cadore
Letter itself. Not until the following June did Russell explain how awk-
wardly the *Packet* case had intruded on his presentation of Madison's
acceptance of the Cadore Letter. The ship itself, he wrote, had cleared
New York for Lisbon, though actually destined for Gibraltar and was

twice visited by British warships en route. The owners' agent had been selling off cargo at Gibraltar when he got word of Madison's proclamation and decided to sail what remained to Bordeaux, careful not to arrive until after 1 November. Quarantined for two weeks off the mouth of the Garonne, the *Packet* reached Bordeaux on 3 December where the authorities seized her for having come from the British port of Gibraltar and been visited by British warships.[15]

Russell had barely filed a protest in the *Packet* case when he learned that the *Essex* had arrived at L'Orient. Knowing its departure date, he felt certain the administration's response to the Cadore Letter was on board. His hopes confirmed, and now furnished with Madison's proclamation of acceptance, he hesitated to forward it to the foreign office. Unless the French government first disavowed its seizure of the *Packet*, the proclamation might appear to be leverage to secure its release. Paris, he wrote, was quite capable of reversing "the order in which these measures ought to stand." However, having already told Cadore the substance of the proclamation at a meeting on the 15th, he saw no reason to delay transmitting it officially inasmuch as it would become public knowledge before by any stretch of optimism the French government could release the vessel. Two days later, he forwarded Madison's proclamation, careful to stipulate that the president had acted in response to France's repeal of her decrees, an action that "did not depend on any condition previously to be performed by the United States."[16]

Naively perhaps, Russell hoped that by divulging the contents of Madison's proclamation before formally transmitting it he could elicit assurances that the offending decrees were now definitively revoked. The president's willingness to reimpose non-intercourse on Britain, he argued, was all that the Cadore Letter required of him. To his chagrin, the author of that letter allowed fecklessly that France had expected non-intercourse to take full effect on 1 November, not after a three-month interval. Irritably, Russell explained that the president felt obliged to give London time to revoke its orders or, failing that, ask Congress to make non-intercourse effective. Cadore responded with an ominous *non sequitur*. He declared "with some vivacity," Russell reported, "that the Emperor was determined to persevere in his system against England—that he had overturned the world in adopting this system & that he would overturn it again to give it effect." Though not usually given to understatement, Russell told Smith, "Upon the whole this interview was not calculated to increase my confidence in the revocation of the decrees."[17]

To his friend Joseph Pitcairn, he wrote, "It seems here that we are still to be kept in suspense till the 2nd of February—They continue however to promise fairly."[18]

As for the *New Orleans Packet*, Russell credited his "remonstrance" with breaking off legal proceedings; the following June, its bond revoked, it was free to depart. The publication of his "remonstrance" in the Paris press, however, brought heated charges from William Pinkney that Russell had misled him to believe the French decrees had "ceased to operate."[19] What riled him was that Russell's December 10 note of protest, now made public, had questioned their repeal. Pinkney, having assured London that repeal was an accomplished fact, had been telling the ministry it had no grounds for retaining its orders-in-council. For Russell even to suggest this might not be so had weakened his position with the ministry. Although Russell later defended the correctness of his exchanges with Pinkney, he tended to split hairs and seemed somewhat disingenuous. Pinkney, he told Madison, had asked for "confirmatory evidence" of repeal, whereas he could only tell him that the decrees were not being enforced. Documentary proof of repeal was not to be had. Then, when French customs seized the *Packet* citing violation of those decrees, he reckoned his first duty was to find out whether some subordinate had acted without authority. Until he had an answer, to have notified Pinkney of the incident might have compromised him, especially if London had discovered he was concealing knowledge of it. Russell had to admit, albeit obliquely, that the publication of his "remonstrance," had reopened doubts about repeal, but he had not foreseen its being published and remarked somewhat lamely that by mid-December London had already made clear it would not retreat from its orders-in-council. In retrospect, Russell's telling Pinkney that he had found no evidence of enforcement appears to have led the latter to overstate the case for their having been repealed. Clearly, ministerial communication across the Channel had not been as forthcoming as it might have been. Russell had said too little; Pinkney had assumed too much. In the aftermath, Russell told Madison he had heard from third parties that Pinkney had attacked him "with all his eloquence to prove at once my imbecility and perversity" and had urged his recall.[20] Madison told him not to worry about it, that he had no reports of "unfriendly language" from Pinkney and fully understood the *chargé*'s need to tread carefully between getting assurances of French repeal while "not weakening the ground on which British repeal was urged." Nor did the president criticize his handling of the *Packet* case.[21]

Napoleon hailed Madison's proclamation as "a first step toward arriving at a good result." The next step was for Congress to reinstate non-intercourse against Britain. By way of encouragement, he made known to both Russell and Serurier that in the interim "I shall . . . do no harm to vessels which really come from America." They need only bring "a letter in cypher joined to the licenses which attest that the boat comes from America and has been laded there."[22] This promise of openness, however, said nothing of releasing American ships and cargoes already in custody. To that end, Russell received Smith's suggestion that he try to negotiate a mutual restoration of property. The secretary noted that although seizures of French property under the Non-Intercourse Act were "little more than nominal," if an offer of reciprocal restoration could pry loose U.S. property whose value was far from nominal, the administration was prepared to go this route.[23] When Russell first put out a feeler, he learned "unofficially" that an exchange proposal would be rejected.[24] Then, on 5 February, the idea of reciprocal restoration seemed to have awakened official interest when the *Moniteur*, whose columns often presaged shifts in government policy, made the proposal public. Having already told Cadore that, yes, he was authorized to negotiate an exchange, Russell figuratively held his breath waiting for the foreign office to make the next move. A welcome silence from that quarter led him to reflect on what might have happened. There were, he wrote, "intrinsic difficulties in the thing itself." Had he taken the initiative—been the first to offer an exchange—France would have seen it as an admission that her reprisals had been justified. But even if France herself had taken the initiative, he told Smith, she might have insisted on a ship-for-ship restoration which obviously would have left a disproportionate amount of American property in French hands.[25]

Grateful to have dodged a risky negotiation, Russell tried a different approach. He urged the release of American vessels in the certain prospect that Congress would follow the president's lead and reimpose non-intercourse on Britain when after the three-month interval London had not revoked its orders-in-council. Not surprisingly, Cadore declined to take congressional action on faith. Although the emperor was "pleased with what the United States had already done," he rejoined, "he could not *throw himself into their arms* until they had accomplished their undertaking," a clear reference to the reimposition of non-intercourse.[26] Disappointed, Russell told one of his correspondents that the president's proclamation has not met "with sufficient good faith here . . . & we are again deferred to a future period for the accomplishment of this revocation." To Pitcairn, he wrote, "They are waiting to learn the precise shape in which our non-intercourse with England will be carried into operation."[27]

Meanwhile, Russell saw fit to vent some timely outrage at France's licensed trade with Great Britain. Americans who were about to forgo their own commerce with the British, he told Cadore, could not "consent" to have this sacrifice "counteracted by any commercial intercourse whatever under licenses or otherwise between France and her enemy. . . ."[28] The shot was nicely aimed but the target out of range. Chiding Napoleon for puncturing his own "System" made for good irony, but threats to withhold "consent" from France's cross-Channel trade stood small alongside the administration's more material concern that French consuls might soon be licensing trade out of U.S. ports. On this point the administration's position was clear. In mid-January, Russell conveyed Smith's stern warning that such "Consular Superintendance" was inadmissible within U.S. jurisdiction.[29] At the same time, he foresaw that American sea captains on his side of the Atlantic would continue to seek licenses as a means of escape. He made clear he would have no part in it.[30]

By late 1810 Napoleon believed he had conceded enough to American sensitivities that Serurier should make the most of them. Objectively considered, these concessions did not amount to much. His announced willingness not to treat stranded American seamen as prisoners of war might be passed off as simple justice. And his readiness to acquiesce in Madison's announced annexation of a sizable chunk of West Florida could be seen as bowing to a *fait accompli.* Even the letters he approved through whose publication two high French officials announced that no U.S. vessel detained since 1 November would be tried under the Berlin and Milan decrees fell short of the assumption in Washington that those decrees had been absolutely revoked.

Curiously, in light of Napoleon's earlier stance on Florida issues, Madison's decision to occupy about one-third of West Florida met with his unqualified approval. In August, land-hungry American settlers having swelled the population of the Baton Rouge region to a critical mass had quietly ousted Spanish authorities, organized themselves politically, and asked for U.S. protection. Madison, responding to the fear that Britain might capitalize on Spain's anarchy to seize that part of her New World empire, had dispatched troops to occupy West Florida as far east as the Pearl river. Congress, similarly alarmed, not only sanctioned this action but in January 1811 authorized the president to occupy East Florida as well.[31] Understandably, in this preemptive context, Napoleon could readily welcome Americans taking on the British in a venue where he himself could not affect the outcome. That he could view Americans as defenders against a common enemy goes far to explain why Russell was told that the United States could "dispose of the Floridas as they pleased," and why Serurier was instructed to repeat these assurances. Always alert for equivocation, Russell asked for Napoleon's acquiescence in writing. Cadore declined, he reported, but "putting his hand on his heart," said he had been "officially" authorized to give such assurances.[32] For the time being, this was enough.

The Berlin and Milan decrees also came in for a placatory gloss when Cadore remarked that the emperor might have kept the decrees in full force until Congress reimposed non-intercourse. Instead, he had graciously sanctioned the publication of two official letters, one from the minister of justice, the duc de Massa, and the other from the minister of finance, the duc de Gaète, both of which confirmed that U.S. vessels arriving since 1 November might be detained but not proceeded against. Of the two letters, both dated 25 December and nearly identical, Massa's promised that if the United States fulfilled its "engagement," ships and cargoes detained since 1 November would be released. More problematical was the fate of vessels detained before that date inasmuch as Gaète's letter said their ultimate disposition "must be the object of a special report."[33] Shown these letters at a meeting on the 22nd, Russell merely remarked that he had hoped ships would be released prior to 2 February. Cadore, however, put his own spin on this meeting, telling Serurier to inform Washington that its minister had not only seen but also approved both letters.[34] Whether in fact Russell had made approving noises when he read the Massa and Gaète letters, he was not likely to have caviled at official communications that seemed to promise the eventual release of at least some U.S. property. To Pinkney he voiced the hope that even this "partial revocation" of French decrees might inspire London to free the U.S. vessels it had taken since 1 November.[35]

Back in Washington, Madison's political enemies gleefully held up the letters as proof of the president's gullibility, pointing out that Massa and Gaète had promised no more than had been vouchsafed to Armstrong three months earlier—that after 1 November 1810, American ships might be detained but not confiscated for alleged violations of the Berlin and Milan decrees. Across the aisle, Madison's supporters could only hope that once Britain had been subjected to non-intercourse, the uncertainty over the status of the French decrees would pass from both the domestic and foreign policy scenes.

As the new year dawned, Russell reported a turn for the worse in the way French port officials were dealing with U.S. vessels on arrival. Once impounded for violating French decrees, now the vessels became the victims of bureaucratic delay. Their captains, crews, and passengers, he wrote, were subjected to lengthy "examinations." Officials took the vessel's papers, drew up a procès verbal, and transmitted the whole to the Director General at Paris [who] "from these documents makes a report to the Emperor or to the Council of Commerce and much time is necessary to obtain a final decision."[36] Russell saw good news on another front, however. In mid-January Cadore sounded what appeared to be a complete about-face on licensing. The foreign minister characterized licensing as a temporary safeguard designed for an earlier era, but now that Madison had made a show of "independence," licensing was no longer expedient. "What was done before that last epoch," he wrote, "can no longer serve as the rule in the present circumstances." Although Cadore did not specify what the new "rule" would be, Russell inferred that licensing was on its way out. Paris, he wrote Smith elatedly, had not only given up the "exceptional powers" it claimed for its consuls, but had abandoned "the system itself." His elation proved short-lived. In fact, Cadore had deliberately deceived him. Telling Serurier what he had told Russell, Cadore wrote, "I cannot assure you that licenses cease to be [issued] although this letter [to Russell] gives it to be so understood by implication."[37] More truthfully, he might have said that France would hold American shipping hostage at least until Congress had made good on Madison's promise to cut off trade with Britain. Meanwhile, licensing still had a future.

But would Congress make a clean break in once more cutting commercial ties with Britain? Distrust ran high among French officials, Russell wrote. Some fully expected to see Congress create a loophole large enough to admit British goods already en route from Liverpool. Any sign of congressional equivocation, he warned, and France would find further reason to detain American vessels. But even if Congress were "faithful and severe," he doubted she would adopt "a prompt & liberal course" because too many French officials were convinced that all seaborne traffic was "directly or indirectly . . . auxiliary" to British commerce.[38] These fears were partly borne out when Congress did decide to admit cargoes that had left British ports prior to 2 February, but the late cutoff date proved less troublesome than the law's failure to make non-intercourse complete. The bill Madison signed on 2 March closed the door firmly to British imports but put no restrictions on exports. Smith later explained this halfway measure. Congress, he told Russell, reflected the public perception that France had not entirely revoked its decrees but had only suspended them.[39] Whatever the accuracy of that perception, the failure of Congress to cut off both legs of the British trade did hand Napoleon a convenient pretext for continuing to detain American shipping.[40] Russell, having warned in vain, now had to deal with the consequences.

CHAPTER 12

RUSSELL STRUGGLES,
NAPOLEON CAVILS

In both capitals that spring, changes in high-level foreign office personnel raised speculation as to what changes in policy might follow. Madison in March and Napoleon the following month replaced their chief foreign policy advisors. In Paris, the duc de Bassano succeeded Cadore as minister of exterior relations; and in Washington, James Monroe replaced Robert Smith in the State Department. In both instances the public wondered whether, based on what was known of their personalities and backgrounds, Bassano and Monroe might be harbingers of new directions in French-American relations.

Bassano's elevation most clearly reflected Napoleon's need to secure an Austrian ally in his fast-approaching military showdown with Russia. Recently returned from Vienna, Bassano had already made a start toward firming up diplomatic and military support in that quarter. He was expected to continue. Confident and widely experienced in diplomatic matters, Bassano had served in most of the major capitals of Europe since the days of the Consulate.[1] Now, at forty-eight and with a newly bestowed ducal title, he was to devote his ministry to avoiding or at least postponing war with Russia while working to assure that France would have allies if war came. By the spring of 1811, Napoleon's simmering quarrel with Russia was already well advanced and, as noted earlier, owed much to Czar Alexander's open and unabashed defiance of the Continental System. Bassano was Napoleon's choice to impress on the czar the dangers of non-compliance and to make up for Cadore's not having conveyed his

wrath to St. Petersburg forcefully enough.[2] No one, of course, could foresee how France's eastward-looking diplomacy would affect its relations
with the United States. In retrospect, it was not surprising that Napoleon,
preparing for a massive campaign against Russia, found even less time to
devote to American issues.

The announcement of this cabinet shuffle was characteristically abrupt;
Cadore, the emperor announced, had not been quick enough to carry out
his instructions. Still, as a placatory gesture, he offered the fallen minister
the Vienna post and on the latter's refusal named him a minister of state.
Whatever he thought of Cadore's shortcomings on the job, his letter of
discharge cordially thanked him for his loyalty. No hard feelings apparently; it was just that Bassano's qualifications better fitted his designs of
the moment.[3]

Monroe's appointment undoubtedly signaled Madison's lingering
hope to patch things up with London. Before accepting, Monroe had
warned the president that he still believed in the soundness of "an accommodation with England," which Madison assured him was not a bar to
his appointment.[4] Remembered for the treaty he and William Pinkney
had concluded there in 1806—the one Jefferson had rejected—Monroe
in a sense personified the conciliatory, though not openly pro-British,
leanings of the Republican party's moderates. To some, he had been a bit
too willing to slide over the impressment issue in 1806; and others recalled
that he had not been well received in Paris during his mission to Madrid.
Despite his supposed pro-British bias, however, the secretary of state
emerged a year later as the administration's point-man in persuading
Congress that if it declared war on Britain, the executive branch would
stand behind it. Toward France, Monroe shared with the president and
doubtless a majority of Congress the view that Napoleon had toyed egre-
giously with the promises made in the Cadore Letter. Louis Serurier
would get an earful from him on this score.

Monroe's accession to the State Department meant ridding it of Robert
Smith, whose political disloyalty had nearly paralyzed the administration
and whose intellectual shortcomings had required Madison to function
virtually as his own secretary of state.[5] More important, in his now unified
cabinet the president had a friend and colleague who, though recently a
halfhearted rival for the presidency, could be counted on in international
crises to share his views of the nation's best interests. Serurier, attentive
to unspoken motives, thought he detected both domestic and foreign
policy overtones in the appointment. Madison, he speculated, may have

thought to neutralize Monroe politically by keeping him close by. He may also have perceived that the British, if they chose to negotiate, would prefer to deal with Monroe, rather than Robert Smith whose treatment of "Copenhagen" Jackson still rankled. The new secretary of state, he mused, was well known and respected in Britain, and that worried him.[6]

Neither Russell nor Serurier took much comfort from these personnel changes at the top. Russell doubted Cadore's successor would be a catalyst for better relations. He described Bassano as having "all the mildness without the apparent weakness of his Predecessor & while he appears more affable & unreserved, it is equally difficult to collect from his conversation the real intentions of his Government."[7] In short, among Bassano's other talents useful to his master was his ability to keep the American chargé d'affaires guessing. William Crawford, who met Bassano in November 1813 just before he left the ministry, described him as taller and bulkier than most Frenchman. "His countenance is indicative of plain good sense, and of good nature and sincerity. [But] There is nothing brilliant or imposing about him,"[8] a judgment that reflects Edward Whitcomb's observation that each of Napoleon's foreign ministers—from Talleyrand to Cadore to Bassano—was "less able and independent than the last."[9]

Arriving in Washington in early February 1811, seven weeks before Monroe's appointment, Serurier settled in amicably enough with Robert Smith. He found the secretary's unabashed francophilia mildly reassuring. Smith, he observed shrewdly, "nourishes a secret admiration for the Emperor which he very wisely conceals." He ascribed the secretary's affinity for Napoleon at least in part to the short-lived marriage of his niece, Elizabeth Patterson, to the emperor's youngest brother, Jerome.[10] Questioned closely only two days after he arrived, Serurier promised the release of vessels detained since May provided Congress, still debating the Eppes Bill, acted decisively to close down commerce with Britain. American property seized earlier, however, would not be restored because it had been taken in just reprisal for the Non-Intercourse Act. (Serurier later paid for his candor when Smith, in his vendetta against the administration, published his comment about "acts of just reprisal.")[11] Serurier hedged when asked if reinstituting non-intercourse would fully satisfy Napoleon's requirement of "making the English respect your rights." He remembered having been instructed not to blurt out, "No, we want you to declare war." Instead, albeit disingenuously, he said the emperor did not presume to tell Americans how to make their rights respected. He assured Smith, however, that "it seemed natural to me to understand by that [requirement, to mean], non-intercourse above all." As for anything else Napoleon might require of American self-respect he left the door ajar.[12]

At a second meeting, Smith again asked whether passage of the Eppes Bill would suffice to improve relations. This time, Serurier pounced on its failure to ban exports. Unlike the Non-Intercourse Act, he noted, this one allowed Americans "to carry their products to England." Smith dismissed the discrepancy as being of no importance. Permitting exports, he argued, benefitted only the American carriers; it did nothing to lessen the hardships Britons would feel at their loss of the American market. Not satisfied, the French minister said he thought the bill was "weak and dilatory." Smith countered that it was strong enough to have angered the British minister, to which Serurier rejoined, "perhaps that is the best that can be said for it."[13]

Nor did the export loophole pass unnoticed in Paris. Russell met with Bassano on 28 April, flourishing a copy of the Eppes Bill and demanding the immediate release of American property on grounds that the United States had now fully complied with the Cadore Letter. Bassano said he would confer with the emperor and two days later told him that Napoleon had found the Congressional action "not entirely satisfactory." The sticking point, as Russell had foreseen, was that U.S. vessels were still permitted to carry cargoes to England. In the exchange that followed, Russell tried to argue from Napoleon's own rationale that one-sided traffic would drain Britain of specie and ultimately bankrupt her. Britons buying without selling, he contended, would deplete British resources "more rapidly . . . than complete non-intercourse." Bassano gave him a steely reply. What would prevent American shipmasters, he countered, from carrying British exports to third-party buyers? American carriers barred from importing British goods directly could sell such cargoes elsewhere. Russell admitted lamely that his instructions were "silent on this point," but said he saw no reason why his government would sanction third-party trafficking from which it derived no benefit. Bassano, he reported, expressed some "doubt and uncertainty,"[14] as well he might, considering the lesson Paris had learned earlier when British and American shipmasters had evaded the Non-Intercourse Act by exchanging cargoes in neutral ports.

Despite Bassano's disparagement of the Eppes Bill, Napoleon asked for advice on how to respond to it. Unaware at first that the law permitted American exports to Britain (until Bassano pointed it out), he roundly declared he would seize any U.S. carrier that so much as dared touch at a British port. Americans, he blustered, should have declared war on Britain long since; a partial non-intercourse was only a "war of sorts." His major concern, however, was still to prevent British goods from reaching the continent. He told his advisors he wanted proposals for more rigorous licensing coupled with greater attention to consular certificates of origin. Then, voicing his frustration over the past failures of such controls, he threatened that if American shipmasters persisted in trading with the British en route to the continent, he would resurrect his Berlin and Milan decrees and pursue them with privateers.[15]

All this preceded the advice he presumably wanted. Bassano's subsequent recommendations dated May 6 were remarkably moderate.[16] Congress, he believed, had responded literally to the requirements of the Cadore Letter, although by permitting exports to Britain it had raised the troubling likelihood that U.S. carriers would pick up British goods to sell in other venues. Still, he urged that because Congress had not forbidden this traffic, France should not interfere with it. He devoted most of his report, however, to arguing for an end to licensing. Licenses, he contended, were too expensive (then selling at 600 francs) and had to be renewed for each voyage. Too, as presently configured, they allowed importers entry at only two French ports and specified only four American cities as ports of departure. In their place, Bassano argued that all French consuls in America, not just a few, be authorized to certify cargoes. Once documented, France could safely receive these cargoes at all metropolitan ports where customs officials could examine them, impose duties, and oversee the subsequent exportation of French commodities of equal value. Moreover, the shipping information now required of licensees—the vessel's tonnage, number of crewmen, and so forth—could just as readily be entered on consular certificates.[17] Most significantly, however, Bassano observed that port officials could already tell the American provenance of most cargoes even without certification. The foreign office had a list of recently imported commodities known to be produced only in the United States. Working from this list, customs officers should have had no difficulty spotting goods of British origin.[18]

Napoleon responded only to this last observation. By a decree of that same day, 6 May he agreed to admit any cargo identified as American from the foreign ministry's "list of products exported from America from the 1st October 1806 to 30 September 1807."[19] Bassano was elated. Foreseeing a potential for easing relations with Washington, he sped the good news to Serurier. The latter could also announce the release of all vessels detained since 2 November, except those taken by privateers. He was not to speculate on the fate of the latter. Much depended on Britain's next move, Bassano told him. If the May 6 decree resulted in an expansion of Franco-American trade, Britain would likely escalate her depredations, hopefully to the point where the United States would declare war. Should that happen, the envoy could promise the unconditional release of all American vessels.[20] Whether Napoleon and his foreign minister truly believed that a greater volume of Franco-American trade would evoke more warlike acts from the British government, they clearly overestimated the growth potential of his May 6 decree. American merchants remained shy and rightly so. In the weeks that followed, France did release a few American vessels, but it still subjected incoming cargoes to licensing and certification, and the list of American products approved for importation excluded virtually all processed or manufactured items.[21]

As summer lengthened, Russell picked up rumors that the French government might prefer to deal with his successor. Since mid-April the capital had known that Joel Barlow would replace Armstrong at full ministerial rank; and for the beleaguered *chargé*, Barlow's arrival could not be soon enough. Russell repeated to his correspondents his fervent hope that Barlow would step off the next U.S. public vessel to make a French landfall.[22] His own future was uncertain. The recent death of his mother and the press of business at home encouraged an early return to Rhode Island. With Pinkney's recall imminent, and the grim prospect of a winter crossing, he kept putting off but finally accepted the administration's offer to post him to London, again as *chargé d'affaires.*[23]

———— ∞ ————

Two months after announcing it would happen, Bassano confirmed to Serurier that U.S. vessels held since 2 November had been released. Well, not quite all. Only three had been allowed to depart, he admitted, but their release should prove to Washington that the Berlin and Milan decrees had been revoked. As to other proofs of revocation, he told Russell that France would welcome "all vessels coming from America except where we are informed that they had been visited by the British, or submitted to payment of an impost, or forced to change their destination when they had been destined to France."[24] Given these qualifications, Russell must have wondered exactly what part of the Berlin and Milan decrees had been revoked. And he regretted "so partial" a release, he told Bassano, especially because the grounds for detaining these three ships "conclusively proved nothing in relation to the revocation of the French edicts."[25]

In everything but name, Russell concluded, the offending decrees were still being enforced. True, some vessels held since 1 November had been freed and others taken by French privateers might also be released, but he warned a prominent mercantile house in Providence "not to adventure on appearances."[26] Still, if French officials no longer cited the decrees, perhaps the British could be persuaded they had been revoked. On this frail hope, he notified the American *chargé* in London that "Since the first of November these decrees have not to my knowledge *in any instance* been executed to the prejudice of American property. . . ."[27] To Monroe, however, he despaired of eliciting any "clear & unequivocal testimony" of revocation. France might show a few favors to American shipping, but Napoleon would never go the length of renouncing the purpose of his decrees altogether. His explanation was simple and it registered strongly in Washington. He was certain that Napoleon would never retreat so far as to give London and Washington grounds for conciliating their own differences.[28] Himself convinced of this stratagem, he told Bassano angrily, "we were not sufficiently dull to be deceived by this kind of management." Nor was he surprised when Bassano sidestepped the question of making an official announcement of revocation and merely promised to do what he could to expedite the release of other ships held since 1 November. In the offshore waters, meanwhile, French privateers continued to search out ships and cargoes tainted by contact with the enemy, and the prizes they brought back became in most cases irrecoverable.

Small numbers of American vessels ventured warily into French ports that spring. When sixteen were admitted in mid-May, Bassano hailed them as fresh evidence of the emperor's new openness to American carriers.[29] As their captains soon discovered, however, easy entry did not guarantee easy departure. From Bordeaux, Vice Consul Christopher Meyer put the recent arrival figure at seventeen (ten in that city, seven others at Bayonne). A month later none had been cleared for departure. His explanations were disheartening. Their captains were hard put to secure return-cargoes equal in value to the ones they had brought in. Worse, Paris officials insisted on determining the value of both incoming and

outgoing cargoes with time-consuming exactitude.[30] To Russell, these delays were a contemptible sequel to the decrees. American vessels were
now being lured into French ports, he wrote, only to find themselves
caught in a bureaucratic web from which few seemed likely to escape.[31]
He warned his correspondents of the risks, some old, some new. Typical
was the letter he wrote to Martin Blake, an American businessman in
Liverpool who asked what his chances were of safely sending an American
vessel with an American cargo. Russell replied that "it would be almost
impossible to *convince* this Government that it was not *English property*
and an everlasting examination would be as ruinous as the prompt operation of any decree."[32] Summing up the situation to Smith in early August,
he sourly characterized French policy toward American shipping as having moved "from prompt confiscation to perpetual detention."[33] Even
those vessels cleared for departure were burdened with the requirement
that silk goods comprise two-thirds of their cargo. As a result, he told
Bassano, French silk merchants overcharged them because they knew of
the requirement, and American buyers, already overstocked, were forced
to sell at a loss. If the silk requirement continued, he predicted, American
carriers would become increasingly scarce.[34] By midsummer, France had
so little external commerce that he was telling his friends and fellow merchants not to bother. "[T]he market here is hardly worth fighting for,"
he wrote David Parish. And to the merchant prince, Henry Higginson,
then in London, he predicted that even if Britain revoked its orders-in-
council, "the trade to this country must be a losing and ruinous business
so long as the present high duties are exacted on importations & two
thirds silks are required to be taken away as returns. Litteraly [*sic*] speaking, there is indeed no demand for any thing we can bring hither." In
sum, high tariffs plus ruinous export requirements had taken a heavy
toll.[35]

   By early summer 1811, detained shipping fell into two categories. Some
vessels recently captured were set free, but the "old" cases, victims of the
Rambouillet and Trianon decrees, were stuck fast in the Council of Prizes
where the legal proceedings against them had recently been suspended.
Bassano did not explain this hiatus; nor did he respond to Russell's request that, for better or worse, the Council resume processing these earlier cases.[36] Nor did it help that the interim U.S. consul in Paris had tried
to force his way into the Prize Council's records. Alexander McRae, David
Warden's temporary replacement, had announced rashly that he intended
to uncover evidence of fraud in those records. As a result, French litiga-

tors had invoked an old law which barred access except to parties to a cause or their lawyers.[37] Like Armstrong before him, Russell had trouble with his consuls.

———— ∞∞∞ ————

As his mission drew to a close, Russell was perhaps most frustrated by his inability to win explicit French approval for his government's avowed and perhaps now fulfilled intentions toward East Florida. Because Napoleon the previous December had voiced no objection to the partial annexation of West Florida, Russell anticipated no difficulty in securing a nod for the administration's contingency plans to occupy the peninsula as well. His instructions also suggested that no one in Washington would take it amiss if France were to approve outright annexation.[38] Accordingly, he explained to Bassano why Congress in January had authorized the president to occupy East Florida and the as-yet-unoccupied portion of West Florida. Although his government had no "intention of wantonly seeking an extension of territory," Spain's loss of control in that quarter had opened the possibility that some foreign power might threaten an opportunistic takeover. In aid of outright annexation, he hinted that if Madrid refused to honor its admitted but unsettled American spoliation claims, France would surely agree the United States might compensate itself by keeping the territory. Annexation would also serve his country's strategic interest in allowing unobstructed communication between its east and gulf coasts. Given these considerations, his question was implicit: would the emperor sanction annexation?[39]

Two days later, on 30 April, Bassano returned with two questions. First, what "foreign power" did Americans fear? Certainly not France or any of her allies, Russell replied. Why, then, the emperor wanted to know, should the administration have "difficulty in ascertaining the proper government with which to negociate for the [annexation of the] Floridas?" Because, Russell replied, Washington had to know whether to negotiate with Paris or Madrid. His mention of Madrid, unfortunately, opened the door to another round of imperial evasiveness. As was evident from Napoleon's earlier influence in Madrid, the emperor had long had it within his power to end the Florida game. Having now placed his brother Joseph on the Spanish throne, he had even less pretext to bow to formalities. Given the opening, he had Bassano tell Russell he saw no reason why the cession could not be negotiated with King Joseph. Plausible though it sounded, this suggestion to deal with Joseph Bonaparte was not an option because, as the French Emperor well knew, the Madison Administration did not and was not about to have official relations with what it regarded as a puppet government. Quite possibly, Napoleon hoped in this instance to tempt the United States into a negotiation which, itself an act of recognition, would help legitimize his brother's regime. Whatever his motives, his lingering disposition to parlay the Floridas into something more substantial than winning American goodwill ended Russell's hope for closure. Thus, together with unresolved maritime matters, the *chargé* was left with the loose ends of the seemingly endless Florida controversy. Nor did he believe Joel Barlow would enjoy any greater success.[40]

Russell left Paris having won no diplomatic laurels, but he had at least furnished Washington with a plausible explanation of France's continued harassment of American shipping. Paris, he firmly believed, would concede nothing to the rights of neutrals lest London make some comparable concession that would pave the way to an Anglo-American reconciliation. Given this strategy of delay, he predicted that France would continue her maritime depredations until British policy became so abusive as to drive Americans to war. Only then could one hope French-American relations would improve. He left the testing of this contingency to Joel Barlow.

CHAPTER 13

SERURIER PARRIES
COMPLAINTS AND REJOICES
AT FOSTER'S UNDOING

What the Madison administration most needed from France in the spring of 1811 was solid proof that the Berlin and Milan decrees had been revoked. From the outset of his mission, it impressed on Louis Serurier that his government's willingness to furnish such proof was as vital to his credibility as it was to its own, for without hard evidence of French revocation, the administration stood no chance of persuading London to repeal its orders-in-council and would remain exposed to Federalist charges that it had been duped by France into complicating relations with Great Britain.

While the matter of proof hung fire, the new French minister settled into an uneasy relationship with Secretary of State Monroe whom he described as friendly,"moderate and well informed," but not as pro-French as his predecessor.[1] When they first met in early April, the two men had little to discuss until they had news of the French response to the latest congressional sanctions against Britain. Serurier did, however, express anger at his first brush with a hostile press. He told Monroe he might sue the editor of the [Baltimore] *Federal Republican* for having greeted him on arrival as the "Minister of rapine and murder," but Monroe talked him out of it, noting that the same editor had called the president "a good vassal of the Emperor." If he took the editor to court, he warned, he would be accused of trying to infringe on Americans' freedom of the press. Having foreseen this argument, which he thought "captious," Serurier agreed to drop the matter so as not to "multiply" the administration's problems, he told the foreign office.[2]

Until the *Essex* arrived in early July—conveying what he later described as an unwelcome "silence" from Paris and "bad reports" from Russell— the French minister applied his considerable charm to create a reservoir of goodwill and soon boasted that "M. Monroe speaks to me of France only with unction and the President himself redoubles his regards and kindliness." He also cultivated minister-designate Joel Barlow, and after spending two weeks as Barlow's house guest assured Paris that the emperor could have every confidence in the goodwill of Armstrong's successor.[3] Their friendship also had a personal payoff. When Barlow left for France, Serurier rented his "Kalorama" estate on a nearby Washington hilltop, a welcome change after living in the cramped quarters of a Georgetown inn.[4]

Unlike Jonathan Russell whose job was to question French policies, Serurier's was to defend them. He realized almost immediately, however, that trying to justify his government's treatment of American shipping did nothing to advance France's larger but unspoken purpose of bringing Americans into the war. Too, he faced the unsettling possibility that if that treatment worsened, France itself might become the target of hostilities. Accordingly, he began to play on the theme that if France expected Americans to stand firm against Britain, she must show more leniency toward American shipping (compatible of course with the Continental System). At all costs, she must avoid giving cause for further alarm.[5] He noted, for example, the distressing effect of a report in late April that American vessels, even those with licenses, were being sequestered under a revival of the Berlin and Milan decrees. The rumor had devastated Americans who were friendly to France, he wrote, and Federalists were knowingly outraged. Even though the rumor proved false, fabricated he believed by the "English Party," he sent his alarmist despatch anyway, warning that such rumors if substantiated would embarrass the Administration and energize its enemies.[6]

While Serurier defended the continued detention of American vessels on grounds that Congress had failed to ban exports to Britain, he impressed on Paris the apparent effectiveness of the ban on imports. The ramifications he believed were significant. Not only were a growing number of American consumers looking to France for commodities they could no longer buy from Britain, but he also thought their stake in this traffic would move them to defend it vigorously against British interference. Accordingly, he urged that France assure the safe and speedy return of American merchantmen from ports under French control.[7] Such pleas for leniency were to become a staple of his despatches throughout his mission.

As time wore on, Serurier found the activities of French-commissioned privateers to be his most recurrent problem. Some, having preyed on American shipping, became targets of reprisal when they ventured into U.S. ports. In mid-April, for example, he sought and won Monroe's promise to prosecute the leaders of a mob which had set fire to a well-known French corsair that had rashly put into Norfolk. At about the same time, American shipowners in New York caused the arrest of the *Diligent*, charging it with the illegal capture of two of their vessels en route from Cadiz and Lisbon. Obliged to make official protests on these occasions, Serurier remarked ironically that his countrymen's private warfare at sea had done more damage to relations with Washington than it had to enemy shipping. He also reminded Paris that such incidents diverted public outrage away from Britain.[8]

The most politically-charged of these "ship" incidents erupted when the owners of the American schooner *Exchange* who had earlier lost their vessel to a French prize court sued for recovery when it turned up in Philadelphia. In the interim, the French navy had thought highly enough of the *Exchange* to make it one of their own, renaming it the *Ballaou*. Thereafter as a public vessel, it had immunities related to national sovereignty. When in July it arrived in Philadelphia under stress of weather, its former owners secured a restraining order. The ensuing legal tug-of-war moved tortuously on appeal from state to federal jurisdictions and ended only when the Supreme Court in February 1812 dismissed the former owners' libel and restored the schooner to French custody. While the outcome remained in doubt, Serurier periodically lectured the secretary of state on the inviolability of public vessels and warned of possible reprisal. An obviously discomfited Monroe took his text from the constitutional separation of powers to explain why the executive could not intervene in matters that were *sub judice*. For nearly seven months, the case resisted Serurier's best efforts to clear it away. In the end, however, the high court found no legal precedent for extending U.S. jurisdiction to a public vessel owned by a "friendly" power. Happily for the administration, the decision also laid to rest—at a time of worsening relations with London—an issue touching on French national honor which, if the court had decided differently, might well have evoked violent reprisal from France's punctilious emperor.[9]

———— ∞∞∞ ————

Through late spring 1811 the French envoy hoped to hear that enough American vessels had been freed to satisfy his hosts that Bonaparte's decrees had been revoked. Madison, too, was hopeful. In early May, he wrote optimistically to Jefferson that "From the jumble of accts. from France, it is probable that the repeal of the decrees is professedly adhered to."[10] Until revocation had been certified, however, Serurier could only hope that his mission might be rescued by an offsetting crisis in Anglo-American relations.

On this score, he exulted when in mid-May an American frigate exchanged fire with and severely damaged a British corvette off Cape Henry. Though the *President's* forty-four guns made quick work of the twenty-gun *Little Belt*, Americans viewed the encounter as a long overdue blow for American national honor, a fitting payback for Britain's countless insults on the high seas, even as belated revenge for the attack on the *Chesapeake*. The *Little Belt* had refused to answer Commodore Rodgers' hail, he reported, and had undoubtedly fired the first shot.[11] Musing over the incident, he supposed the British captain had taken too lightly the approach of an American frigate and "thought that sending a ball would suffice to humiliate it." Had the frigate been French, he added whimsically, the corvette would surely have fled under full canvass.[12] A bit of good news from France at that moment, he predicted, would make war "almost certain." To his American friends, he reported having applauded the commodore's "beautiful conduct," but without "chaleur," he assured Bassano, lest "the Emperor's minister have the appearance of pushing these people into war."[13] In light of Federalist charges that Rodgers had acted on orders from Paris, his circumspection seems warranted. Himself tempted to guess at hidden motives, Serurier wondered if Madison had ordered the attack to divert attention from the anti-French incidents in Norfolk and Philadelphia.[14] Speculation about official motives persisted until all but the most conspiracy-minded were satisfied that happenstance largely explained what had taken place in the twilight off Cape Henry.

The *Little Belt* affair excited strong emotions but fell short of provoking a full-blown crisis. With Congress out of town, taunting articles in the press lacked for oratorical amplification. In the aftermath, London merely asked for an explanation; and its newly appointed minister, Augustus

John Foster, agreed to be satisfied with an official inquiry, although he did find what he called "unaccountable differences" between Rodgers' testimony and that of the captain of the *Little Belt.* On Monroe's plea of "no hostile intention," Foster referred the matter back to London.[15] Both he and Serurier had more pressing issues to deal with.

───⊗⊗⊗───

Besides coping with various ship incidents, Serurier also had to deal with the administration's opposition to French licensing. The issue long smouldering flared up in late June when he learned that Paris had just given French consuls in Boston and Baltimore the same authority to issue export licenses as had been granted earlier to those in New York and Charleston. Though he was prepared to argue the commercial advantages of licensed trade, his instructions gave him no guidance as to how to defend the "legality" of such consular activity. Nor did he have a copy of the flimflamming letter Bassano had sent Russell in January which had characterized licensing as a temporary expedient that "no longer served as the rule."[16] Monroe was in a foul mood when Serurier called at his office. The administration's political enemies, he was told, would pounce on this extension of French licensing as proof that the French decrees were still in force and denounce the administration for tolerating an expansion of consular authority. Why did licensing persist, he asked, when Bassano's letter to Russell of 18 January (he did have a copy) formally announced an end to it? Warming to his exasperation—his face "quite discomposed"—Monroe exclaimed: "Ah, Monsieur, if your sovereign had deigned to imitate the promptness that our President showed in the publication of his proclamation; if he had reopened . . . his ports to our vessels, all American commerce would be gained by France; a thousand vessels would have left, at all risks, for your ports." On balance, Serurier thought Monroe's outburst showed "more discouragement than ill-will." In reply, he hopefully pictured this latest extension of licensing as the final phase of a "system which would make way for more generous arrangements between the two Governments." Mindful now of how prickly the administration had become on this issue, he told Bassano he would caution French consuls not to cause "jealousy or discontent" among those who applied for licenses. He gave Monroe the same assurances, while pointing out that he had no authority to change imperial policy.[17]

A few days later, his troubles multiplied when the arrival of the *Essex* failed to bring news of sweeping concessions from Paris. "I found him icy," Serurier said of Monroe, and he "asked me if I was any happier." Masking his chagrin, the Frenchman pleaded having had no despatches dated later than 1 March and therefore no way of knowing how the emperor had responded to the trade sanctions Congress had taken against Britain in February. He could confirm, however, that his government was admitting more American vessels, even those without licenses. And the secretary should be pleased that the emperor had no objection to American troops occupying the Floridas. Monroe, clearly unmoved, looked at him "coldly." Shifting to safer ground, Serurier spoke optimistically of Barlow's impending departure. Here at least the two could agree on the need for a fully accredited minister in Paris. Monroe promised to draft Barlow's instructions and send him off without further delay.[18]

Almost as dispiriting as the "silence" from Paris was the effect on Washington of the newly arrived British minister. The possibility that Augustus John Foster had brought healing proposals from London, Serurier wrote, had clouded the political atmosphere in the capital dramatically. Persons once eager to talk to him now kept aloof. "They are polite," he wrote, "but under a thousand pretexts, they avoid to be seen even chatting with me." Too, newspapers normally pro-French now seemed to reflect the administration's uncertainty about what might happen next. The possibility of a British rapprochement appeared to have paralyzed it. Still, he perked up when, sitting next to Monroe at a Fourth of July banquet, he was told that Barlow had been ordered to sail. This, he hoped, would help to "neutralize" Foster's presence.[19] Five days later, however, with Barlow still ashore, he asked whether the British minister had proposed something that accounted for the delay. No, indeed, Monroe replied; there would be "no kind of arrangement" unless London revoked its orders-in-council. Rumored elsewhere, Serurier was relieved to hear directly from the secretary of state that the British envoy was not talking revocation. As for the delay in sending Barlow, he had to accept Monroe's explanation that until favorable news came from France, the administration had little choice but to yield to the public's insistence that he not be sent. Though disappointed, Serurier rejoiced quietly at intimations that Foster's mission posed no imminent threat of a reconciliation. Little did he know, Monroe was already framing a lengthy defense of the administration's foreign policy in response to Foster's unforgiving condemnation of it.[20]

Looking ahead, Serurier wished Paris would give him the sort of "good news" he could use to offset British influence in the long run and warned that unless word came that France had opened its ports freely and released sequestered vessels, a reassembled Congress might cut off trade with both belligerents. It would pain him, he wrote, to see "the Emperor's interests in America on the brink of perishing in my hands." His sense of isolation persisted. "Our best friends," he sighed, "are deserting my house . . . and I will not long be able to dispute the ground with these disadvantages."[21] Ten days later, however, his gloom vanished in a burst of optimism. "Everything has changed," he wrote ecstatically, "and M. Barlow leaves in three days." The reason: reliable news coming by way of London that France had released all American vessels held since November. Believing confirmation would soon follow, he and Monroe agreed to publish their expectations in an "unofficial" exchange of public letters.[22] Both had reason to be pleased, Monroe because it vindicated Madison's acceptance of the Cadore Letter, Serurier because the release of American vessels could be used as a "weapon" to rout the troublemakers of the "English party." After weeks of estrangement, he found himself once more in the administration's good graces. "I have never seen [the president] more triumphant," he exulted. As well he might be, he added thoughtfully, for in acting on the Cadore Letter Madison had embarked on "a policy which was altogether his, but which he was beginning not to know how to sustain."[23]

Unfortunately, the news from Paris a few days later fell far short of his and Monroe's expectations. Only those ships that had voluntarily entered French ports since 1 November were being freed; those taken at sea by privateers would continue to be detained on grounds they might have had contact with the enemy.[24] A "deeply disturbed" Madison once more confronted him with the inference that the Berlin and Milan decrees were still in force, leading the envoy to reflect that the official status of those decrees had become "a personal matter" for the president. Without solid proof of their revocation, attacks on his credulity were certain to be renewed when Congress reconvened.[25]

Meanwhile, he kept a watchful eye on Foster's talks with Monroe. Although the secretary was closemouthed about the details, Serurier knew he was trying to persuade the British minister that the Administration had dealt fairly with both belligerents.[26] A former secretary of the British legation here, Foster wasted no time delivering a harsh message from London.[27] Only days after he landed, he asked why the Administration had punished Britain for its response to Napoleon's Berlin Decree. The emperor's announced blockade of the British Isles was so patently frivolous that London might well have responded by closing down all neutral traffic with French dominions. Instead, his government had preserved, indeed encouraged, neutral trade with the continent, channeling it under license through British ports. Nor was the Berlin Decree adequately justified by the supposed ineffectiveness of the earlier Fox's blockade which, he insisted, Britain had maintained "by a sufficient naval force" from its inception.[28] In a later exchange, Foster asked Monroe snidely why when he was posted to London he had not objected to Fox's Blockade at the time. Why only recently had Americans adopted the French view of its insufficiency?[29] Monroe replied evenly that in May 1806, he and Pinkney had been engaged in amicable treaty negotiations with his government, and that "a formal complaint" would have marred the spirit in which both parties were striving to reach a major accord.[30] He might have added that London's willingness at that time to reverse the *Essex* decision had counted for more than whether a short strip of Europe's northern coast was about to be well or badly blockaded.

Enlarging on his most serious allegation, Foster scolded the administration for accepting the promises of the Cadore Letter; Washington knew full well that Napoleon was still enforcing his antineutral decrees. Only the previous month he had told "certain deputies from the free cities of Hamburg, Bremen, and Lubeck . . . that the Berlin and Milan decrees shall be the public code of France as long as England maintains her orders in council." Nor would he countenance the likely rebuttal that Bonaparte had explicitly exempted the United States. If that were true, he went on, why did France continue to capture and detain American vessels? And if, as reported, France was now releasing some of them, why had she not done so before? Was it not likely, he insinuated, that the French emperor was belatedly rewarding Americans for having inflicted non-importation on Britain? If so, what more proof was needed that Americans had become accomplices in the French emperor's "violent, and monstrous system of attack"?[31]

Monroe's response yielded nothing either to the truth or the bellicosity of Foster's accusations. First, as to Fox's Blockade, he scoffed at the notion that London had ever mustered enough naval force to make it effective. His government, however, was not disposed to argue the "priority" of French vs. British offenses against neutral shipping. France had in fact repealed her offending decrees. He offered as proof that "not one vessel has been condemned by French tribunals, on the principle of those decrees, since the 1st of November last." Nor could Foster offer credible evidence to the contrary. Whatever Bonaparte may have told the deputies of the Hanse towns, Foster must accept as fact, not since contradicted by events, that the French emperor had made an exception of American shipping. Nor was the detention of American vessels between November and February proof against repeal. Rather and reasonably so, Paris had waited to see whether, absent Britain's revocation of her orders, Congress would fulfill Madison's call to reimpose sanctions.[32]

What Monroe lacked during these exchanges, of course, was a formal statement of French repeal signed by the imperial hand. Without a disavowal from the highest level, he found himself in the anomalous position of arguing that Napoleon had repealed his decrees while at the same time belaboring Serurier to give him solid evidence of it. Not surprisingly, he fell back on Russell's earlier argument to Pinkney, that is, that proof lay in their nonenforcement. Or as he put it to Foster: ". . . want of proof against the fulfillment of a pledge is proof of the fulfillment."[33] Unimpressed, Foster doubted Monroe himself believed it was so and again reminded him that Napoleon had never explicitly renounced his edicts. Ironically, Russell at the same moment was telling Bassano that neither did the release of a few vessels prove that the decrees had been revoked.[34]

Foster overreached, however, when he asserted that Britain's orders-in-council would remain in force until all carriers once more had access to the same European markets that had been open to them prior to 1806.[35] Monroe rejoined that since 1806 France had extended dominion over many more European ports and could hardly be expected to fling them open, unless London expected her to do away with the universal prohibition against trading with the enemy. Foster bristled; he had proposed nothing so foolish; rather, his government expected the United States to share its outrage that Napoleon had made it a crime for neutrals to have in their possession "the produce of English industry or of the British soil. . . . Against such an abominable and extravagant pretension," he added grandly, "every feeling must revolt."[36]

Not easily revolted, Monroe shot back: Did he mean to suggest that France had no authority to prevent British goods from entering her ports? And did London propose to hold the United States accountable for French import controls?[37] In mid-December, Foster denied having demanded that "America should force the entry of British manufactures into France." This, he wrote, was a "total misconception." Rather, he had meant to record his government's objection to the injustice of being cut off from continental and now American markets as the result of an illegal French blockade which, far from having been revoked, had made the United States an accomplice in "undermining the resources of Great Britain."[38]

Still, Foster could not take back his instructions, and for him to say that the orders-in-council would remain in place until France had opened its European ports to neutral carriers of British goods was patently unreasonable. "Degrading," Monroe called it, to demand that the United States "open the continent to British manufactures," or failing that, "repeal their non-importation act."[39] And to John Quincy Adams, Madison predicted that the British condition would be "hostilely resisted."[40] Serurier rejoiced in its bad effect on public opinion. Reporting now as a Washington insider, he described the outrage of American officials when they realized Foster had made repeal of the orders-in-council contingent on France's revocation of her decrees "not only with respect to America, but with a much greater extension."[41] For the moment, the French minister satisfied himself that Foster had asked too much and that Washington and London seemed more likely than ever to come to blows.

CHAPTER 14

Madison Prepares a French Initiative as British Relations Worsen

adison may have acted unwisely in accepting the Cadore Letter, but nothing is more certain than that Napoleon's erratic treatment of American shipping in the aftermath seriously weakened the administration's case for having embargoed British imports. Madison's Federalist critics, whose disdain for non-importation showed in their tolerance of widespread smuggling, pictured the president as having fallen easy prey to Napoleon's machinations. Even administration loyalists fretted at the mixed signals coming from Paris. To make matters worse, former Secretary of State Robert Smith, writing from sullen exile, now filled the columns of American newspapers with his *Address to the People of the United States,* attacking the administration for the supposed errors and weaknesses of its foreign policy that he had presumably had a hand in framing.[1]

By midsummer 1811, Madison's diplomacy was at a standstill. William Pinkney, fresh off the boat at Annapolis, confirmed London's refusal to budge from its orders-in-council. Nor had Augustus Foster signaled any hope in that respect. In late July the president reached out for a settlement with France, one that he hoped might elicit like concessions from Britain or, failing that, justify his asking Congress to declare war. Prospects for exploiting a tilt toward France seemed fairly good. Napoleon, despite his underlying hostility, claimed he no longer enforced his decrees against American shipping and had, in fact, released a few vessels, exhibiting a flexibility that was largely missing on the British side. Too, there were encouraging noises from Paris. Although news of it arrived after Barlow had left, Napoleon was quoted as having told his *Corps Législatif* in mid-June that "America makes efforts to have the liberty of her flag recognized. I shall support her."[2] To bring France into play, then, Madison hoped to settle outstanding issues, sweetened with enough promises of commercial advantage to persuade Napoleon to sign on.

Once decided, the president moved quickly. On 8 August, barely a month after Foster's arrival but long enough to realize the futility of trying to deal with him, he packed Joel Barlow off to Paris on board the *Constitution*.[3] And to all appearances, Madison had chosen well. This worldly and wealthy merchant-poet had what most of his contemporaries would agree were both the experience and temperament to wield influence in the French capital. An expatriate since 1788, Barlow had spent nearly seventeen years in Paris, first as an agent for the ill-fated Scioto land company and when this enterprise failed, staying on as a successful commodities trader. During the revolution, he lent his literary talents to republican principles and was subsequently awarded honorary French citizenship. With the Terror, he had prudently removed himself and his family to Hamburg where during a fifteen-month interlude he reportedly made enough money as an import broker to free himself from future financial needs.[4] Called to minor diplomatic service in the late 1790s, Barlow successfully completed treaties with Algiers and later with Tunis and Tripoli. Returning home in 1805, he set himself up lavishly in Washington, renewing ties of friendship with Jefferson, Madison, and other Republican leaders and making Kalorama, his estate on a Washington hilltop, a familiar gathering place for the capital's Republican elite.

From his years in Paris, Barlow brought to his mission a command of the language few of his predecessors could equal. Moreover, he had expert knowledge of France's external commerce, having once served as an import agent for a revolutionary Commission des Subsistances. Besides these practical credentials, he was recognized as one of America's few literary figures. His patriotic epic poem, *The Vision of Columbus*, written many years earlier and recently revised under the title of *The Columbiad*, was known to French intellectuals and by association to those French politicos who to this day fancy themselves as members of that nation's intelligentsia. Acceptance at this level guaranteed him entrée to the salons of the elite where moments of social contact often shortened the hours of diplomacy. In Barlow, Madison also had an emissary of extraordinary vitality whose extroverted personality and powerful presence were certain to command a hearing.[5] He had also chosen a man who was determined to make an accommodation with France even if it meant chasing a French emperor all the way across Europe. This, too, was in Barlow's future and he would die in the attempt.

———— ⌘ ————

While Barlow's mission held out hope of better relations with France, Britain's capacity to irritate showed no signs of abating in the fall of 1811. Foster, as noted earlier, made acceptable amends for the attack on the *Chesapeake*, but by year's end he and Monroe were still locked into the hardened positions they had staked out in July. Britain's refusal to repeal its orders-in-council, already talked of as a *casus belli*, would remain at the top of the list of congressional reasons for declaring war the following June. Nor did the *Chesapeake* settlement evoke much good feeling. In light of Britain's continuing maritime offenses, Serurier believed that resolving this grievance had done little to lower public animosity.[6] The historian Bradford Perkins notes, as well, that the administration "had no desire to use it to dampen what they considered a useful spirit of antagonism toward Britain."[7]

Worse, rumors filtering in from the Ohio Valley told of British provocateurs inciting the Indian tribes, and shortly after Barlow's departure, the eminent British jurist Sir William Scott after months of hearings condemned the American ship *Fox* and eighteen others for violating the order-in-council of April 1809. Scott's decision might have been foreseen. Owners of vessels like the *Fox* believing the Cadore Letter had opened more opportunities for direct trade with France increasingly ran afoul of London's 1809 requirement that they stop first at a British port. Scott's decision registered strongly because it supported the ministry's insistence that Britain remain the sole conduit of traffic to the continent. And because Scott based his decision on Napoleon's alleged failure to fulfill the promise of the Cadore Letter, his words added fuel to the partisan flames. Journal readers on this side of the Atlantic now had an inkling of what Foster had been telling Monroe more or less privately: that until Paris produced proof of repeal, the orders-in-council would remain in place, a position now upheld by a British judge who remarked pointedly that the defendants in the *Fox* case had failed "to produce any evidence of the revocation of the French decrees."[8] In sum, nothing in Scott's view, nor presumably in that of the British ministry, had emanated from Paris during the previous year to alter either the *raison d'être* or the legal force of the orders. The *Fox* decision not only sanctioned the Perceval cabinet's position vis-a-vis the French decrees but also revived Federalist charges that Madison had been foolish to believe them rescinded. Dispirited Republicans could only hope that Barlow would extract terms from Paris sufficiently compelling to afford the administration the means to break the impasse which the *Fox* decision seemed certain to prolong.[9]

Oppressive heat and humidity plus the lurking possibility of epidemic emptied Washington of federal officials in August and kept them out of town through most of September. With national politics in abeyance, Serurier mused idly on the flocks of sheep "grazing peaceably" within the city limits and spent his time scanning the press for items Paris might find useful. Editorial columns late that month had alerted readers to the threatening approach of a British naval squadron, perhaps sent to avenge the *Little Belt*. A month later, these alarms subsided when it became clear that London merely intended to reinforce its naval presence in American waters. While war remained on the public mind, Serurier marveled at how confidently Americans spoke of taking Canada and arming swarms of privateers to ravage British commerce. He doubted Britain had any intention of making war over the *Little Belt* incident. She relied too heavily on the American grain ships provisioning Wellington's troops in the peninsular campaign. Meanwhile, he was pleased to report that France's public image had improved as captains arriving from Bordeaux brought news of increasing latitude toward American shipping. This felicitous "contrast in the conduct of the two powers," he wrote, "serves us better than all that I might say."[10]

Until Monroe returned to Washington in mid-October, Serurier managed to set aside some of the more bothersome aspects of his mission. His first fall meeting with the secretary, however, brought a sharp reminder that France's spotty release of American vessels had pushed the administration into a corner in its dealings with London. Monroe, echoing his encounters with Foster, told him bluntly that France's refusal to release all U.S. vessels taken since 1 November had given the British a pretext for clinging to their orders. Serurier responded as best he could. Many vessels remained in custody, he admitted, but Monroe could be certain the French decrees had been revoked. He offered as proof copies of Bassano's letters of 16 May and 13 July, although he must have known these letters did not explain why there had been no general deliverance.

That of 16 May merely listed import commodities known to be of American provenance—items Napoleon had decreed to be admissible. And that of 13 July announced the release of only three of the vessels held since November, a gesture Russell had already disparaged because their detention had not been grounded on the decrees in the first place.[11] Still, each man drew a measure of satisfaction from this meeting. Serurier was pleased to tout his emperor's gracious release of American vessels (some at least) and his opening of French ports to American cargoes (under license to be sure), which he contrasted with Britain's relentless pillaging of American crews and commerce. Monroe, for his part, took up what was to become a recurrent theme in his conversations with the French envoy: that any sign of French leniency toward American shipping bore directly on the willingness of his countrymen to stand up to London. The administration, he told Serurier, was "inflexible on the revocation of the Orders in Council," and "greater ends" would follow if Americans could be certain of French support. Serurier, who seldom missed an opportunity to make the same connection, once more urged Paris to produce some token of goodwill.

In late October a sense of impending crisis quickened as returning members of Congress gathered with mixed expectations to hear why the president had summoned them into session a month earlier than usual. Some guessed he would ask them to declare war. Others hoped not and deplored the prospect. Whatever might transpire, Serurier believed "the gravity of the circumstances" had caught the public's full attention. "We shall soon know, if this sovereign assembly can justify the great hopes that are placed in it." What most concerned him was how France might fare at the hands of angry members once they had spent their wrath on Britain. Much, he believed, depended on how Barlow's reports from Paris might affect deliberations as the session wore on. The president himself had warned him the political debate might turn ugly unless Barlow reported progress.[12]

Read closely, Madison's message to Congress revealed a president soberly analyzing the parlous state of relations with both belligerents—neither of whom escaped his censure—at the same time urging Congress to take appropriate measures of military preparedness. Britain, he charged, had stubbornly refused to revoke its orders on grounds that France had not revoked its decrees. Worse, London had announced it would enforce its orders-in-council until such time as neutrals were permitted to enter all European ports under French control. The absurdity of this "indispensable condition," which no neutral power had the means to satisfy, the president let speak for itself.[13] Writing to Barlow a few days later, he characterized it as "a better subject for ridicule than refutation."[14]

As for the French decrees, Madison had no choice politically but to say they had been revoked. He went on, however, to hold France accountable for seizing and condemning a "great amount of American property," under laws which, though they had no bearing on neutral rights, he was careful to say, were nevertheless "unjust."[15] Nor had Paris offered to make reparations. To these injuries he added what he called the "rigorous and unexpected restrictions" recently placed on American shipping. His message held Britain to be the more incorrigible of the two belligerents and by alluding hopefully to Barlow's mission he implied that differences with Paris might still be negotiated, whereas those with London, as he described them, appeared to be without resolution.[16] Serurier, keen to nuances, welcomed what he believed was Madison's effort to divert public attention away from France.[17]

In the weeks that followed, Congress responded lethargically to the president's call for military preparedness. Madison had warned of a shortfall in tariff revenues, and members instinctively shied at the prospect of voting new taxes. Too, the idea of preparing for war without the certainty of it had yet to find a place in Americans' strategic thinking.[18] While Congress dawdled, Serurier stepped up his efforts to recover the schooner *Exchange*, a.k.a. *Ballaou*, a case once more caught in the toils of the Pennsylvania legal system but soon to be appealed to the U.S. Supreme Court. If the French claim failed there, Monroe had promised him a legislative remedy. Meanwhile, he avoided uttering specific threats lest his official correspondence find its way into the press and call attention to other more serious unsettled issues. He had Monroe's warning not to allude to the emperor's displeasure over the *Ballaou* lest Congress be diverted from its anger toward Britain and the Federalist charge that Napoleon was trying to dictate to it.[19]

More to his liking, in late November Serurier received instructions to invite the United States to join the emperor in liberating Latin America. A sign of the times, Spain's gradual loss of control in that quarter had awakened acquisitive impulses in both belligerents. For Britain the independence movements promised to replace markets lost elsewhere; and for Napoleon market competition was no less important than the prospect of winning for France the hearts and minds of Latin American insurgents.

As Serurier read his instructions, the emperor hoped to use American carriers to convey troops and munitions and counted on Americans' well-known interest in the region's commercial opportunities to make them willing partners. Unfortunately, in extending this invitation, Serurier also had to cope with breaking news that several French sailors had been killed in riots that followed a whorehouse brawl in Savannah. Discomfited at having to mix friendly advances with demands for satisfaction, he nevertheless found both president and secretary of state eager to hear out Napoleon's Latin America project. The president, he wrote later, was so taken by the emperor's "beautiful and decisive plan" that he promised to lay it before his cabinet. Monroe later the same day admitted that his own "sentiments on the emancipation of South America corresponded perfectly with those of His Majesty [and] that we would co-operate on the means." The future progenitor of the Monroe Doctrine apparently had no qualms about transporting French arms to a region where French political influence was sure to follow.[20] Though no official arrangements came of these meetings, private Americans continued to turn a profit, as they had in the past, trading clandestinely with the insurgents.[21]

As the year 1811 drew to a close, the French minister took modest credit for the relative calm that prevailed. Except for Monroe's persistent complaint that Paris had not yet certified the demise of the Berlin and Milan decrees and the unfortunate fallout from the Savannah riots, he believed he had won the confidence of a government that was moving closer to war. He had it on good authority that Madison "had decided to adopt vigorous measures." How vigorous, he was told, would depend on France's willingness to accord better treatment to American shipping, a theme Monroe continued to play and Serurier continued to echo because he believed it was true.[22] For signs of heightened martial spirit in Congress, meanwhile, Serurier needed to look no further than the cadre of militant congressmen, mostly from southern and western districts, whose strident voices began to sharpen that body's deliberations following the Battle of Tippecanoe. Though few in number, these "warhawks," as their Federalist critics called them, kept up a relentless drumbeat of hostility toward Britain starting in the fall of 1811. Though once pictured as highly motivated "frontier" politicians plotting a double-barreled war of conquest that would take Canada from Britain and Florida from Spain, historians have more recently tended to dismiss both the notion of conspiracy and the importance of these militants in the final decisions for war.[23] Still, few would deny that without their spirited oratory, a congressional majority for war might have been difficult to muster.

A major source of Warhawk passion was their moral certainty that British provocateurs from Canada were inciting sporadic outbreaks of Indian hostility in the Old Northwest. This conviction was enhanced by the discovery of British-made rifles that turned up when in early November, William Henry Harrison attacked and laid waste a large Indian encampment called Prophet's Town, situated at the confluence of the Wabash and Tippecanoe rivers. Here the gathered tribesmen, loosely united under the leadership of an able Shawnee chief named Tecumseh, had dug themselves in, claiming that an earlier cession of Indian lands in the Wabash valley had been wrongfully transacted because not all of the indigenous tribes had been consulted. Although Prophet's Town manifested a more or less passive opposition to treaty enforcement, occasional Indian raids the previous summer made it a focus of frontier anxiety, enhanced by paranoid suspicions that Tecumseh had British backing. Evidence later revealed that British officials in Canada, far from agitating the Indians, had tried to restrain them. Harrison, however, yielded to public pressures and, well placed to take action, decided to march against Tecumseh's stronghold. Just before dawn on 7 November, while encamped about a mile from their target, his forces were attacked. Rallying, they repulsed the attackers in a day-long battle and went on to burn the town. When the smoke cleared, Harrison had suffered some 200 casualties, killed an uncounted number of Native Americans, and inadvertently gained enough national name-recognition to pave his way to the White House some thirty years later.[24] The contemporary political fallout was impressive. The odor of British incitement hanging in the smoke over Prophet's Town quickly gave rise, if not credibility, to the Warhawk axiom that American settlers would never be safe on the northern frontier until the last English official had been driven from Canada and those provinces annexed. Less than a year later, "On to Canada" would become one of the excited war cries of 1812.

Thrilled by news of the battle, Serurier wrote optimistically: "Here then began the war with the allies of England. One must hope that the principal actors will not be slow to appear on the scene."[25] He was right on the first count. Britain's so-called "allies," now in a vengeful mood, kept up raids along the frontier. Of the "principal actors," however, Washington was still offstage. Although the executive branch strained for a convincing level of military preparedness, Congress lumbered toward the scene of action in legislative fits and starts. As the politics of preparedness unfolded, Serurier conferred frequently with Monroe and clearly relished getting an inside view of what was transpiring at the congressional committee level. On these occasions Monroe stressed how critically the perception of French conduct would figure in the legislative outcomes. He sometimes overdid it. In early December, Serurier, knowing that Monroe had been in close consultation with Warhawk members of the House Committee on Foreign Relations, leaped to the conclusion that war was imminent.[26] Monroe had told him that the House committee was about to make a compelling case for war with recommendations for marked increases in the military. When the full House rejected most of its recommendations, Serurier consoled himself that at least the committee had acknowledged the repeal of the French decrees while excoriating the British for having grievously injured American ships, cargoes, and seamen.[27] The House did agree to bring existing forces up to statutory strength but postponed the committee's other recommendations.[28] Not until 14 January 1812 did both chambers agree to raise an "additional military force" of ten infantry and two artillery regiments.[29] Despite the meager yield, the French minister believed the committee's report had placed both branches "in one of those positions where, it is no longer possible to pull back. Only the revocation of the Orders in Council can today prevent war."[30]

———— ∞∞∞ ————

Among historians of the era, Harry Ammon has most fully described the behind-the-scenes and perhaps pivotal role of James Monroe in getting Congress pumped up for war through the fall and into the spring of 1812.[31] That Monroe was able to preview to Serurier all of the foreign relations committee's recommendations the day before they were reported bears out this view.[32] What he told Serurier was meant to be heard in Paris, that is, that British intransigence might not be enough to force the war issue, and that Napoleon, too, had a part to play in strengthening Congress's resolve. As a message bearer, Serurier did not disappoint him; he was soon telling Bassano that "war would be infallible" if Barlow were to report the slightest sign of French goodwill.[33] Whether Monroe truly believed that any marked improvement in French policy would make Congress readier for war is problematic. He was, after all, telling Barlow that if the Cadore Letter were honored, London might recall its orders-in-council and thereby remove a major cause for war.[34] He probably did

not believe that either. His best intelligence suggested that neither belligerent would retreat: Britain because she believed herself the aggrieved
party and France because (as Russell had divined) she would do nothing
that London might act on to promote an Anglo-American détente. It
seems fair to conclude that with Congress edging toward war, Monroe
wanted just enough good news from France—or absence of bad news—to
keep that body from being distracted from the main event. At the same
time, he told Barlow not to let Paris assume that an American declaration
of war on Britain would in any way diminish the administration's demands for indemnification.[35]

In exploiting Serurier's instinct to balloon his government's presumed
influence, Monroe knew his man. The envoy promptly conveyed to Paris
the image of France as a major player in a congressional drama where
both belligerents were ostensibly equally capable of writing the script.
Ironically, it escaped him that France was rarely mentioned in the congressional debates. Had he paid closer attention, he might have realized
that in late 1811, its members were so narrowly focused on Britain's
wrongdoing that unless France committed some new outrage of outstanding infamy, it would continue to be largely ignored. Monroe, meanwhile, did what he could to make it stay that way.

Official Paris, though never shy of supposing its importance in the
affairs of other nations, failed to get this message from anything Barlow
had to say. Napoleon was out of town when the American minister arrived and so was Bassano who, except for holding some preliminary talks,
shortly joined his master in Amsterdam, leaving Barlow to hold low-
level talks with Jean-Baptiste Petry. The latter reported that the American
minister had not once hinted that any action by France would affect his
government's readiness to make war. Rather, Petry supposed, the United
States was playing for time, intent on avoiding war with Britain while
hoping to negotiate a treaty by which France would agree to restore its
maritime neutral rights. He warned Bassano that on his return, he could
expect Barlow to lecture him tiresomely on neutral rights issues. Petry
nonetheless shared Serurier's view that France could wield a determining
influence in American councils. To Bassano, he pictured a weary Congress, divided and brinking on disgrace, but capable of being rallied by a
few "amicable measures on our part:" the cession of Florida perhaps or
permission to float a loan in Amsterdam. In any event, he refused to
concede that neutral maritime rights were as important as Barlow made
them out to be.[36] But then, French officials had yet to feel the full force
of Barlow's advocacy.

CHAPTER 15

JOEL BARLOW,
UNDAUNTED OPTIMIST

No one can say for sure whether Napoleon would have signed the commercial treaty Barlow had in hand when, pursuing the emperor's retreating army, he succumbed to pneumonia in the bitter cold of Poland in December 1812. Barlow never quite caught up with the fleeing emperor, but the preliminaries had been agreed to, and Napoleon was reportedly ready to sign both a commercial treaty and a claims convention. But even had Barlow lived to see his treaty completed, it would probably not have weathered the partisan controversy of Madison's wartime presidency. The president's political enemies would surely have labeled it an alliance of sorts and invoked Washington's parting advice against it. And with the war going badly in the spring of 1813, Madison would doubtless have shrunk from touching off a divisive treaty debate in the Senate. At the time Barlow began his mission, however, whatever hope the president had of keeping open the alternative to war seemed to ride on the outcome.

This said, one would hardly guess from the tone and content of Barlow's instructions that Madison expected his emissary to cozen Napoleon into anything resembling a rapprochement. Listed in detail were France's multitudinous offenses against American shipping for which Barlow was to demand full and immediate indemnification. The language was plaintive, argumentative, and unyielding. It painted a picture of unprecedented maritime wickedness for which France was held entirely responsible. And although France could expect commercial opportunities in return for a claims settlement, even here more was asked than offered. At a minimum, Napoleon must loosen his restrictions on imports, lower his tariffs, and generally dredge up the bureaucratic silt that kept American vessels from freely entering and departing French ports. Most emphatically, however, Barlow was to convince the emperor that every French maritime decree affecting neutral commerce since 1806 had not only been damaging but totally unjustified. He was to settle for no less than the return of all U.S. property not yet confiscated and secure indemnification for those Americans whose property had been destroyed by fire or fiat. Either way, the French government was to settle promptly and fully.[1]

Biographer Irving Brant writing of Barlow's mission rightly labels him "Madison's Stubborn Diplomat."[2] Stubbornness, however, only partly describes the man, for Barlow was also the essential pragmatist who from his first week in Paris set himself what he believed was the eminently practical task of negotiating a full-blown commercial treaty. To this end he deliberately put the indemnification issue on hold, later explaining that rather than haggle over past depredations he planned to draw France into an agreement that he hoped would put a halt to future spoliations.[3] With or without an indemnity clause, he was so fixated on making a commercial treaty that by the time he asked Monroe for explicit instructions, he was already drafting articles he hoped Washington would find acceptable.[4] Whether, as Bradford Perkins claims, the French government deliberately enticed him into prolonged negotiations to hide its "unwillingness to settle larger problems,"[5] evidence abounds that Barlow needed no enticement because he saw no other solution to those "larger problems" than to put the remedies within the framework of a treaty.

Strong westerlies favored the *Constitution*'s thirty-four-day passage to Cherbourg, setting a pace Barlow hoped to sustain in Paris. Arriving in the French capital on 19 September, however, he learned that Napoleon had left for Holland that same day. He met only once with the duc de Bassano before he, too, left Paris. He found the foreign minister outwardly friendly and attentive, and appreciated Bassano's promise to show the emperor the envoy's treaty "ideas," many of which he said were new to him.[6] Barlow should not follow him to Holland, however, because the emperor had no fixed headquarters and in any event was expected back in Paris by mid-October. As it turned out, the imperial entourage did not return until early November,[7] and with little to report home, Barlow ordered the *Constitution* to ferry Jonathan Russell to his post across the Channel and settled in for low-level talks with Jean-Baptiste Petry.[8]

The envoy launched his mission in earnest on the afternoon of 10 November when, hearing that Bassano had returned, he called on the foreign minister bearing a note of that date setting forth his major treaty proposals.[9] A formal response was slow in coming.[10] The foreign minister kept asking for more information and expressed surprise, perhaps sincere, at how much he and the emperor had learned about "American affairs" that they had not understood before. His master, he said, accepted the reasoning and conclusions in Barlow's note, but was not yet sure how to "reconcile its principles with his continental system."[11]

What Napoleon had before him was a fully developed prospectus for reviving Franco-American commerce, prefaced by a critique of France's thus far self-defeating decrees, missed opportunities, and mistaken motives, all of which had stood in the way of what should have been—and still could be—a source of material well-being to both countries.[12] American merchants, Barlow noted disapprovingly, had met with extraordinarily high tariffs, constantly shifting municipal regulations, and export requirements for which "all the silk looms of France would not be able to furnish the quantity necessary." Then followed a warning. Now that the United States had fulfilled the "covenant" of the Cadore Letter, it counted on France's becoming a compensatory trade partner. Without the customs revenue derived from duties on European imports, Congress might be forced to repeal the Non-Importation Act which, he argued earnestly, was a form of commercial warfare "more fatal to England & more advantageous to France than any military war between those two nations could be." As matters now stood, France had a timely opportunity to create a permanent clientele for her own manufactures. Then, only in passing did Barlow touch on maritime claims. Now that his government had complied with the Cadore Letter, France should quickly restore American ships and cargoes. For claimants whose property had already been confiscated he proposed a "separate convention" under which payments could be made "in some manner the least onerous to the French treasury," a phrase he doubtless hoped would resonate with a regime whose motto was: pay later if at all. He also offered a solution to the problem of falsified cargo manifests when he wrote that Washington was prepared "to enact and inflict penalties, and agree with the French Government on the marks, signals, and other measures most proper to attain the end."[13] This offer to cooperate in suppressing portside fraud may explain why Napoleon reportedly studied Barlow's note at length and subsequently authorized a treaty negotiation. Barlow, after all, was suggesting that with Washington's blessing French officials might finally find a way to distinguish law-abiding Americans from interloping Britons.

The American minister's first encounter with Napoleon on 17 November left him with mixed feelings. The emperor was gracious, even flattering, but when Barlow voiced hope for a greater understanding of their mutual commercial interests, he picked up echoes of earlier challenges. Napoleon replied that he wished to favor American commerce, "[B]ut on your part you must defend your dignity against my enemies & those of the continent. Wave a flag, and I will do all for you that you can desire." Wisely, Barlow counseled Monroe not to publish this mildly insulting invitation to camaraderie lest U.S. newspapers make "animadversions" that would be unhelpful to him when they got back to France.[14] Privately to Madison, however, he exuded confidence in what he believed were Napoleon's overall good intentions. At the diplomatic audience, he reported, the emperor had announced in a voice loud enough for all to hear that he would respond without delay to Barlow's "interesting" proposals. From this as well as from the friendly remarks of other French dignitaries, he assumed he was about to win not only tariff reductions and free transit for American goods through French entrepots, but also modifications in the licensing system and indemnification for American vessels not restored.[15] A letter he wrote to Mrs. Madison two days later sounded the same optimistic note.[16]

Though convinced that his 10 November note prefigured favorable policy changes, Barlow also caught a glimpse of Napoleon's complacent attitude toward maritime matters. From Bassano he heard the emperor's boast that even without American non-importation his Continental System had already "greatly crippled" British commerce. Moreover, if American vessels flocked to French ports in such numbers as Barlow predicted, the British would simply step up their seizures. Alarmed that Napoleon might decide not to negotiate, Barlow dashed off rebuttals. British commerce, he wrote Bassano, had not been crippled by its loss of European markets. Rather, statistics showed that since the beginning of the continental blockade, Britain had doubled in value what her exports had been to Europe by reaching out to other markets, principally in Latin America and, when not embargoed, in the United States. Only the recent closure of American ports had distressed Britain to the extent the emperor ascribed to his "System."[17] Too, the emperor was mistaken to believe that an increase in France's American commerce would simply increase British depredations. Having remained silent when Petry had earlier voiced the same concern, Barlow now volunteered that his government might authorize armed convoys. He put it to Bassano that if France were to fling open her ports and the resulting commerce proved valuable, Congress would surely act to protect it. Still, Barlow's allusion to convoying had to be tentative if for no other reason than that international law forbade neutral powers to provide their merchantmen with armed escort because it infringed on the right of blockading powers to conduct visit and search.[18] Still, the notion of convoying American traffic in the Atlantic was to have a recurrent appeal, both in Congress and in Paris.

———— ❧ ————

Barlow responded with alacrity when in late December 1811 Bassano announced he was ready to discuss a commercial treaty. As an earnest of good intentions, the American minister suggested they sign a pretreaty agreement by which France would open her ports to certified American cargoes and free such vessels as were still detained.[19] Not unexpectedly, Bassano squirmed at putting his signature on so forthright a statement of intent. There was no need for it, he replied loftily; the emperor had already adopted these principles and the forthcoming treaty would formalize them. When Barlow argued that a signed commitment of this sort would restore the confidence of the American business community, however, Bassano agreed to refer it. The imperial reply came two days later. The emperor, he was told, did not find it "proper" to sign such a document, "but you may notify it to your government, word for word, as if it were signed; for the principles are adopted, and from this day forward they will be in operation."[20]

Barlow took small comfort from oral assurances. One might speculate that Napoleon shied from making a written pledge because it was too much like a treaty but without a *quid pro quo*; or that Barlow may have hoped to obtain the substance of a treaty without negotiating for it. But like others who dealt with Napoleonic France, the envoy suspected he was already skirting a terrain littered with the shards of broken promises and the debris of second thoughts. In this instance, being told that orders had gone out to expedite the legal proceedings against U.S. vessels did not, he knew, guarantee their release. They had not in the past. Nor was he encouraged by Napoleon's blunt refusal to accept certificates of origin as the "only papers" American carriers needed to show. Bassano, who had recently advanced the same view, nonetheless loyally defended licensing as the surest means of shutting out British commodities. If Barlow could propose an effective alternative, the emperor would consider it.[21] Meanwhile, on 11 September Napoleon signed sixty licenses for grain imports, fourteen of them assigned to U.S. carriers.[22] Licensing would remain a problem.

Two months later, Madison echoed his envoy's chagrin at Napoleon's refusal to sign a pretreaty agreement that would have "pledged nothing more than a melioration of formalities as to ownership and origin. . . . The liberation of the remaining Ships & Cargoes could surely have created no difficulty, if any real purpose of friendship or good faith be entertained." As for French licensing, the president continued, it was "a practice that must be abolished, if not by F. by us." Like Barlow, he believed that certificates of origin were an effective alternative.[23]

—————————☙☙☙—————————

Only an incorrigible optimist reading between the dour lines of Bassano's formal reply to his note of 10 November could have seen a basis for negotiation. The rhetoric was somberly familiar: Franco-American commerce was at a standstill not because France restricted it, but because Americans did not respect their flag enough to prevent the British from seizing their merchantmen. Accordingly, any treaty with the United States must "assure the independence of their flag," code words which Barlow must have recognized as meaning measures that would lead to war. Nor did Bassano countenance Barlow's argument that the Trianon tariff had hurt the American trade. American importers had no reason to complain because the burden of higher commodity prices fell on French consumers. It seemed to elude him that the latter would necessarily consume less. Besides, he added, French importers faced the same high rates as did Americans; the tariff did not discriminate.[24]

To anyone less congenitally optimistic Bassano's reply of 27 December would have seemed breezily dismissive. Barlow, however, took it in stride and spoke confidently of the future. Led on, perhaps by earlier conversations in which the critical issues had been muted, he told Madison he had reason to believe that "most if not all the points I have discussed in my note of the 10th November will be accorded." Rather, it worried him not to have been instructed on the finer points of treaty-making. He supposed he was "pursuing" the president's intentions and until he received specific instructions, he said he planned to discuss treaty articles "as if I were specially authorised for that object."[25] William Lee, then acting secretary of legation, gave Madison quite a different impression of Bassano's shattering response. Lee was not acquainted with its details, but he knew enough to write that "the answer to Mr. Barlow's note is not what was expected and most certainly is not what was intended to have been given for many days." He was at a loss to explain why Napoleon had dashed the hopes raised earlier.[26]

In fact, the French foreign office had spent several weeks carefully plotting a course between what Barlow asked for and what it felt could be conceded. Both Petry and Bassano left records of their conversations. Petry was more flexible. He challenged Barlow's complaints where they ran athwart French interests but also heeded arguments he thought were plausible. Thus, while telling Barlow that any reduction of French import duties would wipe out the retail value of current inventories, he ventured to Bassano that a phased reduction of duties might expand the volume of much-needed imports. Again, when Barlow insisted that detained vessels be restored without distinction, Petry reminded him that ships taken in reprisal for the Non-Intercourse Act were beyond recovery. In his report, however, he recommended that all vessels held since 1 November be released forthwith. Petry also urged that a treaty negotiation go forward. If France's American commerce expanded as a result, he argued to Bassano, Congress would have less incentive to lift its Non-Importation Act whose effect, he reminded Bassano, coincided with purposes of the Continental System. France would be ill-served if for want of an alternative trade-partner, the United States lifted its ban on British imports. To keep it in place, he believed Barlow would be satisfied if France were to facilitate the offloading and departure of American vessels, open more French ports for incoming cargoes, and reduce the quantity of silks exporting vessels were required to lade. Even if such measures did not stimulate French-American commerce, they would placate the American maritime community until such time as their government's quarrel with England led to war.[27]

Bassano agreed with Petry's analysis but stepped on his recommendations. Not surprisingly, he echoed the emperor's unflattering judgment that Americans lusting after commercial gain could never be reliable players in his grand scheme to choke off Britain's export trade. Bassano went on to dismiss Barlow's specific complaints. French commercial regulations were not fickle; American shippers had no reason to feel uncertain about them. Tariff levels were not too high, nor did they bear heavily on goods of American production. Requiring American ships to load silks had not flooded the American market; nor were American vessels likely to turn up in greater numbers unless they were able to elude British capture. Only Barlow's mention of convoying evoked a positive response. He wished Petry and Barlow had had something more than "a fugitive conversation" on the subject and told the emperor he would have Serurier sound out Washington.[28] As for the rest, he thought Petry was probably right: Barlow would be satisfied to win a few minor concessions. He doubted, however, that anything France might write into a treaty would induce Congress to move toward war. Barlow himself had not promised such an outcome. Nor could France expect it "from a nation which is always ready to sacrifice its independence and its dignity to its commercial interests." Against this backdrop of distrust and low expectations, Bassano wrote Barlow on 27 December inviting him to open treaty negotiations.

Why Napoleon decided to stage what appeared to be a diplomatic charade Bassano explained to Serurier a few days later. A treaty was not likely to expand commerce, he wrote, but the emperor regarded a negotiation as a way to show goodwill. At some level, he and Barlow might resolve some of American shipowners' minor complaints, but most of their grievances were unfounded and therefore could not be negotiated away. Convoying, however, did hold out a promise of restoring commerce, and he told Serurier to scout its possibilities, albeit unobtrusively. "[A] convoy measure," he wrote, "is the only thing that can effectively protect the commerce of the United States. . . ." Until then, Serurier was to highlight the favors Americans already enjoyed; their certified cargoes arriving "without inquietude in our ports," the formalities "short & simple." Flatter them, too, that France held their new minister in high regard, that Barlow had shown a "very marked spirit of conciliation."[29] In sum, he was to picture a benign France embarking on a round of friendly negotiations whose outcome might hinge on whether the administration saw fit to provide armed protection to its merchant shipping. Despite this instruction, Serurier made no subsequent mention of convoying. If he did not already know it, Monroe may have told him that such protections were impermissible to governments that wished to stay neutral.

Though Barlow wanted to make a good beginning, he brought Bassano up short for repeating the canard that his country had failed to "defend its flag," hotly reminding him that Washington had demanded and received "entire satisfaction" for the attack on the *Chesapeake* and was now standing firm in its demands that London revoke its orders-in-council. Bassano, obviously taken aback, said he intended no reproach but merely meant to describe the unchecked and unpunished depredations committed by the Royal Navy on both sides of the Atlantic. The insult glossed over, the two men turned to the business at hand.[30]

CHAPTER 16

BARLOW FALTERS,
LONDON RETREATS

I f nothing else, Joel Barlow's relentless pursuit of a commercial treaty through the spring and summer of 1812 spoke to the man's energy and resilience. With little encouragement from either Paris or Washington, he threw himself wholeheartedly into this venture, determined to see it through no matter what obstacles others might throw in his way. Without waiting for instructions, he drafted a treaty "projet" that for detail and completeness lacked only the essential prerequisite that it provide for indemnification. Predictably, this oversight did not pass unnoticed in Washington. When the *Constitution* arrived in February with Barlow's early despatches, Monroe flung back a blunt warning that the administration would reject any treaty that failed to hold France accountable for past injuries. Nor, the secretary continued, was it thought advisable at this time to negotiate a commercial treaty, especially if it specified tariff reductions. Given the costs of arming for war, he predicted that Congress would more likely raise tariffs than lower them.[1] Moreover, Monroe found Barlow's treaty projet itself seriously flawed. In April, he sent the envoy a full-dress critique, faulting seven of the proposed articles either for their imprecision or their one-sided favor to France.[2] He directed his heaviest reproof, however, at Barlow's naive supposition that France could be bound to settle spoliation claims at some future time. Such promises were "no adequate security for the attainment of the end," he wrote, and again warned Barlow that if his treaty failed to secure immediate compensation, "you may be assured that it will not be ratified."[3]

In sum, a treaty on the scale Barlow envisioned was not what the administration had in mind and unless its envoy firmly nailed down a French commitment to indemnify he might as well come home.

On 17 January 1812, not yet aware of impending censure, Barlow charged boldly into the diplomatic arena brandishing the draft treaty he hoped would win the emperor's approval in the space of a few weeks. Besides affirming the neutral rights principles of the Franco-American Convention of 1800, he proposed nine new articles, some merely "regulatory," others he proudly hailed as "strangers to all treaties & will be new in the law of nations." His most novel would do away with the concept of contraband, the name given to illicit cargo which, he argued, had been downwardly defined in recent times to mean mostly arms and ammunition which, of course, the United States did not export on a competitive basis and should be got rid of because it was a pretext for harassment. An enlightened emperor would surely agree to jettison this outmoded pretext for plundering the innocent traffic of neutral carriers.[4]

Of some thirty articles, the one calling for tariff reduction topped his list, although only a dogged commitment to the free flow of commerce can explain why he tackled an issue so sensitive to government finance.[5] The odds against his putting this article across were imposing. Not only would lowering duties produce less revenue, but to freeze them by treaty would mean forgoing the option of raising them when future exigencies might require more revenue. Also it required a gambler's act of faith to believe that lower duties would produce greater returns by increasing the volume of dutiable goods. But even if Barlow were to succeed in beating down the prohibitive levels of the Trianon tariff, he had no guarantees his own government would agree to reduce its own. Treasury Secretary Gallatin, he knew, had recently reported a shortfall in customs receipts which made it unlikely the administration would entertain a treaty further curtailing its principal source of revenue. Against such odds, Barlow persisted in calling for lower tariffs to the end of his mission except, of course, when it stood in the way of his larger objectives. Thus, when Bassano pushed this cherished objective off the table in March 1812, Barlow made no attempt to snatch it back. By then, believing that other elements of his negotiation were coming to a head, he expected to have a signed treaty in hand within a few days. The pragmatist in him momentarily prevailed; he was prepared to take what he could get. And because other articles appeared to be acceptable, he was holding the *Hornet* at Cherbourg.[6]

Barlow's hope for a quick treaty-signing died a lingering death. Napoleon saw his "projet" in late February but made no comment; then more weeks passed before Bassano, over-worked and weary of Barlow's importuning, asked the emperor to name someone else to deal with him.[7] Bassano's first choice was Hauterive who, he hinted shrewdly, could best handle Barlow's disappointment if the emperor decided not to press for "immediate results."[8] Rather, in late April Barlow learned that the duc de Dalberg, a French councillor of state, had been appointed to treat with him.[9] Ruefully, he admitted that events had conspired against him; in this instance he knew that Napoleon's approaching showdown with Russia had created a diplomatic whirlwind which had swept aside everything in the French foreign office not connected with it.[10] Bassano had, indeed, been busy. In preparation for the Russian campaign, he had spent the month of March negotiating and then shoring up alliances with both Prussia and Austria. To Barlow he explained apologetically how his ongoing preoccupation with the Russian crisis meant that he must depute their treaty negotiations to an underling.[11]

His treaty hopes temporarily sidelined, Barlow found other reasons to be concerned. In mid-March the *Moniteur* reported a *senatus consultum* during which Napoleon had mentioned that the Berlin and Milan decrees no longer applied to American vessels. Fair enough, Barlow told Bassano, but he had hoped for a more declarative statement. He flinched when the foreign minister replied sourly that the emperor was reluctant to state outright that the United States was "out of the gripe of those decrees," because he had learned that Congress intended to permit the landing of British goods contracted for before the Non-Importation Act went into effect. Flustered, Barlow explained as best he could why Congress might feel compelled to uphold the sanctity of prior contracts, but to no avail. "I have since heard," he told Monroe, "that the Emperor is not well satisfied," adding caustically that Frenchmen were so cynical they saw loopholes in the law where none was intended.[12] He also noted the seizure of a U.S. merchantman, the *Belisarius,* whose detention raised the appalling possibility the French decrees had been revived against American shipping. He warned Bassano that if his countryman believed this was true, it would cause a "sensation," but was more or less reassured when the minister explained that the *Belisarius* had arrived with more cargo than was listed on her manifest. Customs officials would restore the part that was certified.[13]

The smooth course Barlow hoped to chart for his negotiations ran into still more rough weather when he found himself forced to dispel French suspicions of a breakthrough in Washington's dealings with London. Napoleon, on reading a piece translated from the *London Courier* of 10 March, asked whether there was any truth to the writer's speculation that Augustus Foster would arrange an Anglo-American settlement based on terms of the failed Monroe-Pinkney treaty.[14] Someone, perhaps Bassano, may have pointed out that although the 1806 treaty had been rejected for want of a guarantee against impressment, it had promised to resolve other issues. Petry, taking Barlow aside, hinted that Monroe, now strategically positioned as secretary of state, might harbor enough "paternal tenderness" for the once-discarded treaty to revive it. Impatiently, Barlow dismissed the rumor. Fuming over delays in his own negotiation, he told Petry there was no evidence whatever that Washington had made any progress in dealing with Foster. Nothing in Madison's January 16 message, he pointed out, remotely suggested an accommodation, much less a resurrection of the ill-fated treaty. He reminded the Frenchman that the British navy still searched American vessels for deserters and even now, London demanded absurdly that Washington force France to revoke her decrees as they applied to the carriers of all nations. Petry was persuaded. On rereading Madison's message, he told Bassano that he saw no sign of an opening toward London. Moreover, too little time had elapsed since the message to credit rumors of diplomatic forwardness on that front. From what was known, Foster's mission had broken down completely.[15]

Uncertainty over the status of the Berlin and Milan decrees refused to go away. Although the emperor in his *senatus consultum* had confirmed the American exemption, Bassano managed to introduce an unsettling element of doubt. Addressing the Senate on 10 March, Bassano cited the decrees by name and spoke earnestly of the Emperor's unrelenting determination to confiscate any vessel tainted by contact with Britain, her tax collectors, or her naval forces. Unfortunately, he failed to mention the American exemption. When Barlow angrily pointed out that London would take the omission as proof that Americans were still exposed, Bassano, to his credit, tried to set the record straight: he apologized to Barlow and wrote Serurier not to let the American public be misled by what it read of his speech in the British journals. He had not cited the American exemption to the Senate, he explained lamely, because it was not germane; but in any event, Washington must be assured that American shipping did remain exempt from the decrees and was "every day more favored by the French government."[16]

Barlow had another reason to bristle at the untimeliness of the foreign minister's gaffe. He had just sent Jonathan Russell "additional proof" of decretal non-enforcement, citing some seven instances in which U.S. ships technically in violation of the French decrees had been allowed to unload and depart.[17] Now, because Bassano had fecklessly failed to mention the American exception, he was sure the British ministry would draw the opposite conclusion. He did not have long to wait. From London on 21 April came a ministerial pronouncement, soon referred to familiarly as the Prince Regent's decree, which seized on Bassano's undifferentiated defense of the French decrees as reason enough to justify retaining the orders-in-council. Barlow bitterly chided the foreign minister for his "unaccountable reserve." Still, through his irritation, he spotted a passage in the British decree that seemed to open a window of diplomatic opportunity. It promised that if the French emperor were to "publish an authentic act expressly and unconditionally repealing the Berlin and Milan decrees, the Orders in Council, including that of January 7, 1807, should be wholly and absolutely revoked." Grasping this offer for what it was worth, Barlow urged Bassano to come forward with just such an "authentic act." Long overdue in any case, a formal statement of repeal would undercut London's latest rationale for retaining its orders and serve to focus the gathering wrath of the American people on the hypocrisy of their true oppressor. What better way to single out Britain as the principal ravager of neutral rights than for France to renounce her decrees "unclogged with conditions, and unshaded with Doubts, as to the past, the present and the future?" Almost as an afterthought, he suggested that Americans would be even more gratified (and presumably march even more resolutely into battle) if France were also to sign an indemnities convention and a commercial treaty.[18]

Waiting for a reply, Barlow's hopes for a speedy negotiation sank even further. Delay, he knew, was inherent in Dalberg's appointment.[19] But now came Monroe's chastening enjoinder that he backtrack and pick up on the indemnities issue. He must have groaned audibly on reading the secretary's stony admonition that he sign no treaty without securing an ironclad French pledge to indemnify. A letter from Madison of 24 February posted the same warning: no indemnities, no treaty. Without "payments from the [French] Treasury or negotiable substitutes," Madison had written, "there can be neither cordiality nor confidence here . . . nor any formal Treaty on any subject."[20] Barlow replied contritely that he would comply but allowed that engaging Paris on maritime claims at this point would be "dull work, hard to begin and difficult to pursue." Monroe's reproof, he confessed, had "somewhat abated" his zeal. He supposed he had misunderstood the president's wishes. "I am not certain, since the receipt of your letters . . . that I shall consent to any treaty," he wrote Monroe, but added unrepentantly, "I have little doubt that their intention is to offer me one that, under all circumstances, I should think ought to be accepted."[21] His message to Washington was painfully clear: to insist on indemnification at this point would lessen the likelihood of any settlement.

Again, as to why Barlow strayed so far from his original instructions, one might speculate that perhaps some unrecorded conversation either with Madison or Monroe before he left Washington had led him to believe he had greater latitude in carrying out those instructions than lay in their wording. More likely, his abundant self-confidence told him that if France embraced his vision of a treaty so richly rewarding to the commerce of both parties, indemnification would follow as a matter of goodwill. Whatever the explanation, Barlow's despatches now bore a strained quality. Dalberg, he reported, was "an amiable, intelligent man, well disposed, but bound very straight by instructions." Still, he added: "I believe that a treaty may be got out of him that will be worth accepting." Moreover, Dalberg had intimated a readiness to discuss indemnification. How ready he did not say and, as had happened before, external events overtook his preoccupation with treaty clauses.[22]

Having asked Bassano for an "authentic act" revoking the Berlin and Milan decrees, what Barlow got back was an authentic act of Napoleonic deception—an imperial decree so transparently falsified as to astonish contemporaries and leave later historians grimacing at its cynicism. Best described as the phony St. Cloud Decree, the deceit lay in its bearing the date of 28 April 1811. It postulated that a full year before, the emperor, pleased to discover that the United States had complied with the terms of the Cadore Letter, had decreed from his St. Cloud residence that "the Decrees of Berlin and Milan are definitively and from the date of last November 1st considered as non avenue with regard to American vessels." On its face, this was the "authentic act" of revocation American diplomats had ardently sought for more than a year. Yet here was Bassano telling Barlow with all apparent sincerity that the document he requested had been sent to Jonathan Russell a year earlier, insisting that it must be tucked away in the files of the U.S. legation. Feigning perplexity, he exclaimed to Barlow: "I cannot dissimulate to you my surprise at the doubt you express . . . on the revocation of the decrees of Berlin and Milan," and promised to give him a copy of the decree in question. Barlow later told Monroe that when Bassano handed it to him, "I made no comment on the strange manner in which it had been so long concealed from me." The foreign minister did admit that the decree had never been published, but one lie leading to another, he assured Barlow that copies had been sent to both Russell and Serurier. The American envoy replied grimly that he had no such decree in his archives; he had never heard of it, and would Bassano please send him a copy, officially.[23] Not deceived for a moment by its fraudulent date, he wrote Madison he was sure it "was created last week . . . in consequence of my note of the 1st of May."[24] The president later agreed that the St. Cloud Decree would be an "everlasting reproach" to the French government.[25] Even today, though long known to have been manufactured in May of 1812, this document is filed in the French archives among holdings for April 1811.[26]

Probing for motives behind the St. Cloud Decree, Henry Adams suggests that Napoleon, about to leave Paris for his fateful campaign against Russia, "could not entirely disregard the wishes of the United States."[27] Adams may be right, for except as a bone thrown to appease Washington, the decree had no apparent tactical purpose. One can readily imagine Napoleon casually granting Barlow's latest request as he rode off to war, glad to put behind him the annoyance of dealing with the hyperactive envoy of a minor power. Barlow, however, thought the decree a subtle piece of calculation; that Napoleon had read the Prince Regent's decree to mean that war between the United States and Britain was inevitable no matter what action France took. Announcing his own repeal might not hasten an American declaration of war, but neither would it prevent war because news of it would come too late for London to react to it, repeal its orders, and thereby save the peace. Calculated or not, Barlow set out to prove Napoleon wrong in the element of timing. If Russell were to pass the word swiftly, he believed London might still repeal its orders in time to prevent war. Accordingly, he dispatched a copy to London posthaste, warning Russell to observe the utmost secrecy lest the French emperor recant on realizing that he had furnished the means of preventing a war he believed inevitable.[28]

Irving Brant finds Barlow duplicitous in telling Bassano that proof of French repeal would hasten a U.S. declaration of war although, in fact, he hoped to prevent war by providing Russell with the means of persuading London to repeal its orders-in-council.[29] Duplicitous or not, Barlow could hardly have resisted playing out what he must have seen as a win-win opportunity. If Britain chose to ignore the St. Cloud Decree, he truly believed his countrymen would be more united for war. Better yet, if London took the decree to heart and repealed its orders, peace would prevail. In either event, he urged Russell to put the essential question: would London, in light of France's definitive renunciation of her antineutral decrees, revoke her own? How, he wondered, could the Perceval ministry refuse? Later he told Monroe he had done all he could, "to remove the cause of war" and if London refused to respond positively, his countrymen would at least have "the moral advantage."[30]

Despite Barlow's high expectations of it, the St. Cloud Decree played only a cameo role in the British ministry's decision to suspend the orders-in-council. What ultimately prevailed was the long and severe economic depression that had slowly but now decisively energized political forces in Parliament in favor of their recall. Napoleon's preposterous démarche barely stirred the waters of credulity. One historian, summing up the views of his profession, remarks that the St. Cloud Decree was "patently absurd and fooled no one."[31] Certainly not the British. In London, for example, *The Statesman* of 22 May, noting Russell's presentation of the decree, dismissed it as no more than "a paper, which probably never existed, and which, without doubt, has been ante-dated."[32] When on 23 June Lord Castlereagh announced the suspension of the orders of 1807 and 1809, he mentioned the St. Cloud Decree as a pretext, then dismissed it as not having satisfied earlier conditions, and went on without further explanation to say simply that the ministry had decided to re-establish commercial intercourse with neutrals "upon its accustomed principles."[33]

Left unspoken was Britain's severe economic distress, which the historian Bradford Perkins convincingly argues was the major determinant in the ministry's decision. After years of weathering Napoleon's Continental System and America's intermittent trade sanctions, her export position had weakened to the point where she was suffering thousands of business failures and widespread unemployment. For more than a year, the ministry's political foes had blamed the orders, if not for causing, at least for prolonging the distress. Goaded by petitions from distraught merchants, Parliament was on the brink of overriding the ministry. Then, on 11 May the assassination of Spencer Perceval threw the political scene into a brief turmoil. The murder of the prime minister at the hands of a deranged malcontent, Perkins finds, probably delayed the decision to act. Before the ministry's political enemies could renew their attack, Castlereagh announced the government's decision to suspend the orders, but stipulated their reinstatement if the United States did not lift its ban on British imports within fourteen days of receiving notice.

The ministry's retreat is best remembered for having come too late. Congress had already declared war five days earlier, a coincidence that cost those British merchants who, believing the ministry's concession to have lifted non-intercourse, promptly despatched vessels to the American market only to suffer the wartime losses their government had so recently inflicted on neutral Americans.

Never averse to second guessing, Henry Adams speculates that if Jonathan Russell had been a more perceptive diplomat, someone like William Pinkney, he might have warned Madison of the ministry's impending retreat and thereby delayed the president's war message.[34] But even taking into account the slowness of transatlantic communication, such speculation seems to serve little purpose except to illustrate the difficulty diplomats experience when they try to foresee where governmental bodies will come out on matters of war and peace. If Russell missed signs of imminent repeal, so did his counterpart, Augustus John Foster, fail to foresee that the Warhawks were about to carry the day in Congress.

French officials, for their part, doubted that London had retreated far enough and hoped that Washington would notice the British ministry's apparent failure to include Fox's Blockade of 1806 in its suspension order. They were fairly sure the Madison administration would balk at this omission. If not, Serurier was to warn that unless London offered proof of having abandoned its 1806 blockade, the emperor might be obliged to revive his original counterthrust, the Berlin Decree.[35] For a few weeks in July 1812, the tattered dispute as to whether Fox's Blockade had been left intact seemed about to come full circle. In Paris Barlow squared off, promptly telling Petry that he had from Russell Castlereagh's assurances that the ministry's recent suspension had "embraced the blockade of the 16th of May 1806, which having been merged with them in subsequent Orders in Council is now considered to be extinguished with them."[36] Petry, however, after reviewing Pinkney's earlier failed effort to determine whether Fox's Blockade had been superseded, concluded that even now London's position remained "vague and evasive."[37] Only with news reaching Paris that the Madison administration had decided to fight its already declared war for other reasons were the parties spared another round of rancor. Thus when, the following October, Serurier loyally delivered the Napoleon's threat to revive the Berlin Decree, Monroe barely blinked.[38]

CHAPTER 17

Co-belligerency and a
Diplomatic Breakthrough

G reat events were afoot everywhere but in Paris that spring. Napoleon was off to Russia for a calamitous rendezvous with des-
tiny. London was offering a self-interested reprieve to those it
had victimized on the high seas. And in Washington, the Warhawks were
about to restore the nation's honor and take Canada if they could. In
Paris, however, Joel Barlow could only wait and wonder how these events
might affect his mission.

Bassano when he left for Warsaw sometime in late May 1812 made
clear the American minister was to stay behind and continue talks with
Dalberg.[1] Though Barlow doubted he would make little progress toward
completing a treaty, he exulted in London's suspension of its orders-in-
council and claimed modest credit for having acted in time for Russell to
put the St. Cloud Decree to the use he intended. The result, he told
Monroe, was "far more favorable than I expected." On the down side, he
worried that London's retreat might cause Napoleon to lose interest in
making any treaty at all.[2] Mindful of this, he hoped to persuade the
French government that Britain's olive branch had not poked them in
the eye. To Bassano he pictured the ministry's action as a victory for
freedom of the seas, vindicating America's defense of her flag and, most
important, opening fresh opportunities for commerce. Now that neutral
shipping was no longer menaced by the Royal Navy, French manufactures
were free to flow across the Atlantic in exchange for much-needed American raw materials. Make a commercial treaty now, he urged, and France

would snatch the U.S. market away from her enemy. Both Petry in Paris and Serurier in Washington thought they saw the same opportunities.[3]

Then came news that Congress had declared war, an upending of events, he told Bassano, that gave even greater force to his arguments for a commercial treaty.[4] All too aware of Monroe's insistence on indemnification, Barlow began to draft a long note linking the two objectives. Provision for past property losses, he wrote, must either "precede or accompany the treaty in question," whereupon he listed claims against every French decree from that of Berlin to that of Rambouillet.[5] Had he seen Bassano's letter to Serurier written a few weeks before, he would have realized how slim were his near-term chances of concluding either a commercial treaty or a claims convention. Though some of it was persiflage, the foreign minister made a telling point when he described Barlow as obstinately delusional to believe that a mere treaty could restore a commerce so irretrievably thinned out by the Royal Navy. The American was also devious, he told Serurier, in touting commercial benefit to both parties when his real goal was to secure greater advantages for his own countrymen. Any reduction of duties, for example, would principally benefit those Americans who were actively engaged in carrying cargoes between European ports. American vessels are everywhere, he wrote. "Their flag is the best known, the most commonly used in our seas. The advantages they would obtain [from a commercial treaty] would give still greater activity to their commerce." Serurier must make it known that if treaty negotiations lagged, it was because France had to consult her own interests.[6]

Equally ill-omened, had Barlow been privy to this letter, Serurier was to make no promises to indemnify. The potential payout, Bassano told him, would be excessive. Besides, the principle of just reprisal was at stake. If pressed, he might hint at a possible arrangement in the future. As for himself, Bassano wrote that he intended to "put off the question with M. Barlow as much as will be possible." Dalberg, too, had instructions not to discuss indemnification.[7] If the administration complained of the delays in treaty-making, Serurier should lay the blame on the unexpected "innovations" in Barlow's treaty projet which went too far beyond the principles embodied in the now-expired Franco-American Convention of 1800 and therefore "could not be lightly decided." As a softener, he enclosed a list of vessels recently freed, together with the emperor's promise of greater favors if Americans took firmer measures to protect their trade with France. This last was a reminder that Barlow had talked of armed convoys, but nothing had been heard of them since.[8] Even as he cited ironclad legal grounds for resisting American damage claims, Bassano told Serurier that France might resolve the issue by redrawing the western boundary of Louisiana so as cede the United States an additional fifteen million acres, her claimants to be paid from subsequent land sales. This proposal for an *ex post facto* add-on to the Louisiana Purchase was twice blessed. With a bit of cartographic enlargement, Paris might not only settle the nettlesome boundary question but also discharge a financial liability it would not openly admit to. Bassano doubted Washington would accept this scheme but told Serurier to run it by them. In the end, nothing came of it; Serurier never reported it back.[9]

The idea of paying off American claims in the currency of New World acreage was not entirely new. The previous December a high Spanish official had approached Barlow with the suggestion that for roughly two million dollars France might redefine the western boundary of Louisiana in such a way as to augment the original purchase by six million acres. American claimants would be indemnified from subsequent land sales up to the amount of forty-two million francs, thereby liquidating all maritime claims against both France and Spain. Although Barlow had refused to discuss the specifics of this proposal with either French or Spanish officials, he told Madison that both parties seemed sincere and the moment opportune. The draft convention he forwarded was remarkable in several respects. It admitted that the Treaty of San Ildefonso by which Spain had "retroceded" Louisiana to France in 1800 had not clearly defined its western boundary and proposed to expand it with a "supplimentary article." Like the Adams-Onis Treaty of 1819, the northern boundary was to extend westward along the 42nd parallel to the Pacific. Unlike that later treaty, however, which started its south-to-north run from the Sabine River in present-day Louisiana, the draft Barlow had in hand would have started the line from the mouth of the Rio Grande, in short, included Texas and made the Mexican War at least problematical. Nothing came of this overture, however: the Madison papers for this period contain no evidence of a response.[10] Quite possibly, the president was put off by its rather complicated and dubious financial arrangements.

On the eve of America's declaration of war, the Berlin and Milan decrees still refused to go away. In May Barlow heard from detained American captains that both decrees had been cited in the recent capture of their vessels. No one, he learned later, had notified the commanders of French corsairs of the American exemption. Navy Minister Denis Decrès admitted as much to Bassano and offered to post new instructions if His Majesty so ordered.[11] America's entry to the war made it unnecessary.

Momentarily stalled on the larger issues of his mission, Barlow, like his predecessor, did what he could to relieve the distress of stranded American seamen. They were often robbed and left destitute by their French captors, he complained to Bassano, "stripped of their larder, belongings and instruments of navigation." Others had been imprisoned when, as often happened, American seamen pressed into service aboard a British vessel were later jailed when the French captured it. Worse, he pointed out, British prisoners often received daily allowances from charitable subscriptions in England whereas the Americans who shared their confinement received nothing. The American captive, he wrote, "suffers all the calamities of the British prisoner, without sharing his advantages; and to add to the horror of his situation, he has before his eyes the despair of ever being exchanged."[12] Although Barlow, unlike Armstrong, made a concerted effort to rescue jailed American seamen, his appeals for their release began to be heard only after the United States had become a more active belligerent.

French treatment of American seamen, however, was not nearly as shocking as the French navy's torching of American vessels intercepted en route to Spain and Portugal that spring. News of these burnings at sea could not have come at a worse time. For Serurier, it meant facing a public newly outraged at France at the very moment Congress was poised to declare war on Britain. For Barlow, it meant adding more entries to the long list of damage claims, a list that already held France accountable for similar attacks during Armstrong's watch. Now, with reports of more such incidents, he warned Petry that unless France called a halt and agreed to indemnify, Congress might show its teeth.[13] Petry, who needed no persuasion, cautioned Bassano that with Congress preparing for war against England, this was not the time for France to give further offense. The inexplicable burning of U.S. vessels at sea joined with news of Barlow's inability to conclude a treaty might push it into declaring war against both powers.[14]

Up to a point, Petry was right. Members of Congress did react angrily, furious that Napoleon had apparently posted a squadron in the eastern Atlantic with orders to burn all neutral carriers within its reach and, inevitably, some members vowed to revisit the issue of declaring war on

France as well. Madison, too, observed that unless France gave redress, Congress might conclude that "a double war, is the shortest road to peace."[15] Whether Napoleon deliberately ordered this attack on American shipping or merely allowed it to happen is difficult to determine. Henry Adams writes that the French squadron sailing from Nantes in January had "orders to destroy all neutral ships bound to or from an enemy's port," but curiously cites as his source Napoleon's order to Marshall Davoust to seize colonial goods in Swedish Pomerania(!)[16] If the French emperor deliberately ordered ships burned without judicial process, it may have been because he regarded those who supplied enemy forces in an active theater of war deserving of more summary punishment than those caught sneaking British goods through less critical parts of his continental blockade. One might also factor in Napoleon's monumental contempt for Americans' capacity to take abuse. Having often intimated that they were too cowardly to make war on Britain, he could assume they would not declare war on France over a few burned merchantmen. And if they ever screwed up their courage to the point of declaring war on Britain, they would surely recognize the logic of destroying ships caught trading with a common enemy.

Petry, significantly alarmed, warned Bassano in late July that Congress would hold France accountable "for having burned their vessels at sea," and while he was at it added such other French offenses as "the arrest and imprisonment of their seamen [and] the hauteur and disdain with which we receive their remonstrances and demands for justice." From Petry this was strong language, but as usual laced with suggestions for remedial action, and they ran the gamut. Now that the United States had declared war, he urged that France stop seizing American vessels altogether, welcome American privateers, do away with the equal-value export requirement, and permit the export of commodities other than silks.[17] Whether, as Irving Brant suggests, this outpouring of advice was the bid of an ambitious underling to usurp Dalberg's nominal primacy, Petry's frequent meetings with Barlow that summer and the letters he sent to both Dalberg and Bassano suggest that he was genuinely alarmed and sincerely wished to keep a bad situation from worsening.[18] When, for example, Dalberg had a particularly frosty meeting with Barlow, Petry gave him a word-for-word account of the American minister's latest outburst. Barlow had asked him rhetorically: "Do the English treat us worse than you? They capture our vessels by virtue of their orders in council— and you, you capture and burn ours by virtue of the Berlin and Milan decrees which you say no longer exist—You violate maritime rights which you demand we make respected and [demand] that we make war on England who also violates them."[19] The source of this explosion, Petry explained, was the emperor's recently announced dictum that Americans would get "all the commercial advantages they desire" if they declared war with Britain. Because news of the war declaration had not yet arrived, Barlow had rejoined bitterly that "under that condition, there will be no treaty."[20]

By late August Barlow was closing with Dalberg on crucial issues but had heard nothing from Bassano. When he told Petry he was "cruelly wounded" by the silence from Vilna, he doubtless overstated his frustration, counting on Petry to retail it to Napoleon's headquarters from whence to evoke some sign that he was not negotiating in a vacuum. As a bearer of woe, Petry did not disappoint. To Dalberg he quoted Barlow as saying of Bassano: "I have had nothing from the Minister for four months, nothing (he told me) but a single letter on the subject of a blind seaman about whom I had written so long before that I had forgotten about him. He promised me back in January in the most positive manner that the treaty would be made within a few days and the indemnities disposed of to our satisfaction. Now six and a half months have passed and nothing is finished . . . I am always criticized for complaining—[but] Can I see our vessels detained, our vessels burned, our seamen imprisoned . . . without making representations?"[21] Whether Petry realized he was being used to rachet up pressure on Vilna, he told Barlow that little could be done while the emperor was campaigning. Unmollified, Barlow grumbled that distance was no excuse: "Once war is declared, a decision is soon given and transmitted."[22] At the moment, however, Petry had it right; whatever promises Napoleon had in mind, he was too busy fighting Russians to think about showering Americans with concessions.

Until news arrived that Congress had declared war, Barlow's treaty talks were hung up on Dalberg's insistence that American vessels import only American produce and not touch at British ports en route home. Because no treaty could keep Americans from peacetime trading with the British, Dalberg appeared to be stringing out the negotiation until U.S. entry to the war made banning such commerce a matter of joint concern. In fact, he had Bassano's word that no treaty would take effect until the United States had declared war, at which time the emperor would confer other commercial favors. It was this "condition"—the contingency of declaring war—to which Barlow had retorted angrily: "there will be no treaty."

As for resisting Barlow's demands for indemnification, Dalberg also had full-dress instructions. He was to argue that France owed nothing for vessels seized under the Berlin Decree because its enforcement took place in French ports where municipal regulations gave it legal sanction. Nor could France be held financially liable for seizures under the Milan Decree which, though it entailed captures on the high seas, had served to enforce Americans' own embargo legislation. Thereafter, France had rightfully detained vessels in reprisal for the confiscatory Section 3 of the Non-Intercourse Act. In sum, Bassano had furnished Dalberg with seamless arguments for avoiding any serious talk of indemnities.[23] Until the United States entered the war, delay clearly remained the order of the day.

As they got down to business, Barlow asked what had become of his original treaty proposals. Not a morning passed, Dalberg recorded, without his being importuned for a contre-projet. Gradually, Barlow wore him down to the point where Dalberg asked if he might offer the release of U.S. vessels seized before the French decrees were known. Bassano reminded him brusquely to focus on "commercial ties" and leave other matters to the future.[24] It was during these preliminaries that Napoleon had announced (via de Sussy) that if the United States entered the war, Americans would be accorded "all the commercial advantages they could desire." This prompted Dalberg to ask exactly what advantages he could tell Barlow to expect. The American envoy had pressed him on this point.[25] Bassano replied stiffly that Americans must first declare war; only then would they know the extent of the emperor's generosity. He was more concerned, he wrote, by Barlow's intemperate reaction to the burning of American vessels which, he insisted, had nothing to do with the Berlin and Milan decrees. Such "unjust suspicions" troubled him, he continued, because they were certain to have an adverse effect on Washington. With Napoleon absent in the field, however, the foreign minister could do little more than urge that Barlow be reminded of the positive aspects of the emperor's conduct.[26]

Delayed, perhaps, by rumors that Congress had declared war, Barlow's magnum opus on indemnities dated 5 June did not reach Dalberg until mid-July and was not forwarded to Bassano until 1 August. When the rumors were substantiated in mid-August, Barlow again pressed to know what "additional" concessions Napoleon had in mind. This time, Bassano merely told Dalberg not to let Barlow get his hopes up: the emperor was

occupied with more pressing matters. In fact, what mattered most to
Napoleon in August 1812 were the Russians who, having denied him a
military victory in Poland, were shamefully retreating eastward with no
sign they intended to admit defeat. As the emperor forged toward Smo-
lensk, his foreign minister marked time by harping on Barlow's diplomatic change of pace. On first contact, he recalled to Dalberg, he and
the American minister had talked exclusively about commercial matters,
agreeing that indemnification was an "accessory" issue. Now, Barlow had
inexplicably thrust these damage claims "au premier ligne." As for Barlow's long indemnity note of 5 June, Bassano thought it "acerbic," and
again told Dalberg to deny grounds for indemnification. He wanted to
hear no more on the subject, he snapped, although Barlow might be
informed, but not in writing, that "the business of indemnities will not
be lost to view & that legitimate claims will be examined." He still meant
later.[27]

———— ∞∞∞ ————

In mid-August, the log-jam in Paris began to break up when Dalberg
came forward with specific treaty clauses. He explained to Bassano why
he believed he could no longer hold the American envoy at bay. Now that
the United States had entered the war, he wrote, delay was fraught with
peril. Because Barlow threatened to report his failed mission to Washington, he was convinced that Congress would explode in anger on learning
of its minister's fruitless effort to negotiate a treaty. Already incensed by
the recent attacks on American shipping, it might well declare war on
France unless it had some word of diplomatic progress.[28] His contre-
projet, he hoped, would reach Washington in time to keep Congress from
taking any precipitate action. What he offered Barlow was, in fact, fairly
innocuous: to renew certain sections of the Convention of 1800 and permit Americans to bring in items of their own production plus whatever
other cargoes were licensed. France, of course, would continue to confiscate British goods found on American vessels, but might agree to waive
duties on cargoes in transit. Six other articles, lifted from a harmless
commercial treaty the United States had signed with Prussia in 1799, related mostly to legal rights the parties would accord each other's na-
tionals.[29]

Like a long distance runner getting his second wind, Barlow seized
eagerly on Dalberg's contre-projet. With scarcely a backward glance, he
dropped altogether the "new principles" he had proposed in January. Nor

did he voice any objection to working from the text of the Convention of 1800.[30] But to serve his own purposes, he seized on Dalberg's opening to spell out some of the safeguards he believed necessary to protect American property. Hereafter, he insisted, France must agree to detain only those vessels that bore forged papers or had violated a legal blockade; and their owners must have the right to sell cargoes freely or be allowed to store and re-export such goods as were inadmissible. Unfortunately, he also suggested revisiting the tariff issue, once more testifying to his abiding belief that a brighter future for French-American commerce depended on nothing so much as lowering them.[31]

Dalberg replied cautiously. Because the emperor had promised additional concessions, he would respond more fully when he had them in hand. If this were meant to slow the pace Barlow had set, he need not have bothered. Barlow himself had furnished ample grounds for delay. By asking permission for American vessels to carry cargoes between French-controlled ports, he invited the Frenchman's offputting response that he would have to seek instruction on this point as well. Too, higher authority would have to weigh Barlow's request for reducing tariffs, although Dalberg expressed doubt they would agree.[32] His response, in short, clearly implied that if the American minister insisted on bringing up matters he should have known would be controversial, there would be no early signing.

By late August, Dalberg had a fairly clear picture of where the negotiation was headed. Barlow, he believed, could probably be talked out of his "tariff and transit" clauses, leaving his government's demand for indemnification the only major obstacle. To get around it, he appeared to rely on Barlow's ingenuity and on this score was not disappointed. On the 27th, he reported that the American minister had just returned from five or six days in the country where it was known he had discussed the indemnities issue with "a person of confidence."[33] Without doubt, this individual was Daniel Parker, a wealthy American merchant-expatriate and former Barlow business partner whose riverside estate on the Seine was a familiar gathering place for American businessmen.[34] Equally certain, here in late August, Barlow and Parker hatched the "secret" plan by which France would "indemnify" individual American claimants by selling them import licenses guaranteed to show a profit. The licensees were to be granted an eight-month period during which they might import commodities at pre-Trianon tariff levels. To his credit, Barlow insisted that no distinction be made between licensees whose losses had occurred before and after the Cadore Letter which meant that France, too, had a stake in secrecy insofar as its acceptance of this condition would admit claims for property seized when the Berlin and Milan decrees were in full force. By rewarding individual licensees rather than the claimant population as a whole, the plan offered no immediate compensation to those claimants who, for whatever reason, were unable to obtain the gilt-edged licenses. The latter, however, were not overlooked. The plan also stipulated that they would be indemnified from a fund derived from the sale of the licenses themselves.

Barlow orchestrated his "indemnities" plan with creative ambiguity, at first taunting Dalberg to use his imagination. Surely the French negotiator could think of ways to indemnify Americans at little cost to the imperial treasury. It was not up to him to make suggestions, but Dalberg must certainly have picked up various indemnity proposals that were being floated by prominent members of the American business community. When this approach proved too subtle—Dalberg mistakenly supposed Barlow had the cession of Florida in mind—the American envoy put on a showy display of terminal frustration. His mission had virtually ended, he told Dalberg. Having failed to obtain indemnification, he had no reason to stay longer. Simultaneously, he loosed a barrage of similar complaints at Petry who, he knew, would promptly relay them to Bassano. Only then, after urging Dalberg to open his mind to easy solutions while voicing his own despair at finding them, did he come forward with the "plan." Even then, he tried to distance himself from its authorship by leading Dalberg to believe that it came from the American business community at large. Eventually, Dalberg agreed to enclose a copy of the plan, suggestively undated and unsigned, in a despatch he sent to Vilna on 8 September.[35]

Bassano had mixed reactions to these latest developments. He more or less sanctioned Dalberg's taking an initiative but shared the latter's inclination to apply the brakes. Whether from bureaucratic timidity or distrust of his negotiator's judgment or merely a wish to keep matters from spinning out of control while his emperor was otherwise occupied, he instructed Dalberg to consult with his ministerial colleague, Collin de Sussy. He wanted to know what the minister of commerce thought of Barlow's treaty proposals, especially his "very delicate" indemnity plan. Nearly all of the issues Barlow had brought forward, he reminded Dalberg, fell within the operational jurisdiction of de Sussy's ministry. Having thus layered his negotiator with a time-consuming stratum of bureaucratic consultation, Bassano addressed some of the problems he himself foresaw. He dismissed as frivolous the notion that France might lower its tariffs. And as for Barlow"'s indemnity plan, he was not surprised that American businessmen in Paris were elated but, again, he wanted to know what de Sussy thought of it.[36] Two weeks later he addressed the same judgments and doubts to de Sussy directly, perhaps hoping to dilute his responsibility for Dalberg's handiwork when it came under Napoleon's scrutiny.[37]

Whether Barlow's relatively painless plan for indemnification played a role in the Emperor's decision to invite him to Vilna is difficult to determine. De Sussy was too busy to give his colleague an opinion of it, and the latter refrained from attaching any importance to it in subsequent conversations with Barlow. What most fascinated Dalberg were Barlow's frantic efforts to find out where Vilna stood on some of the other issues they had discussed. He reported the envoy had twice importuned Talleyrand to intercede and would have written directly to the emperor had not his friends dissuaded him. Only enormous pressure from the American community in Paris, he believed, could have driven the American minister to consider the latter impropriety.[38]

In the end, Barlow's winning powers of persuasion, seconded by the timely arrival of a war-threatening letter from James Madison, had the most visible impact on breaking the deadlock.[39] After listening to Barlow read excerpts from this letter, Dalberg warned Vilna that unless the emperor did not care one way or the other whether the United States declared war on France, he must "consent to some arrangement," and do it quickly. Madison had written that if, as seemed likely, the British agreed to an early peace, "the full tide of [public] indignation . . . will be directed agst. France." Barlow had also impressed on Dalberg the president's need to show as much "energy" toward France as he had toward Britain, reminding him that under the mere threat of war London had suspended its orders-in-council and was expected to yield on other issues in the face of approaching hostilities.[40] Finally, the president had intimated that he might recall Barlow even before Congress reconvened. Because withdrawing one's ambassador traditionally prefigured a declaration of war, Dalberg needed to say no more. His depiction of Barlow on the brink of winding up his affairs apparently hit its mark. Less than three weeks later, on 11 October, Bassano wrote to invite Barlow to Vilna, thereby setting the stage for the American envoy's last round of diplomacy.[41]

CHAPTER 18

SERURIER FRETS: WILL

CONGRESS DECLARE WAR ON

BOTH BELLIGERENTS?

From his Washington vantage Louis Serurier watched the approaches to war with as much incertitude as those who ultimately voted for it, which may explain why few other acts of Congress have evoked such an effusion of historiography. Writing more than thirty years ago, Marshall Smelser already counted "perhaps as many as fifty historians" who since June 1812 had come up with original explanations of why Congress voted for war. Would-be explicators continue to multiply, although at a slower pace, and recently the profession has shown an inclination to lump lesser "causes" within the spacious parameters of its having been a war fought for national honor or ideological survival. War came, they posit, because majorities in Congress believed that if they continued to put up with Britain's abuse, disdain, and other real or imagined humiliations, their failure to act would bring irreparable dishonor to themselves, fatally injure the Republican party, and perhaps even destroy popular support for republican institutions.[1] Thus, rather than rank the causal significance of such issues as impressment, orders-in-council, expansionism, and so forth, they seem reasonably well satisfied to swing a big net over the multiplicity of grievances, which infuriated those members of Congress who, were they alive today, would say they voted for war because they had had a bellyful of England and weren't going to take it anymore. Certainly the Warhawks said as much, and for them retreat was not an easy option. Riding the crest of their own heated oratory, they seemed to realize that to adjourn without declaring war would discredit both them and their party. Egging them on, Serurier warned his Republican friends to consider "what will become of all these endless declamations and oscillations," which, if they produced no result, would "destroy forever the confidence and esteem of their friends."[2] If such nudging was self-interested, he was also uneasily aware that a wrought-up Congress might declare war on France as well. Madison had warned him repeatedly that reports of ill-treatment at the hands of French authorities made it more difficult for his administration to rebut the Federalist charge that it was submitting to French tyranny.

When in late December 1811, the president complained of French seizures in the Baltic, Serurier guessed aloud that lawless privateers had probably gotten out of control. Two months later, however, with news of French naval frigates systematically burning American vessels off Spain and Portugal, he had to admit, if only to himself, that this smacked of imperial sanction.[3] Until late March, however, the French minister weathered the early weeks of 1812 relatively free of serious controversy. True, Monroe still complained that Paris produced only "plans for accommodation but nothing final," but except for the unpleasantness in Savannah, he was satisfied to watch the downward course of Anglo-American relations. Americans might profit richly from the Iberian grain trade, he wrote, but this "will not prevent them from making war if the Orders in Council are not revoked," and Monroe assured him there was no sign of that. He found it mildly amusing that the British minister in his distress was covering the ruins of his mission with lavish dinner parties. Foster might be an agreeable host, he supposed, but unless circumstances changed, ". . . on leaving his table, the Representatives are going to vote their war bills, just as they would on leaving my house."[4] Unless London revoked its orders, all signs pointed to a Congress moving inexorably toward war.

Though confident of war in the near offing, the French envoy felt obliged to repeat to Paris the misgivings he heard voiced by members of Congress who feared that wartime tax increases would rouse the wrath of their constituents and often recalled the fate of John Adams, who during the Quasi-War had raised taxes for a war that never fully materialized. Conventional wisdom held that Adams's tax levies had cost him and his party the election of 1800. Now, twelve years later, would the fear of popular resistance to tax increases stall the movement toward war? Serurier hoped not and tried to assure Paris that circumstances had changed since Adams's day. Now Britain was the enemy, not France. This time

Americans had Canada to gain, prizes to be taken, and with French blessing the prospect of opening a vast European market. War was just a matter of time, he predicted; Americans might be slow in working up to it,
but once committed, "they will not quit easily." In the event, France
should be ready to offer "real advantages and useful compensations."[5]

The Savannah affair, meanwhile, ruffled the diplomatic waters but in
the end made no great waves. Despite conflicting reports as to what had
transpired in that city the previous November, Serurier felt duty-bound
to denounce the violence done to French sailors. He also suggested that
news of it reaching Paris might explain why two American grain ships
had been burned at sea en route to Lisbon and Cadiz. He put it to Monroe that if his government had had knowledge of the Savannah incident,
which in addition to producing dead Frenchmen involved the burning of
two French privateers, the squadron that sailed from Nantes in mid-January might have had orders to take similar reprisals. Serurier was only
guessing. Word of the Savannah imbroglio had barely reached Paris before the squadron left. With Napoleon on the Russian front, its seems
unlikely that so specific a reprisal had much to do with its subsequent
activity.[6]

Predictably, each side produced exonerating versions of what turned
out to be several days of civil unrest in Savannah. Mayor William B.
Bulloch, who was also U.S. Attorney for the district, reported its origins
in a dockside brothel on the night of 13 November when unruly crewmen
from two French privateers beat up several American sailors. Next evening, the city guard rounded up the still-active brawlers, but only after
two Americans had been killed. Two days later, the situation worsened
when the city's seafaring populace joined by outraged citizenry took to
the streets, creating disturbances that the civil authorities were unable to
control. Late afternoon the next day, the scene shifted to the waterfront
where, reportedly, a group of French seamen holed up in a warehouse
opened fire on a large crowd of locals who had gathered at the wharves.
The crowd, some of them wounded, proceeded to rout the snipers, killing
two of them and wounding others. At nightfall, a few hours after the
warehouse affray, Bulloch learned that one of the privateers, *La Franchise*,
had been cut loose and left to drift up harbor. Before he could recover it,
boarders had set it afire. Its sister ship, *La Vengeance*, suffered the same
fate, although here the U.S. Attorney's account became somewhat hazy.
He pictured a hastily gathered force of "militia," struggling valiantly to
fend off torch-carrying boarders but ultimately forced to abandon the

vessel when they found themselves outnumbered. Left in hostile hands, *La Vengeance*, too, lit up the night sky with its flames.[7]

Serurier from the outset gamely presumed the innocence of the French seamen and demanded punishment of their attackers. Monroe assured him justice would be done but observed, perhaps too casually, that dockside brawls involving foreign seamen were not uncommon. As more details surfaced, the French envoy's protests intensified, as did the administration's efforts to pacify him. Two weeks later, Monroe called him in to say that the administration regretted the incident and had already demanded rigorous inquiries by the governor of Georgia, the customs collector, and the U.S. Attorney.[8] By early January, on receiving more details from Captain Lominé of *La Vengeance*, Serurier charged that the militiamen boarding that vessel under the pretext of defending it had deliberately allowed it to be burned. Worse, the boarders had torn down the imperial flag and raised their own. Her captain later claimed some twenty-five French seamen either killed or drowned. Until the guilty were punished, others would fear for their lives.[9]

Indignation tinged with bitterness eventually subsided into sighs of resignation on both sides. Paris should know, Monroe wrote Barlow, that public attacks on the crews of marauding French privateers left local authorities no recourse but to call out a "posse comitatus." He was not surprised that those summoned to deal with the Savannah rioters "should partake of the general feeling and illy perform their duty." Even so, Barlow was to tell Paris that measures would be taken to prevent a recurrence.[10] Serurier's parting shot, delivered to Monroe two months later, scoffed at charges of provocation and persisted in characterizing the French seamen as innocent victims. Justice had been promised, he reminded the secretary, but had yet to be done. To Bassano he expressed doubt that much would come of the administration's professions. Typically in such cases, plaintiffs were referred to an independent state court system where juries seldom ruled in favor of foreigners.[11] As for his own conduct, he told Bassano, he had assumed the aspect of a "very offended minister," but had avoided language which, if made public, might distract Congress from its approaching showdown with Britain.[12]

The French minister had barely finished jousting with Monroe over who had done what to whom in Savannah when the infamous John Henry Letters burst on to the political scene. Before passions cooled, nearly everyone associated with Henry's disclosures, Serurier among them, had reason to wish the affair had been less cluttered with ambiguities. Still, when he considered how effectively the letters had galvanized hostility toward Britain, he had few regrets.

Captain John Henry, a former American army officer recently employed by the Canadian government, turned up in Washington in early 1812 bearing documents that purported to implicate prominent Federalists in a British plot to separate New England from the Union. Sent to gather intelligence during the waning days of the Embargo, Henry had scouted the northern states, his ears cocked for sounds of disaffection. What he heard seemed to justify his mission; his reports to the Canadian Governor General painted New England's political leaders so dissatisfied with the administration's hostility toward Britain as to be ripe for secession and possibly ready to reaffiliate with the crown if hostilities broke out. The *raison d'être* for Henry's mission dried up in April 1809 when Smith and Erskine negotiated the agreement that had promised to relax Anglo-American tensions.[13] Ironically, Henry's reports might never have come to light had not both Québec and London refused to reimburse him for some of his travel expenses. Stiffed first by the Canadian Governor General, Henry took his case to London where the Liverpool ministry praised his work but gave him neither money nor the political appointment he had hoped for. Thoroughly discouraged, he was on his way back to Canada to renew his claim when a fellow passenger who called himself the Count de Crillon suggested he might turn his frustration to profit by selling his incriminating intelligence to the Madison administration.

———— ⟨⟩ ————

Serurier, approached by Crillon, allowed himself to vouch for the man's credentials to the American officials who were to deal with him. An accomplished con artist, the ersatz count whose real name was Paul Emile Soubiron established his *bon fides* by showing Serurier enough medals and forged letters to satisfy the French minister that he was what he claimed, a patriotic aristocrat fallen on hard times. "His manners were noble and easy," Serurier wrote later, and his motives in brokering the Henry Papers also rang true. He spun a convincing tale of having committed a youthful indiscretion in France for which he wished to make amends and win back the emperor's favor. To this end, he hoped by exposing a British intrigue to be credited with having rendered a worthy service to the French cause in America. Though Serurier later claimed to have harbored misgivings about Crillon, he accepted the authenticity of Henry's letters and on reading them instantly saw their potential for discrediting the administration's political enemies. Though warily refusing to take custody of the documents, he did act as a go-between, directing Crillon and Henry to the State Department where Monroe promptly dipped into the department's contingent fund and paid Henry $50,000 for his letters. At the level of farce, Crillon later got most of John Henry's money by selling him a nonexistent château in the south of France; and Henry himself, with the administration's connivance and careful attention to timing, managed to flee the country before Congress could interrogate him. Crillon, too, departed shortly, though not before deposing himself fancifully before the House Foreign Affairs Committee.[14] By this time, Serurier was glad to see the last of him. Uneasy at the man's dramatically embroidered accounts of his exploits, he feared Federalists might expose him to public ridicule and thereby diminish the impact of the disclosures. At a more serious level, the Henry Letters went to Congress where Federalist members, alarmed by rumors of their contents, squirmed uncomfortably at the calamitous possibility that some of their New England confreres were about to be exposed for having talked treason to a British spy.[15]

Awaiting the dénouement, Serurier predicted that when Henry's correspondence reached Congress, it "will inflame the nation and throw it into enthusiasm for war." Meanwhile, he himself stayed well away from the congressional scene. Wisely, as the moment approached, he declined Monroe's offer to mention his role in bringing the letters to light, allowing modestly that he had done no more than pass them along to the administration. Modesty aside, however, he foresaw that if Federalists discovered that the French minister had figured even remotely behind the scenes, they would cry forgery.[16] The subsequent uproar in Congress focused more volubly on British treachery than on treasonous Federalists. For one thing, Henry's letters did not name names. The Senate asked for names, but Monroe replied there were none. In fact, the names of Henry's contacts had been deleted, which Serurier believed suited the administration's twin purposes of exciting public outrage at proof of British intrigue while not identifying individual conspirators lest the Federalists be driven into angry isolation at a time when the imminence of war called for at least a semblance of national unity.[17]

Serurier's association with Crillon passed largely unnoticed in Washington, but not in Paris. Even before he received a chiding note from

Bassano, he learned from Monroe who had it from Barlow that on his return to France, Crillon had not only been exposed as an imposter but also jailed for passing forged letters of credit. Glimpsing a rebuke in his future, Serurier minimized the collateral damage. Republicans, he admitted, felt chagrined at having wined and dined the man, but Bassano should know that he himself had not been linked to Crillon publicly. Nor had the bogus count bilked the French treasury of a single penny. Having earlier led Bassano to believe that Crillon's credentials were impeccable, he now recalled by way of exculpation that "a thousand things [about him] kept rousing my doubts." Whatever the fleeting embarrassment, he exulted quietly at having helped to furnish authentic evidence of British meddling which, he was sure, had propelled Congress a step closer to war.[18]

Whether it would be one war or two, Serurier feared the worst when news broke in late March that more American grain ships had been torched en route to Lisbon. Outraged members of Congress, he learned, were asking themselves why they should do battle with Britain and not with France as well. Summoned to Monroe's office on the 23rd, he found the secretary angrily brandishing affidavits sworn out by two American sea captains whose vessels had been destroyed. The envoy was partly prepared for the tense scene that followed. Besides two confirmed kills, the French squadron was rumored to have orders to burn all the carriers they encountered. Still, Monroe was "more agitated, more discomposed" than he had ever before seen him, greeting him with " 'well, Monsieur, so it is decided that we will receive nothing but outrages from France, and at what a moment, at the very instant when we were going to war with her enemy!' " The timing could not be worse, he went on; London had given no sign of recalling her orders and the administration was within a week of asking Congress for a prewar embargo. Moreover, the anger now directed at France had offset the effect of the Henry Letters and would surely hurt Republican candidates in the upcoming congressional elections. If the French frigate commanders had acted without orders, he warned, the administration would want them punished; if the destruction were intentional, the truth would be known when the *Hornet* arrived within the next few days.

Serurier responded tightly that even if the reports were true, the secretary of state must realize how sorely France resented American grain ships supplying British forces in Spain and Portugal at a time when French troops there were suffering great privation. Without American provisioners, he observed, Wellington would have long since evacuated. Monroe subsided a bit. He tried to explain that absent a blockade neutral parties had a right to sell noncontraband to belligerents; American grain ships would supply French forces, too, if France could provide a safe port of entry. American carriers would flock to it. As matters stood, the government had no authority to prevent American vessels from provisioning British forces until Congress declared war or imposed an embargo.[19]

By mid-April 1812, top administration figures had devised a ritual for dealing with Serurier whenever France committed some new offense. They would brace him with a heated protest, listen to his on-the-spot explanations and then, having pronounced the explanations unsatisfactory, either Monroe or the president would end the session with the formulaic "let's hope we hear good news from Barlow," often capped with the warning that although the administration had set its course for a war with Britain, Congress might not be content to stop there. In this way they reinforced what they knew Serurier already believed: that a show of French goodwill might hasten a declaration of war but that unless France mended its ways it, too, might find itself at war.

⊷∞⊶

As Congress debated the merits of another embargo, Serurier waded through political shallows increasingly awash with unresolved issues, partisan passions, and momentarily a rumor of potentially devastating impact. For a time in April, until it proved false, London succeeded in spreading the word that France had avenged itself for the detention of the *Ballaou* by confiscating eleven American vessels, including the U.S. government's aviso, *Wasp*. Even if the rumor were false, he wrote Bassano, coming in the wake of the ship-burnings, "the effect of all this news on the two chambers has been terrible." Though Congress met in secret, it leaked enough threats for him to worry about legislative retribution. Monroe had reassured him that sanctions against France were not yet on the congressional docket, but unless the *Hornet* brought better news from Barlow, "the administration would find itself in a most difficult situation." At worst, it might be forced to recommend war against both belligerents which, he added somewhat superfluously, would not be in his country's best interests.[20]

Serurier consoled himself that an embargo, if enacted, would at least cut off Wellington from his American suppliers. Predictably, the imminent threat of a lockdown sent shipmasters hurriedly clearing for sea before it took effect. His legation secretary, George de Caraman, visiting Baltimore reported the city "in complete combustion" as last-minute cargoes of grain were laded for Lisbon. Few would risk a French port, he noted unhappily, lest they join the ships reportedly seized in reprisal for the *Ballaou*. While these rumors persisted, Serurier grumbled that American sea captains refused to carry his despatches without a written note assuring them safe passage.[21]

Through April, the French envoy's spirits rose and fell on the tide of news from Europe. Private letters from Barlow spoke optimistically of a treaty soon to be signed that would resolve all problems. Happily, too, the *Hornet* brought word that France had not made retaliatory seizures of American vessels. Heartened Republicans, he reported, had rallied to the good news and were once more focused on having it out with Britain. Talk of repealing the Non-Importation Act, till recently noised about in Federalist circles, also had died away. He took a moment to tell Bassano why his portrayal of the public mood had been so conflicted. His problem was the "perpetually changing colors of the indecisive events and men that I have painted." He hoped, too, that Bassano might excuse him for fretting over the French navy's burning of grain ships. The bad news had arrived at the very moment the emperor seemed about to "reap the fruits" of his restraint.[22]

Just as Serurier had begun to hope that Britain was once more in the crosshairs of public hostility, Madison called him in to review the now familiar list of complaints against France. Besides her continuing harassment of U.S. vessels in the Baltic, her navy's egregious burning of American grain ships en route to Spain and Portugal had raised further doubt as to whether the Berlin and Milan decrees had been revoked. Equally disturbing was the lack of progress on the diplomatic front. Not for a moment should Serurier credit the optimism Barlow had voiced in private letters.[23] The truth was that after seven months, Barlow had not persuaded the French government, even provisionally, to ease up on American shipping. Issues that should have been resolved long ago were still pending, and even if Barlow succeeded in signing a treaty, the president cited the slowness of Atlantic crossings and the likelihood of Senate amendments that would further delay its taking effect. Meanwhile, without a commercial treaty or the expectation of one, Americans continued to suffer the ruinous strictures France had inflicted on their commerce.

How could Americans, he asked, now on the brink of war with England, rely on France as a trade partner when they met with prohibitively high tariffs, long delays, and a licensing system that favored French but not American carriers? His countrymen, Madison concluded testily, might be better off relinquishing their trade with France altogether.[24]

Serurier responded gamely: fraudulent traffic in the Baltic had grievously breached the emperor's continental blockade. Nor could he explain the burning of American grain ships, except to say that his government could hardly be blamed for regarding them as "floating stores for the English army." The commercial problems the president complained of were regrettable, he admitted, but given the administration's well-known opposition to licenses, his government had found it "simpler to furnish them to those who would accept them." Then, hoping to lighten the president's mood, he praised the administration for its determined stand against London which, if it led to war, would put an end to licensing and bring forth a favorable commercial treaty more quickly than the president imagined. Madison had shrugged doubtfully, he later recalled. None of his explanations had satisfied, although the president did allow grudgingly that relations might improve if the *Hornet* whose arrival was expected momentarily brought good news from Barlow.[25]

Next day, Monroe did what he could to restore Serurier's battered spirits; the president's remarks did not reflect a lack of resolve toward Britain; the administration was steadfastly committed to war. The grain ships recently cleared for Lisbon had been warned of the dangers, and the government would not alter its course in Congress. Unless London recalled its orders-in-council, a declaration of war would follow as soon as other vessels due in from Europe and the Far East had safely returned. Serurier, for his part, felt only moderately reassured; Congress was volatile and if more grain ships were destroyed, the administration might not be able to keep its partisans focused exclusively on British offenses.

Ten days later, despite reports of more burnings, he took heart from several offsetting developments. Warhawks in the House, he was pleased to report, had rebuffed the Senate's bid for adjournment and seemed determined to see the crisis through. True, Congress as a whole was still of many minds, and the Treasury's first offering of "war bonds" had reached only half of its $11 million goal, a shortfall ascribed to the antiwar sentiments of moneyed New Englanders. But reports from the south and west told of recruits enthusiastically flocking to the colors. All in all, sectional differences notwithstanding, he believed he was witnessing an aroused citizenry girding for war.[26] Auspicious, too, was the outbreak of hostilities along the southern frontier where in early May local militia led by General George Mathews invaded Spanish East Florida. London, he was sure, would lodge a diplomatic protest on behalf of the Spanish Junta, which if Congress took it as a sign of Britain's own designs in that quarter might well spur it to jump the remaining hurdles.[27]

Serurier listened skeptically to Monroe's solemn denial of any official complicity in the Mathews invasion. What the French minister heard was that in leading troops south of the St. Mary's River, the seventy-three-year-old former governor of Georgia had inexplicably exceeded Washington's instructions and, of course, had since been disavowed. Mathews' forces would not be pulled back, however, because, as Monroe explained blandly, there was "more danger in retreating than in advancing." Serurier caught a whiff of duplicity. They disavow "the precipitate conduct of the General," he wrote, but "they maintain the occupation." Doubtless, Mathews' "spirit of enterprise" had not displeased, and he expected to hear soon that the American flag was flying over St. Augustine.[28]

In fact, the envoy's cynical prediction spoke to an episode marked by a number of half-answered questions. Whether Mathews received official encouragement by wink or by word, his orders, now more than a year old, had put him on a long leash. The Florida Resolution of January 1811 had authorized the occupation of East Florida contingent on "any attempt to take possession by a foreign power," or if invited to do so either by the Spanish governor or by "existing local authorities."[29] Absent the first two, Mathews set out to create the requisite "local authorities." It took him about a year to win the support of American power brokers residing south of the St. Mary's, but once assured of armed support, they staged a "revolution," declared independence, and invited annexation. On cue, Mathews' "Georgia Boys" invaded, seizing Amelia Island and nearby towns, ultimately carrying their conquest as far as the outskirts of St. Augustine.[30]

This sequence was not quite what Congress or the president had in mind. Irving Brant suggests that Monroe had fore-knowledge of Mathews' preparations and perhaps his intentions but did nothing to stop him. He allows Madison, however, to testify to his own innocence by quoting a letter he wrote to Jefferson on 24 April saying that "Mathews has been playing strange comedy in the face of common sense, as well as of his instructions."[31] That the administration subsequently decided to keep occupation forces in north Florida (where they remained until 1815) tarnished somewhat its decorous disavowal of the man who had put them there. Serurier, not one to linger over the vagaries of official self-deception, rejoiced in the cheering thought that Mathews' expedition had "the advantage of compromising the administration with England more than ever." Americans were another step closer to war.[32]

Less welcome, the *Hornet* brought no word of a diplomatic breakthrough in Paris. Serurier read the administration's chagrin in the columns of the *National Intelligencer* but thought he also detected an element of friendly calculation in the simultaneous publication of the Barlow-Bassano correspondence. Readers, he hoped, would recognize the "tone of moderation and goodwill" in these exchanges and conclude that despite delays, France was negotiating in good faith.[33] As he expected, Federalist outcries redoubled and for a period of two or three days after the *Hornet*'s arrival it unnerved him to hear more talk of declaring war on both powers. Noised about in public places, the two-war possibility also echoed in Congress until, much to his relief, Republicans in the House rejected by a comfortable seventy-two to thirty-seven vote John Randolph's motion to treat both belligerents equally. This margin led him to reflect that members of Congress might already be weighing the cost–benefit differences between fighting an English war and a French one. He reminded himself that Americans took pride in their practical wisdom, and although some members talked of making war on both, others pointed out there was no easy way to attack France whereas a war on Britain would raise profitable havoc with her merchant fleet and open the way to Canada. Both belligerents, he mused, had wounded Americans' sense of national honor, but only Britain could be made to pay a steep price. Once this truth sank in, Americans would keep peace with France if only to use her continental ports for privateering sorties.[34]

Privately, Madison agreed and for the same reason. "To go to war agst both," he wrote Jefferson, "presents a thousand difficulties, above all, that of shutting all the ports of the Continent of Europe agst. our Cruisers who can do little without the use of them." Using France as a base for privateers was still in the future, however, whereas merely keeping at peace with that power, Madison told his predecessor, was becoming ever more difficult. Barlow's most recent despatches indicated that "France has done nothing towards adjusting our differences with her." Rather, she appeared to be toying with Barlow's "wishes & hopes," presumably until such time as Washington's quarrel with London broke out in war. Having insisted publicly that Napoleon had revoked his decrees, Madison said he now found "positive cases [that] rebut the allegation." Over all, he wrote, Napoleon's conduct "betrays the design of leaving G.B. a pretext for enforcing her O. in C."—a conclusion Jonathan Russell had reached ten months earlier.[35]

While no good news came from Paris, what came from London by way of the *Hornet* clinched Madison's decision to ask Congress for war. Put simply, he felt he had no choice inasmuch as Russell's negotiations with Castlereagh had failed to budge the British ministry from its offending orders-in-council.[36] But he may also have perceived a timely opportunity to take on the British when they were most vulnerable. If Napoleon defeated Russia, as seemed likely, his closure of all European ports would likely destroy Britain's vital export economy and make her more amenable to American demands.[37] Too, his timing may have been influenced by an awareness that Britain's naval power, in decline since 1809, might soon be overmatched by France, thanks to the latter's recent and vigorous naval building program.[38]

Whether Madison should have waited for further news from London before sending his war message to Congress remains an open question. Henry Adams, always the critic, believes that the president should have known of and heeded signs of British retreat. He also questions whether American grievances were any more war-provoking in June 1812 than they had been earlier, a view that tends to overlook their cumulative effect.[39] A political insider close to the scene, however, defended the timing of Madison's decision. George Joy, the president's well-informed and well-connected correspondent in London, wrote of having chided Viscount Sidmouth, a recent addition to the post-Perceval ministry, for characterizing the decision for war as "precipitate." Not so, Joy had replied: the Prince Regent's decree of 21 April had signaled more rigorous enforcement of the orders, and he doubted Madison knew of the momentum in Parliament to suspend them.[40]

For Serurier, the president's not-so-secret war message of 1 June seemed likely to produce its intended result. Surveying the political scene with a now practiced eye, he predicted the Republican-controlled House would yield a substantial majority for war, and he doubted Federalists could block it in the other chamber. Federalist merchants and shipowners, erstwhile opponents of war, he mused, would doubtless embrace its opportunities, mount cannon on their vessels, and take up privateering on a grand scale.[41] At a personal level, he rejoiced to see the great unspoken object of his mission fulfilled. On 18 June the House of Representatives concurred, seventy-nine to forty-nine, in a war resolution the Senate had passed, nineteen to thirteen, the day before. Still, he was not sure France was in the clear. The day after the House voted for war, chilling news arrived that French frigates had burned more American grain ships.[42]

The United States' entry to the war had remarkably little effect on the conduct of the European belligerents or, for that matter, on the larger objectives of American foreign policy. Madison immediately set out to mend the rupture he had tried to avoid even before he learned that London had suspended its offending orders. He had sent Jonathan Russell what he believed were reasonable terms for an armistice: that if Britain revoked her orders and gave up impressment, he would ask Congress to forbid the employment of British seamen on all American vessels.[43] This offer, however, fell on deaf ears. Russell was told that the ministry's gracious suspension of its orders-in-council should suffice to bring about a cease-fire without the Royal Navy's forgoing its "ancient and accustomed" right to recover deserters.[44] In the end, impressment more than any other issue thwarted an early settlement; and in the weeks that followed, the war became more narrowly what many felt it should be in any case: a payback for insults too long endured.

Likewise from France Madison received no intimation that joining the fray would restore American vessels or get indemnification for their owners. What most exasperated the administration was the continued torching of American grain ships. Less than a week after Congress declared war Monroe told Serurier that given these new acts of violence, he might have to tell his friends "they had been too weak toward France and perhaps too quick toward England." Hardly weak, Serurier retorted: the president had, after all, threatened at one time to make common cause against France if Britain repealed her orders-in-council. Still, he urged they put aside past differences. Americans now faced a "formidable enemy," but could take heart in having a "powerful friend." Monroe, in no mood for generalities, rejoined tartly that France could best support the American war effort by facilitating a freer exchange of goods. Unless imports from European France replaced those from Britain, the federal government's loss of tariff revenue would make it "impossible to sustain the war." Serurier relayed this warning to Paris, where Barlow repeated it.[45]

Shaken by this encounter, the envoy was relieved when Congress adjourned. It might have declared war on both belligerents, he told Bassano, if the administration had not opposed it.[46] He recalled later how narrowly the Senate had defeated a resolution on 12 June that would have authorized taking reprisals against all French vessels, a measure tantamount to a declaration of war. Had two members of the Senate voted the other way and had the House concurred in the motion, it stood to reason that Congress might have altered the future of American relations with Europe in ways that can only be imagined. It still might happen, Serurier warned, unless Paris could explain why American ships were being burned and why Barlow had failed to make a treaty.[47] He also took the occasion to pass along Monroe's warning that unless France took Britain's place as a trade partner, the loss of customs revenues might force Americans to sue for peace.[48]

Having voiced his worst fears, Serurier headed north in early July. He intended to mingle with the people and encourage their war spirit, he told Paris. Along the way, he asked the French consuls in Philadelphia and New York to keep Paris abreast of events in his absence.[49] There was little more he could do. If France were to draw advantage from Americans' wartime status, the initiative must come from Paris.

CHAPTER 19

BARLOW GOES TO VILNA AS THE
RUSSIAN CAMPAIGN COLLAPSES

N apoleon's absence from Paris when Congress declared war meant that Barlow had to ask questions of French officials who were not quite sure how to deal with their new co-belligerent. When he made clear his countrymen expected France to welcome their privateers and allow them to sell off captured British ships and cargoes, the reactions he got were tentative but fairly positive.[1] His closest contact, Jean-Baptiste Petry, urged Bassano to let Americans sell captured property as long as they continued to take away French produce of equal value.[2] As the reality of American privateering took shape, others puzzled over questions of jurisdiction. The chief of the Navy's Prize Division, a man named Rivière, asked Bassano whether the U.S. consul at Quimper should be permitted to dispose of a prize taken by the privateer *Decatur*. Rivière's reading of earlier Franco-American treaties favored the consul's request, but he was not sure. Two weeks later, equally perplexed, Navy Minister Denis Decrès told Bassano that he, too, leaned toward giving the American consul oversight, but asked for a directive from the emperor.[3] Barlow later learned the consul's request for jurisdiction had been granted.[4] Considering the *Decatur*'s success, she would have been hard to turn away. A well-armed sloop out of Newburyport, she had already taken eight prizes from the British that summer and had been instrumental in directing the *Constitution* to its stunning rendezvous with the *Guerriere* in late August.[5]

Collin de Sussy, the recently named minister of manufactures and commerce, took a tougher line on prize-related issues, arguing that Barlow had overreached in asking that American prizemasters be permitted to sell off cargoes of non-British origin, re-export those that were British, and not be bound by the equal-value export requirement. Americans, he told Bassano, ought to have the same but no greater rights than Frenchmen, that is, they might sell captured vessels, but the cargoes should be sequestered pending a determination of their admissibility.[6] In time, thanks largely to Barlow's initiative, French officials did allow the sale of captured vessels; and the following April Napoleon agreed that Americans might re-export captured goods not lawfully permitted entry. It was one of his few concessions to wartime America.[7]

Although Barlow eventually won most of the privateering privileges he asked for, he was unable to free American vessels long held in custody. Nor do records of this period explain why the French Council of Prizes continued to suspend hearings even as the number of detentions rose.[8] Meanwhile, Consul David Warden found considerable variation in the dangers to which American vessels were exposed in nearby waters. Those navigating the Baltic, he reported, were safe only under British convoy, but those in the Atlantic appeared to come and go freely as long as their incoming cargoes were of U.S. origin or, in the case of sugar and coffee, licensed. As for cross-Channel trade, some members of the American mercantile community, he noted irritably, had affiliated themselves with French business houses in order to share in the licensed importation of "colonial" products directly from Britain. Most of these individuals, he fumed, because they were long-term residents unlikely to return to U.S. jurisdiction, would surely escape punishment for trading with the enemy.[9]

War also rekindled Barlow's efforts to free American seamen imprisoned for no other crime than having been impressed aboard a British vessel later taken by the French.[10] Ultimately, his best argument for their release was to volunteer them to serve on board French or American privateers. To highlight the injustice of imprisoning them, he recounted the plight of four American seamen who, pressed into service aboard a British frigate, had struck for freedom when, as members of a British prize crew put aboard a captured American despatch boat, they had assisted the American captain and his crew to retake the vessel. Inexplicably, they had been jailed when they subsequently put into a French port.[11]

The idea of freeing American seamen to man short-handed privateers got a major boost later that fall when Captain Nathan Haley, erstwhile State Department courier and one-time French naval officer, announced plans to buy and arm a vessel to ravage British shipping in the waters off Brest. Haley induced Barlow to make the case that these seamen would doubtless welcome the opportunity to serve their country under his command. Impressed, Barlow promptly asked Bassano to consign to Haley's custody some seventy-seven seamen detained at various "depots" throughout France while agreeing to vouch for their American citizenship. A month later, by this time in Vilna, he had positively identified a pool of fifty or more seamen detained at Cambray, Arras, and Valenciennes. Haley, he wrote, vowed to bring in two British prisoners for every American he signed on, a promise, the minister observed wryly, that "may resemble the premature sale of the Bear Skin, but I have little doubt he will keep his word."[12]

Haley ultimately got his liberated crewmen but only after the ministers of war, external relations, and navy had resolved one another's hesitations and checked with Napoleon. It was typical bureaucratic second-guessing. Ultimately, the duc de Feltre, minister of war, notified his colleagues that the emperor had authorized him to release fifty-four Americans on condition they serve on board American privateers. Suspecting there might be Britons among them, however, he reported having insisted that Barlow verify the U.S. citizenship of those whose names were on his list.[13] In the aftermath, David Warden managed to secure the release of others still in custody, diligently weeding out those who he believed falsely claimed U.S. citizenship.[14]

Haley's 16-gun French-built sloop, *True Blooded Yankee,* lived up to its skipper's promise. Sailing from Brest in March 1813 on the first of three voyages, it ultimately netted ships and cargoes worth an estimated $400,000. When the British finally captured the Yankee *"scourge"* that fall, her complement of 200 was so depleted by manning prizes that only 23 persons remained on board. They and Haley spent the rest of the war in a Gibraltar prison.[15]

───── ❦ ─────

As Barlow and Dalberg waited to hear from Vilna, Jean-Baptiste Petry got wind of Barlow's indemnity plan and denounced it on all counts. For one thing, the American envoy must know that his government opposed all forms of licensing, but worse, his estimate of indemnities at twenty million francs fell far short of what American claimants counted as their actual losses. Moreover, the favored licensees stood to profit by an amount three or four times that figure. Finally, allowing Barlow to designate the licensees secretly struck him as an invitation to fast dealing. He was not surprised at the "impure source," he wrote Bassano, recalling that Barlow and his associates had royally bilked an earlier generation of French investors by persuading them to invest in the Scioto land company.[16]

Nearly a year later, the foreign office sent a full text of the plan to William Crawford, Barlow's successor. Crawford must already have had some knowledge of it because Bassano had disclosed the plan to Serurier who, in turn, had outlined its major features to Monroe well before Crawford left Washington.[17] Like Petry, Crawford suspected corruption in Barlow's insistence on naming the licensees while keeping the plan secret.[18] Whether Barlow's plan deserved such mistrust, a case can be made for his good intentions. What he proposed, in effect, was a short-term means of indemnifying those members of the American business community who had suffered losses from French confiscations. Special licenses would enable them import cargoes at pre-Trianon tariff levels for a period of eight months; other claimants would be paid from a fund generated by sales of the licenses themselves. His insistence on secrecy may only have meant that he intended to keep Washington in the dark until the plan was up and running. Mindful of the administration's dead set against licensing, he may have hoped his success in devising a two-tiered instrument of indemnification would speak for itself. In his defense, it might also be noted that not all members of Congress shared the executive's abhorrence of licensed trade. Had Barlow lived into the spring of 1813, he would have felt vindicated when after more than three months of intermittent debate, the Senate had let die a House resolution "to prohibit the use of foreign licenses."[19] Clearly, there were others who believed that a licensed trade was better than none.

Whether, as Crawford later suggested, Barlow's proposal would have injured American commerce as a whole, William Lee reported a new-found prosperity among those Americans who had obtained licenses even without special favor. Writing from Bordeaux in mid-January 1813, he saw no reason to question *le Moniteur*'s recent boast that despite the British blockade, some fifty American vessels had arrived during December alone, most of them licensed and all of them "richly laden."[20]

The diplomatic breakthrough Barlow had long awaited came in late October: a cordial letter from Bassano announced the emperor's eagerness to "conclude an arrangement without delay." Come to Vilna at once, he promised, and they could put the finishing touches on both a commercial treaty and a claims convention.[21] For Barlow, his hopes shriveled by months of inactivity, the invitation must have been irresistible. On the 25th he wrote back that he would set out the next day, bringing with him the documents that he and Dalberg had put in draft.[22] He told Monroe he hardly relished the prospect of a carriage ride across Europe but felt he could not refuse the invitation without giving offense. The alacrity with which he accepted, however, showed less concern for offending than it did a readiness to go whatever distance was necessary to bring his diplomacy to fruition. After months of delay in Paris and little encouragement from Washington, he now had an opportunity to confound those who had disparaged his efforts. Having looked to this moment for more than a year, he meant to seize it. Personal vindication rode on his hopes and, on its face, his optimism seemed warranted: why else would Napoleon have asked him to travel the breadth of the continent unless he was prepared to sign what he and Dalberg had agreed to? And perhaps feeling a need to reassure Washington, he promised not go beyond matters of commerce and indemnity. If Napoleon offered a treaty of alliance, he assured Monroe that "I shall not be at a loss how to answer."[23] Lee, who kept in close touch with Barlow, shared his optimism. Bassano's letter, he believed, promised "a fair adjustment of all differences," and although "quite an unbeliever for several months past I now entertain great hopes of his coming to a prosperous arrangement."[24]

Little of this enthusiasm crossed the Atlantic. Madison later expressed "much dissatisfaction," not so much with Barlow's decision as with the invitation itself. Napoleon, he grumbled to Monroe, should have treated with Barlow before he left for Russia or, if too distracted by campaigning, transferred negotiations to Washington.[25]

———— ∞∞∞ ————

In company with his nephew Thomas and two servants, the American minister set off across Europe, not altogether unmindful that despite his best efforts, failure might greet him in the end. That he would die in the cold emptiness of the Polish countryside adds an element of tragedy to his mission, whose last chapter he began to write as he described the devastation of war unfolding outside his carriage window. A witness now

to the ragged retreat of the Grande Armée, he described the terrain he
passed through as "a mass of mud, lined alternately with rocks, deep
sands & wooden causeways and bordered with dead horses, sick & dying
soldiers, broken waggon wheels & burnt villages, the fruits of glorious
war."[26]

Weary and depressed, he reached Vilna on 18 November only to learn
that Napoleon was still several hundred miles to the east. Bassano assured
him, however, that the emperor had been sent copies of the treaty and
claims convention and would soon return orders "to conclude the business in both its parts." In fact, the foreign minister was sure enough of
Napoleon's approval that he sent the emperor an instrument of ratifica-
tion ready for signature.[27] Despite assurances, Barlow was skeptical. What
he had seen on the road to Vilna spoke more to chaos than to moments
of fruitful deliberation. "The emperor's present retrograde movement,"
he wrote prophetically, "may occasion further delay."[28] His misgivings
soon proved correct. Napoleon, now on the run and traveling day and
night incognito, in fact bypassed Vilna, reportedly not wanting its citizens
to know that he had left his army behind. He paused outside the city only
long enough to meet briefly with Bassano and then sped on through
Warsaw and Dresden to reach Paris on 18 December.[29] Whether he and
Bassano found time to discuss Barlow's treaties when they met in the
outskirts of Vilna on the night of the sixth is not recorded, though it
seems unlikely.

Meanwhile, Barlow's fatigue and the onset of diarrhea began to take
their toll. Hoping for better roads and warmer weather, he planned to
return to Paris by way of Vienna and Munich. Even as he left Vilna, he
was not well. Petry and young Barlow later told of the envoy's steadily
worsening health as their carriage drove hard through the bitter Polish
countryside. Putting Warsaw behind them and near Cracow they reached
the small town of Zarnovich. Here on the 22nd, feverish, unable to speak,
and clearly unable to travel further, Barlow bedded down in what his
companions later described as a house belonging to an excellent family.
Though two physicians attended him over the next few days, neither offered hope for recovery. As Petry and his nephew stood vigil, Joel Barlow
succumbed to pneumonia on 26 December 1812. He was buried in Zarnovich the next day and with him whatever faint hope for an accommodation with France.[30]

Although historians tend to eschew the "what ifs" of their craft, Barlow's mission having been taken this far invites speculation. Arguably, the commercial treaty Bassano asked Napoleon's permission to sign in late 1812 was a document both parties might have accepted. Not so, the accompanying claims convention, but the treaty of commerce was a well considered, no frills document scrupulously protective of France's core interests but also marginally generous to America's maritime entrepreneurs. It contained none of the new canons of maritime law Barlow had so grandly proposed the previous January; nor did it respond to the American envoy's earlier pleas for tariff reduction. But on the positive side, it resurrected enough of the 1800 Convention to promise an eventual reestablishment of the principle of free ships, free goods. Also, had the treaty lived, American importers would have had greater freedom in choosing export cargoes though still required to take away cargoes equal in value to those they brought in. American prizemasters were exempted from this requirement altogether. As Bassano explained, France could not expect commerce raiders to master the intricacies of French export practices. Too, Americans might freely sell prize vessels and re-export any captured cargoes judged inadmissible. For ordinary importers, Barlow also won a six-month grace period for the payment of duties, a victory for his argument that shipmasters needed this length of time to sell off enough of their cargoes to keep them solvent during layovers. In all, his commercial treaty had a good deal to recommend it. His indemnity plan was another matter.

In forwarding the commercial treaty, Bassano noted that the American minister would not sign it without some provision for indemnification. Apparently he felt uneasy enough about Barlow's indemnity plan to solicit an opinion from the comte de Sussy. The latter raised no objection to selling special import licenses to Americans but drew the line at favoring them with tariff concessions. French importers of the same goods, he pointed out, would be hard put to compete.[31] Whether de Sussy's advisory caught up with Bassano's submission to the emperor seems problematical. Still, even without the tariff benefit, American interests might have been satisfied if Napoleon had agreed to put the proceeds from selling the licenses into an indemnity fund. Unfortunately, the emperor's correspondence gives no clue as to how he regarded the plan, although Bassano later explained to Serurier why it had been found "inadmissible." It was because the American minister had overstepped his authority. "Your letters," he told Serurier, "confirmed me in the opinion I already had that he [Barlow] was not authorized by his government to take such a course."[32] And as Petry later told Crawford, French officials had never taken the claims convention seriously because they were sure Washington would not approve its licensing feature.[33] This explanation, while both plausible and exonerating from the French standpoint, also closed down any serious effort to come to terms with the indemnification issue.

Ironically, Barlow's plan prefigured at least part of what he envisioned for it, that is, greater licensing opportunities for American importers. Although, in the event, such licenses were not purchased through the American legation, as Barlow intended, nor were sales receipts set aside for later indemnity payouts, Napoleon did authorize the sale of two hundred more of them to any and all buyers only a few weeks after Barlow died.

───── ∞∞∞ ─────

News of the American minister's death stunned members of the expatriate community in Paris to whom he was a familiar and likeable figure. An obituary translated from an unnamed Paris newspaper appeared in the *National Intelligencer* of May 4. It described the late minister as a hard-driving, witty, sensitive man, "sincerely beloved by all those whom he admitted to his society." Mourning quickly turned to contention, however, when it became clear that Barlow's failure to name a chargé d'affaires would touch off a nasty struggle for control of the U.S. legation. Controversy centered on whether the interim appointment of his nephew, Thomas Barlow, as legation secretary sufficed to warrant the latter's taking charge.[34] The French foreign office thought not and, despite heated protests from such would-be claimants as William Lee and Isaac Cox Barnet, decided that until a new minister arrived it would transact lesser matters of state with David Bailie Warden, the U.S. consul residing in Paris. Objectively considered, this choice seems to have made sense inasmuch as neither Lee nor Barnet could document their claims, and young Barlow managed to weaken his own candidacy by first asking leave to carry home the news of his uncle's death, then demanding to be accredited, and finally seeming to disqualify himself by invoking the Logan Act. Inflamed members of the Barlow faction, however, proceeded to make Warden's life miserable.[35] The feuding ended only when William H. Crawford arrived six months later. Meanwhile, substantive issues in Franco-American relations slumbered quietly at the legation on rue Vaugirard.

CHAPTER 20

Serurier Reports on Wartime Washington; From Paris a Long Silence

Napoleon Bonaparte's remarkable staying power in the wake of his Russian disaster gave Americans another sixteen months to wage war without attracting Britain's undivided attention. For a while it appeared the French emperor might recoup his losses completely. In the spring of 1813, he rebuilt an army of 250,000 and marched it into Germany where it won battles against both Russians and Prussians. It soon became clear, however, that military genius alone could not make up for the men and horses he had lost the previous winter. Unable now to mount the formidable cavalry charges with which he had once pursued his enemies to convincing defeat, he concluded an armistice with both powers on 4 June, hoping to regroup in the interim. During this lull, the final coalition that would bring him down came into being. Two weeks into the armistice, British plenipotentiaries promising generous subsidies made treaties with Russia and Prussia that stipulated no separate peace, and on 12 August Austria, too, declared war on France.[1] The allies, fortified by the perception that Napoleon was no longer invincible, soon began to gain the upper hand militarily. Although their combined forces were defeated near Dresden in late August, they gradually pushed the French back, winning a decisive victory at Leipzig in October. Pressing on toward Paris even as the emperor's army continued to win minor battles, the allies occupied the French capital in late March 1814.

Not surprisingly, the final months of the Napoleonic era brought less urgency to relations between Washington and Paris. The beleaguered emperor had little opportunity to mend those relations or, for that matter, the means to worsen them. If anything, U.S. entry to the war lessened the immediacy of once critical issues. Neutral rights, so passionately defended against French transgressions, dropped out of sight the moment Americans themselves ceased to be neutral. Nor was it any longer useful to talk of expanding each other's markets when American carriers were the prey of every British warship. And with the fate of France itself in the balance, the American prospects for securing reparations diminished with each passing month. What remains to be considered, then, is how French and American officials came to regard each other's *fin de guerre* convulsions as the French imperium drew to a close. The end game is about to be played out.

⸻ ◅◆▻ ⸻

Serurier returned in late August to a capital awash in heavy rains and reeling at the news of General William Hull's bloodless surrender of Detroit. This was "a deplorable debut for the campaign," he wrote, but reminded Bassano that he had predicted Americans would fight badly at first.[2] A few days later, the cabinet having returned, he called on Monroe. He had fresh instructions to repeat basically what Barlow had been told: that France owed nothing for having seized American vessels in retaliation for Section 3 of the Non-Intercourse Act. He seemed nonplused when Monroe observed mildly that someday both parties might seek indemnification; but when asked to elaborate, the secretary declined.[3] Hoping to sound a positive note, Serurier began to expound on the favors the United States could expect from France now that they were fighting a common enemy. This brought the sharp rejoinder that what Americans expected was justice and not merely because they had become co-belligerents. Monroe told him the public was still angry at the torching of their grain ships. By one count, as many as seventeen had perished at the hands of the French navy, an outrage not forgotten. For Serurier, the only comfort he took from this meeting was the secretary's solemn word there would be no peace with Britain until she had renounced impressment, that a mere suspension of its orders-in-council was not enough. Considering how far London had retreated, however, the envoy thought the administration might find it difficult to prosecute war at whose outset it had won a major concession.[4]

Instructed to do so and before the meeting ended, Serurier pursued London's retreat a step further. Although the orders of 1807 and 1809 had been recalled, the administration must realize, he warned, that unless London had also suspended Fox's Blockade of 1806, the emperor might be compelled to revive and enforce his Berlin Decree. Monroe, he related, took the warning without demur.[5] As well he might. With all three parties at war, the notion of Fox's Blockade or the Berlin Decree putting further strains on French-American relations must have struck the Secretary of State as singularly conjectural.

As American military operations unfolded, most of them disastrous, the French envoy took a lively interest in the outcomes, cheerfully parading his enthusiasm for the campaigns against Canada while managing to hide his chagrin when they went awry. As Paris would expect of him, however, he saw as his major task to weigh the shifting fortunes of war on the military stamina of his host government. Thus, in early September he sat silent but attentive as the secretary of state deplored Hull's inexplicable surrender of Detroit. Not all the details were known, Monroe told him, but clearly Hull "had lost his head." By all odds, it was "a shameful capitulation."[6]

Although the campaigns against Canada continued to go badly, the war at sea was a different matter. Like most Americans, the French minister could scarcely contain his exuberance at the early performance of the American Navy. A week after his dispirited meeting with Monroe, the *Constitution* won a smashing victory over the *Guerriere*. A boost to American morale, it came at a critical time, he wrote, for although Madison's re-election might depend on whether William Henry Harrison could retake Detroit before the electors met, the *Constitution's* victory had so revived the country's flagging spirits as to make it unlikely Washington would sue for an early peace whatever the electoral outcome. The *Constitution*, he reported, had reduced the *Guerriere* to a floating hulk thanks to "the prodigious quickness of the American maneuvers . . . the accuracy of fire . . . the fearlessness of the attack." A British frigate had met its match and France should rejoice at "le début de cette nouvelle rivale de l'Angleterre."[7] By way of support, he urged his government to welcome American privateers which had reportedly captured several hundred British merchantmen during the first months of the war. It would "produce the worst effect," he warned, if France prevented these far-ranging and "daring filibusters," so successful in their home waters, from selling off their prizes in French ports. Admittedly, American shipmasters were notorious for slipping British goods into the continent and would doubtless continue to do so, but he hoped that some way could be found to accommodate those who were now "desolating English commerce."[8]

Predictably, the French navy ministry countered with a request that French privateers be permitted to operate out of American ports and in late May 1813 it furnished the French consul in New York with blank letters of marque. The ministry's approach was wary, however. Doubtless recalling the furor touched off by Citizen Genet's unsanctioned privateering activities two decades before, it cautioned Lescallier not to issue the commissions until Serurier cleared it with Washington. Eventually, Monroe was receptive, to a point. French corsairs, he agreed, might bring in merchantmen captured from the British, but not from the Spanish because the administration regarded Spain as a neutral.[9] In making free with this offer, however, the secretary apparently forgot that after the Genet affair, Congress had enacted a neutrality law barring U.S. ports to all warring privateers. Once reminded, he had to explain to Serurier that unless Congress changed the law the executive had no authority to admit French privateers or allow them to fit out. To its credit, the administration later made at least a halfhearted effort to persuade Congress to accord reciprocity but gave it up when a House committee in the spring of 1814 declined to report out a bill to that effect. Serurier was told the committee feared the measure would fail of passage. More likely, he supposed, the administration feared being exposed to more Federalist cries of French influence.[10]

Ironically, even as Serurier urged Paris to come forward with acts of goodwill that might strengthen his hand with the administration, the substance of his despatches weakened his advocacy. Readers in Paris might wonder if France had much to gain from extending commercial or other concessions when its envoy was reporting how well the United States was doing without them. British peace overtures had been rejected; a majority in Congress supported the war effort; and American morale, though shaken by Hull's surrender, had recovered in the flush of naval victories. Clearly, a disconnect existed between the French minister's perceived need to offer concessions and a government which, by his own account, looked primarily to itself.

With nothing from Paris, the French minister was reduced to tugging peevishly at the skirts of the administration for its failure to curb the flow of provisions to British forces in the Iberian campaign.[11] Reproachfully, he asked Monroe how Americans could expect to earn the emperor's goodwill when their government tolerated such a self-defeating traffic.

Americans must know that provisioning the enemy hardly comported with sound military doctrine. The secretary replied coolly that his government allowed such commerce because it still regarded Spain and Portugal as neutral parties. As for the charge of trading with the enemy, Monroe must have savored the moment. Belligerents often showed "commercial tolerances" toward one another, he noted; indeed, was not France herself engaged in such commerce? Had she not for some time trafficked with the British in colonial goods? Serurier admitted a parallel but countered irritably that trading modest amounts of French wine for British colonial sugar could hardly compare with the "immense provisioning" of an enemy army. As the meeting ended, Monroe warned him not to expect Congress to cut off the Iberian trade; too many members had too many constituents who profited from it.[12] Monroe knew whereof he spoke. In the year 1811 alone, American exporters had shipped more than 380,000 barrels of flour to Spain's Atlantic ports.[13] The secretary also read Congress correctly: in November a motion to forbid the export of all foodstuffs failed in the House. Introduced by a member whom Serurier described as "more ardent than able," the motion was voted down resoundingly, seventy-six to twenty-six. Worse, he wrote, some who voted against it did so from a "feeling against us."[14] By the end of February, however, the issue was more or less mooted by a tight British blockade off Chesapeake Bay.

————— ✺ —————

Madison's address to Congress on 4 November dwelt mostly on military matters, but also complained briefly of French foot-dragging in treaty negotiations and expressed mystification at Napoleon's St. Cloud Decree. Though the president's reproofs were mild, Serurier called them "cold and defiant." Paris, he knew, expected him to complain. Not so, Monroe rejoined: considering the long silence from Paris, the president's allusions to France might better be characterized as a "feebly expressed discontent." Serurier declined to be drawn out.[15]

Of greater significance, the envoy was pleased to report no danger of an early Anglo-American peace. Jonathan Russell had returned from London in early November and his exchanges with Castlereagh, soon published, left no doubt that the British ministry had flatly rejected Madison's terms for a cease-fire. Russell himself called on Serurier and gave him the same message: London believed it had conceded enough in suspending the orders-in-council. On reflection, what struck Serurier as most heartening were the irreconcilable positions each side had taken on the impressment issue. He doubted Britain could retreat from so recent an affirmation of its navy's right to recover deserters; and for political reasons equally compelling, he believed Madison had no choice but to insist that she do so. Impressment alone, he predicted, would keep the war going until American attacks on Canada forced London to give it up. Meanwhile, Madison's electoral triumph over the antiwar Republican De Witt Clinton and the spectacle of a feisty Congress churning out military bills lent weight to his belief that Americans would not quit soon.[16]

Though loathe to distract the administration from military matters, the envoy nonetheless kept a watchful eye on events which might affect French interests even remotely, lest he be thought lax in his official duties, which explains why in late November he protested the arrival of a ship flying a Haitian flag which put into Philadelphia and later sailed on to New York. Not wanting to be thought negligent, he recounted having told Monroe how scandalized he was to learn (from the French consul in Philadelphia) that the United States allowed entry to all foreign vessels without distinction. Surely, he objected, such openness did not apply to the ships of insurrectionists, in this instance coming from a Haitian populace over whom France still claimed sovereignty.[17] His exchanges with Monroe on this subject illuminated some shadowy perceptions on both sides.

Though any serious French claim to Saint Domingue in late 1812 flew in the face of reality, the fact that the United States had not recognized Haitian independence gave the envoy at least a pretext for complaint. Under the law of nations, he reminded the secretary, a friendly power did not give aid to another's rebels. France had long overlooked Americans' profitable trade with the island but had to draw the line at their welcoming rebel vessels. Monroe rejoined that U.S. policy toward Haiti was mutually beneficial, pointing out that Washington's "arrangements" with the island chieftain, Alexandre Pétion, also served French interests inasmuch as Yankee privateers operating out of Haitian ports were wreaking the sort of havoc on British shipping that France ought to welcome. This explained why a vessel flying Pétion's flag had not been turned away. But, Serurier rejoined, by receiving a rebel vessel the United States had appeared to extend diplomatic recognition. This thrust struck home. Monroe, clearly at a loss to explain how Washington could deal with a political entity without formally recognizing it, replied blandly that recognition was not intended—Pétion did not expect it.[18] Serurier, however, continued to insist that the rebel ship, the *Courier* by name, be sent away; and when the French consul in New York failed to make it happen, he heard more from Monroe on the administration's gingerly approach to this first black republic. Although Haiti was an ideal base for privateering, Washington had to deal cautiously with Pétion lest by appearing to give its blessing to a successful slave rebellion it create unrest among its own slave population. Already, Monroe told him, the president had reliable reports of British provocateurs conspiring to touch off an uprising in the southern states. As a countermeasure, Pétion would be told as tactfully as possible why in deference to France, Washington could receive no emissaries. Nor would it, for reasons of domestic tranquillity, hereafter admit her vessels to American ports. Accordingly, Monroe promised to have the *Courier* sent away. Serurier felt obliged to file a written protest, however, when Lescallier reported the vessel still in New York harbor two weeks later. He did so reluctantly, he told Bassano, because Washington still resented the long "silence" from Paris with respect to the Barlow negotiations. In all, he thought it best to accept Monroe's word that future relations with Pétion would be minimal and was gratified when shortly thereafter Congress voted to close U.S. ports to Haitian vessels.[19]

As the year 1812 drew to a close, Serurier gave a mixed assessment of the American war effort. Canada would not soon fall hostage to other issues, he admitted, because American land forces were "all indiscipline, disorder, and ignorance." Henry Dearborn's army had been forced into winter quarters by low morale and the refusal of state militia to cross the Canadian frontier. Similarly, the Niagara campaign had bogged down for want of militia support and competent leadership. Even the hopes for Harrison's retaking Detroit had been dashed by short supplies and heavy snows. Paris, however, should not underrate the long-term significance of the U.S. navy's show of mettle. Isaac Hull's destruction of the *Guerriere* and Decatur's capture of the *Macedonia*, he wrote, will make Britain "tremble for the future . . . a new rival declares itself, still very feeble if one considers only the number of its vessels, but intrepid, enterprising, and supported by a hundred thousand sailors from the best merchant marine in existence."[20]

Congress, too, had shown its mettle by voting funds for more frigates and raising pay for its regulars. What troubled him, he wrote, was how little France figured in this great struggle. Administration figures, he wrote Bassano, "are too proud and bitter to complain to my face, but I learned again yesterday, that in the latest Cabinet meeting, M. Madison cried out several times: 'Six months of declared and effective war against England, and not a word from France!' and that three Secretaries expressed themselves with even greater bitterness. I employ all that my zeal suggests to sustain confidence, but they no longer believe me and my position was never more difficult."[21]

In early 1813, Serurier's gloom lightened with news that Napoleon had invited Barlow to Vilna. If, as rumor also had it, treaty negotiations might be transferred to Washington, he knew he stood to advance his own career.[22] For the moment, however, it was enough that members of the Republican party recognized the invitation as "decisive proof" the emperor intended to bring those negotiations to a swift conclusion. Federalists, he reported, likened the invitation to a master summoning a servant and even some of his Republican friends had to be instructed that for a sovereign to single out an ambassador for special attention was a "mark of regard," and in this instance a harbinger of Barlow's imminent success.[23] A prevailing optimism now ran through his despatches. Both Congress and the president, he believed, were measuring up to wartime challenges. Republican majorities in both Houses appeared to have no difficulty winning support for new military appropriations, and Madison's recent cabinet appointments promised greater vigor in the executive. He seemed pleased that John Armstrong had been named to the War Department. Armstrong, he noted superfluously, "is already known to Your Excellency."[24] What he did not know was how grudgingly Madison had decided to put up with the general's difficult personality, having made the appointment largely to strengthen the party's base in New York.[25] Serurier also confidently described the new Navy secretary, William Jones, as a man of "worthy talents," a prominent Philadelphia merchant and onetime naval officer. Noting that the war and navy departments had had no peacetime importance whatever, he was satisfied that Madison's cabinet now had "two more strong voices for continuing the war."[26]

What troubled him most by late January was the "extravagant news" of French disasters on the Russian front.[27] Talk of French military reverses, he wrote, had dominated public discourse for the past two weeks, fueled by British and Russian war bulletins flooding into Washington conjuring up what he called a "fantastic tableau" of French forces repeatedly thrown back and captured in large numbers. Fortunately, more recent reports had minimized the gravity of the military situation and had restored confidence in the emperor's "genius," at least among Republicans, most of whom, he wrote, had remained supportive of France throughout the worst of the bad news. They understood that if France left the field, Britain would turn on the United States with "redoubled" vigor. Still, with the Grande Armée clearly in retreat, Serurier reported sourly that the Russian chargé, Andrei de Daschkoff, closeted since the fall of Moscow, now strutted ostentatiously across Washington's social scene.[28] News of Napoleon's safe return to Paris brought further cheer, although at a presidential levee Madison took the opportunity to chide Serurier for the emperor's having called Barlow more than half way across Europe to discuss matters that should have been settled long before. The envoy offered what he thought were reasonable explanations but on being brusquely rebuffed broke off a conversation he said served "no useful purpose."[29]

Serurier particularly disliked having to stand on ministerial dignity whenever he sensed some ceremonial impropriety. Madison's second inauguration was such an instance. Half apologetically, he explained to Bassano how he had handled his non-role in this "grand solemnity." An uncomfortable episode, it ended better than he had expected. He refused to attend the ceremony, he wrote, because he had not been invited to sit at the president's right hand as had Turreau and all previous French ministers. Because the Senate was no longer in session, Madison had announced he would take the oath of office "in the presence of the people." Well versed in the partisanship of the day, Serurier suspected that the president had found a convenient pretext not to appear in public with the French minister, lest Federalists renew their charges that he was under French domination. A State Department messenger had promised him a good seat at the swearing-in, but he had declined.[30]

Alarmed that he might have given offense, he was put at ease by a conversation he had with Madison on the morning of the inauguration. The president, apparently softened by the recent news of Barlow's death, spoke to him "in a tone altogether different from that of the preceding days." Both men expressed personal regret at Barlow's loss but also, in Madison's words, "for the damage to our affairs, already long delayed." More was to follow. At the inaugural ball that evening, Madison remarked on the likelihood that Barlow had probably not had time to appoint a chargé d'affaires. The president then left him for a whispered conference with Monroe, and a few moments later the secretary strolled over to inform him that the president had named William Crawford, president *pro tempore* of the Senate, to replace Barlow. Serurier, gratified by the eminence of the appointee, reported that Crawford had already left for Georgia to wind up his affairs and would leave for France as soon as possible.[31] A new phase in French-American relations was about to open.

Looking back on America's first year at war, the French envoy doubtless had mixed feelings about the role he and his government had played in the unfolding drama. He could take modest pride in having muted the administration's anger at his emperor's continued ill treatment of American vessels, his refusal to deal substantively with Joel Barlow, and his apparent unwillingness to lend moral support to a co-belligerent. He had done his best to impress on Paris the importance of cultivating American goodwill, arguing that despite its bumbling war effort, the United States was a rising power whom France might someday usefully enlist in support of her own larger interests. Meanwhile, he was all too aware that his calls for conciliatory measures had not been heard. The here and now of French interests were far away, and for Serurier worse was to come.

CHAPTER 21

SERURIER CHAGRINED AS
MADISON LOOKS FOR PEACE

Although Serurier never doubted his emperor would ultimately prevail, continued reports of Allied battlefield successes put his mission to its severest test. At a personal level, he was appalled at the spectacle of Federalists rejoicing every time a bulletin arrived signaling a new French defeat. His "salons," he told Bassano, had always been open to guests of both political parties, but when a group of Federalists dining in Georgetown toasted the Russians for having killed a hundred thousand Frenchmen, he said he would invite thereafter only those persons who showed "decency and politeness."[1] The Russian factor took on more serious overtones when, shortly after Madison's inauguration, Monroe told him "confidentially" that the president was considering a Russian offer of mediation. Forewarned and having rehearsed what he should say, Serurier responded loftily that "the mediation of so intimate an ally by one of the belligerents was highly equivocal and did not promise a great impartiality." Passing over the gratuitous reference to being an "ally," Monroe admitted the offer was awkward but said the administration could not afford to "disoblige" a power against whom it had no complaints and to whom a rebuff might pose some danger. Serurier supposed the czar's gesture was either mere "politesse," in which case nothing would come of it, or—and here he guessed correctly—the British had covertly enlisted their Russian ally to give them a face-saving way out of their war in America.[2] Whatever the czar's motives, he warned, the peace process might well go forward; Congress had removed the sting from the impressment issue by forbidding foreigners to serve on American vessels;[3] and although some members still thirsted for revenge, they might be tempted if a third party were to give them a way out. He might be able to prevent this, but only if the next packet from France brought a treaty from Barlow. Without it, he wrote despondently, "I can do nothing."

Two weeks later, he learned that Madison had accepted the Russian offer.[4] In the event, Monroe took pains to assure him that the administration had not sought out the czar's good offices, nor had it relinquished its war aims. There would be no peace until there were "no orders in council, no paper blockades, no impressment aboard American vessels. . . ."[5] Then, subsiding into a reflective mood, the secretary mused that both France and Russia had traditionally championed the rights of neutral carriers and would doubtless do so someday in company with the United States. Serurier felt no need to respond to these ruminations. His political antennae told him that Washington's newfound hope for peace meant that France and French policy would count for even less with Washington than they had in the recent past. Madison and Monroe, he noted uneasily, no longer murmured about "our supposed wrongs, our delays, and our silence," and he confessed to Bassano that he preferred the earlier times when they complained, "even with bitterness."[6]

Nostalgic whimsy notwithstanding, the French minister had the last word on the Barlow mission. In late April, Monroe broke his own three-month silence to express his government's "lively discontent" at having received word from Paris that "nothing had been concluded at Vilna." The conduct of the French government was inexplicable. But before Monroe could continue, Serurier cut him off. He had just received Bassano's damning explanation of Barlow's indemnity plan and made the most of it. The secretary of state was aghast, he wrote, when told how Barlow had ultimately come to grips with the indemnity issue, dismayed to learn that Barlow had proposed to indemnify American claimants by arranging to have them buy some eighty French import licenses. Visibly shaken, Monroe protested that the administration would never have sanctioned this sort of private arrangement; it opposed licensing in all its forms. Having caught the secretary's full attention, Serurier went on to give him the foreign office version of what had transpired. Barlow and Dalberg, he recounted, had been quietly working on treaty clauses along the lines of the Convention of 1800 when Barlow had suddenly insisted on dealing with this "secondary matter of indemnities." Until then, discussion had touched on the possibility that the United States might satisfy its citizens' claims by acquiring the Floridas, but Barlow had shown no interest. When indemnification again surfaced, Bassano had invited Barlow to produce an alternative remedy and was "much surprised to find him looking for a mode of redress for American losses in the same system which the [American] government . . . rejects with so much perseverance." Indeed, it had, Monroe replied. A licensing proposal of this sort ran entirely counter to Barlow's instructions. The administration had told its envoy merely to secure recognition for the principle of indemnification and to arrange for an "amicable" means of satisfying American claims. This said, Monroe took another blow when Serurier asked whether Barlow had been furnished with a precise roster of ships and cargoes for which indemnification would be sought. When Monroe said he had, Serurier replied smugly that none had been presented. There the meeting ended. Satisfied that Barlow's scheme was now in ruins, the French envoy predicted that Crawford would press for indemnification by other means and suggested helpfully that the emperor might once again offer up the Floridas in lieu of cash.[7] Serurier could not help but gloat. Barlow's own government had disavowed his diplomacy. He would hear no more from Monroe on why Barlow's diplomacy had stalled out in Paris.

───── ✎ ─────

Powerless to prevent the administration's dalliance with Russian mediation, the French minister nonetheless tried to reassure Paris that peace would not come soon. Gallatin might sail for St. Petersburg in May, but the time-distance factor and the uncertainty of Britain's willingness to treat under Russian auspices foretold more months of active warfare. By all accounts, the government clearly intended to launch new campaigns against Canada if only to wipe out the disgrace of earlier forays; and congressional appropriations for a second year of warfare, he added knowingly, signaled a government in no hurry to end hostilities.[8] As for consummating the Russian offer, Madison himself had cautioned Congress that "time only can decide."[9]

Meanwhile, Serurier made subtle use of the president's having told Congress that Crawford would be instructed to avoid any "connexion of their fortunes with the system of other powers." The French minister was well aware of George Washington's cautionary Farewell but pretended to believe that Madison particularly objected to linking the fortunes of the United States to those of his emperor. Huffily, he let it be known how absurd it was to "repulse an alliance that has never been offered." Alliances with France, he told Monroe, were eagerly sought by the leading powers of Europe, but "had never been lightly given, nor readily offered." Behind this posturing, Serurier told Bassano he knew "perfectly well" that Madison's only purpose had been "to dismiss the eternal reproach of French influence, but I did not wish to appear to have guessed the motive. I also knew that in thus satisfying what the dignity of the Emperor requires, I did not disserve the administration, that my reproaches serve to justify their own."[10]

Predictably, perhaps, with talk of peace in the air, Serurier and Monroe speculated on how their governments would relate to Britain in a postwar era. The French envoy recorded a conversation in late May which revealed a seductive paradigm in the foreign policy thinking of French and American statesmen of the time, a shared conviction that if the past were a guide, Great Britain would continue to frustrate the aspirations of both powers, denying France her well deserved prominence in world affairs while blocking the expansionist and maritime ambitions of the United States. For his part, Serurier voiced certainty that Britain would always remain France's "implacable rival," while Monroe predicted that peace would mark "only the beginning of our quarrels with England" over "[t]he Floridas, Canada, the savages, our commercial rivalry, our pretensions above all to become a maritime power. . . ." In this light, he was sure France and the United States would find many opportunities to make common cause against Britain, though nothing, he warned pointedly, could be "more troublesome for . . . our political interests in the future" than a failure to settle the indemnities issue.[11]

Animated by Monroe's vision, Serurier eagerly embraced the likelihood that the United States and France would find occasions to join forces in contesting British pretensions in the future. To encourage this shared interest, he wrote Paris that France should give free rein to Americans in their maritime sphere, set aside fears of their commerce, open her ports to them, not begrudge them their profits, and furnish them with arms if the need arose. This, he wrote "is the great reckoning to which all others ought to be subordinated."[12]

Neither man could foresee, of course, that in the years ahead, except for occasional skirmishes, most of them diplomatic, neither Frenchmen nor Americans would again offer a serious military challenge to Great Britain. Nor for all the importance Monroe gave to spoliation claims could either foresee how quickly indemnification would become only a minor irritant in French-American relations. But like those who embraced "containment" in the Soviet era, this readiness to believe in Britain's enduring hostility would serve a variety of useful foreign policy purposes for both powers as they went their separate ways throughout most of the next hundred years.

The summer of 1813 passed fitfully for the American cause, as it did for Serurier. General Dearborn's indecisive campaign south of the Great Lakes made him wish he could report offsetting naval victories, but U.S. frigates were now bottled up. Congress, too, disappointed him by passing a tax bill whose prospective revenues he thought insufficient. Nor was all quiet on the diplomatic front. In June, he stood by helplessly as Napoleon's inexplicable St. Cloud Decree caught fire in the press. Congressional Federalists fanned the flames, demanding to know how the administration could explain why an explicit revocation of the Berlin and Milan decrees dated 28 April 1811 had not been divulged to its minister until May 1812. Monroe, again fronting for the administration, asked Serurier hopefully whether he himself had received a more timely notice of revocation. The French minister replied evasively that many of the previous year's communications had been intercepted at sea, implying that the St. Cloud Decree had been among them. To satisfy Congress, Monroe told him he was drafting a report on the subject and predicted it would "produce a good effect." He offered to give the envoy a preview of his draft, but must have thought better of it for Serurier never received an advance copy and later complained to Bassano that it was "not exactly what he had promised me." The French minister was understandably piqued. Monroe's report virtually confirmed the predating of the decree when he verified that neither Russell nor Serurier had been told of it at its supposed time of issuance. The secretary chose instead to direct his fire at London for refusing to acknowledge the repeal of the Berlin and Milan decrees at the time of the Cadore Letter. Hard put to explain the inexplicable, Monroe obviously preferred to dwell on British bad faith than to guess why Napoleon had ostensibly wiped the slate clean in April 1811 but kept its erasure secret for more than a year.[13] Federalists had their own explanation. As one New York congressman put it, "Napoleon knew very well that when proper evidence of the repeal of his decrees was furnished, the English orders in council would be repealed, and the U.S. would not go to war with G. Britain."[14] Madison himself had reached the same conclusion some months before, as had Russell and Barlow.

Having junketed once more to the Canadian front, the French minister returned in September to find the Federalists churning up another "scandal," this time over the intemperate letter Turreau had sent to Robert Smith in June 1809. Responding to a flurry of speculation in the press, House Federalists in late December hoped to balloon Madison's tardiness in rejecting Turreau's insulting remarks into possible grounds for impeachment.[15] As for the letter itself, written shortly after news broke of the Erskine Agreement, Turreau had scolded the administration for yielding to British blandishments while having the gall to offer a renewal of the Franco-American Convention of 1800. He also accused the administration and its predecessor of having unjustly characterized the French decrees as violative of neutral rights, permitting illicit trade with St. Domingue, encouraging Francisco Miranda, knuckling under to British policy, and so forth. In all, it totted up French grievances with enough acerbity to reflect accurately Napoleon's own bitter feelings about Americans and the problems they had caused him up to that time. But was the letter threatening? Federalists thought so. Turreau's call for American "political sacrifice" suggested that a right-minded United States should have joined the French-backed league of armed neutrals. From this Federalists extrapolated that Turreau would not have voiced this expectation unless he believed Madison would submit to French direction. Not unlike partisan attacks on the executive, then and later, Federalists demanded full disclosure, documents, and blood if they could get it. Where, they asked, was the original letter? Had it been secretly removed from the State Department files? Had Turreau thrice refused to take it back? Had he been persuaded only after "Copenhagen" Jackson had been recalled? Across the aisle, administration defenders at first challenged the accuracy, even the existence, of what was, after all, a translated copy. Failing to make a case for forgery, they belittled its contents as nothing more than "impertinence," and finally pronounced the administration's refusal to accept the letter as proof that no French influence had been at work. With administration supporters complaining of time wasted, a copy of the letter was read into the record, and on 11 January a House resolution demanding to know the whereabouts of the original was defeated, ninety-six to sixty-five.[16]

Serurier was appalled by the uproar. He thought Turreau's reaction to the Erskine Agreement was "perfectly just," though he wished his predecessor had kept his anger to himself. The clamor in the press, unfortunately, led him to worsen a moderately unpleasant situation. He told Monroe he was not surprised that Federalist newspapers had maligned Turreau but was shocked to read equally harsh pieces in the *Intelligencer.* Unwilling to listen to Monroe's familiar lecture on freedom of the press, he said he knew the government had no power to silence these critics, even if it were so disposed, but could it not curb its own people? If the attacks on Turreau continued, he warned, French publicists might see fit to attack Crawford's predecessors. If it came to a *guerre de presse*, he warned, "We too have persons in France who know how to write about governments." He did not recommend such reprisals, he later told Bassano, but merely wanted to give the administration something to "reflect on."[17]

Amid conflicting military bulletins from Europe, the French minister himself had much to reflect on. Most Americans, he hoped, would continue to realize how vital the success of French arms was to their own war effort, that without France they would face the full might of Great Britain. He believed they knew this truth "from the first Magistrate down to the last citizen."[18] By early November, however, moved by reports of more allied victories and sensing the need to "sustain confidence," he resorted to the time-honored device of planting optimistic articles in the press. Reliable intelligence was hard to come by, he told Bassano and begged him to send the kind of information he could use to offset the obviously biased reports emanating from London.[19] By early 1814, however, he must have known that he was waging a rear-guard action against growing evidence that the emperor might not prevail. Discouraged by news of the French defeat at Leipzig, he looked hopefully to the administration for moral support. He was not disappointed, although in conversation with Monroe he may have missed the fullness of Washington's motives. The secretary told him that the president fervently wished for the success of French arms but what he neglected to mention was that the administration hoped Napoleon would stay in the field long enough to persuade the British to cut their losses in America and make peace. The extent to which peace dominated the administration's agenda that spring became clear when Monroe asked a favor of Serurier. Because the Senate had persistently refused to approve the appointment of Albert Gallatin to the U.S. peace commission, he wanted to know whether France would permit Crawford a temporary leave of absence to take his place? The president intended to return Crawford to his post afterwards, which should guarantee that France would find nothing contrary to her interests in an Anglo-American peace treaty. Serurier answered, though not officially, that he believed Paris would not object.[20] The request was mooted, however, when on 7 February, Madison broke the deadlock over Gallatin's confirmation by nominating Senator George Campbell of Tennessee to take the treasury post, thereby meeting the Senate's earlier objection to Gallatin's holding two federal offices.[21]

As the Napoleonic era drew to its tumultuous close, Serurier had reason to consider his own uncertain future. He sounded a plaintive note in welcoming Bassano's successor to the foreign office. He was sure, he told the duc de Caulincourt, that the emperor was too busy to deal with American affairs but urged that the importance of the Washington post not be overlooked. America's growing "maritime power," he predicted, would figure importantly in the future and could likely be harnessed to serve French interests in the postwar.[22] His own immediate future, it turned out, was secure. A note from Antoine de LaForest heralding the return of the Bourbons made clear that Louis XVIII's soon-to-be government would keep him in place, indeed counted on him to convey its "amicable dispositions" and the promise of better relations.[23]

Though he remained loyal to Napoleon to the end, when the end came the French envoy took refuge in professional formalities and managed fairly well to hide his personal feelings. Congress was out of session and Serurier himself in New York when news broke that the Allies had occupied Paris. Despite this calamity, he put on a brave face. France need not despair, he wrote Caulincourt, "as long as there exists a French Army commanded by the Emperor."[24] In mid-June, however, LaForest's note confirming the worst reached him shortly after he returned to Washington. With what must have been a heavy heart at the passing of imperial splendors, he conveyed the restored monarchy's goodwill to members of the administration.[25] On his own initiative, he circularized a terse statement to French consuls, officially notifying them of the emperor's abdication and the impending return of the house of Bourbon. This "great revolution" he observed neutrally, would be of interest to "all Frenchmen in the New World." Consuls were asked to signify their allegiance by an "acte d'adhésion," and were told hereafter to display the "cocarde Blanche."[26] With this muted finale, except for the passing thunder of the Hundred Days, the American echo chamber of the Napoleonic era fell silent.

CHAPTER 22

END OF AN ERA:
THE CRAWFORD MISSION

E xplaining William H. Crawford's failed mission to France, his biographer Chase Mooney finds it "reasonable to assume that no one could have settled the issues with the French government at that time."[1] Yet, if the time was not right for a settlement, Crawford perhaps did less to make it right than his biographer is prepared to concede. Though Mooney assigns Crawford "abilities of a high order," he admits the American envoy spoke no French and had no previous diplomatic experience. What abilities Crawford did possess were those of a skilled politician, coupled in his case with a streak of independence of the type foreign offices tend not to appreciate in an emissary. To the extent that Crawford was his own man, much like Joel Barlow in this respect, he conducted his mission to Paris pretty much as he pleased, certainly at his own pace; and as the record also suggests, he was too easily distracted from its principal objects.

One might also question whether Crawford's biographer is quite on the mark in denying that his subject's "temper in any way affected negotiations."[2] If not his temper, certainly his temperament affected his mission. The time and energy he devoted to picayune consular matters, for example, he might better have spent in a more concerted effort to connect himself to the power centers of the French government. Here, after all, was a diplomat who arrived in Paris on 25 July 1813, decided not to pursue Napoleon to his camp at Dresden, and as a result made no personal contact with the emperor until 14 November. To be sure, he and Bassano exchanged notes in the interim, but it seems reasonable to conclude that William H. Crawford lacked both the temperament and the inclination to pursue his mission with anything approaching the zeal Barlow had shown. Thus, it also seems fair to say that if the time was not right for settling issues with the French government, Crawford did not put that time to best use. On its face, his performance in Paris exhibited a timidity all the more curious given his reputation as a forceful standard-bearer for the administration in Congress.

In the eyes of his contemporaries, the Senator from Georgia cut an impressive figure. Joined to an imposing physique—he stood six foot three and was well fleshed out—he showed an intellectual vitality that led Henry Adams to call him "the only vigorous Republican leader in the Senate."[3] By way of background, Crawford came from a Virginia family of small planters who had resettled in Georgia during the Revolution. Trained locally in the law, he rose to prominence in the turbulence of Georgia state politics at the turn of the century and in late 1807, on the eve of the embargo, was elected to the Senate seat left by the death of its longtime incumbent, Abraham Baldwin. From this beginning in national politics, the freshman Senator quickly contracted debts with the party's leaders which, consciously intended or not, assured him of political preferment. From James Monroe he earned a measure of goodwill for having supported the latter's lackadaisical bid for the presidency in 1808. He also won thanks from Treasury Secretary Albert Gallatin for having led the administration's battle in Congress to recharter the Bank of the United States, albeit unsuccessfully. Madison, too, appreciated the support Crawford gave to administration measures on the floor of the Senate when, as often happened, they came under attack from dissident members of their own party.[4] Owed by such persons in high places, the forty-one-year-old Senator was well positioned to be rewarded politically when the time came to name Barlow's successor.

Though usually faithful to Republican principles, the Georgia Senator showed a maverick tendency when it came to supporting his party's policies. He voted against the embargo, then supported it, but voted against the Non-Intercourse Act because he thought it both weak and unavailing. He also opposed the administration's navy bill in the spring of 1812. Despite these and other lapses from party regularity, however, he sided fairly consistently with the party's Warhawks up to and including the vote for war.[5]

Monroe must have felt the press of events when he wrote Crawford's instructions in late May. From Paris Thomas Barlow had written that except for Napoleon's helter-skelter retreat from Moscow his uncle would have signed both a commercial treaty and a claims convention. If Washington moved quickly, young Barlow assured him, a new minister could wind up the business in short order.[6] Accordingly, Monroe instructed Crawford to make a judgment call as to whether Barlow's diplomacy had provided adequately for indemnification and for putting commerce back on a "reciprocal" footing. Above all, he was to make very certain that France had made a firm commitment to indemnify Americans not only for property seized under the Bayonne and Rambouillet decrees but also for the vessels burned en route to Lisbon and Cadiz. Alternatively, if he found flaws in Barlow's indemnity arrangements, and if he himself were unable to secure the necessary commitment, he was to request that the emperor merely issue a series of decrees releasing American property and reopening trade on "a just, solid, and stable foundation." In light of Crawford's later conduct, it bears repeating that Monroe told him explicitly that the president preferred this step-by-step return to normal relations, paraphrasing Madison to the effect that "It was by edicts that our relations with France were first violated. By edicts they may be completely restored."[7] Beyond this, he was to promise no injury to French interests in the event that the czar's mediation produced an Anglo-American peace treaty. Nor would the United States form a "political connexion" with either power in the postwar. If, however, France refused to indemnify, the president would have to decide what further actions to take. In sum, France's willingness to indemnify for American property losses became both the major focus of Crawford's instructions and the touchstone of future good relations.

Crawford's earliest letters from France showed a decided inclination to feel his way cautiously. Physically drained by a cold and rough crossing, he arrived in L'Orient feverish and still suffering the effects of seasickness. His diary suggests a quick recovery, but health concerns possibly explain why more than a month elapsed before he wrote his first full-length despatch from Paris.[8] On arrival in the capital, he found other reasons to proceed cautiously. Rumors circulated that Napoleon was seeking a general peace settlement. If the war ended in Europe, he feared he might have to wait for additional instructions. He was also uncomfortably aware that France took a dim view of the czar's offer of mediation inasmuch as peace on the American front would potentially free up British soldiery to

join the allied forces arrayed against it in Europe. Finally, Crawford stick-
led at opening his mission officially until he had formally presented his
credentials. With the emperor still campaigning in Germany and, he believed, too busy to receive him, he was reluctant to make contact with
the French foreign minister.[9] Although Petry suggested to Bassano that
Crawford's punctilio might be satisfied if he were to present his credentials to the empress in her capacity as regent, no record exists of a reply.[10]
Petry passed the word, meanwhile, that the new minister was "very but-
toned up (*très boutonné*)," silent on the nature of his instructions, and
disapprovingly tight-lipped at any mention of Barlow's indemnity plan.[11]

Although Crawford did receive a letter from Bassano dated 1 August
inviting an overture, he told Monroe he had not replied because no one
in Paris knew how to reach the emperor's headquarters. More likely, as
he also told Monroe, he held back because he believed his first face-to-
face meeting with Napoleon would determine the success of his mission
and therefore thought it best to await his return. In the interim, he noted
grimly that rumors had spread through the capital describing him as "an
impetuous and unaccommodating man, who will be disposed to say, and
do harsh things." This effort to discredit him, he supposed, was the work
of Federalist enemies in the homefront press. Whatever the source, he
took care not to give it substance.[12]

The fruits of Barlow's earlier diplomacy also gave him pause. His predecessor's draft commercial treaty, he believed, had lost its allure because
the licensed importation of colonial goods had succeeded in glutting the
French market. Napoleon's offering of 200 more licenses on his return
from Moscow seemed to render a commercial treaty superfluous. Accordingly, he told Monroe he would put aside commercial matters and focus
instead on nailing down indemnification. But here, too, he sounded a
negative note. Although the details of Barlow's licensing plan were still
shrouded in secrecy, he doubted he could agree to it even if he knew its
full extent.[13] He enclosed a copy of the plan he had received from the
foreign office but said he could not attest to its completeness. Only later
did he learn from Petry that Paris had long since rejected it because it
knew Washington would never accept its licensing feature.[14]

He also discovered that if the plan had been implemented, the foreign
ministry would have turned over to Daniel Parker the "indemnity" funds
to be derived from selling the licenses. Knowing the shady reputation
of Barlow's former business associate, he suspected Parker would have
pocketed a fat percentage of the take. Four months later, Parker braced

him with a version of the plan that envisioned the duties on French-imported tobacco being paid in the United States where they would ultimately amount to an "indemnity fund" he reckoned at $10 million. By this time, Crawford had gathered his thoughts on the subject and told Parker bluntly that France could set aside any revenues she wished for indemnity purposes, "but we have a right to refuse to become parties to an engagement, which will . . . tend to create a monopoly during its continuance." Not until January 1814 did Crawford finally lay Barlow's indemnity plan to rest.[15] No indemnity funds ever accrued from sales of licenses.

As he settled down in Paris that fall having decided to start afresh on the indemnity issue when the emperor returned, the American minister filled his days trying to restore a semblance of order to the chaos American consuls had created for lack of ministerial oversight. To be sure, he had instructions to discipline them, but the extent to which he became enmeshed in their personality clashes almost certainly distracted him from the main purposes of his mission. First to be rebuked was David Bailie Warden, the prickly Irish-born U.S. consul for Paris, whose officious conduct had rankled both Washington and his fellow consuls. Bassano's decision to do official business with Warden after Barlow died had left the other would-be chargés—specifically William Lee and Isaac Cox Barnet—angry and quarrelsome.

Typical of the disarray, Crawford arrived to find Lee and Warden contesting control over two prize vessels brought in by Commodore Rodgers. Lee's consular position in Bordeaux gave him a better claim to handle these cases but, as Crawford related, Warden had persuaded Rodgers that Lee was a bankrupt and would probably cheat him. At stake was a 2 percent consular fee.[16] Aloof at first, Crawford ultimately decided that Lee was the aggrieved party and "reprehended" Warden severely for having twice leaned on French authorities in his efforts to gain jurisdiction.[17] As for charges of usurpation, Warden heard it again from Crawford who told him he had wrongfully solicited the office of chargé on Barlow's death and had had no authority to act without presidential sanction. Warden replied tartly that he would do the same again, if only to keep the legation's papers from Parker who would surely have used the government's secrets for "selfish and private purposes." Troubled by Warden's mystifyingly intricate relations with low-ranking officials in the foreign office, the minister offered to find replacements for both Warden and Lee, if the president so desired.[18] A month later, his feelings about Warden further inflamed, he left a damning description of the man's demeanor, characterizing it as "a tissue of arrogance and civility—of ambition & weakness—of apparent simplicity with the most unblushing duplicity." He could understand why Armstrong had wanted to get rid of him.[19]

Isaac Cox Barnet, U.S. consul for Le Havre, was another battle-scarred figure from an earlier era. Barnet had made the mistake of crossing swords with Armstrong over which of two American claimants was entitled to be indemnified for a cargo which an earlier French regime had paid for in depreciated *assignats*. Armstrong's claimant had won his case, but not before Barnet had accused the man of fraud and had him jailed for assault. Fired for this impertinence, Barnet was later reinstated at Le Havre in March 1812, thanks to a presidential inquiry and a good word from Joel Barlow.[20] When Crawford came on the scene, Barnet and Warden were competing for consular fees swollen by the sale of prize vessels now being brought in by American privateers. Warden, fuming at encroachments on what he regarded as his exclusive preserve, charged Barnet with maintaining an office in Paris (which was true) and with claiming to be the U.S. consul-general (which may also have been true). As Armstrong observed wearily, the two men had merely entered a more intense phase of longstanding competition for the consular business that ultimately found its way to the capital.[21] Barnet's claim to the title of consul-general, he told Monroe, was part of their "open war with each other, [adding] I will not trouble you with their writings."[22] His own writings, however, dwelt increasingly on David Warden's propensity for causing the kinds of problems that reflected badly on the government. In May 1814 Crawford fired him and turned the Paris consulate over to Barnet, a measure that might be seen as an act of desperation, having earlier described Barnet as hardworking but "not very able."[23] Warden did not go quietly. Crawford had to threaten to withhold funds that were owed him before Warden grudgingly handed over some forty pieces of official correspondence he had exchanged with the foreign office.[24]

───— ✦✦✦ ——───

Crawford's preoccupation with consular squabbles almost certainly diverted him from the loftier purposes of his mission. A month passed after Bassano had invited him to open "communication" in early August, two months since his arrival at L'Orient.[25] Troubled that the foreign minister had not renewed his overture, he sent Bassano a blockbuster note on 11 September. Ignoring Monroe's preference that he simply request the release of American property still in custody, he launched a frontal assault on the touchy issue of what he called the French navy's "lawless and wanton" burning of American grain ships.[26] Although Barlow's unanswered protest on this score made a logical starting point, there was also something anomalous, if not also digressive, in Crawford's defending the right of American carriers to supply the armed forces of a nation with whom both parties were now at war. Bassano must have marveled at Crawford's arguing the case for "free ships, free goods" in the context of a common war effort. To his credit, Crawford seems to have recognized this anomaly when he later told Monroe he hoped Congress would place a ban on the Iberian grain trade.[27] As an diplomatic opener, however, his note seemed to make too much of France's efforts to accomplish the same end by more summary means.

Toward France's more distant offenses he merely warned that Americans would lose all confidence in French goodwill unless they were indemnified for property seized under the Bayonne and Rambouillet decrees. He said he believed the emperor had already approved the "principle of indemnity," and had signified his willingness to sign Barlow's draft of a commercial treaty. Whatever preliminaries his predecessor had agreed to, he stood ready to carry them forward.[28]

Had Crawford at this point merely asked for the release of American property not already confiscated, he might at least have had a response from Dresden. As it was, he had no word from Bassano until Napoleon returned to Paris two months later. Impatient in the interim, he carped at relatively minor afflictions. When the French police seized some of his incoming despatches, he thought he might quit. "If I cannot prevent this practice," he wrote Monroe, "I shall certainly not remain here even if this court conduct itself as it ought to do in the more essential points."[29] Too, for what it was worth, he sent Bassano a three-and-a-half-page letter detailing the misadventures of an American sailor who had been caught in the toils of the French justice system.[30] Made fretful by inactivity, he nonetheless kept a watchful eye on the military scene. Napoleon was still winning battles, he wrote, but his armies were clearly in retreat; should he sue for peace, the United States would face Britain's full military might alone. Like other Americans, Crawford dreaded the prospect of Wellington's veterans, once freed from the Peninsular Campaign, advancing along a front stretching from Plattsburg to Detroit.[31]

Behind the scenes, Madison had already taken the first steps toward peace. In May 1813, responding to Russia's offer of mediation, he named a team of five to meet with British negotiators under Russian auspices. They included Albert Gallatin, his erstwhile treasury secretary whose appointment the Senate at first refused to approve; Henry Clay, the War-hawk Speaker of the House whose signature on a peace treaty would presumably assure its acceptance in that quarter, and Senator James F. Bayard of Delaware, whose moderate Federalist principles added a touch of bipartisanship to the endeavor. These three were to rendezvous in St. Petersburg with John Quincy Adams and Jonathan Russell. In taking this initiative, the president also took a major risk that London would not accept the czar's mediation. What Crawford learned from John Quincy Adams, however, well before the news reached Washington, was that although the British were willing to talk peace, they would not meet under Russian auspices, not in St. Petersburg, nor in Russian-occupied Gothenburg, to which Gallatin and Bayard hopefully repaired in November 1813.[32] Not surprisingly, the British shied at having a Russian presence at the peace table lest that nation's well-known attachment to maritime neutral rights become an issue they had no intention of discussing. Ultimately, the U.S. commissioners met their British counterparts in the supposedly "neutral" though British-occupied Belgian city of Ghent, and from the sidelines Crawford offered them advice through the summer and fall of 1814.

⸻ ❧ ⸻

Allied armies were crossing the Rhine when the American envoy had his first and only encounter with Napoleon. They met at an imperial reception on 14 November shortly after the latter's return. Decked out in imperial finery and apparently untroubled by military reverses, the French emperor circulated amiably among the assembled dignitaries. Crawford presented his credentials and gave the short speech required on such occasions, but spoke in English. His interpreter let him know that the emperor supported the American war effort and promised to "do everything in his power to make the relations between the two countries as friendly and as beneficial as possible."[33] A few days later, Napoleon's abrupt shuffle of ministerial personnel caught Crawford by surprise. Apparently sensing that he might have to negotiate if his military operations faltered, the emperor replaced Bassano in the foreign office with the duc de Vicence, Armand-Augustin-Louis de Caulincourt, a diplomat whose assets included his having befriended the czar when he was posted to St. Petersburg in the halcyon days following the Treaty of Tilsit.[34] It was no secret in Paris, Crawford reported, that Napoleon counted on the duc de Vicence to strike acceptable peace terms if the need arose,[35] and in the weeks that followed Caulincourt did figure prominently in various efforts to come to terms with the advancing allies.

Crawford first met the new foreign minister a few days after the imperial reception and was sharply taken aback when told that Barlow's indemnity plan had created a wave of "speculations" in licenses which had deprived the French government of much-needed revenues. Caulincourt characterized the plan as shamefully unworthy of their two governments and called on the envoy to disavow it. Crawford replied truthfully that far from sanctioning Barlow's arrangements, his government was "most decidedly opposed to the license system in every form." American shipowners, he supposed, had acted in their private capacities. If they also profited from acquiring licenses, he added, they were merely reimbursing themselves for French depredations. If speculation had followed, it was not because Washington had sanctioned Barlow's plan or had even known of its existence until recently. Inasmuch as Caulincourt later reminded Napoleon that Barlow's plan had never been implemented, he probably meant merely to put Crawford on the defensive at their first meeting. But if he also meant to distract the envoy from raising the indemnification issue, he was less successful. As their meeting drew to a close, Crawford said he believed both parties had recognized a French obligation to indemnify and asked how the emperor intended to proceed.[36]

Three weeks later, on hearing from Caulincourt that the emperor had agreed to discuss indemnification, Crawford decided to push for an "immediate decision," one that would smoke out the French government's readiness to deal with the details. The note he drafted listed meticulously all "the classes of cases for which Indemnity should be made." To his dismay, however, before the note could be delivered, the emperor and his entourage left Paris. The reason was soon obvious. The twilight battles around the French capital were about to begin in earnest. Cut off in midstroke, Crawford blamed himself for not acting more swiftly; his note had been ready for delivery, he told Monroe, but he had mistaken the hour of the emperor's departure. "I have been six months in France." he wrote cheerlessly, "and I am not certain that I have advanced one step closer to the great object of my mission."[37]

As before, the American minister made a conscious decision not to follow Napoleon into the field, convinced that appeals for indemnifica-

tion would be drowned out by the din of battle.[38] The previous fall, perhaps, when the fighting east of the Rhine was intermittent, he might at
least have received a hearing. Now, in February and March 1814, with
allied forces closing on Paris, he could hardly expect to make himself
heard. Still, believing that Bonaparte's government would survive its military reverses, he made one last bid for indemnification. He wrote Caulincourt that if the war ended in Europe, the United States might have to
"retire from the contest." His countrymen, however, might be encouraged to fight on if France were to accord "a prompt & just, and liberal
remuneration for the injuries it has inflicted."[39] A weak argument, he
almost certainly expected no more of this note than to put the central
purpose of his mission on the record. And yet, remarkably, it almost
found its mark. Even as allied forces descended on Paris, Caulincourt
made a concerted effort to persuade Napoleon to sign Barlow's commercial treaty, hinting that the indemnification issue could be finessed. A
commercial treaty, he argued, if it revived France's American commerce
would so enrich both parties as to reduce the indemnities issue to manageable proportions. The cost to France they could haggle over later. That
Caulincourt was serious about restarting a treaty negotiation is confirmed
by the indemnity schedules he drew up, assigning monetary values to
various classes of claims he believed were valid.[40] Whether Napoleon ever
responded to his foreign minister's initiative is not recorded. His days in
power were growing short. Nor is there any evidence that Crawford knew
that the principal aim of his mission had finally caught the attention of
the French foreign office.

As Napoleon fought his last battles, Crawford followed events with
both hope and foreboding. In mid-February, he speculated that the emperor's best chance for survival lay in making a separate peace with Austria, a possibility that was clearly in the wind. Later, catching at a moment
when Prussian and Austrian forces were temporarily retreating north, he
hoped French forces might reach Belgium. If so, the British for time-
honored strategic reasons would be bound to keep troops there. Unless
Britain remained militarily engaged in that or some other quarter, he
reminded himself, her soldiers would soon be on the Canadian front.[41]

Despite rumors of Austrian mediation, the time for diplomacy soon
passed. Napoleon, still believing he could out-general his enemies, let slip
whatever opportunities he may have had to come to terms. On March 9,
as peace talks languished at Chatillon, British diplomacy moved decisively. Lord Castlereagh, offering subsidies amounting to five million

pounds, managed to coax enough unity from his Russian, Prussian, and Austrian allies to bind them to a treaty by which they agreed to fight until they had rid the continent of their nemesis. A week later, although Crawford reported hearing of minor military actions between Reims and Soissons, the end had arrived.[42] On March 31, the allied sovereigns meeting at Talleyrand's house in Paris renewed their commitment not to treat with the French emperor; and at their behest and in swift succession, the French legislature declared Napoleon deposed, patched together a constitution, and called on Louis XVIII to take the throne.[43]

During the April interregnum, while Paris waited for Louis to approve the new constitution, the allied leaders dealt amicably enough with a French provisional government headed by Charles Maurice de Talleyrand, who once again proved himself to be one of history's most agile political survivors. Paris newspapers, Crawford noted, obsequiously touted a return of "good government," and fickle Parisians who a few weeks earlier had shouted for their emperor now shamelessly took to the streets to cheer the czar. Looking ahead, he prophesied (accurately) that France was not likely to achieve political stability under a constitution that the old aristocracy detested for its liberality and republicans deplored for its failure to safeguard individual liberty. "I hope a better state of things will spring up," he wrote, "but I rather hope, than expect it."[44] His thoughts turning to home, he told Monroe he would make a "fair experiment with the new government," but added plaintively, "the longer I remain here, the more strongly I desire to return to my native country." Still, he was curious to see how the new regime might function. Two days later he wrote Monroe asking for six copies of Jefferson's "manual" on parliamentary procedure. France had boasted a legislative body for twenty-five years, he remarked sardonically, "without knowing anything of the principles of order in their proceedings. They are now desirous of knowing and applying them."[45]

Still troubled as to whether peace in Europe might inspire the British to prosecute their war in America more vigorously, what Crawford learned of British intentions allayed at least some of his anxiety. London had yet to signal a time and place, he wrote, but conversations with British officials in Paris led him to believe that negotiations were at hand. He worried, however, that British peace terms might not be acceptable. Seated at a dinner with French and British officials—among them Lords Castlereagh and Cathcart—he gladly drank a toast to "universal peace" offered by the comte de Marbois, "but noted warily that Castlereagh had added: "upon just principles."[46] Did such principles, he wondered, include the continued impressment of American seamen? Other Englishmen had told him that London would demand nothing less than control of the Great Lakes and, yes, a recognition of its Navy's right to recover deserters.[47] By mid-May, however, he concluded—as would the Ghent commissioners when they omitted it from the peace treaty—that impressment was fast becoming a nonissue, no longer worth contesting. With the British navy discharging seamen and dry-docking its men-of-war, he urged Monroe to see the reasonableness of dropping it altogether. Because further military action was unlikely to change London's position, "why should we not consent to a Peace which shall leave the principle unsettled?"[48] This advice, also offered to the American peace commissioners, may well have weighed in their decision not to pursue the matter. The Ghent treaty made no mention of impressment.

⎯⎯⎯ ∞ ⎯⎯⎯

Whether indemnification could be wrung from any of the four regimes that succeeded Napoleon's first exile seemed to depend on how each felt about actually having to pay up. Crawford's earliest contacts with the provisional government in March and April of 1814 sounded promising. He was told by Dupont de Nemours who, as "secretary" of the interim regime was well placed to know its intentions, that France would pay for "all of the illegal confiscations and condemnations which had been committed by the [previous] government."[49] Early in Louis's first restoration, however, Crawford found the "permanent" government much less receptive. Talleyrand, who served as Louis XVIII's foreign minister both before and after the Hundred Days, showed a decided aversion to addressing spoliation claims. Twice in conference he refused even to discuss the matter and when he left Paris for the Congress of Vienna, Crawford regretted not having put those claims in writing at the outset. A written note on the subject, he assured Monroe, would await the French foreign minister on his return.[50] Before the issue could be revisited, however, France was treated briefly to Napoleon's triumphal return from Elba, and Crawford again found himself talking to Caulincourt. The latter's "countenance immediately changed," he reported, when asked the emperor's intentions with respect to American spoliation claims. There followed some artless dodging on the part of the foreign minister who said he assumed Crawford had settled the matter with the provisional government. When told this was not the case, he allowed fecklessly that perhaps the issue had been resolved during the Anglo-American treaty negotiations in Ghent. Crawford replied irritably that "the wrongs committed by France could not possibly have been arranged in a treaty between the United States and England, to which France was not even a party." An obviously confused Caulincourt said he would look into the matter.[51] He never had time. Waterloo put an end to it.[52]

Though what remains of the indemnities issue is a long story, it can be summarized roughly as follows. For American claimants the peace that came to Europe after Bonaparte's final exile reduced their chances for an early payoff in large part because dramatic changes were overtaking the American economy. Venture capital, once substantially invested in commerce, shifted increasingly away from the Atlantic and into mill towns like Lowell and Lawrence and into the economic development of a rapidly expanding frontier. The consequent growth of domestic manufacture, together with the development of internal markets, meant that Americans looked less needfully to Europe for either manufactured goods or markets. Not surprisingly, amid the excitement of building factories and staking out a western frontier, maritime claimants had difficulty making their voices heard. Seizures of American property in the past no longer quickened the public's political pulse, and with the shrinking importance of the mercantile community in the nation's economy as a whole, its once vocal spokesmen gradually faded from the political scene. Concurrently, as a new generation of Americans turned their energies inward and away from the sea, it was relatively easy for Louis XVIII's restored government to ignore their claims for damages. Each year the issue drifted further into the past without causing serious incident. Nor were Louis' successors any more willing than he to make restitution. Like a persistent but minor case of indigestion, the claims issue rumbled around in the background of French-American relations for nearly two decades. Not until 1831, and only then under Andrew Jackson's threat of reprisal, did the government of Louis Philippe agree to settle. And not until 1836, after further delays, did France pay the agreed-upon sum of twenty-five million francs.[53] When the American Minister William Rives negotiated the final settlement, he said he believed "the sum sufficient, in all probability, to pay every cent justly due. . . ."[54] Only then did Americans finally settle their accounts with Napoleon Bonaparte.

Napoleon's Case
Against Americans:
Summarizing the Evidence

A major purpose of this study has been to explore Napoleon's growing hostility toward the United States in the last ten years of his reign to determine whether his rationales for despoiling American commerce merit positive consideration. A corollary purpose has been to flesh out the roles of French and American diplomats as they grappled with these elements of Napoleonic hostility and to assess the responsibility of each party for not coming to terms with the other's perception of its national interests.

Although the French emperor's preoccupation with European affairs always came first, he did periodically turn his wrath on Americans largely because he perceived them to stand in the way of his defeating Great Britain, the power that in turn stood in the way of his permanently dominating the continent. Americans came into this crossfire of Anglo-French warfare when Napoleon, forced by his naval defeat at Trafalgar to give up any thought of invading the British Isles, believed that by closing the ports of Europe to Britain's manufactures he could destroy her export-dependent economy and bring her to her knees as surely as if his armies had crossed the Channel. American shipmasters who at the time were the principal carriers of British products to continental markets inevitably began to pay a steep price in vessels seized and confiscated as Napoleon gradually tightened his continental blockade. Contemporaneous British efforts to control American trade with the continent, despite Napoleon's efforts to block it, gave rise to protests from Washington that charged both belligerents with violating America's maritime rights as a neutral power. Students of the era are familiar with the economic sanctions Congress enacted in response to these spoliations: first a nonimportation act aimed at Britain, then an embargo intended to cut off trade with all nations, followed by a nonintercourse act aimed only at the two major combatants, and finally a perilous permutation of the latter known as Macon's Bill No. 2. Broadly speaking, Congress hoped to coerce the belligerents into honoring the maritime principle known as "free ships make free goods," which holds that neutral-flag vessels may safely carry noncontraband goods to any belligerent port unless that port is "legally," which is to say, effectively, blockaded. By late 1807, both belligerents were clearly violating this standard of effectiveness, Napoleon's corsairs by randomly seizing American vessels on the high seas, Britain's navy by patrolling laxly enforced blockades along the European coast.

As events unfolded, Napoleon arrived at several unsettling truths about the Anglo-American nexus. Once the spoliations began, he believed Britain to be far more abusive of American shipping than he and Congressional sanctions more severely and unjustly damaging to France than to his enemy. And because those sanctions never succeeded in cutting off trade with Britain completely, he concluded indignantly that no matter how severely the British damaged American shipping interests, the latter were not likely to forgo the profits they drew from commerce with their major trade partner. His day-to-day anger, however, focused mainly on those American shipmasters who sought tirelessly to penetrate his "Continental System," thereby frustrating his efforts to strangle Britain's export trade.

Beginning in May 1806, Napoleon caught his first glimpse of the role Americans would play in his own economic warfare when London initiated a naval blockade along a stretch of Europe's Channel coastline so extensive that both Washington and Paris agreed it failed to meet the standard of effectiveness. Six months later he struck back. By then, he had succeeded in closing the ports of northern Europe to British exports and quite likely believed he stood a fair chance to deprive Britain of her European markets altogether. His Berlin Decree of November 1806 declared a French blockade of the British Isles that, although ostensibly an answer to "Fox's blockade," anticipated his design to make all of Europe proof against cargoes from that source.

The Berlin Decree created only mild tensions in French-American rela-

tions because its enforcement consisted mostly of confiscating such cargoes of British origin as Americans and others tried to slip past French
customs officials. At this early stage, the Jefferson administration had no
grounds for protest. The prevailing view in Washington held that France
did no violence to the maritime rights of neutrals by seizing "enemy"
goods on their arrival, that she was simply exercising a well-established
right to enforce "domestic regulations" at her ports of entry. When
French privateers began to make captures on the high seas, however,
those relations took a decided turn for the worse. Those captures began
when in November 1807 British orders-in-council required neutral carriers bound for Europe to stop first at a British port, obtain custom certificates, and purchase licenses. A month later, from his headquarters in
Milan Napoleon retaliated by threatening to seize any vessel caught submitting to these British controls—wherever it might be apprehended.
From Washington's perspective, the likely confiscation of American ships
taken at sea was a far cry from what befell those that arrived voluntarily
in French ports. From this time forward, Washington's quarrel with
France came to center on this vital distinction between permissible and
impermissible venues of capture. In the long run, the toll of American
vessels taken at sea became a major grievance against France and the basis
for later American demands for indemnification.

By early 1808, Napoleon was so sure Americans would declare war
rather than submit to Britain's November orders-in-council that he offered the United States an alliance, promised to release the U.S. vessels
that up to that time he had only sequestered, and held out the lure of
persuading Spain to hand over East and West Florida. Jefferson, to his
credit, considering how much he wanted to annex the Floridas, refused
to be entangled. Instead, Congress, fed up with both belligerents, responded to French and British interference by levying a general embargo,
a more or less effective lockdown of American shipping, which lasted
from early 1808 until March 1809.

The embargo was barely in place when, to the indignation of official
Washington, Napoleon volunteered to help enforce it. An imperial decree
issued from Bayonne in April 1808 ordered the seizure of all American
merchantmen still at sea in European waters. The emperor's rationale,
not entirely frivolous, was that American vessels having eluded the embargo had not only violated their own government's law but were almost
certainly operating under forged registries, most likely in collusion with
the British. If the United States government were powerless to take them

into custody, France would. Moreover, Paris officials, speaking for the emperor, took serious exception to the embargo itself, complaining that France had been unfairly lumped with Britain as a target of a trade cutoff when it was obvious that their enemy had committed far more serious offenses. Britain, not France, they pointed out, had initiated the illegal paper blockades, impressed American seamen, attacked an American warship (the *Chesapeake*), and most recently had presumed to license American trade with the continent. By contrast, the emperor had done no more than take retaliatory measures, an argument that would seem to stand on its merits although the accompanying French seizures of American property strongly suggests a profit motive as well.

The French emperor had even more righteous cause for complaint when in the spring of 1809 Congress replaced the embargo with its Non-Intercourse Act. This legislative sequel continued to forbid direct commerce with Britain and France but permitted Americans to trade with others, a loophole that enabled British and American merchants to circumvent the law's intent by exchanging cargoes in neutral ports. Moreover, this commerce conducted in third-party venues had the protection of the British navy whose ubiquitous presence denied like opportunities to France. Also, though perhaps unaware of its consequences, Congress wrote into the Non-Intercourse Act a blatant defiance of Napoleon's Continental System. By not closing off trade to the Dutch ports then under French control, it figuratively thumbed its nose at the emperor's efforts to plug one of the leakiest spots in his continental dyke. And finally, because section 3 of the law threatened to confiscate any belligerent merchant ship which entered an American port, Napoleon was handed a thin but at least arguable rationale for the sweeping confiscations he announced in his Rambouillet Decree of May 1810.

It would be hard to deny that Congress bore a major share of responsibility for worsening French relations. Often a blunt instrument in foreign policy matters even today, in this era it was so intent on beating concessions out of Britain—the nation's more valuable trade partner—that it paid scant attention to how its legislative actions might affect France. Members debating the Non-Intercourse Act, for example, predicted precisely how British and American merchants would evade it. At the same time, they shrugged at the likelihood that the law would effectively cut off trade with France. The same indifference to consequences resurfaced in early 1811 when Congress responded imperfectly to Napoleon's supposed revocation of his Berlin and Milan decrees. Finding the emperor's revocation to have been conditional, it enacted a halfway measure against Britain that cut off British imports but put no restrictions on exports. Thus, instead of cutting off all trade with Britain, as Paris had anticipated, Congress once more created opportunities for American and British ship-owners to exchange cargoes in third-party ports. In sum, at nearly every legislative turn, Congressional sanctions against Britain were never tight enough to persuade French officials of their sincerity. What Congress paraded as evenhandedness they saw as damaging to France and blatantly hypocritical.

In May 1812, a month before the United States joined France as a co-belligerent, the French foreign minister offered a full-dress argument for rejecting American claims for property losses. The duc de Bassano began with the earliest of the emperor's countermeasures. Ships and cargoes taken under the Berlin Decree, he wrote, offered no basis for indemnification because, as Americans themselves admitted, their property had been taken at port-side under the permissible dictum of "domestic regulation." Likewise, the Milan Decree, though it entailed captures on the high seas, had affected only those vessels already in violation of their government's embargo. By implication, it made no difference whose government confiscated the property of these lawbreakers; France had no obligation to indemnify them. Finally, the property confiscated under the Rambouillet Decree of March 1810 was justly taken in reprisal for that part of the Non-Intercourse Act which threatened to confiscate any French merchantman entering an American port. Again, it made no difference whether none or only a few had actually been confiscated. It was the principle of the thing. Although some of Bassano's arguments were rebuttable, they clearly set forth plausible grounds for resisting American demands for indemnification.

In a broader sense, the French emperor had no compunctions about seizing the property of Americans because he believed they and their government were fundamentally hostile to a whole range of France's vital national interests. Not only had congressional economic sanctions made France their principal victim, but Washington had also allowed its citizens to engage in a variety of activities repugnant to those interests. For want of governmental restraint, Americans had paid "tribute" to London for the privilege of assaulting his continental blockade, traded with rebels in Haiti, and beginning in 1808 had become major suppliers of provisions to the British forces he was fighting in Spain. But above all, he resented their ceaselessly inventive efforts to penetrate his Continental System, routinely using forged documents to land British cargoes falsely certified as American. Highlighting his resentment on this score was the frustration expressed by French port officials at their inability to tell the difference between Americans and Britons who looked alike, spoke alike, brought documents couched in the same strange language, and had similar reputations for practicing profitable deceits, most likely in collusion with one another. Evidence of the latter American consuls in France amply substantiated. At this level of daily contact, the crosscultural distrust was pandemic and though Napoleon was at one remove from it, he was not immune to its infection.

Too, the French emperor angrily brushed aside complaints that French tariffs were too high, French export requirements too restrictive, and the departures of vessels too often delayed. His answers came to this: if Americans thought his tariffs excessive, they were reminded that the duties bore equally on all importers, French and American alike. If they objected to exporting French commodities equal in value to the cargoes they brought in, it was because France prudently sought to prevent a flight of specie and not least to deter American shipmasters from rounding out their cargoes with British commodities on return voyages. As for his port officials tying up their vessels on arrival and often delaying their departures, from what he knew of Americans' skill in circumventing his system, he made no apologies for taking reasonable safeguards against the fraudulent landing of forbidden cargoes.

Where personalities touched on foreign policy, Napoleon took a keen dislike to most of the American diplomats he dealt with. John Armstrong, along with special emissaries like George Erving and James Monroe, frayed his patience with their efforts to bully his Spanish ally into relinquishing West Florida, pretending it had been part of the Louisiana purchase. For Napoleon, and reasonably so, East and West Florida were and remained tightly held bargaining chips to be spent at Spain's expense—or annexed—as circumstances might dictate. He particularly disliked Armstrong for what he saw as the latter's misdirected belligerence in defense of American neutral rights, his "morose" personality, and his often unintelligible diplomatic notes. And although he gave Joel Barlow, Armstrong's successor, a more cordial welcome and might have dealt with him on substantive issues, he had by late 1811 decided to wait out American demands for indemnification hoping that America's entry to war would sweep the matter aside. Although they faithfully represented U.S. interests, these American diplomats were never able to find those conjunctures of mutual self-interest that could convince the French emperor of their sincerity.

By contrast, his own diplomats served him well insofar as they succeeded in putting a comfortable distance between these troublesome Americans and his main theater of military operations. In his economic warfare against Britain, he could count on such ministers as Talleyrand, Cadore, and Bassano to defend the integrity of his Continental System without suggesting that he make concessions to the United States they knew he would not accept. And by replacing Louis Turreau, Armstrong's equally bellicose counterpart in Washington, he had in Louis Serurier a loyal and personable diplomat who was able to soften, if not deflect, Americans' reactions to his retaliatory treatment of their shipping.

Only as a potential player in his war games did Napoleon pay even half-friendly attention to the United States. On one occasion he nodded approvingly when Washington proposed to occupy Florida to keep the British out. And when Joel Barlow hinted that Americans might put their France-bound merchant ships under protective convoy, he wanted to hear more. But although he might have encouraged such enterprise, at no time did he delude himself that Americans would take up arms against Britain for any reasons but their own. Neither he nor his foreign office ever accepted the argument, so often put by American diplomats and sometimes echoed by his own, that if he eased up on American shipping, Congress would leap to declare war on his British enemy. Rather, he was convinced that Americans possessed an inglorious capacity to absorb insult and would not lightly forsake the profits of neutral carriage for the honorable alternative of war. Consequently, he saw fit to treat Americans according to what he regarded as the righteous principles of reprisal until such time as London's abuses would register strongly enough to awaken them to self-respecting battle. President Madison, who saw through these purposeful delays, ultimately had to accept the harsh reality that Paris would make no meaningful concessions to American shipping lest London by matching them open the way to an Anglo-American rapprochement. Rather, the president concluded, and rightly so, that France would persist in rejecting American protests, shifting its grounds for seizing ships and cargoes until Britain's more serious offenses led the United States to war.

Finally, it should be noted that whenever French and American diplomats spoke of mending relations in this era, they invariably fetched up on the formidable presence of the British navy. Napoleon repeatedly set as a minimum requirement that Americans pledge not to allow British warships to visit their merchant vessels. "You must defend your flag," he often insisted. And yet, as noted earlier, no American shipmaster could ignore the order of a British naval commander to heave to. What took place on such encounters—Napoleon suspected the payment of "tribute"—was beyond anyone's control. Napoleon knew it; so did American diplomats. Thus, his repeated demand that they resist such encounters became a key element in his strategy of delay. Similarly, when those same diplomats pictured how profitably France could expand her American trade if she no longer threatened to seize their carriers, he reminded them of the British navy's well-demonstrated power to prevent it. In sum, what Napoleon expected of American conduct on the high seas both parties knew could not be delivered.

By the time the United States entered the war, the French emperor's military fortunes were in decline. Though lukewarm to American co-belligerency, Napoleon did open French ports to American prizemasters allowing them to sell off vessels captured from the British—a privilege which, as noted, Washington did not reciprocate. At some point, he might have signed Joel Barlow's commercial treaty, although his reluctance to indemnify for past depredations would surely have kept that treaty from being ratified. In the end, unpaid claims for questionable spoliations would be Napoleon Bonaparte's principal legacy to French-American relations of the era. If Americans looking back believed that he had treated them with unwarranted severity, the evidence suggests that although he managed them harshly and to his own advantage, his conduct was not altogether unjustified.

Notes

INTRODUCTION

1. See, most recently, Doron Ben-Atar, *The Origins of Jeffersonian Commercial Policy and Diplomacy* (London: St. Martin's Press, 1993), 170.

2. For a recent and illuminating critique of Napoleon's Continental System, see Geoffrey Ellis, *Napoleon* (New York: Longman, 1997), 102–12.

3. Quoted from Raoul Brice in a 1937 translation of his work, *The Riddle of Napoleon* (New York: G. P. Putnam's Sons), 125.

4. American statesmen of the day often cited the writings of publicist Emmerich de Vattel but went beyond Vattel's dictum that belligerents might seize enemy cargoes from neutral vessels as long as they paid for them. See, for example, Daniel Lang, *Foreign Policy in the Early Republic: The Law of Nations and the Balance of Power* (Baton Rouge: Louisiana State University Press, 1985), 117–18.

5. Madison described these rare instances in a lengthy essay, published anonymously in Washington in late 1806, *The Writings of James Madison*, ed. Gaillard Hunt (New York: Putnam's Sons, 1908), Vol. VII, 204–395.

6. For the politics of naval philosophy in this era, see Craig L. Symonds, *Navalists and Antinavalists: the Naval Policy Debate in the United States, 1785–1837* (Newark, DE: University of Delaware Press, 1980).

7. George Minot, *Reports of Cases Argued and Determined in the High Court of Admiralty*, (Boston: Little, Brown and Company, 1822–38), Vol. 2, 361–62. For more on Scott's reasoning in the case and his part in the later *Essex* decision, see Bradford Perkins, "Sir William Scott and the *Essex*," *William and Mary Quarterly*, 3rd Series, 22, (1956), 169–83.

8. The overall value of U.S. exports rose from $94 million in 1801 to $108 million by 1807. See William S. Dudley, ed., *The Naval War of 1812: A Documentary History* (Washington: Naval Historical Center, 1985), I, 16.

9. *Prologue to War: England and the United States, 1805–1812*, (Berkeley: University of California Press, 1961), 77.

10. For the full text of the *Essex* decision, see Dudley, *Naval War of 1812*, 17–21. By the time of the British orders-in-council of November 1807, Britain had seized 528 U.S. vessels. A year earlier, France had detained 206. *Ibid.*, 17.

CHAPTER 1

1. *History of the United States of America* (New York: C. Scribner's Sons, 1889–91), II, 246–47.

2. More recently, Robert W. Tucker and David C. Hendrickson also find Jefferson's reading of the retrocession treaty "plainly at odds with the interpretation given by the parties to that treaty," *Empire of Liberty: the Statecraft of Thomas Jefferson* (New York: Oxford University Press, 1990), 144.

3. *James Madison, Secretary of State, 1800–1809* (Indianapolis: Bobbs Merrill, 1953), 149.

4. Harry Ammon, in his *James Monroe: the Quest for National Identity* (New York: McGraw-Hill, 1971), 317.

5. Monticello, 13 Sept. 1808, Madison Papers, reel 10, comparing Armstrong's turgid correspondence with that of General Turreau. See also Napoleon to Cadore, 19 Jan. 1810, *Correspondance de Napoléon Ier* (Paris: H. Plon, 1858–60), XX, 132.

6. Monticello, 20 Aug. 1807, Madison Papers, reel 9.

7. Joel Barlow to James Monroe (private), 21 Nov. 1811, State Department, Diplomatic Despatches, France (hereinafter DD-F), Vol. 13.

8. For the financial benefits Armstrong derived from this marriage, see C. Edward Skeen, *John Armstrong, Jr. 1753–1843: A Biography* (Syracuse University Press, 1981), 30–32.

9. *Neither Peace Nor War: Franco-American Relations, 1803–1812* (Baton Rouge: Louisiana State University Press, 1983), 17.

10. Erving as quoted by Consul Isaac Cox Barnet in a letter to Secretary of State James Monroe, 8 July 1811, Despatches from U.S. Consuls, 1890–1906 (hereinafter CD), Vol. 3.

11. Monticello, 20 Aug. 1807, Madison Papers, reel 9. For a detailed account of the Monroe-Pinckney negotiation in Madrid, see Harry Ammon, *James Monroe*, 233–47.

12. Talleyrand to Armstrong, Paris, 30 frimaire, an 13 [21 Dec., 1804], enclosed in Armstrong to Madison, 30 Dec. 1804, DD-F, Vol. 10.

13. See Charles Callan Tansill, *The United States and Santo Domingo, 1798–1873* (Baltimore: Johns Hopkins Press, 1938), 105–06.

14. 5 March 1805, Department of State, DI, Vol. 6, 269.

15. Madison to Armstrong, 5 March 1805, DI, Vol. 6, 269; also to George Erving (minister designate to Madrid), 18 March 1805, *Ibid.*, 278–82.

16. Louis Marie Turreau de Garambouville was best known to his contemporaries as the harsh suppressor of the 1793 Vendéean uprising. Clifford Egan describes him as a crude, tough, arrogant soldier sent to Washington either as a favor or to get him out of France, *Neither Peace Nor War*, 38.

17. "Extrait d'une lettre de S. M. du 22 Thermidor an 13" [10 Aug. 1805], Archives étrangères, Correspondance politique-Etats-Unis (hereinafter AECP-EU), Vol. 58, 251.

18. See Madison to Turreau, 6 Jan. 1806, and Turreau's reply of 13 Jan., AECP-EU, Vol. 59, 14v and 16–16v.

19. Jefferson to Armstrong, 14 Feb. 1806, Ford, *Works*, Vol 10, 230–31. See Rayford W. Logan's *The Diplomatic Relations of the United States with Haiti, 1776–1891* (Chapel Hill: University of North Carolina Press, 1941), 177–180, for the political controversy over cutting off trade with Haiti.

20. Armstrong to Madison, Paris, letters of 12 and 24 Nov. 1804, DD-F, Vol. 10.

21. Same to same, Paris, 30 Dec. 1804, *Ibid.*, enclosing Talleyrand to Armstrong of 21 Dec. 1804.

22. To Monroe, Paris, 12 March, 1805, *Ibid.* (copy sent to Madison). For the Quasi-War and a more favorable view of Talleyrand in an earlier era, see Alexander DeConde, *The Quasi-War: The Politics and Diplomacy of the Undeclared War with France* (New York, Scribners, 1966).

23. Armstrong to Monroe, 12 March 1805, DD-F, Vol. 10.

24. Same to same, Paris, 18 March 1805, *Ibid.*

25. Madison to Monroe and Pinckney, 23 May 1805, DI, Vol. 6, 295–98.

26. Beurnonville to Talleyrand, Aranjuez, le 12 prairial, an 13 [1 June 1805], AECP-EU, Vol. 58, 153–54v, enclosing copies of the U.S. Ministers' final proposal to Cevallos, dated 12 May 1805, *Ibid.*, 156–57v; Cevallos' reply of 15 May, *Ibid.*, 158–59v; and Monroe's angry letter to Beurnonville of 23 May 1805, *Ibid.*, 160–61.

27. *Ibid.*

28. Talleyrand's note enclosed in Armstrong to Madison, Paris, 5 April 1805, DD-F., Vol. 10.

29. To Monroe, 1 April 1805; to Madison, 3 July 1805, *Ibid.*

30. Its port of collection at Ft. Stoddert was well north of the West Florida boundary, and Jefferson made no effort to establish it. Revocation of the act, however, became one of Madrid's conditions for negotiating. See Tucker and Hendrickson, 150–51.

31. "Résultat de la mission de M.M. C. Pinckney & J. Monroe auprès de S.M.C. en 1805," florial, an 13 [21 April-20 May 1805], AECP-EU, 58, 130–30v.

32. To Madison, Bordeaux, 16 Dec. 1804, Stanislaus Murray Hamilton, ed., *The Writings of James Monroe* (New York: G. P. Putnam's Sons, 1900), IV, 277–97.

33. Department of State, 6 June 1805, DI, Vol. 6, 301–02.

34. To Talleyrand, No. 29, Baltimore, 20 messidor, an 13 [9 July 1805], AECP-EU, Vol. 58, 204–04v, 206. By mid-April 1805, both U.S. envoys had also detected a deliberate French tactic of delay. See Monroe to Armstrong, Madrid, 16 April 1805, and Armstrong to Monroe, Paris, 4 May 1805, DD-F, Vol. 10.

35. See Armstrong's despatches to Madison of 10 Sept. and 3 Oct., 1805 DD-F, Vol. 10.

36. Armstrong enclosed both the one-page proposal and his "Notes of a Conversation" in a coded despatch, dated 10 Sept. 1805, *Ibid.*

37. Washington, 23 Oct. 1805, in Paul Leicester Ford, ed., *The Works of Thomas Jefferson* (New York: G. P. Putnam's Sons, 1905), Vol. 10, 177.

CHAPTER 2

1. To Madison, Paris, 9 March 1805, DD-F, Vol. 10.

2. *Ibid.*

3. Department of State, 13 March 1806, DI, Vol. 6, 315–21.

4. Madison to Armstrong, Department of State, 18 Oct. 1807, *Ibid.*, 434.

5. Paris, 4 May 1806, DD-F, Vol. 10.

6. Paris, 10 Oct. 1806, *Ibid.*

7. See Armstrong's despatches to Madison of 28 March, 26 May, and 4 June, 1806; also Talleyrand to Armstrong, 4 June, 1806, *Ibid.*

8. See Armstrong's despatch to Madison of 17 July (in which he described Izquierdo as the real, though not the official, Spanish representative in Paris), that of 9 August, and especially that of 10 Oct. 1806, in which Armstrong recapitulated the course of his Florida diplomacy since the previous May. DD-F, Vol. 10.

9. To Madison, 10 Oct. 1806, *Ibid.*

10. Armstrong to Izquierdo, Paris, 30 Sept. 1806 enclosed the outlines of both treaties. Izquierdo replied on 1 Oct., *Ibid.* Armstrong could only report that Napoleon had read both documents "attentively" before he left. To Madison, Paris, 10 Oct. 1806, *Ibid.*

11. Paris, 10 Oct. 1806, *Ibid.*

12. "Rapport à Sa Majesté," 6 May 1806, unsigned but certainly written by Talleyrand or at his direction. AECP-EU, Vol. 59, 133–138v.

13. Turreau to the Ministre des Relations Extérieures (MRE) of 22 Feb. 1806, *Ibid.* 59, 51. For other "Florida despatches," see those of 20 Jan., 12 Feb., 13 Feb. (enclosing Turreau to Madison, 8 Feb., Madison to Turreau, 10 Feb., and Madison to Irujo, 15 Jan.), and those of 22 Feb. and 19 March, 1806, *ibid., ff.* 59, and 21–94, *passim.*

14. To MRE, No. 17, Baltimore, AECP-EU, Vol. 59, 144v–45.

15. Masserano to Talleyrand, Paris, 16 June 1806; and Talleyrand to Masserano, 24 June 1806, *Ibid.,* 186–88v, and 213–14, respectively.

16. For Talleyrand to Vandeul, Paris, 27 June 1806, see *Ibid.,* 221–21v; for extensive quotations from Vandeul's letter of 23 June and Talleyrand's replies of 3 and 12 July, see Adams, *History,* III, 380–84.

17. 31 July 1806, No. 3, Paris, AECP-EU, Vol. 59, 233–36.

18. Prussia was offended by Napoleon's offer of Hanover to Britain and by his exclusion of Prussia from his newly created Confederation of the Rhine. Popular anger joined official displeasure when the Emperor had a Nuremburg bookseller shot for publishing a pamphlet critical of his treatment of Germany. See, for example, Felix Markham, *Napoleon* (New York: New American Library, 1964), 110–14.

19. For these letters of 5 February and 5 March, 1807, see DD-F, Vol. 10, and AECP-EU, Vol. 60, 69 and 70, respectively.

20. Letters of 12 and 16 June 1807, DD-F, Vol. 10.

21. Talleyrand to Armstrong, Tilsit, 6 July 1806; same to same, Konigsberg, 13 July 1806, *Ibid.*

22. Talleyrand to Armstrong, Paris, 10 Aug. 1807. Replying the next day, Armstrong told Talleyrand he appreciated his efforts "to preserve the friendship and confidence which so happily subsist between the two countries." *Ibid.*

23. Jean Baptiste Nompère, comte de Champagny, had served three years as ambassador to Vienna and most recently three years as minister of interior. For details of his career, see Edward A. Whitcomb, *Napoleon's Diplomatic Service* (Durham, NC: University of North Carolina Press, 1979), 27.

24. Champagny to Armstrong, Paris, 19 Aug. 1807; Armstrong to Madison, Paris, 23 Aug. DD-F, Vol. 10.

25. To Champagny, Paris, *Ibid.*

26. See the report of the Garde des Archives de l'Empire to Champagny, Paris, 26 August 1807. AECP-EU, Vol. 60, 189–189v; and Champagny to Armstrong, 13 September 1807, DD-F, Vol. 10.

27. Armstrong to Madison, Paris, 29 Sept. 1807, *Ibid.,* responding to Madison's letter of 15 July and possibly to that of 2 August to Armstrong and Bowdoin. DI, Vol. 6, 429–31, and 436–37.

28. Armstrong to Masserano, Paris, 16 Oct. 1807; Masserano to Armstrong, Fontainebleau, 20 Oct., DD-F, Vol. 10.

29. To Madison, Paris, 15 Nov. 1807, *Ibid.*

30. To Champagny, Paris, 27 Jan. 1808, DD-F, Vol. 10. The Correspondance politique contains two Armstrong letters to Champagny on Florida, but dated 28 and 29 Jan. Vol. 61, 15–16, 19–19v.

31. See Armstrong's notes on his meeting with Champagny, 4 Feb. 1808, and a confirmatory letter he wrote to the foreign minister the following day. DD-F, Vol. 11.

32. Champagny to Armstrong, 15 Jan. 1808, and Armstrong's notes of 4 Feb. on his meeting with Champagny, *Ibid.*

33. Champagny to Armstrong, Paris, 13 Feb. 1808, DD-F, Vol. 11.

34. Same to same, 12 January 1808, *Ibid.* For the Administration's rebuff of the alliance proposal, see Madison to Armstrong, 2 May 1808, *ASP FR*, III, 252.

CHAPTER 3

1. For an extended account and analysis of the origins of the Non-Importation Act, see Burton Spivak, *Jefferson's English Crisis: Commerce, Embargo, and the Republican Revolution* (Charlottesville, VA: University Press of Virginia, 1979), 31–47. And for its scope and weaknesses, see Herbert Heaton, "Non-Importation, 1806–1812," *Journal of Economic History*, I, (May 1941), 178–98.

2. An early but thoroughgoing analysis of the impressment issue as seen from both sides of the Atlantic is Anthony Steele's "Impressment in the Monroe-Pinkney Negotiation, 1806–07," *American Historical Review*, 57, No. 2 (Jan. 1952), 352–69.

3. Washington, 20 March 1807, Madison Papers, Reel 9.

4. Marie-Jeanne Rossignol finds impressment so offensive to Jefferson's sense of nationhood that he rejected a treaty which otherwise exceeded his expectations. *The Nationalist Ferment: the Origins of U. S. Foreign Policy, 1789–1812* (Columbus OH: Ohio State University Press, 2004), 294–301.

5. AECP-EU, Vol. 59, 169 shows a French translation of an English-language news clipping of Fox's 16 May l806 letter to Monroe, announcing the blockade and justifying it on grounds of French harassment of British commerce.

6. Chapter IV of Perkins's *Prologue to War* offers a thoroughgoing and cogent explanation of the origins of Fox's Blockade.

7. See Monroe to Madison, London, 8 June 1806; and Coxe to Madison, Philadelphia, 20 June 1806, Madison Papers, Reel 9.

8. "Rapport historique sur les Relations de la France avec les Etats-Unis depuis la Convention du 8 Vendémiaire an 9, 30 septembre 1800," with Champagny's cover letter to Napoleon, dated 19 Feb. 1810. AFIV 1681A doss. 3.

9. Also in dossier 3, among contemporary documents translated from English sources.

10. *Prologue to War*, 106.

11. Clifford Egan calls the decree "a convenient pretext for action Napoleon would have taken anyway." *Neither War Nor Peace*, 29.

12. See his *The Continental System: An Economic Interpretation* (Oxford: Clarendon Press, 1922, reprinted in 1960), Ch. III.

13. "Rapport historique," *loc. cit.*

14. Letters to Madison, Paris, 9 and 28 March 1806. DD-F, Vol. 10.

15. To Madison, Bordeaux, 11 Dec., and to Armstrong, 7 Dec. 1806. CD (Bordeaux), Vol. 2.

16. To Jefferson, Washington, 23 April 1809, in Robert A. Rutland et al, ed., *The Papers of James Madison: Presidential Series* (Charlottesville, VA: University Press of Virginia, 1984), Vol. 2, 322.

17. Armstrong to Lee, letters of 20 and 24 Dec., CD (Bordeaux), Vol. 2.

18. See Armstrong to Decrès, 20 Dec.; and Decrès' reply of 24 Dec., 1806, AECP-EU, Vol. 59, 346–46v, 347–48; and Armstrong to Madison, 24 Dec. 1806, DD-F, Vol. 10.

19. To Talleyrand, No. 9, Washington, 23 Feb. 1807, AECP-EU, Vol. 60, 66–66v;

20. To Madison, Paris, 29 March 1807, DD-F, Vol. 10.

21. To Talleyrand, No. 11, Baltimore, 1 April 1807, AECP-EU, 60, 71–73v.

22. Same to same, No. 13, Baltimore, 8 April, *Ibid.*, 76.

23. The Monroe-Pinkney treaty arrived in Washington on 15 March. Madison's fresh instructions dated 20 May called for six major changes, among them that the U.S. would be free to treat other belligerents as it treated Britain, this in lieu of the earlier "declaratory note on the subject of the French decree of Nov. 21, 1806." DI, Vol. 6.

24. Paris, 10 Feb. 1807, AECP-EU, Vol. 60, 49–51. This letter probably reached Warsaw at about the same time Armstrong's "outline" of the treaty arrived. Paris, 13 February 1807, *Ibid.*, 51–53v.

25. Talleyrand first learned of the order from the French consul in Copenhagen. He described it to Napoleon without comment in a letter dated 9 February 1807 from Warsaw. Mémoires et documents, Vol. 659, 112.

26. The French government had the text of the January order-in-council from the *London Gazette* of January 10, a French translation of which appears in AECP-EU, Vol. 60, 3–3v.

27. *History*, III, 421.

28. Madison to Monroe and Pinkney, Department of State, 31 March 1807, DI, Vol. 6, 384–85.

29. To Armstrong, Department of State, 22 May 1807, *Ibid.*, 411–12.

30. An extract of Armstrong's letter to Monroe of 7 July, enclosed in Armstrong's to Madison of 12 July, 1807, DD-F, Vol. 10.

31. Masserano to Talleyrand, Paris, 1 July 1807, AECP-EU, Vol. 60, 151–52v; Talleyrand to Decrès, 14 Aug., and Decrès to Talleyrand, 21 Aug. 1807, *Ibid.*, 183–84, 187.

32. See Armstrong to Talleyrand, 9 Aug. 1807; and Armstrong to Madison, 23 Aug. and 20 Sept. 1807. DD-F, Vol. 10.

33. For a detailed account of Jefferson's diplomacy in the wake of the *Chesapeake* attack, see Ch. 3 of Spivak's *Jefferson's English Crisis*. See specifically Madison's instructions to Monroe and Pinkney to secure "ample reparation" for the attack, but also "an entire abolition of impressments." Department of State, 7 July 1807, DI, Vol. 6, 423–29.

34. Armstrong to Madison, Paris, 3 August 1807, DD-F, Vol. 10. See also Armstrong to Lee, Paris. 5 September 1807, CD (Bordeaux), Vol. 2.

35. To Talleyrand, No. 29, Baltimore, 18 July 1807, AECP-EU, Vol. 60, 166–71.

36. *Ibid.* Turreau also suggested that the appearance of a French naval squadron off the coast would make "a favorable impression."

37. To Minister of Exterior Relations, No. 43, Baltimore, 4 September 1807, AECP-EU, Vol. 60, 199–201v.

38. Department of State, 15 July 1807, DI, Vol. 6, 430.

CHAPTER 4

1. Monroe and Pinkney to Armstrong, London, 10 Oct., DD-F, Vol. 10; Madison to James Bowdoin, 17 July, DI, Vol. 6, 419–21; and Armstrong to Madison, 27 Aug. 1807, DD-F, Vol. 10.

2. See Regnier, Grand Juge Ministre de la Justice, to the Procureur Général Impériale près le Conseil des Prises, 18 Sept. 1807; the latter to the Ministre des Relations Extérieures,

Paris, 26 Sept., 1807, in AECP-EU, Vol. 60. 218–18v, 216–17; and Champagny to Armstrong. 7 Oct., 1807, *Ibid.*, 220–21.

3. Champagny to Armstrong, Fontainebleau, 7 Oct. 1807, AECP-EU, Vol. 60, 220–20v. See also Armstrong's same-day reply in DD-F, Vol. 10, and Armstrong to Champagny, Paris, 12 Oct. 1807, AECP-EU, Vol. 60, 224–24v.

4. See Armstrong to Madison, Paris, 20 and 24 Sept. 1807, DD-F, Vol. 10.

5. See Armstrong's "Private Circular" to U.S. consuls in France, Paris, 6 Oct. 1807, CD (Paris), Vol. 2.

6. To Madison, Paris, 9 Oct. 1807, DD-F, Vol. 10.

7. Napoleon to Champagny, 9 Oct. 1807, *Corres.*, XVI, 76; and to Finance Minister Martin Gaudin, 13 Oct., *Ibid.* 84–85.

8. *Continental System*, 114, 117. One order applied only to neutral vessels laded with re-exported colonial goods. Another threatened confiscation of any vessel bearing a French consul's certificate of origin, and a third declared good prize any vessel originally owned by the enemy. Champagny took note of these orders in his "Rapport historique" of 19 Feb. 1810, *loc. cit.* Texts appear in *Debates and Proceedings of the Congress of the United States*, 10th Cong. 2nd sess. (Washington: Gales and Seaton, 1834–56), 1698–1701, hereinafter referred to as *Annals.*

9. *Prologue to War*, 197.

10. *History*, IV, 97, 99–100, 219. The French archives contain a translated copy of Bathurst's letter of 21 November explaining the licensing requirements to U.S. businessmen. AFIV, 1681A, Doss. 3

11. *Continental System*, 177.

12. Milan, 24 Nov. 1807, DD-F, Vol. 10. For Napoleon's instructions to Champagny, dated 15 Nov. 1807, see *Corres.*, XVI, 165.

13. For the text, see *Annals* (10th Cong., 2nd Sess.), 1751–52. Frank Melvin suggests that the preamble to the Milan Decree specifically denoting its retaliatory nature was added later, that news of the British orders, dated 11 November, may not have reached Milan by 17 December. See *Napoleon's Navigation System: A Study of Trade Control During the Continental Blockade* (New York: AMS Press, 1970, reprint), 41.

14. Paris, 27 Dec. 1807, DD-F, Vol. 10.

15. *Ibid.*

16. To Madison, 16 Jan. 1808, CD (Bordeaux), Vol. 2. Armstrong relied heavily on Lee for front-line intelligence. Other consuls, most of them at odds with the minister, preferred to report either to Madison or Consul General Fulwar Skipwith.

17. AECP-EU, Vol. 61, 11.

18. Armstrong to Madison, Paris, 22 Jan. 1808, DD-F, Vol. 11; Lee to Madison, letters of 27 Jan. and 13 Feb. 1808, CD (Bordeaux), Vol. 2.

19. Louis Sears' early work, *Jefferson and the Embargo* (Durham: Octagon Books, 1966) has been superseded most notably by Burton Spivak's sophisticated inquiry into motives and misgivings. See his *Jefferson's English Crisis*, Ch. 4.

20. *Entangling Alliances with None: American Foreign Policy in the Age of Jefferson* (Kent OH: Kent State University Press, 1987), 116.

21. *Corres.*, XVI, 244.

22. Champagny to Armstrong, Paris, 15 Jan. 1808, DD-F, Vol. 11.

23. Armstrong to Champagny, 8 Feb. 1808; Champagny to Armstrong, 13 Feb., *Ibid.*

24. Armstrong to Madison, 22 Feb. 1808, *ASP FR*, III, 250.

25. "Rapport historique," Feb. 1810, AFIV, 1681A. doss. 3.

26. Madison to Armstrong, 2 May 1808, *ASP FR*, III, 252–53.

27. *Ibid.*

28. To Armstrong, 21 and 22 July, 1808, *Ibid.*, 254.

29. Cf. Madison to Armstrong, 8 Feb. 1808, *ASP FR*, III, 249; Champagny to Turreau, 15 Feb. 1808, AECP-EU, Vol. 61, 44–45.

30. Cf. Armstrong to Madison, 5 April 1808, enclosing his formal representation to Champagny of 2 April, *ASP FR*, III, 251–52; Madison to Armstrong, 8 Feb. 1808, *Ibid.*, 249–50.

31. Cf. Turreau to Champagny, Washington, 30 Jan. 1808, and Champagny to Turreau, 15 Feb. 1808, AECP-EU, Vol. 61, 22 and 44–45, respectively.

32. 8 Feb. 1808, *ASP FR*, III, 250.

33. To Champagny, 2 April 1808, *Ibid.*, 252.

34. Turreau to Champagny, No. 13, Baltimore, 20 May 1808, AECP-EU, Vol. 61, 119v.

35. "Memo of American Vessels lately captured and detained in the Ports of France & her allies, since the order to enforce the decree of 21 Nov. 1806 and the Decree of 17th December 1807," enclosed in Lee to Madison, 13 Feb. 1808. CD (Bordeaux), Vol. 2.

36. Champagny to Armstrong, Milan, 24 Nov. 1807, *ASP FR*, III, 248.

37. To Madison, 17 Dec. 1807. CD (Bordeaux), Vol. 2.

38. To Secretary of State, 1 Nov. 1808, *Ibid.*

39. To Secretary of State, Paris, 14 April 1809. CD (Paris), Vol. 3.

CHAPTER 5

1. Armstrong to Madison, 28 Feb. 1808, DD-F, Vol. 11.

2. For details, see Skipwith to Armstrong, Paris, 28 Jan. 1808; Armstrong to Madison, 29 Jan 1808; Armstrong to Messrs. Israel, Gross, Collins, etc., Paris 29 Feb. 1808, in DD-F, Vol. 11; and Skipwith to _____, 8 Feb. 1808, CD (Paris), Vol. 3.

3. To Madison, Paris, 7 April 1808, enclosing his earlier authorization from Armstrong, dated 16 July 1806. CD (Paris), Vol. 3.

4. See Skipwith to John Graham [State Department clerk], Paris, 20 June 1808; to Jefferson, Paris, 8 March 1808, *Ibid.*; and to Champagny, 23 Feb. 1808, *Ibid.*

5. Letters to Madison of 13 Feb. and 1 Nov. 1808. CD (Bordeaux), Vol. 2.

6. Napoleon was directing his campaign in Spain from Bayonne in April 1808.

7. This was exactly the view Napoleon expressed to his Minister of Finance, A. M. Gaudin, writing from Bayonne on 17 April 1808. *Corres.*, XVII, 16.

8. Madison to Armstrong, 22 July 1808, *ASP FR*, III, 254; Armstrong to Madison, Paris, 23 April 1808, DD-F, Vol. 11.

9. Merrill Peterson, *Thomas Jefferson and the New Nation: A Biography* (New York: Oxford University Press, 1970), 902.

10. To Madison, Bordeaux, 26 March 1808, CD (Bordeaux), Vol. 2.

11. See Paul Butel, "Crise et mutation de l'activité économique à Bordeaux sous le consulat et l'Empire," *Revue d'histoire moderne et contemporaine*, XVII (July–Sept. 1970), 552–58. Butel confirms a staggering decline in Bordeaux's port activity in 1807–08, caused in large part by the U.S. embargo.

12. Monticello, 12 Aug. 1808, Ford, *Works*, XI, 43. See also his letter to Madison of the same date, *Ibid.*, 44.

13. Enclosed in Armstrong's despatch to Madison of 8 July 1808, were his note to

Champagny of 10 June, the latter's reply of 22 June, and Armstrong's remonstrance of 8 July. DD-F, Vol. 11.

14. Champagny first mentioned the appearance of American vessels carrying goods to Cadiz in his letter to Turreau, Bayonne, 26 May 1808. AECP-EU, Vol. 61, 138v.

15. No. 13, Baltimore, 20 May 1808. AECP-EU, Vol. 61, 108v–109, 116v–17, 120v–21. This long despatch runs 59 folio pages and covers events dating back several months. Henry Adams sees its primary importance to express Turreau's ultimate despair of any congressional action against Britain. *History*, IV, 228.

16. Turreau to Champagny, No. 16, Baltimore, 28 June 1808. AECP-EU, Vol. 61, 167v.

17. *Ibid.*, 171–74.

18. Turreau to Champagny, No. 16, Baltimore, 28 June 1808. AECP-EU, Vol. 61, 175v–76v; and same to same, No. 13, Baltimore, 20 May 1808. *Ibid.*, 132–32v.

19. Bayonne, 18 May 1808, enclosed in Armstrong to Madison, Paris, 23 July 1808. DD-F, Vol. 11.

20. See Melvin, *Napoleon's Navigation System*, 73–76.

21. It was Madison's instructions of 8 Feb. 1808 that informed Armstrong's Aug. 6 note to Champagny, *ASP FR*, III, 249.

22. See DD-F, Vol. 11, for Armstrong's notes to Champagny of 6 and 28 Aug. 1808.

23. St. Cloud, 7 Sept., 1808, AECP-EU, Vol. 61, f. 383.

24. The outcome of the first Champagny-Haley conference is contained in an unsigned memorandum dated September and entitled "Etats Unis d'Amérique." AECP-EU, Vol. 61, 385–89. The unsigned critique dated 15 September appears to be Collin de Sussy's adverse critique of what Haley had written. *Ibid.*, 400–01v. Haley's reply to Napoleon's earlier request for clarification, addressed to Champagny, bears the date 20 October, *Ibid.*, 425–26v. Melvin also cites critiques from de Sussy and Decrès from dossiers 24 and 25, AFIV 1318. He finds that Decrès generally favored Haley's proposals, whereas de Sussy argued to keep the decrees in place. See Melvin, 74–75.

25. On this last point, Armstrong agreed: the unlikelihood of an accord with Britain "more than any other single circumstance [has served] to prolong the imperial policy, of which we complain." To Madison, Bourbon l'Archambault, 28 Aug. 1808, DD-F, Vol. 11.

26. To Napoleon, Paris, 28 Oct. 1808, AECP-EU, Vol. 61, 439–40.

27. Madison Papers, Reel 11.

28. Armstrong to Champagny, Paris, 18 Oct. 1808. DD-F, Vol. 11.

29. Cf. Armstrong to Madison, 24 Nov. 1808, DD-F, Vol. 11; Smith to Armstrong, 15 March 1809, DI, Vol. 7, 36–37.

30. *Madison the President*, 287. For a succinct and more recent account of Madison's problems with Smith, see Robert A. Rutland. *The Presidency of James Madison* (Lawrence, KS: University Press of Kansas, 1990), 74–75.

31. No. 8, Paris, 10 Dec. 1808, AECP-EU, Vol. 61, 10–10v.

CHAPTER 6

1. Secretary of State Robert Smith received a copy of this decree on 2 August 1809, enclosed in a despatch from Consul General David Bailie Warden, Paris, 2 May 1809. CD (Paris), Vol. 3.

2. See Champagny's "Projet de Traité avec les Etats-Unis d'Amérique," enclosed in his report to the Emperor, Paris, 8 March 1810, in AFIV 1681A Doss. 4.

3. Cadore's "Circulaire du Ministre des Relations Extérieures aux Consuls de France," 20 August 1810, AECP-EU, Vol. 64, 189.

4. To John Graham, Paris, 4 Jan. 1813. CD (Paris), Vol. 4.

5. See Melvin, 88; also John Holland Rose, *The Life of Napoleon I* (New York: The Macmillan Company, 1907), 203–06, and Audrey Cunningham, *British Credit in the Last Napoleonic War*, 60, all of whom tie the distress of French grain producers to Napoleon's initial foray into licensing.

6. Emmanuel de Las Casas, *Memorial de Sainte-Hélene [par]Las Casas* (Paris: Edition Garnier frères, 1961), IV, 200.

7. Melvin, 123. Copies of licenses and related ministerial correspondence are in Doss. 4, Série AFIV, côte 1706E, ANF.

8. See Armstrong to Madison, 16 and 20 Feb., 1809, in DD-F, Vol. 11.; also Armstrong to Champagny, Paris, 13 Feb., noting that Congress had set "severe penalties" for navigating under British license or paying any of the taxes imposed by one of the November 1807 orders-in-council. AECP-EU, 62, 42. See also Champagny to Armstrong, 16 Feb., *Ibid.*, 44; Armstrong to Champagny, 18 Feb., *Ibid.*, 46; and again to Madison, 22 March 1809 in DD-F, Vol. 11.

9. To Secretary of State, Paris, 10 April, enclosing Champagny to Armstrong, Paris, 20 March 1809, *Ibid.* See also same to same, Paris, 26 April, and Armstrong to Secretary of State, 27 April, *Ibid.*

10. Melvin, 102.

11. Minister of Finance to the Emperor, No. 30, Paris (undated). AECP-EU, Vol. 62, 135–36v.

12. See *Annals* (10th Cong., 2nd Sess.,) 1426–1553, *passim.*

13. Perkins, *Prologue to War*, 232. Madison hoped the expense of "double voyages" would serve as a deterrent. To Pinkney, 10 Feb. 1809, DI, Vol. 7, 27. The French Consul General in Philadelphia later bore out Madison's prediction of the high costs. See Beaujour to Champagny, No. 49, 18 Aug. 1809, AECP-EU, Vol. 62, 312–13v.

14. "Rapport historique," Feb. 1810, AFIV 1681A Doss. 3.

15. Armstrong to Madison (private), 25 May 1810, *Papers of James Madison: Presidential Series*, Vol. 2, 355.

16. Section 3 read that all French and British vessels together with their cargoes "shall be forfeited, and may be seized and condemned by any court of the United States." *Annals* (10th Cong., 2nd Sess.), 1826.

17. See Armstrong to Champagny, 2 April 1808; Madison to Armstrong, 21 July, in *ASP FR*, III, 251–52, and 254, respectively, and the latter's reply in full of 28 August, DD-F, Vol. 11. See also Smith to Armstrong, 15 March 1809, explaining the linkage between ship-burnings and the closure of U.S. ports to French warships. DI, Vol. 7, 37.

18. Smith to Armstrong, 1 July 1809. DI, Vol. 7, 46.

19. For secondary accounts, see Rutland, *Presidency of James Madison*, 39–41; Perkins, *Prologue to War*, 211–18; Brant, *Madison the President*, 43–48. Henry Adams blames Erskine's failure on Canning's contradictory instructions. *History*, V, 55–57.

20. Paris learned of Canning's repudiation in the *Gazette de France* (No. 155) of 5 June 1809. French officials, on reading Erskine's instructions, were shocked at the terms Canning had thought the U.S. would submit to.

21. Turreau to Champagny, No. 19, Baltimore, 1 June 1809, AECP-EU, Vol. 62, 196–96v.

22. Two despatches to Champagny, both dated 19 March 1809, *Ibid.*, 70–73.

23. To Champagny, 15 April 1808, *Ibid.*, 110–13v.

24. To Champagny, No. 14, Baltimore, 20 April 1809, *Ibid.*, 118.

25. For the original of Turreau's angry letter, see AECP-EU, Vol. 62, 221–31. Translated copies appeared first in the *Federal Republican* (Baltimore) and then in the *National Intelligencer* of 28 August 1813.

26. Smith to Pinkney and Armstrong, 15 March 1809, DI, Vol. 7, 29–33 and 33–36, respectively. Turreau knew nothing of this threat. See Brant, M*adison: The President*, 41.

27. To Armstrong, 15 March 1809, DI, Vol. 7, 35.

28. Cf. letters of 21 and 27 April 1809, DI, Vol. 7, 40, 40–43.

29. The 27 April instructions warned Armstrong not to relinquish claims based on their earlier enforcement. Nor was he to acquiesce in Napoleon's likely closure of Spain's colonial ports as the price of obtaining the Floridas. See also Smith to Armstrong, 1 May 1809, *Ibid.*, 43–44.

CHAPTER 7

1. To Secretary of State, Paris, 27 April 1809. DD-F, Vol. 11.

2. To Champagny, 2 May 1809, copy enclosed in Armstrong to Secretary of State, 3 May, *Ibid.* He also enclosed a copy of his first, more general notification to the French minister, dated 29 April.

3. See his note to Champagny of 4 May; the latter's shocked reply on 12 May that Armstrong might consider leaving his post without the Emperor's consent; and Armstrong's assurance dated the 19th that he would certainly not depart without permission, all in DD-F Vol. 11.

4. To Secretary of State, Paris, 3 May 1809, *Ibid.*

5. To Secretary of State, Paris, 3 and 26 May 1809. *Ibid.*

6. See *ASP FR*, III, 241, for the text of the 26 April order. Smith wrote Pinkney on 16 June that he was sure it would be revoked as soon as London learned of the Erskine Agreement, DI, Vol 7, 45–46. Madison, however, concluded that one form of blockade had merely replaced another.

7. To Champagny, 26 May and 5 June 1809, DD-F, Vol. 11.

8. To Champagny, 12 June 1809, enclosing a copy to Smith in his dispatch of 30 June, *Ibid.*

9. To Smith, 30 June 1809, *Ibid.* Hauterive (Alexandre Maurice Blanc de la Nautte) had been named chief of foreign ministry's second division in 1803. When he began conversations with Armstrong, he also bore the title of Councillor of State.

10. To Napoleon, Vienna, 26 May 1809. AECP-EU, Vol. 62, 187–89v.

11. Champagny had already drafted Hauterive's instructions, dated 13 May, when he sent them to Napoleon, along with his analysis and recommendations of 26 May.

12. "Note pour le général Armstrong, ministre des Etats-unis d'Amérique à Paris," 18 May 1809. *Corres.*, Vol. 19, 21–22. Napoleon dictated this note from Schoenbrunn Palace and left for his command headquarters at Ebersdorf the next day.

13. Champagny, writing to Vienna on 12 May, alluded only briefly to Armstrong's May 2 exposition of the Non-Intercourse Act, presumably preferring to wait until he reached Vienna before discussing its details.

14. This draft decree, neither signed nor dated, appears in the June and August folios of AECP-EU, Vol. 62, 215–15v, and 295–96. The August version offered to revoke both decrees, provided London revoked its blockade order of April 26. Neither decree was

issued, but the latter formed the basis for Napoleon's "Altenberg Letter" of 22 August. See *Corres.*, Vol. 19, 353, 374–76.

15. To Champagny, Paris, 21 June 1809, AECP-EU, Vol. 62, 249–50v.

16. To Smith, Paris, 22 July 1809, DD-F, Vol. 11.

17. To Champagny, Paris, 21 and 25 June 1809, AECP-EU, Vol. 62, 249–50v, 251–53v.

18. To Smith, Paris, 24 July 1809, DD-F, Vol. 11.

19. Vienna, 13 June 1809, AECP-EU, Vol. 62, ff. 213–14v.

20. Napoleon in Vienna wrote Champagny (then in Altenberg) on 17 August: "Send me the project of the letter for the minister of the United States, so that I can send it back to you if it is to be sent." Having edited Champagny's draft, he authorized it be sent on 21 Aug. *Corres.*, Vol. 19, 353, 374–75.

21. To Jefferson, Washington, 6 Nov. 1809. *Works*, II, 460.

22. Armstrong to Smith, Paris, 18 Oct. 1809, DD-F, Vol. 11.

23. See same to same of 16 Sept. and 18 Oct., and Armstrong to Champagny of 8 Sept. 1809, *Ibid.*

24. Despite its August date, this draft decree originated in June in response to Denis Decrès' query as to whether to detain an American vessel which had put into the Spanish port of St. Sebastien, but had not touched at a British port or been visited by a British warship. The response is an undated "Minute de Decrèt Impérial," [June 1809], AECP-EU, Vol. 62, 263–63v.

25. *History*, Vol. 5, 144.

26. Cf., Champagny's "Rapport Historique" (19 Feb. 1810), and his 13 June letter to Hauterive, AECP-EU, Vol. 62, 214v. See also Champagny to Turreau, 26 June 1809, *Ibid.*, 253–55v.

27. 31 July 1809, Madison Papers, series 2, reel 25.

28. Richardson, *Messages*, I, 473.

29. See Smith to Madison, Washington, 31 July 1809, Madison Papers, series 2, reel 25; and Madison to Jefferson, Montpellier, 16 Aug. 1809, *Works*, II, 450.

30. Smith to Jackson, 8 Nov. 1809. *ASP FR*, III, 318–19.

31. See Armstrong to Champagny, Paris, 16 Sept. 1809, and Champagny's acknowledgment from Vienna, dated 7 Oct. DD-F, Vol. 11.

32. Armstrong to Smith, Amsterdam, 20 Aug. 1809, *Ibid.*

33. *Ibid.* Armstrong biographer C. Edward Skeen offers a more detailed account of this visit to the Netherlands, 103.

34. Champagny to Armstrong, Altenberg, 28 Aug. 1809; Armstrong to Smith, Paris, 16 Sept. DD-F, Vol. 11.

35. To Champagny, Paris, 7 Aug. 1809, AECP-EU, Vol. 62, 302–03. Petry had also served as consul in Charleston during the 1790s. Never considered for a ministerial post, he was nevertheless regularly consulted on American policy.

CHAPTER 8

1. Smith to Pinkney, 11 Nov. 1809, DI, Vol. 7, 65–66. Armstrong was to impress on Champagny that the Administration would not, however, protest a blockade if it were effective. *ASP FR*, III, 326.

2. Armstrong to Smith, Paris, 28 Jan. 1810, *Ibid.*, III, 326.

3. Pinkney to Armstrong, 6 April 1810, DD-F, Vol. 11. For Pinkney's persistence on

this issue, see especially his letters to Wellesley, 30 April; to Smith, 13 June; to Wellesley, 23 June; and to Smith, 1 July. See also Smith to Pinkney, 2 July 1810, in *ASP FR*, III, 357–61, as well as Armstrong to Smith, 4 April; Pinkney to Armstrong, 23 and 27 March; and Armstrong to Smith, 3 May and 18 July, DD-F, Vol. 11.

4. To Pinkney, Paris, 2 May 1810, copy enclosed in the packet he sent to Smith the next day, *Ibid.*; Smith to Pinkney, 5 July, *ASP FR*, III, 362.

5. See Smith to Pinkney, 25 Nov. 1809, DI, Vol. 7, 72. Pinkney was told, however, that the Dutch trade counted less than Erskine's failure to bind the United States not to restore intercourse with France. See Adams, *History*, V, 91–93.

6. On 25 Dec. 1809, Smith wrote Pinkney that Armstrong's despatches, the most recent dated 1 November, held out little hope of change in French policy. DI, Vol. 7, 83.

7. See, for example, Armstrong's berating J. M. Forbes, [Hamburg], for allowing the departure of a U.S. vessel suspected of having false papers. To Smith, Paris, 10 Dec. 1809, DD-F, Vol 11; and the Armstrong-Forbes correspondence of 22 Nov. and 3 Dec. 1809, *Ibid.*

8. To Champagny, No. 6, Washington, 15 Dec. 1809, AECP-EU, Vol. 62, 432–34. For his "political" report, *Ibid.*, 435–46v.

9. Washington, 18 Dec., 1809. AF IV, 1681A, doss. 2.

10. Washington, 11 Nov. 1809, DI, Vol. 7, 63–64; and for Lee's letter to his wife Susan (in Bordeaux), Paris, 10 Dec. 1810, see Mary Lee Mann, ed., *A Yankee Jeffersonian: Selections from the Diary and Letter of William Lee of Massachusetts, written from 1796 to 1840* (Cambridge, MA: Belknap Press, 1958), 94.

11. See Armstrong to Smith, Paris, 4 Sept. 1809 (DD-F, Vol. 11) for Warden's notice of prize court activity; and William Lee to Smith, 31 March 1810, CD (Paris), Vol. 3, enclosing a year-end report showing that only five U.S. vessels had cleared Bordeaux during the last six months of 1809.

12. See "Copie d'une lettre écrite à S.E. le Ministre de l'intérieure, par M. Collin, Directeur général des Douanes," Paris, 26 Dec. 1809, AECP-EU, Vol. 62, 460; also Adams, *History*, Vol. 5, 151–52.

13. *Ibid*, 226.

14. *Corres.*, XX, 78, 80–81.

15. The *National Intelligencer* published this letter on 26 May 1810.

16. Certificates of origin figured at least peripherally in the internal ministerial debate. Montalivet thought them sufficient, but Bonaparte's finance minister, the duc de Gaète, found them "a weak guarantee against abuses." See "Rapport du Ministre des finances à Sa Majesté, l'Empéreur et Roi," 4 Jan. 1810. AECP-EU, Vol. 64, 54–56v.

17. To Smith, Paris, 22 Dec. 1809, DD-F, Vol. 11.

18. To Smith, letters of 1 and 6 Jan. 1810, *Ibid.*

19. Armstrong to Smith, Paris, 10 Jan. 1810; Lee to his wife, Paris, 13 Jan. 1810, *Yankee Jeffersonian*, 107. According to Lee, Napoleon after cancelling the Council of State "set off in a most violent rage to Malmaison to see Josephine." Same to same, 16 Jan., *Ibid.*, 108.

20. *Ibid.*, 103.

21. To his wife, letters of 16 Jan. and 15 Feb. 1810, *Ibid.*, 109, 115.

22. *History*, V, 226–28.

23. *Corres.*, XX, 109–10.

24. *History*, V, 228.

25. "Rapport historique," 19 Feb., 1810, AFIV, 1681A, doss. 3.

26. See Cadore's letters from Consul Gohier and French Minister Bourrienne, posted in Amsterdam and Hamburg, respectively, and dated 27 and 29 Jan. 1810, *Ibid.*

27. *Napoleon's Navigation System*, 207–08.

28. Armstrong to Smith, Paris, 28 Jan. 1810, DD-F, Vol. 11.

29. 19 Jan. 1810, *Corres.*, XX, 132.

30. Armstrong's letter to Smith of 28 Jan. enclosed documents marked "A" through "E." "Document "A" was a one-page report of events in Holland, Spain, and Britain; "B" reported rumors of Napoleon's marriage plans; "C" was Armstrong's first treaty "proposition" (the note Napoleon deplored); "D" was the fleshed-out version of "C"; and "E" reported U.S. maritime problems with Denmark. DD-F, Vol. 11.

31. *Ibid.*

32. See Cadore's "Draft Note to the Minister of America," undated but sent to Napoleon for his approval on 25 Jan. 1810, in *Corres.* XX, 141. Cadore modified this note slightly and sent to Armstrong on 14 Feb. DD-F, Vol. 11.

33. See Henry Adams's conjectures, *History*, V, 230.

34. *Ibid.*, 144, 233.

35. See, for example, Melvin, *op. cit.*, 158, also Mary Phoebe Heath, *Napoleon I and the Origins of the Anglo-American War of 1812* (Paris and Toulouse, 1929). Heath writes (p. 124) that by insisting on indemnity, Armstrong "confused the whole affair, and thereby lost his greatest moment of opportunity."

36. Cadore to Armstrong, Paris, 14 Feb. 1810. AECP-EU, Vol. 64, 67–68v.

CHAPTER 9

1. See his letters to Smith of 17 and 18 Feb. 1810, enclosing a copy of his note to Cadore of 18 Feb., DD-F, Vol. 11.

2. Armstrong to Smith, Paris, 25 Feb. 1810, *Ibid.*

3. Smith to Armstrong, 20 June 1810, DI, Vol 7, 101–02. The changes Madison proposed to Armstrong would have made new articles (28 and 29) in the Convention of 1800 more explicit without fundamentally altering their content.

4. Armstrong expressed these misgivings to Cadore who conveyed them to Napoleon on 18 May 1810. See AFIV 1706E Doss. 5 (1810).

5. To Cadore, Rambouillet, 22 Feb. 1810, *Corres*, XX, 237.

6. See Cadore to Turreau, Paris, 22 Feb. 1810. AECP-EU, Vol. 64, 89–89v, and Napoleon to Cadore, 19 Jan. 1810. *Corres.*, XX, 132.

7. *Ibid.*, 109.

8. See Cadore's "Rapport sur le choix d'un agent à envoyer en amérique," Paris, 16 Feb., 1810. AFIV, 1681A, Doss. 3.

9. To Cadore, 22 Feb. 1810. *Corres.*, XX, 237–38. Moustier was sent instead to Morlaix to arrange a prisoner exchange.

10. Armstrong to Cadore, Paris, 10 March 1810, *ASP FR*, III., 381–82; and notifying Smith of his remonstrance the same day. DD-F, Vol. 11. Publication of the 14 February letter may also have moved Armstrong to set the record straight. See *Le Moniteur Universel*, 22 Feb. 1810.

11. To Monroe, 13 April 1811, *Writings*, Vol. IV, 48–54.

12. To Armstrong, Washington, 21 May 1810, *ASP FR*, III, 384–85.

13. In a cover note to the two documents cited below.

14. Cadore to Napoleon, Paris, 17 March 1810. AFIV 1681A Doss. 4.

15. Napoleon to Cadore, 20 March 1810, *Corres.*, XX, 273; and Cadore to Napoleon, 21 March 1810, AFIV 1681A Doss. 4.

16. *History*, V, 236.

17. Cadore to Napoleon, Paris, 21 March 1810. AFIV 1681A Doss. 4.

18. *Ibid.*

19. Armstrong on 8 March asked permission to depart and on 20 March reminded Cadore of his request. See AECP-EU, Vol. 64 and 63, 90 and 63, respectively. On 20 April he learned from Petry that the Emperor would consent to his taking temporary leave, *Ibid.*, Vol. 63, 100.

20. *History*, V, 243–44.

21. Armstrong learned of the Rambouillet Decree in mid-May. He described it in a brief note to Madison on the 24th, Madison Papers, Reel 12.

22. "Decret impériale qui ordonne la saisie et la vente des Batimens sous le pavillon des Etats-Unis, entrés dans les ports de l'Empire, à compter du 20 mai, 1809," en palais de Rambouillet, le 23 Mars 1810, *Bulletin des Lois*, No. 286, 375–76.

23. This printed list appears between folios 110 and 116 in AECP-EU, Vol. 64. Dated 1 April 1810, its title is "A List of Vessels and Cargoes captured and sequestred [*sic*] in the Ports of France, Spain, Holland and Naples since the 1st of April 1809."

24. To Sec. of State, 31 March 1810, CD (Bordeaux), Vol. 3.

25. "Copie d'une Circulaire adressée aux Consuls par le Ministre des Relations Extérieures," Paris, 12 April 1810, AECP-EU, Vol. 64, 116–17.

26. *Ibid.* Armstrong referred to this new agency in a postscript dated 13 July and enclosed a copy of the decree dated 6 June which had established it.

27. To Smith, Paris, 4 April 1810, DD-F, Vol. 11.

28. See Armstrong's summary of his correspondence with Pinkney, to Smith, Paris, 3 May 1810, *Ibid.*

CHAPTER 10

1. From the remarks of Thomas Gholson, *Annals* (11th Cong., 2nd Sess.), II, 1772.

2. For a sampling of negative views, see Rutland, *Presidency of James Madison*, 62; Brant, *James Madison the President*, 140, 147; Perkins, *Prologue to War*, 242–43; Marshall Smelser, *The Democratic Republic* (New York: Harper and Row, 1968), 196–97; and Henry Adams, *History*, V, 194–98.

3. Washington, 23 May 1810, Madison Papers, Reel 26. Smith sent Pinkney a copy of the bill on 4 May but made only passing reference to it in his letter of 22 May. *ASP FR*, III, 358–59.

4. To Jefferson, 7 and 24 May 1810, Madison Papers, Reel 12; see also *National Intelligencer* of 24 May. The even more encompassing Rambouillet Decree Armstrong described in a letter to Madison of 24 May, Madison Papers, Reel 12.

5. Smith to Pinkney and Armstrong, 5 July 1810, *ASP FR*, III, 362, 385.

6. *History*, V, 294–300.

7. To Armstrong, 29 Oct. 1810, Madison Papers, Reel 12. From Cadore's letter of 14 February, the administration labored under the mistaken impression that American ships in Spanish (and Dutch) ports had merely been sequestered.

8. See Turreau to Cadore, New York, 15 May 1810, AECP-EU, Vol. 63, 111; Armstrong

to Smith Paris, 10 July, DD-F, Vol. 11. For Napoleon's pique at having received a press clipping and Armstrong's explanation of the delay in transmitting an official copy, see Armstrong to Cadore, 8 Aug. 1810, DD-F, Vol. 11, and Cadore to Napoleon 9 Aug. 1810, AF IV 1681A Doss. 4.

9. "Note pour le Ministre de l'Intérieur," Saint Cloud, 25 June 1810. *Corres.*, XX, 431–42.

10. In a postscript to his 8 July despatch (incorrectly dated the 18th), Armstrong reported that an unpublished decree dated the 5th would admit thirty American cargoes "under special licenses." He held up this despatch long enough to enclose a published copy.

11. This translation of the Cadore Letter is from the French original. It differs in minor respects from the translation published in *ASP FR*, III, 387, and both differ slightly from Armstrong's translation in the Madison Papers.

12. Cf. Napoleon to Cadore, Saint Cloud, 31 July, *Corres.*, XX, 554–55; and "Projet de Note au Ministre des Etats-Unis," 2 August, *Ibid.*, XXI, 1–2.)

13. He believed that re-instatement of non-intercourse would leave America "like Europe, armed against English tyranny." "Projet de Circulaire," 12 Aug. 1810, AFIV 1681A Doss. 4.

14. For Pinkney's notification of 25 August and Wellesley's response of 31 August, see *ASP FR*, III, 365, 366.

15. See Richardson, *Messages*, I, 481–82.

16. To Jefferson, 19 Oct. 1810, Madison Papers, Reel 12.

17. Paris, 27 August 1810. DD-F, Vol. 11. Armstrong sent Pinkney a hasty note on 6 August quoting only the first two lines of the Cadore Letter. Consequently Pinkney notified Wellesley flatly that the Berlin and Milan decrees "are revoked." Napoleon's qualifiers had to be dealt with after the full text arrived. See *ASP FR*, III, 365; and AECP-EU, Vol. 63, 183–86.

18. For Cadore's advice, see his "fragment de rapport à L'Empereur," 30 July 1810, AECP-EU, Vol. 64, 144–45v. This document is unsigned; only the marginalia appears to be in Cadore's hand.

19. See Cadore to Armstrong, 7 Sept. 1810, *ASP FR*, III, 388.

20. Armstrong's despatch of 10 Sept. summarized Cadore's responses to his questions. DD-F, Vol. 11. Exchanges of correspondence on these issues often overlapped. See Armstrong to Cadore, 8 August and 8 Sept., *ibid.*; also Cadore to Armstrong, 9 Aug. and Armstrong's reply of 20 Aug., both in AFIV 1681A Doss. 4, and Cadore to Armstrong, 12 Sept. 1810. *ASP FR*, III, 388–89.

21. To Smith, 10 Sept. 1810. DD-F, Vol. 11.

22. *Ibid.*

23. To Armstrong, *ASP FR*, III, 389. For Cadore's earlier advice, see his "Projet de réponse à la note de Mr. Armstrong du 20 Août." Paris, 31 August 1810. AFIV 1681A Doss. 4.

24. Armstrong to Smith, Paris, 10 July 1810. DD-F, Vol. 11.

25. Bordeaux, 29 Sept. 1810. *ASP FR*, III, 389.

26. St. Cloud, 22 Aug. 1810, *Corres.*, XXI, 57. For details of the incident, see Cadore's "Rapport," Palais de Trianon, 5 Aug. 1810. AFIV 324 (Relations Extérieures); Turreau to Cadore, No. 18, Baltimore, 1 July 1810, AECP-EU, Vol. 63, 129–32v, enclosing his protest to Smith of 6 April; Smith to Turreau, 4 May, and Turreau's response of 22 May, *Ibid.*, 133–36v. Armstrong first heard of the incident in Cadore's note of 27 August (AECP-EU,

Vol. 64, 179–80). See also Cadore to Napoleon, 28 August in AFIV 1681A Doss. 4; Napoleon's response to Cadore, 6 Sept., AECP-EU, Vol. 64, 192–94; and Armstrong's reply to Cadore's note of 10 Sept., DD-F, Vol. 11.

27. Smith to Jonathan Russell, 15 Nov. 1810. DI, Vol. 7, 131–32. Turreau also admitted having mishandled the case. See his No. 24, Baltimore, 20 Aug. 1810, AECP-EU, Vol. 63, 196–97.

28. If all the Merino sheep requested by American diplomats departing France were marshaled tail to nose, the line might stretch from Monticello to Morrisania. For Cadore's role in making the arrangements, see AECP-EU, Vol. 63, 201–01v, 211.

29. The original text of the Trianon Decree appears in Napoleon's response to Cadore's "Rapport" of 5 August 1810, AFIV (Relations Extérieures), 324. Irving Brant dates the decree from 12 September, noting that because it superseded the Rambouillet Decree, Napoleon backdated it to 5 August to coincide with the Cadore Letter. *Madison the President*, 219–20.)

CHAPTER 11

1. Samuel Flagg Bemis describes at length Adams's unmasking of Russell's forgery in his *John Quincy Adams and the Foundations of American Foreign Policy* (New York: A. A. Knopf, 1949), 498–509. See also *Dictionary of American Biography* (New York: C. Scribner's sons, 1928–68), VIII, 245.

2. Serurier was *chargé* at The Hague following annexation. Russell described him in his despatches of 27 Sept. and 4 Dec. 1810. DD-F, Vol. 12. For autobiographical details, see the Serurier Papers (Kent State University), Reel 1 for an overview, Reels 2–5 for duplicate despatches.

3. Recalled in 1818, Serurier returned to Washington in 1830 and served there until 1835. See Serurier Papers.

4. "Copie des instructions de M. Serurier, Ministre Plénipotentiaire aux Etats-Unis," No. 1, Fontainebleau, October [?] 1810. AFIV 1681A Doss. 4.

5. Serurier to Cadore, Paris, 7 Nov., and Petry to Cadore, 20 Nov. 1810, AECP-EU, Vol. 64, 263–66 and 233–35v, respectively.

6. To Smith, Paris, 17 Nov, 1810. DD-F, Vol. 12.

7. Cf. Russell's note of 1 Oct. and Cadore's reply of 8 Oct. *Ibid.*; and Cadore's "Copie des instructions de M. Serurier," dated Oct. 1810, AFIV 1681A Doss. 4.

8. See Russell to Cadore, 8 and 14 Oct., and to Robert Smith, 15 Nov., 1810 in DD-F, Vol. 12. For his frustration over licensing issues, see also his letters of 11 and 19 October to Capt. Merrit Bates and Messrs. John Lewis Brown and Cie., respectively [in Bordeaux]. Jonathan Russell Letter Books (Brown University Library, 2 vols.), I, 47 and 51.

9. To Smith, Paris, 4 Dec. 1810. DD-F, Vol. 12.

10. See Pinkney to Russell, London, 7 Oct. 1810, ASP FR, III, 389; Russell to Pinkney, Paris, 11 Dec. 1810, *Ibid.*, 390.

11. To Smith, Paris, 1 Dec. 1810, DD-F, Vol. 12.

12. To Smith, 4 Dec. 1810, *Ibid.*

13. *Ibid.*

14. Paris, 6 July 1811. Letter Books, II, 193. William Lee made the same disclaimer to Madison while on a home visit in early 1811. (New York, 11 Feb. 1811, Madison Papers, Reel 13.)

15. To Smith, Paris, 7 June 1811. DD-F, Vol. 12.

16. Russell to Cadore, 17 Dec. 1810, and Russell to Smith, 7 June 1811, *Ibid.*

17. Paris, 29 Dec. 1810, *Ibid.*

18. Paris, 4 Jan, 1811. Letter Books, I, 149.

19. To Smith, 27 Dec. 1810 DD-F, Vol. 12.

20. Russell to Madison, Paris, 10 June 1811, enclosing a copy of his letter to Pinkney of 26 Sept. and an extract from the letter he received from Pinkney, dated 7 October. Also among the Madison Papers (Reel 26) are copies of Russell's letters to Pinkney of 1, 11, 13, and 27 Dec. 1810.

21. To Russell, (private), 15 Nov. 1811. DD-F, Vol. 12.

22. To Cadore, Paris, 13 Dec. 1810. *Corres.*, XXI, 316–17.

23. Smith to [Armstrong], 2 and 5 Nov. 1810. *ASP FR*, III, 389–90.

24. To Smith, Paris, 25 Jan. 1811. DD-F, Vol. 12.

25. To Smith, Paris, 13 Feb. 1811, *Ibid.*

26. To Smith, Paris, 29 Dec. 1810, *Ibid.*

27. To R. Rogers, care of S. G. Lamatt [Naples], Paris, 17 Jan. 1811. Letter Books, I, 163; and to Pitcairn [Hamburg], 27 March 1811, *Ibid.*, II, 44–45

28. To Cadore, 17 Dec. 1810. DD-F, Vol. 12.

29. Russell to Cadore, 12 Jan. 1811, AECP-EU, Vol. 64, 299–99v.

30. To Joseph Pitcairn [Hamburg], 8 Dec. 1810, Letter Books, I, 120.

31. For secondary accounts of the West Florida takeover and the ensuing Florida Resolution, see Brant's *Madison the President,* Chaps. XIII and XVI; and the first eight chapters in Rembert W. Patrick, *Florida Fiasco: Rampant Rebels on the Georgia-Florida Border, 1810–1815* (Athens, GA: University of Georgia Press, 1954).

32. To Smith, 29 Dec. 1811, DD-F, Vol. 12. See also Russell to Cadore, 18 Dec. 1810, and to Smith, 4 Jan. 1811, *Ibid.*; also Cadore to Serurier, 29 Dec. 1810, AECP-EU, Vol. 64, 295–95v.

33. Cadore sent drafts of both letters to Napoleon for his approval on 20 Dec. 1810. (AFIV 1706E Doss. 5). Translated versions appear in *ASP FR*, III, 393–94. Massa's original, addressed to the President of the Council of Prizes, and Gaèté's to the Director General of Customs, are in AECP-EU, Vol. 64, 292–93 and 294–94v, respectively.

34. Cf. Cadore to Serurier, No. 4, 30 Dec. 1810. AECP-EU, Vol. 64, 297–98; Russell to Smith, 29 Dec. 1810, DD-F, Vol. 12.

35. Paris, 27 Dec. 1810, copy enclosed in Russell to Smith, 15 Jan. 1811, *Ibid.*

36. See Russell to Smith, 25 Jan. and 15 March 1811; and Russell to Cadore, 7 Feb. DD-F, Vol. 12.

37. Russell to Cadore, 12 Jan. 1811; Cadore to Russell, 18 Jan.; Russell to Smith, 21 Jan., *ASP FR*, III, 501; Cadore to Serurier, No. 5, Paris, 9 Feb. AECP-EU, Vol. 65, 43–44.

38. To Smith, Paris, 15 March 1811, DD-F, Vol. 12.

39. See Smith's explanation to Russell, 6 March 1811, DI, Vol. 7, 148–49.

40. Titled the "supplementary act," this piece of legislation re-imposed the non-importation provisions of the 1809 Non-Intercourse Act (sections 3 through 10 and 18), but not its sections 12 and 13 banning exports. Cf. *Annals* (11th Cong., 3rd Sess. (1810–11), 1338–39; and (10th Cong., 2nd Sess. (1808–09), 1824–1830.

CHAPTER 12

1. Born Hugues-Bernard Maret, a native of Dijon, Bassano wrote on political issues during the Revolution, saw military service in Belgium in the early 1790s, then served in

various diplomatic posts throughout Europe. At the time of his appointment, he was Secretary General of Consuls, later a Minister of State.

2. Edward Whitcomb maintains that Bassano's appointment reflected Napoleon's already made decision to invade Russia. *Napoleon's Diplomatic Service*, 148.

3. See Napoleon's letter of discharge in *Corres*, XXII, 71.

4. See their correspondence of March 20, 23, 26, and 29, 1811 in Monroe, *Writings*, V, 181–84. See also Adams, *History*, IV, 373–74.

5. Madison offered to post Smith to the legation in St. Petersburg. Smith decided instead to attack the administration publicly for its foreign policy weaknesses and inconsistencies. For details of this uproar, see Brant, *Madison the President*, Ch. XIX.

6. To Minister of Exterior Relations (MRE), No. 14, Washington, 24 May 1811, AECP-EU, Vol. 65, 217–17v.

7. To Smith, Paris, 4 and 25 April 1811. DD-F, Vol. 12.

8. *The Journal of William H. Crawford*, Daniel Chauncey Knowlton, ed., in the *Smith College Studies in History*, IX, No. 1 (Oct. 1925), 51.

9. *Napoleon's Diplomatic Service*, 126.

10. See his despatch No. 1, 3 Feb. 1811, Reel No. 1, Serurier Papers (Kent State University); and his No. 5 [March 1811] AECP-EU, Vol. 65, 105v.

11. Same to same, No. 21, 20 July 1811, *Ibid.*, 320v-21.

12. Same to same, No. 3, Washington, 17 Feb. 1811, *Ibid.*, 50–64.

13. To Cadore, No. 5, [March 1811], AECP-EU, Vol. 65, 104v.

14. Russell to Smith, Paris, 2 May 1811. DD-F, Vol. 12.

15. "Note dictée en conseil d'administration du commerce," St. Cloud, 29 April 1811. *Corres.*, Vol. 22, 144–47. His Council on Commerce and Manufactures also believing that Congress had enacted a complete embargo recommended seizure of all U.S. vessels that violated it, AECP-EU, Vol. 67, 44–45v.

16. AECP-EU, Vol. 64, 309–16v.

17. *Ibid.*, 312v.

18. *Ibid.*, 313.

19. "Décision de l'Empereur," 6 May 1811, *Ibid.*, 317.

20. Bassano's No. 8 to Serurier, 16 May 1811 (AECP-EU, Vol. 64, 320–24) also enclosed a list of some 91 products known to be of American origin which Serurier submitted to Monroe on 23 July. See *ASP FR*, III, 509. The *National Intelligencer* published the list on 6 August.

21. Bassano's No. 8, Paris, 16 May 1811, *op. cit.* See also Bassano to Collin de Sussy, Paris, 24 June 1811, and to Serurier, 8 July, AECP-EU, Vol. 64, 325–25v and 326.

22. Russell first noted Barlow's appointment in a letter he wrote to Joseph Pitcairn on 22 April. Letter Books, I, 94. For Russell's eagerness to be relieved, see his Letter Books, II, e.g., letters to Bourne, 2 June; to David Parish [Hamburg], 6 July and 7 Aug.; and to Joseph Patterson [St. Petersburg], 15 Aug, 162–63, 191, 240, and 250, respectively.

23. As late as 14 September, five days before Barlow arrived in Paris, he wrote Pitcairn that he had not yet decided whether to accept the appointment. Two months later he was in London. Letter Book II, 15.

24. To Serurier, No. 10, Paris, 13 July 1811. AECP-EU, Vol. 64, 328–29v, relating what he had told Russell.

25. Russell to Monroe, Paris, 15 July 1811. DD-F, Vol. 12.

26. To Brown and Ives, Paris, 8 May 1811. Letter Books, II, 119.

27. To John Speare Smith, Paris, 5 July 1811, DD-F, Vol. 12.

28. To Monroe (private and confidential), Paris, 13 July 1811, *Ibid.* Madison had reached much the same conclusion when he first heard of the Altenberg Letter. See his letter to Jefferson of 6 Nov. 1809, *Papers of James Madison: Presidential Series*, Vol 2, 55.

29. Bassano to Russell, 4 May 1811, enclosed in Russell to John Speare Smith (U.S. *chargé d'affaires* in London), 10 May. DD-F, Vol. 12. See also Russell to Meyer [Bordeaux], Paris, 6 May 1811. Letter Books, II, 116, list eight of the admitted vessels by name.

30. Meyer to Secretary of State, Bordeaux, 11 May and 11 June 1811. CD (Bordeaux), Vol. 3.

31. To John Speare Smith, 10 May 1811, DD-F, Vol. 12.

32. Paris, 25 Feb. 1811, Letter Books, III, 13.

33. August 8, 1811, DD-F, Vol. 12.

34. To Bassano, 10 June 1811, ASP FR, III, 508. Russell explained to Monroe that he was struck by the apparent inflexibility of these cargo requirements. See despatch of 15 July 1811. DD-F, Vol. 12.

35. To David Parish [Hamburg] and Henry Higginson [London], Paris, 6 July. Letter Books, II, 193 and 191.

36. See Russell to Bassano, 11 May 1811, AECP-EU, Vol. 67, 51–51v, and Russell to Smith, Paris, 2 June 1811, DD-F, Vol. 12. Russell noted that eight American vessels taken by French privateers had been held for trial since 1 November. To Smith, 11 May 1811, *ASP FR*, III, 506.

37. For this and other of Russell's problems with McRae, see CD (Paris), Vol. 3 for McRae to Smith, 3 Jan. and 4 April, 1811; McRae to Russell, 29 Jan., 19 Feb., 13 May; Russell to McRae, 28 Jan., 19 Feb., and 14 May; and Russell to Smith, 6 April; also Russell to McRae, 18 May, Letter Books, II, 148.

38. Although neither *American State Papers* nor Instructions to U.S. Ministers contains a copy of Smith's instructions to Russell respecting the Florida Resolution, some of the phrases Russell used in reporting his conversations with Bassano suggest that he had received a copy identical to the one sent to Pinkney on 22 January. See Smith to Pinkney in DI, VII, 140–142.

39. Russell to Bassano, Paris, 30 April 1811. DD-F, Vol. 12.

40. To Smith, 13 July 1811, *Ibid.*; and to Sylvanus Bourne, 2 June 1811, Letter Books, II, 162.

CHAPTER 13

1. To Ministre des Relations Extérieure, No. 7, Washington, 26 March 1811, AECP-EU, Vol. 65, 122v.

2. No. 10, Washington, 20 April 1811, AECP-EU, Vol. 65, 171–78.

3. No. 12, Washington, 5 May 1811, *Ibid.*, 199–202.

4. See his secretary's entry of 10 April 1811 in "Journal of George de Caraman," Archives privées, ANF.

5. Serurier to Bassano, No. 14, Washington, 24 May 1811. AECP-EU, Vol. 65, 213v-15.

6. No. 11, Washington, 26 April, 1811, *Ibid.*, 182–85v.

7. No. 14, Washington, 24 May 1811, *Ibid.*, 212–18v.

8. Nos. 12 and 13, of 5 and 13 May 1811, *Ibid.*, 200v, 205–07v. Serurier later reported that no one had been apprehended, in his No. 30, 9 Oct. 1811, AECP-EU, Vol. 66, 121–24.

9. The case of *The Schooner Exchange v. McFadden and Others* is detailed in Cranch,

Reports of Cases Argued and Adjudged by the Supreme Court of the United States in February Term 1812 (Washington: John Conrad and Co., 1804–61), VII, 116–47. For Serurier's efforts to secure the vessel's release, see his despatches in AECP-EU, Vol. 66, dated 9 Oct., 121–24v; 8 Nov., 262–71; 18 Nov., 296–300v, and in AECP-EU, Vol. 67 dated 31 Jan. 1812, 151–54, and 12 March 1812, 176–76v. His letters of protest to Monroe are enclosed in his despatches of 3 Sept., 272–73v; 14 Sept., 276–77; 3 Nov., 274–75; and 17 Nov., 301, in AECP-EU, Vol. 66.

10. Washington, 3 May 1811, Madison Papers, Reel 13.

11. A naval inquiry later established that the *President* returned *Little Belt*'s first shot and then silenced her with a broadside when the corvette returned fire a few minutes later. After a second crippling broadside, Rodgers expressed regret and offered assistance which the British captain refused. For the testimony of the *President's* officers and crew, see *ASP FR*, III, 477–98.

12. To Bassano, No. 15, Washington, 29 May 1811, AECP-EU, Vol. 65, 219–27v.

13. *Ibid.*

14. Same to same, No. 16, Washington, 10 June 1811, *Ibid.*, 239–40.

15. For the Monroe-Foster correspondence, see *ASP FR*, III, 499–500, and the *National Intelligencer* of 14 November 1811.

16. To Bassano, No. 17, Washington, 25 June 1811, AECP-EU, Vol. 65, 252–54.

17. To Bassano, No. 18, Washington, 30 June 1811, *Ibid*, 265–69v. For exchanges on this issue, see Monroe to Serurier, 29 June, and Serurier to Monroe, 30 June, *Ibid.*, 323–23v, 324–25.

18. Serurier's No. 19, 5 July 1811, *Ibid.*, 283–93v.

19. *Ibid.*

20. To Bassano, No. 20, Washington, 10 July 1811, AECP-EU, Vol. 65, 299–301v.

21. *Ibid.*

22. See Serurier to Bassano, No. 21, 20 July 1811, *Ibid.*, 317, also the *National Intelligencer* of 18 July; and Serurier to Monroe, 23 July, *ASP FR*, III, 508–09. For the drafts of the public letters they planned to exchange but apparently never published, see Monroe to Serurier, 18 July; Serurier to Monroe, 19 July, in AECP-EU, Vol. 65, 326, 327–28.

23. To Bassano, No. 21, 20 July 1811, *Ibid.*, 317–22.

24. In a despatch dated 24 July, Serurier acknowledged receipt of Bassano's No. 9 of 17 June, *Ibid.*, 334–46v, and AECP-EU, Vol. 67, 60–61. From what he told Monroe, Serurier must also have received Bassano's No. 8 of 16 May, AECP-EU, Vol. 64, 320–24. Disappointment doubtless explains why publishing a congratulatory exchange of public letters never took place.

25. Serurier's, No. 22, 24 July 1811, AECP-EU, Vol. 65, 334–46v.

26. *Ibid.*

27. Madison officially received Foster on July 3, only three days after he landed at Annapolis. See Monroe to George Hay (Richmond), Washington, 3 July 1811, Monroe Papers (New York Public Library), Box 4.

28. Foster to Monroe, 3 July 1811. *ASP FR*, III, 435–37.

29. 26 July 1811. *Ibid.*, 443.

30. To Foster, 1 Oct. 1811, *Ibid.*, 446.

31. Foster to Monroe, Washington, 3 July 1811, *Ibid.*, 435–37, a charge he repeated in his letter to Monroe of 22 Oct., *Ibid.*, 449.

32. To Foster, 23 July 1811, *Ibid.*, 439–42.

33. *Ibid.*, 441. That France had recently taken fewer American ships Foster ascribed to

Britain's success in bottling up the French navy, not to Napoleon's retreat from his decrees. To Monroe, 31 Oct. 1811, *Ibid.,* 450.

34. Paris, 8 Aug. 1811, DD-F, Vol. 12.

35. See Wellesley to Foster, No. 1, London, 10 April 1811, Bernard Mayo, ed., *Instructions to the British Ministers to the United States, 1791–1812,* Volume III in the *Annual Report of the American Historical Association,* 1936, (Washington: U. S. Government Printing office, 1941), 312.

36. See Foster's note of 16 July, *ASP FR,* III, 439. Monroe questioned the reasonableness of this condition on 23 July. *Ibid.,* 440, and Foster's reply of 26 July gave the first of several unsatisfactory explanations, *Ibid.,* 443.

37. To Foster, 1 Oct. 1811, *Ibid.,* 445–46. Official Washington's summer recess explains Monroe's delay in responding to Foster's communication of 26 July.

38. To Monroe, 17 Dec. 1811, *Ibid.,* 451.

39. Probably to Lord Aukland with whom he negotiated in 1806, [fall of 1811], *Writings,* V, 191–94.

40. Washington, 15 Nov. 1811, Madison Papers, Reel 13.

41. Serurier's No. 22 of 24 July (AECP-EU, Vol. 65, 343) and No. 24 of 8 Aug 1811 (AECP-EU, Vol 66, 19).

CHAPTER 14

1. Editorially disapproving, the *National Intelligencer* published Smith's pamphlet on July 2. Madison explained to Jefferson why he had avoided any public challenge to Smith's twisted interpretation of the Erskine negotiation. Letter of 8 July 1811, Madison Papers, Reel 13.

2. Bassano sent Serurier this quotation the day after it appeared in the *Moniteur* of 16 June, AECP-EU, Vol. 67, 61. Three months later, the French envoy reported having used it to advantage. To Bassano, No. 28, 18 Sept. 1811, AECP-EU, Vol. 66, 102v.

3. For Monroe's 26 July instructions to Barlow and the latter's hasty departure, see *ASP FR,* III, 509–12.

4. For a lively account of Barlow's early years in Paris and his business success later in Hamburg, see James Woodress, *A Yankee's Odyssey: the Life of Joel Barlow* (Philadelphia: Lippincott, 1958).

5. An anonymous undated memorandum in the foreign office archives referred to Barlow as one of "the most lettered men of the United States," a man who "speaks little and appears cold at first aspect but he feels strongly and deeply. . . ." AECP-EU, Vol. 65, 93–94v.

6. To Bassano, No. 36, 18 Nov. 1811, *Ibid.,* 93–94v.

7. *Prologue to War,* 154.

8. Scott's ruling appeared in the *Intelligencer* of 6 August, but only from its November 6 issue did the public learn the full extent of the Foster-Monroe impasse.

9. Petry in Paris deplored Scott's refusal to admit that it was the earlier Fox's Blockade which had evoked the Berlin Decree. (To Bassano, Paris, 3 July 1811, AECP-EU, Vol. 65, 276–76v.)

10. For this interlude, see Serurier's despatches, Nos. 24, 26, 27, and 28, of 8 and 31 Aug., 8 and 18 Sept., in AECP-EU, Vol. 66, 18–22, 73–78, 82–84v, 101–05v, respectively.

11. Serurier's No. 31 of 23 Oct. 1811, *Ibid.*, 129–33. For Bassano's letters of 16 May and 13 July, see AECP-EU, Vol. 64, 320–24, and 328–29v, respectively.

12. To Bassano, No. 32, 31 Oct. 1811, AECP-EU-, Vol. 66, 144–45v. For Serurier's continuing concern as to how Barlow's despatches might affect congressional action, see his despatches of 10, 14, and 18 Nov., *Ibid.*, 279v, 284, and 296v.

13. See Richardson, *Messages*, I, 491–96.

14. Washington, 17 Nov. 1811, Madison Papers, Reel 13.

15. See Jonathan Russell's elaboration on this distinction in his despatch of 14 July, DD-F Vol. 12.

16. Richardson, *Messages*, I, 493.

17. To Bassano, No. 33, 5 Nov. 1811, AECP-EU, Vol. 66, 146.

18. Congress enacted a very modest army bill on 21 Feb. 1812. *Annals* (12th Cong., 1st Sess.), 2241.

19. No. 33 bis, 8 Nov. 1811, AECP-EU, Vol. 66, 262–71.

20. No. 37, 28 Nov. 1811, *Ibid.*, 331.

21. No. 39, 9 Dec. 1811, *Ibid.*, 361.

22. *Ibid.*, 325v.

23. Julius W. Pratt first developed the thesis of a conspiracy among militants in his *Expansionists of 1812* (New York: Macmillan company, 1925). Roger Brown, however, finds "no firm evidence of reckless bellicosity either among Republican leaders or the great rank and file in *The Republic in Peril* (New York: Columbia University Press, 1971), 44. Bradford Perkins notes the Warhawks' lack of cohesion, *Prologue to War*, 372–76.

24. For a fuller account of this sequence, see J. Leitch Wright, Jr., *Britain and the American Frontier, 1783–1815* (Athens, GA: University of Georgia Press, 1975), 152–54.

25. No. 37, 28 Nov. 1811, AECP-EU, Vol. 66, 327v.

26. *Ibid.*, 331v.

27. See *Annals* (12th Cong., 1st Sess.), 373–77.

28. *Ibid.*, 414–20.

29. *Ibid.*, 2229–34 (Appendix).

30. To Bassano, No. 39, 9 Dec. 1811, AECP-EU, Vol. 66, 361.

31. *James Monroe: the Quest for National Identity*, 300–02.

32. Serurier's No. 37 of 28 Nov. 1811, AECP-EU, Vol. 66, 325v.

33. Serurier's No. 41, 2 Jan., 1812, AECP-EU, Vol. 67, 110.

34. Letter of 21 Nov. 1811, *ASP FR*, III, 514.

35. To Barlow, 24 Feb. 1812, *Writings*, V, 199.

36. To Bassano, 15 Nov. 1811, AECP-EU, Vol. 66, 285–95.

CHAPTER 15

1. See Monroe to Barlow, 26 July 1881, *ASP FR*, III, 509–12. Madison doubtless intended his insistence on indemnification to disarm his political foes in Congress.

2. See *William and Mary Quarterly*, 3rd Series, Vol. 15, No. 4 (Oct. 1958), 438–51.

3. Barlow said as much the following spring when, under a brisk reminder from Monroe, he turned grudgingly to the task of adding indemnification clauses to his treaty. See his despatch, No. 11, 22 April 1812, DD-F, Vol. 13.

4. To Monroe, Paris, 31 Dec, 1811, *ASP FR*, III, 515.

5. Perkins also believes that Barlow's treaty-making efforts "injected new, confusing issues into Franco-American discussions." *Prologue to War*, 367–68.

6. Barlow to Monroe, Paris, 29 Sept. 1811, DD-F, Vol. 13; extract in *ASP FR*, III, 512. See also Russell to Monroe, 17 Sept., DD-F, Vol. 12; and Bassano to Serurier, No. 13, Amsterdam, 24 Oct. 1811, AECP-EU, Vol. 64, 336v.

7. Perkins sees this hiatus as a deliberate snub, although other members of the Paris diplomatic corps were similarly distanced by Napoleon's sojourn in the Netherlands. *Prologue to War*, 367.

8. Barlow to Monroe, 29 Oct. 1811, DD-F, Vol. 13, *ASP FR*, III, 512–13.

9. *Ibid.*, 513.

10. See Barlow to Oliver Wolcott, Paris, 26 Sept. 1811, Barlow Papers, Houghton Library, Harvard University.

11. To Monroe, Paris, 19 Dec., 1811, *ASP FR*, III, 515.

12. The full text of Barlow's 10 November note appears in DD-F, Vol. 13. The copy he sent Monroe on 21 November is very briefly extracted in *ASP FR*, III, 513.

13. Note of 10 November, *op. cit.*

14. "Translation of Mr. Barlows address to the Emperor on presenting his letter of Credence—on 17th Nov. 1811," enclosed in Barlow to Monroe, No. 3, Paris, 21 Nov. 1811, DD-F, Vol. 13. French-language copies of both Barlow's address and Napoleon's reply are in the Barlow Papers.

15. Paris, 19 Nov., 1811, Madison Papers, Reel 13.

16. Paris, 21 Nov. 1811, Barlow Papers.

17. Barlow noted Napoleon's misgivings in his despatch No. 4, 12 Dec. 1811, DD-F, Vol. 13. Barlow's rebuttals appear in two unsigned notes to Bassano, both dated 30 November with copies enclosed in his despatch No. 5, 31 Dec. 1811, *Ibid.*

18. See Petry's record of his meetings with Barlow. To Bassano, Paris, 15 Nov. 1811, AECP-EU, Vol. 66, 285–95.

19. Barlow enclosed his pre-treaty proposal, labeled "Dispatch No. 5-A," in his No. 5 to Monroe of 31 Dec. 1811, DD-F, Vol. 13. He had already told Petry he believed that licenses were unnecessary, that certificates of origin would accomplish the same purpose. See Petry to Bassano, 15 Nov. 1811, AECP-EU, Vol. 66, 288–88v.

20. See Barlow's No. 5 of 31 Dec., *ASP FR*, III, 515–16.

21. *Ibid.*

22. A documentary collection in the French National Archives, (Licenses AE BIII 451) makes clear that by the end of 1811, American importers were secure only if they had a license specifying the cargo and port of entry, plus a consular certificate of origin issued in cipher and a consular letter confirming that both documents were in order.

23. To Barlow, Washington, 24 February 1812, Hunt, *Writings*, VIII, 177–82. See also Monroe to Barlow, 24 February 1812, DI, VII, 191–94.

24. Barlow enclosed a copy of this Bassano letter of 27 Dec., in his No. 6 to Monroe of 28 Jan. 1812, along with the "project for a Treaty," he sent Bassano on 17 Jan.; he also enclosed his cover letter to Bassano of the same date. See DD-F, Vol. 13. Only the letter of 27 Dec. was made public in the United States; no copy of it can be found in the French archives.

25. To Madison (private), Paris, 1 Jan. 1812, Madison Papers, Reel 13.

26. To Madison, 1 Jan. 1812, Madison Papers, Reel 13.

27. Petry to Bassano, Paris, 1 December 1811, AECP-EU, Vol. 64, 378–85v, in which he also noted that the largest number of still-detained U.S. merchantmen had been taken by French privateers since November 1810.

28. "Rapport à Sa Majesté," 5 Dec. 1811, AECP-EU, Vol, 64, 386–94.

29. Two instructions to Serurier, Nos. 16 and 17, both dated 30 Dec. 1811, *Ibid.*, 407–14.
30. Bassano recorded the incident in his No. 17 to Serurier of 30 Dec., *Ibid.*, 413–13v.

CHAPTER 16

1. Department of State, 23 Feb. 1812. DI, Vol. 7, 191–94.
2. A copy of Barlow's 17 January draft annotated with critical marginalia is in the Madison Papers, Reel 13.
3. Washington, 23 April 1812, DI, Vol. 7, 200–05.
4. An extract of Barlow's despatch, No. 6, dated 28 Jan. 1812 appears in *ASP FR*, III, 518. The despatch itself, in DD-F, Vol. 13, enclosed copies of the draft treaty and the "explanatory" letter Barlow sent Bassano on 17 Jan. A French-language version of Barlow's "projet" is in AECP-EU, Vol. 69, 7–16.
5. He proposed a maximum rate of 20 percent, but invited Bassano to make a counter-proposal. He told Monroe he would yield to a French offer as high as 30 percent. See his No. 6 of 28 Jan., *op. cit.*
6. See his despatches Nos. 7 and 8, of 8 Feb. and 3 March 1812, respectively, DD-F, Vol. 13.
7. "Rapport à Sa Majesté," Paris, 27 Feb. 1812. AECP-EU, Vol. 69, 18–19.
8. "Rapport à Sa Majesté," Paris, 17 April 1812, *Ibid.*, 22–25.
9. Bassano to Barlow, 20 April 1812, *Ibid*, 26–27.
10. Barlow first noted the effects of Napoleon's consuming involvement with Russia in his despatch of 8 February 1812, *ASP FR*, II, 518.
11. Bassano's note of 20 April was enclosed in Barlow's No 11 to Monroe, 22 April 1812, DD-F, Vol. 13.
12. No. 9, Paris, 16 March 1812, *Ibid.*
13. For correspondence on the *Belisarius* case, see Barlow to Bassano, 6 and 16 March; Bassano to Barlow, 15 March; and Barlow to Monroe, No. 9, 16 March, reporting that a resolution was "in progress," *Ibid.*
14. Napoleon put his request to Bassano on the margin of the French-translation of the *Courier* article. AECP-EU, Vol. 68, 117–19.
15. Petry to Bassano of 22 March, *Ibid.*, 138–39v.
16. See Barlow to Bassano, 20 April, copy enclosed in his despatch No. 11 of 1 May, DD-F, Vol. 13; and Bassano to Serurier, Paris, 27 April 1812, AECP-EU, Vol. 69, 36–36v.
17. To Russell, Paris, 2 March, copy enclosed in Barlow's No. 8 to Monroe of 3 March, *ASP FR*, III, 518–19. Barlow also pointed out that being licensed would have been no guarantee against seizure if the decrees were still in force.
18. See Barlow's chiding letter to Bassano, 1 May 1812, copy enclosed in his No. 11 of 22 April. DD-F, Vol. 13.
19. Barlow enclosed notification of Dalberg's appointment, dated 20 April (AECP-EU, Vol. 69, 26–27) in his despatch No. 11 of 22 April.
20. For Monroe's letters of 23 and 24 February, see DI, Vol. 7; and for Madison's of 24 Feb., Hunt, *Writings*, Vol. 8, 177–82.
21. His No. 10, DD-F, Vol. 13.
22. For allusions to Dalberg, see despatches, Nos. 12 and 13 of 12 and 22 May, respectively. DD-F, Vol. 13
23. Barlow to Monroe, No. 12, Paris, 12 May 1812, enclosing Bassano's note of 10 May.

DD-F, Vol. 13. External evidence confirms the fraudulent nature of the decree. No reference to it appears in the *procès verbal* recorded at St Cloud on 29 April 1811. See "Note dictée" entitled "Note dictée en conseil," *Corres.*, Vol. 22, 144–47.

24. 12 May 1812, Madison Papers, reel 26.

25. 11 August 1812, *Writings*, VIII, 208. For Bassano's insistence, even to Serurier, that the St. Cloud Decree was genuine, see his letter of 26 May 1812, AECP-EU, Vol. 69, 56–58v.

26. "Extrait du Procès-verbal . . . le 29 avril 1811," AECP-EU, Vol. 67, 44–45v.

27. *History*, VI, 258.

28. To Russell, 11 May 1812. DD-F, Vol. 13.

29. *Madison the President*, 443.

30. Barlow notified Monroe of having alerted Russell in his No. 13 of 22 May, and expressed satisfaction at the outcome in his No. 14 of 13 July. DD-F, Vol. 13.

31. Harry Ammon, *James Monroe*, 311.

32. A translation quickly found its way to Paris, now archived under "English Journals, The Statesman," 22 May 1812, AECP-EU, Vol. 68, 192–92v.

33. Perkins, *Prologue to War*, Ch. IX, offers the most detailed secondary account of the politics surrounding the ministry's decision to suspend the orders. For the text of the suspension order and Russell's cover letter of 26 June, see *Annals* (12th Cong., 1st Sess.), 1777–79.

34. *History*, VI, 282–83.

35. Bassano to Serurier, No. 27, Vilna, 18 July 1812, AECP-EU, Vol. 69, 169–71v.

36. See Russell to Barlow, 27 June 1812, enclosing Castlereagh to Russell of the same date, both enclosed in Barlow to Dalberg, 17 July, *Ibid.*, 177–8v, 185–86v.

37. To Bassano, Paris, 15 July 1812, AECP-EU, Vol. 68, 250.

38. Serurier to Bassano, No. 73, 21 Oct. 1813, AECP-EU, Vol. 70, 313–314v.

CHAPTER 17

1. Bassano to Barlow, Paris, 10 May 1812. DD-F, Vol. 13.

2. Despatch, No. 14, 13 July 1812, *Ibid.*

3. Cf. Barlow to Bassano, 17 July 1812, enclosed in Barlow's despatch, No. 15 of 11 August, DD-F, Vol. 13; Petry to Bassano, 31 July 1812, AECP-EU, Vol. 69, 262–72v; and Serurier to Bassano, No. 61, 6 July 1812, AECP-EU, Vol. 67, 254–54v.

4. To Bassano via Dalberg, Paris, 17 July 1812, with a postscript dated 31 July noting the U.S. declaration of war, AECP-EU, Vol. 69, 177–80. Barlow enclosed a copy to Monroe in his No. 15, 11 August, DD-F, Vol. 13.

5. Barlow to Dalberg, Paris, 5 June 1812, copies enclosed in both Barlow's Nos. 14 and 15 of 13 July and 11 August, respectively, *Ibid.* This note, though dated 5 June, did not reach Bassano (via Dalberg) until mid-August.

6. To Serurier, Paris, 24 April 1812, AECP-EU, Vol. 69, 30–35.

7. Bassano to Dalberg, 10 May 1812, AECP-EU, Vol. 69, ff. 60–76.

8. *Ibid.*

9. *Ibid.* Bassano identified the proposal as having come from Boston, presumably from a French resident there or possibly the French consul (signature illegible).

10. See Barlow to Madison (private), Paris, 30 Dec. 1811; and a copy of the unsigned and undated boundary/claims convention in Madison Papers, Reel 13.

11. See Barlow to Bassano, Paris, 28 May 1812; and Decrès to Bassano, Paris, 6 June,

detailing Barlow's complaint. AECP-EU, Vol. 68, 208–08v, 200–02, respectively. An unsigned "Rapport à Sa Majesté" dated 28 and possibly drafted by Petry at Bassano's direction reminded Napoleon of this oversight. AECP-EU, Vol. 69, 165–66v.

12. To Bassano, Paris, 28 July 1812, AECP-EU, Vol 68, 259–60v.

13. Barlow picked up reports of ships being burned at sea in March. Monroe confirmed them later that month. See Barlow to Bassano, Paris, 12 March 1812, *ASP FR*, III, 520; Monroe to Barlow, 21 March, DI, Vol., 7, 196–98. For Barlow's insistence on immediate indemnification, see Dalberg to Bassano, 12 June 1812, AECP-EU, Vol. 69, 136–37v.

14. Paris, 17 June 1812, AECP-EU, Vol. 68, 243–44v.

15. Washington, 11 Aug. 1812, *Writings*, VIII, 208–10.

16. *History*, VI, 251, citing *Corres.*, XXIII, 182. Neither source specifies motive.

17. To Bassano (Vilna), Paris, 31 July 1812, AECP-EU, Vol. 68, 262–71.

18. "Joel Barlow, Madison's Stubborn Minister," *William and Mary Quarterly*, 3rd Series, 15, No. 4 (Oct. 1958), 444–45.

19. Petry to Dalberg, 13 June 1812, AECP-EU, Vol. 69, 139–41; Dalberg relayed this account to Bassano, 18 June 1812, *Ibid.*, 138–38v.

20. Dalberg and Petry learned of this "condition" circuitously through Collin de Sussy whom the Emperor authorized to impart it to Barlow. See Dalberg to Bassano, 12 June 1812, *Ibid.*, 136–37v; and Petry's report to Dalberg on Barlow's angry reaction, 13 June 1812, *Ibid*, 139.

21. To Bassano, 26 Aug. 1812, AECP-EU, Vol. 68, 295–96v.

22. *Ibid.*

23. Bassano's instructions to Dalberg are dated 10 May 1812. AECP-EU, Vol. 69, 60–76.

24. For Dalberg's correspondence, see ff. 78–79v, 80–89v; and Bassano's reply of 9 June from Thorn [Prussia], ff. 133–135v, *Ibid.*

25. To Bassano, Paris, 12 June 1812, *Ibid.*, 136–37v, enclosing a copy of Petry's report of 13 June detailing a heated conversation with Barlow over the reported burning of seventeen more U.S. grain ships.

26. To Dalberg, Vilna, 11 July 1812, *Ibid.* This note responded to Dalberg's of 24 June, as well.

27. See Bassano to Dalberg, Vilna, 10 and 24 Aug. 1812, AECP-EU, Vol. 69, 198–200v, 228–29.

28. To Bassano, 11 Aug. 1812, *Ibid.*, 201–04.

29. "Contre-Projet remis à M. Barlow par le Duc de Dalberg," undated, *Ibid.*, 205–12. The proposed treaty stipulated "reciprocity" and was to remain in force as long as the parties were at war with Britain. Clauses to be "retained" from the text of the 1800 Convention are on f. 212, undated.

30. Paris, 13 Aug. 1812, *Ibid.*, 213–13v.

31. Barlow separately specified the re-export of tobacco whenever the government's monopolistic "régie" refused to buy it. He also listed for renewal some 18 sections of the 1800 Convention. *Ibid.*, 214–17.

32. For Dalberg's "Observations" to Barlow, 17 Aug. 1812, and his subsequent account of Barlow's response in his letter to Bassano of 21 Aug., see *Ibid.*, 218–19v, 220–21.

33. To Bassano, *Ibid.*, 231–31v.

34. Parker had a reputation for questionable business ventures. See, for example, Russell's comment that he had undoubtedly "made those sacrifices to interest which honest men avoid." To Madison, 2 Jan. 1811, Madison Papers, Reel 12.

35. See Dalberg's despatches of 30 Aug. and 8 Sept., and a two-page copy of Barlow's

indemnity plan, AECP-EU, Vol. 69, 233–33v, 236–36v, and 238–38v. The original plan specified that the proceeds from the sale of 30 licenses would indemnify the owners of approximately 100 vessels captured prior to July 1809. Proceeds from the sale of another 30 licenses, but for imports at current tariff levels, would be designated to indemnify for property seized after July 1809.

36. Vilna, 28 Sept. 1812, *Ibid.*, 242–45.

37. *Ibid.*, 255–57.

38. To Bassano, Paris, 5 Oct. 1812, *Ibid.*, 248–49. By the time this despatch reached Bassano, the invitation to Barlow had already been sent.

39. Washington, 11 Aug. 1812, *Writings*, VIII, 208–10.

40. Dalberg to Bassano, 5 Oct. 1812, AECP-EU, Vol. 69, 248–49.

41. *Ibid.*, 252–52v for the invitation to Barlow and ff. 248–49 for Bassano's same day letter to Dalberg notifying him of the invitation and still asking for de Sussy's opinion.

CHAPTER 18

1. National honor as a cause is ably developed by Bradford Perkins in his *Prologue to War* and by Roger H. Brown in *The Republic in Peril.* Quoted passages from the writings of earlier explicators of "causes" appear in Perkins, *The Causes of the War of 1812: National Honor or National Interest?* (Malabar, FL: Krieger Publishing Co., 1983). The so-called "Republican synthesis" has been modified most recently by Peter S. Onuf in his "A Declaration of Independence for Diplomatic Historians," *Diplomatic History*, 22 (Winter 1998), 71–83 and by Doron S. Ben-Atar, *The Origins of Jeffersonian Commercial Policy and Diplomacy*, and somewhat earlier by Ronald L. Hatzenbueler and Robert L. Ivie, *Congress Declares War: Rhetoric, Leadership and Partisanship in the Early Republic* (Kent State University Press, 1983). See also Reginald Horsman's "Feature Review: The War of 1812 Revisited," *Diplomatic History*, 15, (Winter 1991), 115–24.

2. To Bassano, No. 53, Washington, 19 April 1812, AECP-EU, Vol. 67, 206.

3. To Bassano, No. 41, Washington, 2 Jan. 1812, AECP-EU, Vol. 67, 107–17. Much of this long despatch described congressional politicking over war measures.

4. See his No. 43, Washington, 21 Jan., and No. 47, 2 March, *Ibid.*, 146–48, and 165–71v, respectively.

5. To Bassano, No. 42, Washington, 12 Jan. 1812, *Ibid.*, 123–31; also No. 47 of 2 March, 167.

6. To Bassano, No. 49, Washington, 22 March 1812, *Ibid.*, 184–89; and Barlow to Bassano, 6 Jan. 1812, *Ibid.*, 121.

7. Bulloch to Monroe, Savannah, 26 Dec. 1811, copy enclosed in Serurier's No. 44 of 31 Jan. 1812, *Ibid.*, 155–58. Not forwarded were some 18 depositions testifying to the good conduct of local authorities. For a more detailed account of the riots, see the author's article in the winter 2004 issue of the *Georgia Historical Quarterly.*

8. See Serurier's No. 37 and 38 of 28 Nov. and 1 Dec. 1811, respectively, AECP-EU, Vol. 66, 324–25, 346–49v; and Serurier to Monroe, 27 Nov., *Ibid.*, 336–37v.

9. See Lominé to Serurier, Savannah, n.d., *Ibid.*, 332–335v; and Serurier to Monroe, n.d., [Jan. 1812], AECP-EU, Vol. 67, 118–18v.

10. To Barlow, 29 Nov. 1811, DI, VII, 184–86.

11. No. 44, Washington, 31 Jan. 1812. AECP-EU, Vol. 67, 151–54.

12. No. 38, Washington, 1 Dec. 1811. AECP-EU, Vol. 66, 349.

13. Conveying the Henry Letters to Congress on 9 March, Madison wrote that "in the midst of amicable professions and negotiations on the part of the British Government," her secret agent was "fomenting disaffection to the constituted authorities of the nation." In Richardson, *Messages*, I, 498.

14. To Bassano, No. 49, 22 March 1812, AECP-EU, Vol. 67, 185–85v. Serurier began writing about his contacts with Crillon in his despatches of 8 and 18 February.

15. See *ASP FR*, III, 545–57 for Henry's letters and the report of the House Foreign Relations Committee after it took testimony from Crillon. The fullest secondary account is "The Henry-Crillon Affair of 1812," in *By Land and By Sea: Essays and Address by Samuel Eliot Morison* (New York: Knopf, 1953), Ch. XII.

16. To Bassano, Nos. 47 and 48 of March 2 and 12, AECP-EU, Vol. 67, 171–71v, 175–76, respectively.

17. *Ibid.* Monroe viewed their publication principally as a warning to Federalists to steer clear of subversive activities in the future. To Jefferson, 9 March 1812, *Writings*, 200.

18. Bassano to Serurier, No. 22, 1 May 1812, AECP-EU, Vol. 67, 226–26v; Serurier to Bassano, No. 57, 27 May 1812, *Ibid.*, 237–42. Pretending injured innocence, Crillon bombarded Bassano with explanations. See AECP-EU, Vol. 68, 299–315.

19. To Bassano, No. 49, Washington, 22 March 1812. AECP-EU, Vol. 67, 184–89.

20. To Bassano, No. 52, 9 April 1812, *Ibid.*, 198–202.

21. Serurier's No. 52, *op. cit.*

22. To Bassano, No. 53, 19 April 1812. AECP-EU, Vol 67, 206–09.

23. Madison referred here specifically to a letter written to Postmaster General Gideon Granger. To Jefferson, 24 April 1812, in Hunt, *Writings*, VII, 189.

24. To Bassano, No. 54, 24 April 1812. AECP-EU, Vol. 67, 216–20.

25. *Ibid.*

26. To Bassano, No. 56, 14 May 1812. *Ibid.*, 233–35. Serurier doubtless drew some of his optimism from the *National Intelligencer*, which in June carried upbeat items on the progress of recruitment, even in New England.

27. To Bassano, No. 55, 4 May 1812. AECP-EU, Vol. 67, 228–31.

28. *Ibid.*

29. Smith to Mathews, 26 Jan. 1811, *ASP FR*, III, 571.

30. For the Mathews expedition, see Rembert W. Patrick, *Florida Fiasco*; also Isaac J. Cox, "The Border Missions of General George Mathews," *Mississippi Valley Historical Review*, 12 (Nov. 1925), 303–33, still useful.

31. See *Madison the President*, 445–46, and Ford, *Works*, VIII, 190.

32. Despatch No. 55 of 4 May 1812, *op. cit.*, 229.

33. To Bassano, No. 57, 27 May 1812, AECP-EU, Vol. 67, ff. 237–37v.

34. To Bassano, No. 57, 27 May 1812, *Ibid.*, 237–42. Serurier devoted much of this despatch to explaining his dealings with Crillon.

35. To Jefferson, Washington, 25 May 1812. *Writings*, VIII, 191. See Russell to Monroe, 13 July 1811, DD-F, Vol. 12.

36. Bradford Perkins cites Madison's "no choice" reaction to his journal entry of April 18, 1830. *Prologue to War*, 400–02.

37. For Madison's having seen advantages for the United States in Europe's continued warfare, see Kaplan's development of this thesis in his *Entangling Alliances With None*, 136.

38. Richard Glover argues this possibility in his article, "The French Fleet, 1807–1814: Britain's Problem and Madison's Opportunity," *Journal of Modern History*, 39, No. 3 (Sept. 1967), 233–52.

39. *History*, VI, 221.

40. To Madison, London, 25 July 1812, Madison Papers, Reel 26.

41. To Bassano, No. 58, 7 June 1812. AECP-EU, Vol. 67, 243–46v.

42. To Bassano, No. 59, 19 June 1812, *Ibid.*, 249.

43. Monroe to Russell, 27 July 1812, *ASP FR*, III, 586.

44. Castlereagh to Russell, 29 Aug. 1812, *Ibid.*, 590.

45. To Bassano, No. 60, 23 June 1812, AECP-EU, Vol. 67, 250–54.

46. The vote was 17 to 15. See *Annals* (12th Cong., 1st Sess.), 270.

47. Serurier gratefully reported its adjournment on 6 July in his No. 60 of 23 June, AECP-EU, Vol. 67, 250.

48. Despatch No. 61, 6 July 1812, *Ibid.* 254–54v.

49. To Bassano, No. 62, Baltimore, 12 July 1812, *Ibid.*, 257–61v. See subsequent reports sent to Bassano by Consuls Douzy and Lescallier, *Ibid.*, 262–64, 265–66.

CHAPTER 19

1. Barlow to Bassano, Paris, 8 Aug. 1812 (copy enclosed in his No. 15 to Monroe, 11 Aug., DD-F, Vol. 13.

2. Paris, 31 July 1812, AECP-EU, Vol. 68, 270.

3. See Rivière to Bassano, Paris, 2 Oct. 1812; and Decrès' "Rapport à l'Empereur," 14 Oct. 1812, AECP-EU, Vol. 68, 356–57, 367–67v, respectively.

4. Bassano to Barlow, Vilna, 18 Sept. 1812, DD-F, Vol. 13.

5. See Dudley, *The Naval War of 1812*, I, 233n.

6. De Sussy to Bassano, Paris, 9 Sept. 1812, AECP-EU, Vol. 68. 318–20v. See also Bassano's earlier note to de Sussy in AECP-EU, Vol. 69, 227–27v.

7. This imperial decree of 14 April 1813 clearly favored American prizemasters inasmuch as such goods brought in by French prizemasters were ordered burned. Warden to Monroe, Paris, 26 April 1813, CD (Paris), Vol. 4.

8. To John Graham (State Department), 23 Aug. 1812, *Ibid.*

9. See same to same, 23 Aug., 1 Nov., and 10 Dec. 1812, *Ibid.*

10. In late October, Barlow counted 77 Americans indiscriminately locked up with British POWs at eight different locations, but two months later Consul Isaac Cox Barnet put the figure at 138 and listed them by name. See the Barlow and Barnet letters to Bassano of 26 Oct. and 19 Dec. 1812, respectively, in AECP-EU, Vol. 68, 276–78v, 495–97.

11. To Bassano, Paris, 4 Sept. 1812, AECP-EU, *Ibid.*, 308–09.

12. For Barlow's letters to Bassano of 26 Oct. and 28 Nov. 1812, *Ibid.*, 276–78v, 465–65v.

13. For this exchange of correspondence, see Bassano to Feltre, 30 Nov. 1812, and Feltre's reply of 3 Dec., AECP-EU, Vol. 68, 462–63v and 471–72; and Bassano's notification to Barlow on 9 Dec., *Ibid.*, 489–89v.

14. See, for example, Warden's letter to Bassano of 6 Feb. 1813, AECP-EU, Vol. 70, 61–61v.

15. For a more detailed account of Haley's exploits, see Edgar Stanton Maclay, *A History of American Privateers* (New York: D. Appleton, 1899), 275–77.

16. See his letters to Bassano of 10 and 18 Sept. 1812, AECP-EU, Vol. 68, 321–22v and 329–32.

17. Serurier to Bassano, No. 94, 20 April 1813, AECP-EU, Vol. 70, 188–89.

18. Crawford transmitted this document with a cover note in his No. 6 to Monroe, 15 Aug. 1813, DD-F, Vol. 14.

19. The House passed the measure on 1 March 1813, but the advocates of postponement won out in the Senate. *Annals* (12th Cong., 2nd Sess), 193, 1134–42; and (13th Cong., 1st Sess.), 121. For Serurier's account of its end-of-session demise, see his No. 89, 6 March 1813, AECP-EU, Vol. 70, 100–100v. A law signed 2 August 1813, however, did forbid American citizens to accept British licenses. *Annals* (13th Cong., 2nd Sess.), 2777–79.

20. Lee to Monroe, letters of 15 and 17 Jan. 1813, CD (Bordeaux), Vol. 3.

21. Vilna, 11 Oct., 1812, AECP-EU, Vol. 69, 252–52v. Bassano wrote Dalberg the same day, requesting that he forward documents related to the negotiation. *Ibid.* 254–54v.

22. See Barlow to Monroe, letters of 20 and 26 Oct., 1812, DD-F, Vol. 13. For Bassano's letter of invitation, see *ASP FR*, III, 604.

23. To Monroe, Paris, 25 Oct. 1812, DD-F, Vol. 13.

24. To Monroe, 30 Oct. and 1 Nov. 1812, CD (Bordeaux), Vol. 3.

25. Monroe to Crawford, 29 May 1813, DI, Vol. 7, 291.

26. To Monroe, No. 21, Vilna, 23 Nov. 1812, DD-F, Vol. 13. The Harvard collection of Barlow Papers contains a detailed account of his trip and his impressions of Vilna in letters written to his sister-in-law, Clara Baldwin (from Konigsburg 12 Nov. and Vilna 26 Nov. 1812.) Clara lived with the Barlows in Paris.

27. For a text of the commercial treaty, see his "Rapport à Sa Majesté," 15 Oct. 1812, AECP-EU, Vol. 69, 258–65, and enclosure, ff. 267–67v.

28. To Monroe, No. 21, 23 Nov. 1812, *op. cit.*

29. For Napoleon's retreat, see Alan Palmer, *Napoleon in Russia* (New York: Simon and Schuster, 1967), 251–58. Barlow left his own account, entitled "Napoleon's passage at Warsaw," (undated), in the Barlow papers.

30. For Barlow's last days, see Petry's letter to Bassano, Zarnovich, 27 Dec. 1812, forwarded to Daniel Parker, who broke the news to Barlow's wife. Bassano's cover note dated 13 Jan. 1813, offered condolences, DD-F, Vol. 13. See also Jh. Marcadier (Barlow's private secretary) to Monroe, Paris, 13 Jan. 1813; and Thomas Barlow to Monroe, Paris, 25 Jan., *Ibid.*

31. To Bassano, Paris, 22 Oct. 1812, AECP-EU, 49, 342–47.

32. Dresden, 23 July 1813, AECP-EU, Vol. 70, 315.

33. See Knowlton, *Journal of William H. Crawford*, 34.

34. Barlow hoped to complete his nephew's appointment. From Vilna he wrote asking Monroe to secure Senate approval. See his despatch No. 22 (23 Nov. 1812) and a private letter to Monroe of the same date, DD-F, Vol. 13.

35. For a more detailed description of this episode, see the author's article, "Who's In Charge," in the Winter 2001 issue of the *Newsletter* of the Society for Historians of American Foreign Relations.

CHAPTER 20

1. Although the three continental powers signed an alliance on 27 June, Austria declined to take an active part without first offering to mediate. Georges Lefebvre concludes that even if Napoleon had accepted all of Austria's terms, Wellington's victory at Vittoria was too inviting an opportunity for the allies not to resume military action. See his *Napo-*

leon from Tilsit to Waterloo, 1807–1815 (New York: Columbia University Press, 1965), 331–33.

2. To Bassano, No. 66, Washington, 28 Aug. 1812, Serurier Papers, reel 3.

3. To Bassano, No. 67, Washington, 2 Sept. 1812, AECP-EU, Vol. 67, 274–82.

4. _Ibid._

5. To Bassano, No. 73, Washington, 21 Oct. 1812, _Ibid._, 313v–14.

6. _Ibid._

7. To Bassano, No. 68, Washington, 10 Sept. 1812, _Ibid._, 283–87v.

8. To Bassano, No. 69, 19 Sept. 1812, _Ibid._, 289–93.

9. No. 94, 28 May 1813, AECP-EU, Vol. 70, 240v–42.

10. For Serurier's account, see his despatch No. 116 of 14 Jan. 1814, AECP, Vol. 71, 35–43v, enclosing a letter from Monroe dated 31 Jan.; and his No. 122 of 25 April 1814, _Ibid._, 101–02v.

11. To Bassano, No. 70, 28 Sept. 1812, AECP-EU, Vol. 67, 298–302.

12. No. 71, Washington, 14 Oct. 1812, _Ibid._, 308–10. Seven months later, Serurier got the same response: Spain and Portugal were regarded as neutral parties; and France was equally guilty of trading with the enemy. To Bassano, No. 94, 28 May 1813, AECP-EU, Vol. 70, 242v–243v.

13. See _New American State Papers: Commerce and Navigation_ (Wilmington, DE: Scholarly Resources, 1973), III, 245.

14. For the House action, see _Annals_ (12th Cong., 2nd Sess.), 43.

15. To Bassano, No. 75, Washington, 9 Nov. 1812, AECP-EU, Vol. 67, 326. For Madison's opening address, see Richardson, _Messages_, I, 518.

16. See his despatches Nos. 75 and 76, of 9 and 18 Nov. 1812, respectively, Washington, AECP-EU, Vol. 67, 324–29v, 330–35v. Madison's margin of 128 electoral votes to Clinton's 89 came from a sweep of Southern and Western states plus Pennsylvania and Vermont. With Federalist support Clinton carried all other states north of the Potomac.

17. Despatch No. 78, Washington, 5 Dec. 1812, AECP-EU, Vol. 67, 344–48.

18. _Ibid._ See also Rossignol, _The Nationalist Ferment,_ for a recent analysis of the bipartisan opposition to recognizing Haitian independence.

19. To Bassano, Nos. 86 and 87 of 14 and 20 Feb. 1813, AECP-EU, Vol. 70, 68–75v, and 84, respectively.

20. Despatch No. 79, Washington, 18 Dec. 1812, AECP-EU, Vol. 67, 360–69. See, too, his No. 92, 9 April 1813, AECP-EU, Vol. 70, 151–51v.

21. Despatch No. 80, Washington, 27 Dec. 1812, AECP-EU, Vol. 67, 360–69.

22. For Serurier's hopes to conclude the Barlow negotiations, see his despatches, Nos. 89 (6 March) and 91 (25 March), AECP-EU, Vol. 70, 107 and 128, respectively.

23. To Bassano, No. 85, 8 Jan. 1813, _Ibid._, 13–13v.

24. _Ibid._, 14v.

25. Skeen, _Armstrong,_ 121–25.

26. Despatch No. 85, _op. cit.,_ 14.

27. To Bassano, No. 84, 28 Jan. 1813, _Ibid._, 36–37.

28. To Bassano, No. 85, 7 Feb. 1813, _Ibid._, 64–66v.

29. To Bassano, No. 87, 20 Feb. 1813, _Ibid._, 79–79v.

30. No. 89, 6 March 1813, _Ibid._, 100–07. Madison's second inauguration took place on 4 March.

31. _Ibid._ Washington learned of Barlow's death on March 1. See Serurier's No. 88, 2

March 1813, *Ibid.*, 99bis. Madison publicly announced Crawford's appointment to Congress on May 25, Richardson, *Messages*, I, 526–30.

CHAPTER 21

1. See his No. 98, 10 June 1813, AECP-EU, Vol. 70, 264–64v.
2. To Bassano, No. 89, 6 March 1813, *Ibid.*, 105–06. When John Quincy Adams had asked whether London had been consulted about the offer, Count Romanzoff had replied that the British ambassador, Lord Cathcart, had suggested it. Adams to Monroe, St. Petersburg, 30 Sept. 1812, in Worthington Chauncey Ford, ed., *Writings of John Quincy Adams* (New York: Macmillan Company, 1913–17), Vol. 4, 389–91.
3. This prohibition became law on 3 March 1813, but was not to take effect until after the war. See *Annals* (12th Cong., 2nd Sess.), 1339–42.
4. See Despatch Nos. 89 of 6 March and 91 of 25 March, AECP-EU, Vol. 70, 107, 125–25v, respectively.
5. Despatch No. 93, 10 April 1813, *Ibid.*, 164–64v.
6. *Ibid.*, 168–68v.
7. No. 94, 20 April 1813, AECP-EU, Vol. 70, 187–92v. What Serurier told Monroe came from a letter Bassano had posted from Vilna dated 29 November 1812.
8. Despatch No. 92, 9 April 1813, *Ibid.*, 150–55v.
9. Richardson, *Messages*, I, 527.
10. Serurier's, No. 97, 28 May 1813, AECP-EU, Vol. 70, 248–49.
11. His No. 97 ran 32 folio pages, *Ibid.*, 238–53v.
12. *Ibid.*, 249–53v.
13. See Serurier's despatches, Nos. 99 and 102, of 21 June and 21 July, respectively, in AECP-EU, Vol. 70, 275v–76, 310–11; and Monroe's 12 July report to Congress in the *National Intelligencer* of 14 July 1813.
14. The speaker was Congressman Harmanus Bleecker, as reported in the *Intelligencer* of 3 Feb. 1814.
15. A translated text first appeared that summer in the *Federal Republican,* a Baltimore newspaper edited by Alexander Contee Hanson, a Federalist congressman who introduced two probative resolutions 28 December. Both were tabled. When Hanson renewed his attack on 11 January, he charged that Madison's withholding letter made him guilty of a high misdemeanor. See *Annals,* (13th Cong., 2nd Sess.), 808–12 and 894.
16. *Ibid.*, 922–27, and for the full text of the debates, 808–12, 888–927.
17. See despatches Nos. 106 and 107 of 5 and 15 Oct., 1813, respectively, AECP-EU, Vol. 70, 393–400v, 404–08v.
18. No. 108, 28 Oct., *Ibid.*, 420–21v.
19. No. 109, 9 Nov., *Ibid.*, 425–28.
20. See his despatches, No. 114 and 115 of 3 and 14 Jan. 1814, respectively, AECP-EU, Vol. 71, 2–7v, 21–26.
21. *Annals* (13th Cong., 1st Sess.), 625.
22. Unnumbered despatch, 4 Feb. 1814, AECP-EU, Vol. 71, 57–57v.
23. Antoine de LaForest, Commissaire provisoire de Départment des affaires étrangères, to Serurier, 16 April 1814. *Ibid.*, 80–81.
24. 15 May 1814 (un-numbered), *Ibid.*, 111–12.

25. Despatch No. 1, 18 June 1813, *Ibid.*, 121–22v.
26. See "Notification to Frenchmen," 13 June 1814, *Ibid.*, 20.

CHAPTER 22

1. Chase C. Mooney, *William H. Crawford, 1771–1834* (Lexington, KY: University Press of Kentucky, 1974), 76.
2. *Ibid.* Henry Adams also finds Crawford's "temper and manners were little suited to the very difficult situation in which he was placed." *Life of Albert Gallatin* (Philadelphia: J. B. Lippincott, 1879), I, 510. For a favorable view of Crawford's talents, see Kaplan's *Entangling Alliances with None*, Ch. 11.
3. *History*, VII, 49.
4. See, for example, John S. Pancake, "The 'Invisibles:' A Chapter in the Opposition to President Madison," *Journal of Southern History*, 21, No. 1 (Feb. 1955), 17–37; and for the role of these dissenters in Madison's decision for war, J. C. A. Stagg, "James Madison and the 'Malcontents:' the Political Origins of the War of 1812," *William and Mary Quarterly*, 3rd series, 33, No. 4 (Oct. 1976), 557–85.
5. See Mooney for these and other biographical details.
6. To Monroe (private), Paris, 10 Feb. 1813, DD-F, Vol. 13.
7. Monroe to Crawford, Washington, 29 May 1813, DI, Vol. 7, 285–91.
8. To Monroe, on board the Brig Argus in the harbor of L'Orient, 12 July 1813, DD-F, Vol. 14; and his No. 4, Paris, 15 Aug., *Ibid.* Crawford found time, however, to write a detailed description of his carriage ride to Paris. See his *Journal*, 9–30.
9. Despatch, No. 3, 15 Aug. 1813, DD-F, Vol.14.
10. Paris, 5 Oct. 1813, AECP-EU, Vol. 70, 392–92v.
11. Paris, 7 Sept. 1813, *Ibid.*, 355–56.
12. Crawford's No. 3, 15 Aug. 1813, DD-F, Vol. 14.
13. *Ibid.*
14. As reported to Bassano, 7 Sept. 1813, AECP-EU, Vol. 71, 355–56.
15. Cf. Crawford to Monroe, enclosure No. 3 (private and confidential) in despatch No. 7, Paris, 22 Sept. 1813, and same to same, (private and confidential), Paris, 16 Jan. 1814, both in DD-F, Vol. 14. Parker's proposal was enclosed in the latter.
16. To Monroe, No. 3, Paris, 15 Aug. 1813, DD-F, Vol. 14.
17. To Monroe, No 7 (private), 20 Sept. 1813, *Ibid.* Although angered by what he described as Warden's arrogance and duplicity, Crawford thought Lee equally reprehensible for trying to win Bassano's support in this case. Crawford's *Journal*, 44–46.
18. To Monroe, No. 4 (private), 25 August 1813. DD-F, Vol. 14.
19. See his No. 7 of 22 Sept., *Ibid.*
20. See Barnet's heated correspondence with Armstrong in January 1806. The paper trail thereafter runs through CD (Paris), Vols. 2 and 3; DI, Vol. 7, and DD-F, Vol. 13
21. See Barnet to Warden, 2 July 1812; Warden to Barnet, 13 July, and Warden to John Graham [State Department], 12 Nov., CD (Paris), Vol. 4.
22. Crawford's No. 7 of 20 Sept. 1813, DD-F, Vol. 13; and Warden to Crawford, 15 Sept. 1813, CD (Paris), Vol. 5.
23. To Monroe, No. 23, Paris, 28 May 1814, DD-F, Vol. 14.
24. For Warden's defense of his conduct and anger at his accusers, see his letters to

Crawford of 16 Sept. 1813, 6 June, and 8 Aug. 1814; to Madison, 26 July; and to John Graham, 4 Aug. 1814, all in CD (Paris), Vol. 5.

25. Paris, 8 Sept. 1813, DD-F, Vol. 14.

26. See Crawford's letters to Bassano of 10 and 11 Sept., 1813, copies enclosed in his No. 7, to Monroe, Paris, 20 Sept., *Ibid.*

27. To Monroe, No. 8, Paris, 15 Oct. 1813, *Ibid.*

28. To Bassano, Paris, 11 Sept. 1813, *Ibid.*

29. No. 8, Paris, 15 Oct. 1813 (enclosure #1), *Ibid.*

30. Paris, 11 and 15 Oct. 1813 (enclosed in Crawford's No. 9), *Ibid.*

31. To Monroe, No. 10, Paris, 10 Nov. 1813, *Ibid.*

32. Adams to Crawford, St. Petersburg, 15 Nov. 1813, and to Monroe, 22 Nov., *Writings,* IV, 530–32 and 532–33.

33. See his No. 11, Paris, 19 Nov. 1813, DD-F, Vol. 14; and his *Journal,* 51–52.

34. A former military aide-de-camp, Caulincourt had warned Napoleon against invading Russia and shared his carriage during the retreat. He served again as foreign minister during the Hundred Days. For details of his career, see Louis G. Michaud, ed., *Biographie Universelle ancienne et moderne* (Paris: Michaud frères, 1811–62), VII, 247–51.

35. To Monroe, No. 11, Paris, 19 Nov. 1813, DD-F, Vol. 14. For Caulincourt's negotiations with allied leaders, see Lefebvre, *Napoleon from Tilsit to Waterloo,* 342–48.

36. To Monroe, No. 12 (private), 1 Dec. 1813, DD-F, Vol. 14. For Caulincourt's later explanation, see his "Rapport à Sa Majesté," 4 Jan. 1814, AECP-EU, Vol. 71, 8–10v.

37. To Monroe, No. 12, Paris, 16 Jan. 1814, DD-F, Vol. 14, in which reported his 19 December meeting with Caulincourt and its disappointing aftermath.

38. That he deliberately decided not to follow the French government outside of Paris may be inferred from the private letter he wrote to Monroe, Paris, 15 Feb. 1814, *Ibid.*

39. Same to same, 18 Jan. 1814, *Ibid.*

40. He proposed paying 1.7 million francs to indemnify those whose property had been seized before they could have known of the Rambouillet Decree; 1.8 million for property seized after 1 Nov. 1810; and 2.2 million for vessels burned by the French Navy. He later added a fourth class of claims amounting to 7.3 million francs, apparently to indemnify those whose property had been confiscated in Spanish ports under French control. See his "Rapport à Sa Majesté" of 4 Jan. and that of 24 Jan. 1814, AECP-EU, Vol. 71, 8–10v, 33–34v.

41. To Monroe (private), Paris, 15 Feb. 1814, DD-F, Vol. 14.

42. See his despatch No. 16 of 16 March 1814, and a private letter to Monroe of 26 March, *Ibid.*

43. At the czar's insistence, Napoleon on April 6 abdicated at Fontainebleau. Two weeks later he said farewell to his troops and departed for Elba.

44. To Monroe, No. 17 (private), Paris, 11 April 1814, DD-F, Vol. 14.

45. See his despatches, Nos. 19 and 20 of 18 and 20 April 1814, *Ibid.* The following September Crawford was pleased to distribute copies of Jefferson's manual to Talleyrand, Marbois, and others, who found them "most acceptable." To Monroe, 20 Sept. 1814, DD-F, Vol. 15.

46. To Monroe, No. 20 (private) April 1814, *Ibid.*

47. Private, Paris, 26 March 1814, *Ibid.*

48. No. 22, Paris, 11 May 1814, *Ibid.*

49. Cf. Crawford to Monroe (private), 26 March, and Crawford's despatch No. 18 of 12 April 1814, DD-F, Vol. 14.

50. Cf. Crawford, Despatches, Nos. 22 and 23 of 11 and 28 May 1814, *Ibid.*, and his No. 26 (private) of 10 Sept., DD-F, Vol. 15.

51. Crawford to Monroe, 18 April 1815, DD-F, Vol. 16.

52. A recent and detailed account of this era is Alan Schom's *One Hundred Days: Napoleon's Road to Waterloo* (New York: Atheneum, 1992).

53. For a detailed account of claims diplomacy in the post-Napoleonic era, see Richard Aubrey McLemore's *Franco-American Diplomatic Relations, 1816–1836* (Ft. Washington, NY: Kennikat Press, 1941).

54. To Secretary of State Livingston, 8 July 1831, Richardson, *Messages*, II, 558.

BIBLIOGRAPHY

MANUSCRIPT SOURCES:

National Archives of the United States

Records of the Department of State, United States Ministers, Instructions, All Countries (cited as DI)
Vol. 6 (2 October 1801 to 2 May 1808)
Vol. 7 (1 May 1808 to 21 July 1815)
State Department, Diplomatic Despatches, France (cited as DD-F, by volume number and date of despatch)
Vol. 9 (26 December 1803 to 23 October 1804)
Vol. 10 (12 November 1804 to 27 December 1807)
Vol. 11 (22 January 1808 to 14 September 1810)
Vol. 12 (26 September 1810 to 29 October 1811)
Vol. 13 (29 September 1811 to 26 March 1813)
Vol. 14 (25 July 1813 to 17 August 1814)
Vol. 15 (22 August 1814 to 12 December 1814)
Vol. 16 (20 February 1815 to 2 August 1815)
Despatches from United States Consuls, 1790–1906
(From microfilm copies in the Archives Nationales)
Vol. 2 (Paris, March 1806 to February 1808)
Vol. 3 (Paris, January 1808 to August 1813)
Vol. 4 (Paris, August 1813 to August 1814)
Vol. 2 (Bordeaux, March 1806 to April 1809)
Vol. 3 (Bordeaux, March 1810 to February 1813)

Archives Etrangères de France

Correspondance Politique, Etats-Unis
(cited herein as AECP-EU by volume and folio number)
Mémoires et Documents
Vol. 658 (1800–1805)
Vol. 659 (1806–1809)

Archives Nationales de France

Série AE BIII, cote 451 (Etats-Unis, 1692–1892) (Licenses d'importation, 1811–1812)
Série AFIV, cote 324 (Relations extérieures, An XII-1810) (copies d'actes impériaux) (Contains

Cadore's analysis of the U.S. Non-Intercourse Act of 1 March 1809, transmitted to Napoleon on 5 August 1810)

Série AFIV, cote 1681A (Etats-Unis)

Dossier 2 (1810) (Translations of intercepted letters; General Turreau's domestic problems)

Dossier 3 (1810) (Feasibility of Aaron Burr's proposals for liberating Latin America; Champagny's "Rapport historique" on Franco-American relations, February; translated texts of official British documents, 1806 to 1810, and U.S. presidential proclamations and acts of Congress affecting France, February 1805 to 1810)

Dossier 4 (1810–1811)

—For 1810: Champagny's draft proposal for a treaty with the United States, and draft instructions to Turreau's successor, March; Foreign Office summary of Burr's proposals for liberating Latin America and Canada, March; Cadore's circular explaining the Cadore Letter, August; status of French maritime decrees in March and July;

—For 1811: instructions to Serurier, October, various reports from Cadore to Napoleon of March, April, and May, and extracts from Serurier's despatches of August through November.

Série AFIV, cote 1704 (Etats Unis)

Data relating to the Convention of 1800 and the Louisiana purchase treaty, cited by dossier number.

Série AFIV, cote 1706E (Rapports ministériels, Relations extérieures, Correspondance générale du ministre adressée à Napoléon, an VIII–1814)

Dossier 3 (Scattered reports from Cadore to Napoleon, 1808) Dossier 4 (Correspondence relating to French maritime policy and French licensing of U.S. vessels, 1809) Dossier 5 (Scattered reports from Cadore to Napoleon, 1810)

Archives de la Marine

Série BB1 (Reports from the Minister to the Chief of State, and reports to the Minister, decisions from 1789 to 1864)

Série BB2 (Ministerial correspondence, letters sent between 1789 and 1869)

Série BB3 (Ministerial correspondence, letters received between 1789 and 1869)

Joel Barlow Papers (Harvard University)

James Madison Papers (microfilm)

Series 1: General Correspondence, 90 volumes, 1723–1859

Series 2: Additional Correspondence and Related Items, 8 volumes, 1674–1837

James Monroe Papers (New York Public Library)

Box 4 (1803–1812)

Box 13 Miscellaneous Papers and Undated Letters

Jonathan Russell, Letter Books, I and II (29 Aug. 1811–2 March 1813), Brown University Library

Louis Serurier Papers (Kent State University) (4 reels)

PUBLISHED SOURCES:

American State Papers, Foreign Relations. 6 vols. Washington D.C.: Gales and Seaton, 1832–59. (Cited as ASP FR).

Biographical Directory of the American Congress, 1774–1971. Washington: U.S. Government Printing Office, 1971.

Burr, Samuel Engel, Jr. *Napoleon's Dossier on Aaron Burr: Proposals of Col. Aaron Burr to the Emperor Napoleon.* San Antonio, TX: Naylor Co., 1969.

Correspondance de Napoleon Ier. 34 vols. Paris: H. Plon, 1858-1870.

Cranch, William. *Reports of Cases Argued and Adjudged by the Supreme Court of the United States.* 64 vols. Washington D.C.: John Conrad and Co., 1804–61.

Debates and Proceedings in the Congress of the United States. 42 vols. Washington: Gales and Seaton, 1834–56. (Cited as *Annals*).

Dictionary of American Biography. New York: C. Scribner's Sons, 1928–58.

Dudley, William S., ed. *The Naval War of 1812: A Documentary History.* 3 vols. Washington: Naval Historical Society, 1985.

Federal Republican (Baltimore).

Fitzpatrick, John C., ed. *The Writings of George Washington.* 39 vols. Washington, D.C.: U.S. Government Printing Office, 1933–44.

Ford, Worthington Chauncey, ed. *Writings of John Quincy Adams.* 7 vols. New York: Macmillan Company, 1913–17.

Ford, Paul Leicester, ed. *The Works of Thomas Jefferson.* 12 vols. New York: G. P. Putnam's Sons, 1904–05.

Foster, Augustus John. *Jeffersonian America: Notes on the United States of America, Collected in the Years 1805–6–7 and 11–12,* Richard B. Davis, ed. Westport, CT: Greenwood Press, 1980.

Gazette Nationale ou le Moniteur Universel. (Paris).

Hamilton, Stanislaus Murray, ed. *The Writings of James Monroe.* 7 vols. New York: G. P. Putnam's Sons, 1898–1903.

Hunt, Gaillard, ed. *The Writings of James Madison.* 9 vols. New York: Putnam's Sons, 1900–10.

Knowlton, Daniel Chauncey, ed. *The Journal of William H. Crawford.* Smith College Studies in History, Vol. IX, No. 1 (Oct. 1925).

Mayo, Bernard, ed. *Instructions to the British Ministers to the United States, 1791–1812.* Vol. III, *Annual Report of the American Historical Association, 1936.* Washington D.C.: U.S. Government Printing Office, 1941.

Michaud, Louis G., ed. *Biographie universelle ancienne et moderne.* 85 vols. Paris: Michaud frères, 1811–62.

Minot, George. *Reports of Cases Argued and Determined in the High Court of Admiralty.* 3 vols. Boston: Little, Brown and Company, 1822–38.

National Intelligencer. (Washington D.C., Library of Congress microfilm).

The Naval War of 1812: A Documentary History. 3 vols. Washington D.C.: Naval Historical Center, 1985.

New American State Papers: Commerce and Navigation. 47 vols. Wilmington, DE: Scholarly Resources, 1973.

Richardson, James D. *A Compilation of the Messages and Papers of the Presidents.* 10 vols. Washington D.C.: U.S. Government Printing Office, 1896–99.

Rutland, Robert A. et al, eds. *The Papers of James Madison: Presidential Series.* 4 vols. Charlottesville, VA: University Press of Virginia, 1984–

SECONDARY WORKS:

Adams, Henry. *History of the United States of America.* 9 vols. New York: C. Scribner's Sons, 1889–91.

———— *The Life of Albert Gallatin.* Philadelphia: J. B. Lippincott, 1879.

———— *Documents Relating to New England Federalism.* Boston: Little, Brown and Company, 1905.

Ammon, Harry. *James Monroe: the Quest for National Identity.* New York: McGraw-Hill, 1971.

Barnett, Corelli. *Bonaparte.* New York: Hill and Wang, 1978.

Beirne, Francis F. *The War of 1812.* Hamden, CT: Archon Books, 1965.

Bemis, Samuel Flagg. *Jay's Treaty: a Study in Commerce and Diplomacy.* New York: Macmillan Company, 1923.

———— *Pinckney's Treaty: A Study in America's Advantage from Europe's Distress, 1783–1800.* Baltimore: The Johns Hopkins Press, 1926.

———— *John Quincy Adams and the Foundations of American Foreign Policy.* New York: A. A. Knopf, 1949.

———— Ed., *American Secretaries of States and Their Diplomacy.* 10 vols. New York: A. A. Knopf, 1927–67.

Ben-Atar, Doron S. *The Origins of Jeffersonian Commercial Policy and Diplomacy.* New York: St. Martin's Press, 1993.

Bernstein, Samuel. 1985. *Joel Barlow: A Connecticut Yankee in an Age of Revolution.* New York: Rutledge Books, 1985.

Brant, Irving. *James Madison, Secretary of State, 1800–1809.* Vol. III in *James Madison.* 6 vols. Indianapolis, IN: Bobbs-Merrill, 1941–61.

———— *James Madison, the President, 1809–1812.* Vol. IV in *James Madison.* Indianapolis IN: Bobbs-Merrill.

———— "Joel Barlow, Madison's Stubborn Minister." *William and Mary Quarterly*, 3rd Series, 15, No. 4 (Oct. 1958), 438–51.

Brice, Raoul. *The Riddle of Napoleon.* New York: G. P. Putnam's Sons, 1937.

Brown, Roger H. *The Republic in Peril.* New York: Columbia University Press, 1971

Brown, Stuart Gerry. *The First Republicans: Political Philosophy and Public Policy in the Party of Jefferson and Madison.* Syracuse, NY: Syracuse University Press, 1954.

Bruun, Geoffrey. *Europe and the French Imperium, 1799–1814.* New York: Harper and Brothers, 1938.

Buel, Richard. *Securing the Revolution: Ideology in American Politics, 1789–1815.* Ithaca, NY: Cornell University Press, 1972.

Burt, A. L. *The United States, Great Britain and British North America: From the Revolution to the Establishment of Peace After the War of 1812.* New Haven, CT: Yale University Press, 1940.

Butel, Paul. "Crise et mutation de l'activité économique à Bordeaux sous le consulat et l'Empire," *Revue d'histoire moderne at contemporaine,* (July-Sept. 1970), 552–58.

Butterfield, Herbert. 1939. *Napoleon.* New York: Macmillan Company, 1956.

Christie, Ian R. *Wars and Revolutions: Britain, 1760–1815.* Cambridge, MA: Harvard University Press, 1982.

Clauder, Anna C. *American Commerce as Affected by the Wars of the French Revolution, 1793–1815.* Philadelphia, 1932.

Coles, Harry L. *The War of 1812.* Chicago: University of Chicago Press, 1965.

Combs, Jerald A. *American Diplomatic History: Two Centuries of Changing Interpretations.* Berkeley: University of California Press, 1983.

Cox, Isaac J. *The West Florida Controversy, 1798–1813.* Baltimore: Johns Hopkins Press, 1918.

———— "The Border Missions of General George Mathews." *Mississippi Valley Historical Review*, 12, No. 3 (1925), 303–33.

Cress, Lawrence Delbert. *Citizens in Arms: the Army and the Militia in American Society to the War of 1812.* Chapel Hill: University of North Carolina Press, 1982.

Cresson, William P. *James Monroe.* Chapel Hill: University of North Carolina Press, 1946.

Cunliffe, Marcus. "Madison (1812–1815)." In Ernest R. May, *The Ultimate Decision: the President as Commander in Chief.* New York: G. Braziller, 1960.

Cunningham, Noble E., Jr. *The Jeffersonian Republicans in Power: Party Operations, 1801–1809.* Chapel Hill: University of North Carolina Press, 1963.

Dangerfield, George. *Chancellor Robert R. Livingston of New York.* New York: G. Braziller, 1960.

DeConde, Alexander. *This Affair of Louisiana.* New York: Scribners, 1976.

———— *The Quasi-War: The Politics and Diplomacy of the Undeclared War with France, 1797–1801.* New York: Scribners, 1966.

Durden, Robert F. "Joel Barlow in the French Revolution." *William and Mary Quarterly,* 3rd Series, 8, No. 3 (July 1951), 327–54.

Egan, Clifford L. *Neither Peace nor War: Franco-American Relations, 1803–1812.* Baton Rouge: Louisiana State University Press, 1983.

Ellis, Geoffrey. *Napoleon.* New York: Longman, 1997.

Engelman, Fred L. *The Peace of Christmas Eve.* London: Hart-Davis, 1962.

Forester, Cecil S. *The Age of Fighting Sail: The Story of the Naval War of 1812.* New York: Doubleday, 1956.

Garitee, Jerome. *The Republic's Private Navy: the American Privateering Business as Practiced by Baltimore During the War of 1812.* Middletown, CT: Wesleyan University Press, 1977.

Geyl, Pieter. *Napoleon, For and Against.* New Haven: Yale University Press, 1963.

Gilpin, Alec R. *The War of 1812 in the Old Northwest.* East Lansing, MI: Michigan State University Press, 1958.

Glover, Richard. "The French Fleet, 1807–1814: Britain's Problem and Madison's Opportunity." *Journal of Modern History,* 39 (September 1967), 233–52.

Green, Philip Jackson, "William H. Crawford and the War of 1812." *Georgia Historical Quarterly,* 26 (March 1942), 27–29.

Hatzenbueler, Ronald L., and Robert L. Ivie. *Congress Declares War: Rhetoric, Leadership, and Partisanship in the Early Republic.* Kent State, OH: Kent State University Press, 1983.

Heaton, Herbert. "Non-Importation, 1806–1812." *Journal of Economic History,* I (Nov., 1941), 178–98.

Hecksher, Eli F. *The Continental System: an Economic Interpretation.* Oxford: The Clarendon Press, 1922.

Hickey, Donald R. *The War of 1812: A Forgotten Conflict.* Urbana, IL: University of Illinois Press, 1989.

———— "American Trade Restrictions during the War of 1812." *Journal of American History,* 68, No. 3 (Dec. 1981), 517–38.

———— "The Monroe-Pinkney Treaty, A Reappraisal," *William and Mary Quarterly,* 3rd Ser., 44, No. 1 (Jan. 1987), 66–88.

Horsman, Reginald. *The Causes of the War of 1812.* Philadelphia: The University of Pennsylvania Press, 1962.

———— The Diplomacy of the New Republic, 1776–1815. Arlington Heights, IL: H. Davidson, 1985.

———— "Feature Review: The War of 1812 Revisited." Diplomatic History, 15 (Winter 1991), 115–24.

Howard, Leon, "Joel Barlow and Napoleon." Huntington Library Quarterly, 2 (Oct. 1938).

Hunt, Michael H. Ideology and U.S. Foreign Policy. New Haven: Yale University Press, 1987.

James, C. L. R. The Black Jacobins: Toussaint L'Ouverture and the San Domingo Revolution. New York: Vintage Books, 1963.

Kaplan, Lawrence S. 1987. Entangling Alliances with None: American Foreign Policy in the Age of Jefferson. (Kent, OH: Kent State University Press, 1987.

———— Jefferson and France. New Haven: Yale University Press, 1967.

———— "France and Madison's Decision for War, 1812." Journal of American History, 57, No. 1 (Jan. 1970), 36–47.

Ketcham, Ralph. James Madison: A Biography. New York: Macmillan, 1971.

Knox, Dudley W. A History of the United States Navy. New York: G. P. Putnam's Sons, 1936.

Lang, Daniel G. Foreign Policy in the Early Republic: The Law of Nations and the Balance of Power. Baton Rouge: Louisiana State University Press, 1985.

Las Casas, Emmanuel, comte de. Memorial de Sainte-Hélene [par] Las Casas. Paris: Edition Garnier frères, 1961.

Lefebvre, Georges. Napoleon from Tilsit to Waterloo, 1807–1815. New York: Columbia University Press, 1969.

———— Napoleon. 2 vols. London: Rutledge and K. Paul, 1969.

Lewis, James E., Jr. John Quincy Adams: Policymaker for the Union. Wilmington, DE: SR Books, 2001.

Lingelbach, W. E., "England and Neutral Trade." Military Historian and Economist, II (1917–18), 156–65.

Logan, Rayford W. The Diplomatic Relations of the United States with Haiti, 1776–1891. Chapel Hill: University of North Carolina Press, 1941.

Lyon, E. Wilson. Louisiana in French Diplomacy, 1759–1804. Norman, OK: University of Oklahoma Press, 1934.

Maclay, Edgar Stanton. A History of American Privateers. New York: D. Appleton and Co., 1899.

Malone, Dumas. Jefferson the President: Second Term, 1805–1809. Boston: Little, Brown and Company, 1974.

Mann, Mary Lee, ed. A Yankee Jeffersonian: Selections from the Diary and Letters of William Lee of Massachusetts, Written from 1796 to 1840. Cambridge, MA: Belknap Press, 1958.

Marcus, J. G. A. A Naval History of England. Boston: Little, Brown and Company, 1961.

Markham, Felix. Napoleon. New York: New American Library, 1964.

McCoy, Drew R. The Elusive Republic: Political Economy in Jeffersonian America. Chapel Hill, NC: University of North Carolina Press, 1980.

McDonald, Forrest. The Presidency of Thomas Jefferson. Lawrence, KS: University Press of Kansas, 1976.

McLemore, Richard Aubrey. Franco-American Diplomatic Relations, 1816–1836. Pt. Washington, NY: Kennikat Press, 1941.

Melvin, Frank Edgar. Napoleon's Navigation System: A Study of Trade Control During the Continental Blockade. 1919. Reprint. New York: AMS Press, 1970.

Mooney, Chase C. *William H. Crawford, 1772–1834.* Lexington, KY: University Press of Kentucky, 1974.

Morison, Samuel Eliot. 1953. *By Land and By Sea: Essays and Addresses by Samuel Eliot Morison.* New York: Knopf, 1953.

Onuf, Peter S. "A Declaration of Independence for Diplomatic Historians." *Diplomatic History*, 22 (Winter 1998), 71–83.

Ott, Thomas C. *The Haitian Revolution, 1764–1804.* Knoxville, KY: University of Tennessee Press, 1973.

Palmer, Alan. *Napoleon in Russia.* New York: Simon and Schuster, 1967.

Pancake, John S. "The 'Invisibles:' A Chapter in the Opposition to President Madison." *Journal of Southern History*, 21, No. 1 (Feb. 1955), 17–37.

Patrick, Rembert W. *Florida Fiasco: Rampant Rebels on the Georgia-Florida Border, 1810–1815.* Athens, GA: University of Georgia Press, 1954.

Perkins, Bradford. *Prologue to War: England and the United States, 1805–1812.* Berkeley, CA: University of California Press, 1961.

——— *Castlereagh and Adams: England the United States, 1815–1823.* Berkeley, CA: University of California Press, 1964.

——— "Sir William Scott and *Essex.*" *William and Mary Quarterly*, 3rd Series, 22 (1956), 169–83.

——— *The Causes of the War of 1812: National Honor or National Interest?* Malabar, FL: R.E. Krieger Publishing Co., 1983.

——— *The Creation of a Republican Empire, 1776–1865.* Vol. I in *The Cambridge History of American Foreign Relations.* New York: Cambridge University Press, 1993.

Peterson, Merrill D. *Thomas Jefferson and the New Nation: a Biography.* New York: Oxford University Press, 1970.

Phillips, Allison W., and Arthur H. Reede. *Neutrality, Its History, Economics, and Law: the Napoleonic Period,* II. New York: Columbia University Press, 1936.

Pratt, Julius W. *Expansionists of 1812.* New York: The Macmillan Company, 1925.

Risjord, Norman K. *The Old Republicans: Southern Conservatism in the Age of Jefferson.* New York: Columbia University Press, 1965.

——— "1812: Conservatives, War Hawks, and the Nation's Honor." *William and Mary Quarterly*, 3rd Series, 18, No. 2 (April 1961), 196–210.

Robertson, William S. *The Life of Miranda.* 2 vols. Chapel Hill: University of North Carolina Press, 1929.

Robinson, Donald L. *Slavery in the Structure of American Politics, 1765–1820.* New York: Harcourt Brace Jovanovich, 1971.

Rose, John Holland. *The Life of Napoleon.* New York: The Macmillan Company, 1907.

Rossignol, Marie-Jeanne. *The Nationalist Ferment: the Origins of U. S. Foreign Policy, 1789–1812.* Columbus, OH: Ohio State University Press, 2004.

Russell, Greg. *John Quincy Adams and the Public Virtues of Diplomacy.* Columbia, MO: University of Missouri Press, 1995.

Rutland, Robert Allen. *The Presidency of James Madison.* Lawrence, KS: University of Kansas Press, 1990.

——— *Madison's Alternative: The Jeffersonian Republicans and the Coming of War, 1805–1812.* Philadelphia: Lippincott, 1970.

——— *James Madison, The Founding Father.* New York: Macmillan and Company, 1987.

Schama, Simon. *Patriots and Liberators: Revolution in the Netherlands, 1780–1813.* New York: Knopf, 1977.

Schom, Alan. *One Hundred Days: Napoleon's Road to Waterloo.* New York: Atheneum, 1992.

Sears, Louis Martin. *Jefferson and the Embargo.* New York: Octagon Books, 1966.

Skeen, C. Edward. *John Armstrong, Jr., 1758–1843: A Biography.* Syracuse, NY: Syracuse University Press, 1981.

Smelser, Marshall. *The Democratic Republic, 1801–1815.* New York: Harper and Row, 1968.

Smith, Margaret Bayard. *The First Forty Years of Washington Society.* Gaillard Hunt, ed. New York: Scribner, 1906.

Spivak, Bernard. *Jefferson's English Crisis: Commerce, Embargo, and the Republican Revolution.* Charlottesville, VA: University Press of Virginia, 1979.

Stagg, J. C. A. *Mr. Madison's War: Politics, Diplomacy, and Warfare in the Early American Republic, 1783–1830.* Princeton: Princeton University Press, 1983.

——— "James Madison and the 'Malcontents:' the Political Origins of the War of 1812." *William and Mary Quarterly,* 3rd Series, 33, No. 4 (Oct. 1976), 557–85.

——— "James Madison and the Coercion of Great Britain: Canada, the West Indies, and the War of 1812." *William and Mary Quarterly,* 3rd Series, 38, No. 1 (Jan. 1981), 3–34.

Steel, Anthony, "Impressment in the Monroe-Pinkney Negotiation, 1806–07." *American Historical Review,* 57, No. 2 (Jan. 1952), 352–69.

Stevens, Kenneth R. "Thomas Jefferson and John Quincy Adams, and the Foreign Policy of the Early Republic." *Diplomatic History,* 19 (Fall 1995), 705–11.

Symonds, Craig L. *1980. Navalists and Antinavalists: The National Policy Debate in the United States, 1785–1827.* Newark, DE: University of Delaware Press, 1980.

Tansill, Charles Callan. *The United States and Santo Domingo, 1798–1873.* Baltimore: The Johns Hopkins Press, 1938.

Todd, Charles B. *Life and Letters of Joel Barlow.* New York: G. P. Putnam's Sons, 1886.

Tucker, Robert W., and David C. Hendrickson. *Empire of Liberty: the Statecraft of Thomas Jefferson.* New York: Oxford University Press, 1990.

Walters, Raymond Jr. *Albert Gallatin: Jeffersonian Financier and Diplomat.* New York: Macmillan and Company, 1957.

Weeks, William Earl. "New Directions in the Study of Early American Foreign Relations." *Diplomatic History,* 17 (Winter 1994), 73–96.

Whitaker, Arthur P. *The United States and the Independence of Latin America, 1800–1830.* New York: W. W. Norton, 1964.

——— *The Mississippi Question, 1795–1803: Study in Trade, Politics, and Diplomacy.* New York: C. Appleton-Century, 1934.

Whitcomb, Edward A. *Napoleon's Diplomatic Service.* Durham, NC: Duke University Press, 1979.

White, Leonard D. *The Jeffersonians: A Study in Administrative History, 1801–1829.* New York: Macmillan, 1951.

Woodress, James. *A Yankee's Odyssey: the Life of Joel Barlow.* Philadelphia: Lippincott, 1958.

Wright, J. Leitch, Jr. *Britain and the American Frontier, 1783–1815.* Athens, GA: University of Georgia Press, 1975.

Zimmerman, James F. *Impressment of American Seamen.* New York: Columbia University Press, 1925.

Zunder, Theodore A. *1934. The Early Days of Joel Barlow.* Hamden, CT: Archon Press, 1969.

Index

About the Author

Peter P. Hill is professor of history emeritus at George Washington University. His previous books include *William Vans Murray, Federalist Diplomat: The Shaping of Peace with France, 1797–1801, French Perceptions of the Early American Republic, 1783–1793*, and *The Elliot School of International Affairs: A History of International Studies at The George Washington University*. He lives in Brunswick, Maine.